The
Handbook of
BANK
ACCOUNTING

Understanding and Applying
Standards and Regulations

Charles J. Woelfel

Professional Publishing®
Chicago • London • Singapore

A Bankline Publication

ISBN 1-55738-338-3

Printed in the United States of America

BB

2 3 4 5 6 7 8 9 0

To Colette

Contents

Preface

This book deals with bank accounting and regulation. The current banking environment is focused on banking regulation and compliance, capital adequacy, asset/liability management, operating performance, mark-to-market valuation, nonperforming loans, evolving financial instruments, bank examinations and audits, and many other significant banking concerns. Regulatory agencies—including the Federal Reserve System, the Comptroller of the Currency, The Securities and Exchange Commission, and the Federal Deposit Insurance Corporation—interact with banks almost on a day-to-day basis. *Handbook of Bank Accounting* deals with these and other banking topics as they relate to contemporary bank accounting and regulation.

The book was written to meet the needs of senior- and middle-level bank accountants; bank controllers; managers of commercial banks, thrift institutions, and investment bankers; CEOs and CFOs; bank regulators; bank directors; attorneys and legal staff; CPAs associated with banking institutions; academicians involved with economics, finance, and accounting as applied to banking; students of banking; and libraries. The author focuses on the practical needs of this extended audience for tried and tested concepts and applications.

The book features both financial and managerial accounting topics. Part I establishes a foundation for understanding the current environment of bank accounting and regulation. Part II describes the underlying theory and practice of bank accounting and regulation. Part III discusses income taxes as they relate to banks and the interperiod tax allocation problem. Part IV analyzes the financial reporting problems associated with international banking and business combinations. Part V presents a comprehensive overview of financial statement analysis of banks. Part VI is devoted to major managerial accounting topics related to bank accounting. Part VII discusses bank examinations and auditing. Part VIII provides an evaluation and application of the time value of money.

This book on current bank accounting and reporting issues has 17 chapters organized as follows:

Part I   **The Environment of Bank Accounting and Regulation**
Ch. 1   Financial Reporting
Ch. 2   Bank Regulation and Reporting
Part II   **Bank Accounting: Theory and Practice**

It is the author's goal to attain the following subject-matter objectives: comprehensiveness, reliability, accuracy, practicality, relevance, and convenience. It is our expectation that this *Handbook* will be above all else user-friendly.

This book discusses in depth both financial and managerial accounting topics that are of interest to bankers and other professionals. It emphasizes reporting practices promulgated by the leading accounting and regulatory authorities. The author believes that the study of bank accounting concepts develops an understanding of banking practice. Theory and practice are so interrelated that they cannot be studies in isolation. They are mutually reinforcing.

The book includes many special learning techniques. Key definitions are provided at the end of each chapter. An acronyms glossary appears in Appendix A. Authoritative and relevant references, examples, and illustrations are widely used throughout the book. The effect is to deliver a user-oriented text on bank accounting and regulation.

In writing this book, the author placed major emphasis on content, fitness, and language. It is hoped that the style is clear, concise, complete, and appropriate to the task. Attention to detail added accuracy and thoroughness—a necessary dimension—to the undertaking.

The author has utilized original sources wherever possible and verified secondary sources whenever relied upon. The author has drawn heavily from official documents and publications, especially those of regulatory agencies, The American Institute of Public Accountants (AICPA), and the Financial Accounting Standards Board (FASB). He also communicated with many individuals, organizations, U.S. government departments, regulatory agencies, Senate and House banking committees, banks, public records, periodicals, and various other sources.

The author is especially indebted to the staff of Probus for conceptualizing this book and for keeping deeply committed and involved with its development and publication.

Finally, my wife Colette has played an important part by providing support and understanding during the book's development and production. I am grateful to her and hope that this edition justifies the sacrifices required during the entire process.

Charles J. Woelfel

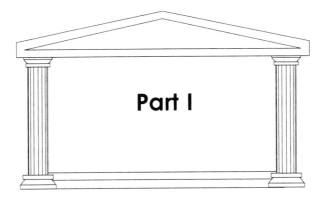

Part I

The Environment of Bank Accounting and Regulation

Chapter 1

Financial Reporting

oday's bankers need relevant and reliable financial information for making economic decisions affecting their banks. Bank accounting can provide much of this financial and managerial information. A knowledge of accounting is essential to making reasoned choices among alternative uses of scarce resources in the conduct of banking activities. This chapter develops an understanding of underlying concepts and principles that influence financial accounting. The development of accounting standards and regulations as applied to certain financial institutions are also discussed, primarily commercial banks and thrifts.

FINANCIAL INSTITUTIONS

Financial institutions are organizations that typically accept deposits and then lend or invest them. Financial institutions bring together net savers with the net users of funds: Commercial banks, investment banks (merchant banks), savings and loan associations, savings banks, and credit unions and major depository financial institutions. Savings banks, savings and loan associations, and credit unions are referred to as thrift institutions. Financial institutions deal in one basic commodity—money and money equivalents. This commodity exists more often than not in book entry form.

Financial institutions use their funds chiefly to purchase financial assets (deposits, loans, securities) as opposed to tangible property. Financial institutions can be classified according to the nature of the principal claims they issue:

- Nondeposit intermediaries include, among others, life and property/casualty insurance companies and pensions funds, whose claims are the policies they sell, or the promise to provide income after retirement;

- Depository intermediaries obtain funds mainly by accepting deposits from the public. The powers of nonbank depository institutions have been broadened in recent years. For example, NOW accounts, credit union share drafts, and other services similar to checking accounts may be offered by thrift institutions.

Financial instruments or products developed for and by financial institutions can be broadly classified into categories: debt instruments, equity instruments, asset-backed securities, hedging instruments, and hybrid instruments. Banks participate actively in various capacities with financial instruments and are discussed throughout this book.

Financial institutions are subject to major risks: interest rate risk, market risk, inflation risk, business risk, financial risk, liquidity risk, credit risk, and currency risk.

- Interest rate risk results from changes in the level of interest rates. Security prices move inversely to interest rates.

- Market risk refers to the variability in returns resulting from fluctuations in the market. All investments in securities are subject to market risk.

- Inflation risk refers to a loss in purchasing power due to the changes in the general purchasing power of the dollar.

- Business risk refers to the risk of investing in operating a particular business or industry.

- Financial risk refers to the risk related to the use of debt financing by companies (leverage).

- Liquidity risk is the risk associated with securities that cannot be purchased or sold quickly and without major price concessions.

- Credit risk results from the possibility that a party to a credit transaction will be unwilling or unable to fulfill its obligations.

- Currency (or foreign exchange) risk is the risk of loss arising from adverse movements in foreign exchange rates.

Additional risks include governmental and political risk, expropriation risk, risk of war, and many others.

Because of the nature of their operations and their impact on the national economy and the public welfare, financial institutions have come to be highly regulated and supervised by governmental agencies. These matters are major topics of this book.

ACCOUNTING

Accounting is the process of identifying, measuring, recording, and communicating economic information to permit informed judgments and decisions by users of accounting information. Accounting has also been viewed as an information system that provides quantitative information, primarily financial in nature, about economic entities that is intended to be useful in making economic decisions. Economic decisions largely determine how scarce resources are allocated within and among business enterprises, what goods and services are produced, and for whom they are to be produced.

Financial Reporting

Financial reporting is a broad term that encompasses not only financial statements but also other means of communicating information that relates directly or indirectly to the financial accounting and reporting process. Corporate officers and managers may communicate financial information outside of the financial statements. These reports often include various kinds of nonfinancial information, such as descriptions of major products, a listing of corporate officers and directors, and other information. Financial reporting is designed to fulfill the objectives of general purpose external financial reporting by banks and other business enterprises. *General purpose financial statements* are designed to meet the needs of many diverse users, particularly present and potential owners and creditors. Financial statements are a basic element of financial reporting. Financial statements are used primarily to communicate accounting information to parties outside an enterprise (e.g., stockholders, creditors, and others).

Figure 1-1 distinguishes between basic financial statements, financial reporting, and all information useful for making investment, credit, and similar decisions.

The major outputs of the financial accounting process are general purpose financial statements:

1. A balance sheet, which summarizes a bank's or other enterprise's financial position at a particular point in time.

2. An income statement, which summarizes an entity's income and the components of income over a period of time.

3. A statement of cash flows, which summarizes an entity's cash receipts and cash payments during a period of time.

4. A statement of retained earnings, which describes changes in an entity's retained earnings during a period, or a statement of stockholders' equity, which describes the changes in retained earnings as well as in other accounts that comprise stockholders' equity.

Financial statements are historical reports that are primarily financial in nature. Statements report information relevant to individual business entities. The information reported often reflects estimates and professional judgments. The information is summarized and classified. Financial statements are interrelated because measuring and reporting on financial position is related to the earnings, cash flows, and other changes in equity of an enterprise.

Figure 1-1
Relationship of Financial Reporting to Other Information Services

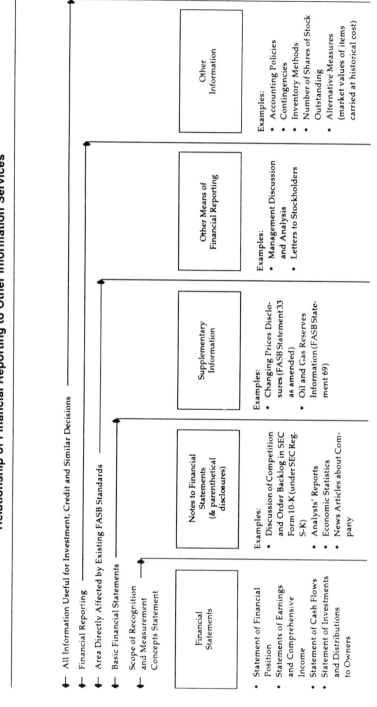

↓ All Information Useful for Investment, Credit and Similar Decisions

↓ Financial Reporting

↓ Area Directly Affected by Existing FASB Standards

↓ Basic Financial Statements

↓ Scope of Recognition and Measurement Concepts Statement

Financial Statements

- Statement of Financial Position
- Statements of Earnings and Comprehensive Income
- Statement of Cash Flows
- Statement of Investments and Distributions to Owners

Notes to Financial Statements (& parenthetical disclosures)

Examples:
- Discussion of Competition and Order Backlog in SEC Form 10-K (under SEC Reg. S-K)
- Analysts' Reports
- Economic Statistics
- News Articles about Company

Supplementary Information

Examples:
- Changing Prices Disclosures (FASB Statement 33 as amended)
- Oil and Gas Reserves Information (FASB Statement 69)

Other Means of Financial Reporting

Examples:
- Management Discussion and Analysis
- Letters to Stockholders

Other Information

Examples:
- Accounting Policies
- Contingencies
- Inventory Methods
- Number of Shares of Stock Outstanding
- Alternative Measures (market values of items carried at historical cost)

Financial statements of banks and other business enterprises are audited by independent accountants to enhance their reliability and to increase confidence in what they report. Bank regulators are also involved in determining the form and content of a bank's financial statements.

Users of Accounting Information: Decision Makers

Decision makers who rely on accounting information are usually identified as external users and internal users. These two classes of users typically have different information needs. External (to the firm) users include investors, creditors, regulators, and others. *Financial accounting* is the major source of information required to satisfy the investment and credit decision-making needs of external users. The main output of financial statements is general purpose financial statements.

Internal users of financial information include the enterprise's managers and officers who are responsible for planning and controlling the policies, operations and procedures of the enterprise. *Managerial accounting* is the major source of information required to satisfy the needs of internal users. Figure 1-2 outlines some of the major differences between financial and managerial accounting.

Both internal and external accounting are discussed in this book. Chapters 1 through 12 deal primarily with financial reporting requirements and objectives. Managerial accounting as it relates to banking is discussed in Chapters 13 and 14.

OBJECTIVES OF FINANCIAL REPORTING

General purpose external financial reporting is directed toward the common investment and credits needs of users in the ability of an enterprise to generate favorable cash flows. The

Figure 1-2
Financial and Managerial Accounting Relationships

	Financial Accounting	Managerial Accounting
Source of authority	Generally accepted	Management
Time reference	Mostly historical	Current and future
Decision emphasis	External	Internal
Type of information	Primarily quantitative	Quantitative and qualitative
Reporting	Determined by GAAP	Decision focused
Scope	Total enterprise	Total enterprise, departments, divisions, products

Financial Accounting Standards Board described the objectives of financial reporting in *Statement of Financial Accounting Concepts No. 1*, "Objectives of Financial Reporting by Business Enterprises." The objectives represent a foundation upon which financial accounting and financial statements are based. The objectives of financial reporting as prescribed by the FASB can be summarized as follows:

General objectives	Provide information that is useful to present and potential investors, creditors, and other users in making rational investment, credit, and similar decisions
Derived external user objectives	Provide information that is useful to present and potential investors, creditors, and other users in assessing the amounts, timing, and uncertainty of prospective cash receipts from dividends or interest and the proceeds from the sale, redemption, or maturity of securities or loans
Derived enterprise objectives	Provide information to help investors, creditors, and others in assessing the amounts, timing, and uncertainty of prospective net cash inflows to the related enterprise
Specific objectives	Provide information about an enterprise's economic resources, obligations, and owners' equity Provide information about an enterprise's comprehensive income and its components Provide information about an enterprise's funds flows

The first objective is the most general. The next three are progressively more specific. The objectives relate primarily to the important needs of external users who do not have the authority to require the information that they want about a given enterprise.

QUALITATIVE CHARACTERISTICS OF ACCOUNTING INFORMATION

The qualitative characteristics of accounting information distinguish more useful information from less useful information for decision-making purposes. *FASB Concepts Statement No. 2*, "Qualitative Characteristics of Accounting Information," identifies the major qualities of accounting information and certain constraints (cost-benefit and materiality).

The qualitative characteristics of accounting information can be viewed as a hierarchy, as illustrated in Figure 1-3. To be useful, financial information must have each of the qualities shown to a minimum degree. These characteristics include (1) decision usefulness, (2) relevance (predictive value, feedback value, timeliness), (3) reliability (verifiability, neutrality, and representational faithfulness), (4) comparability and consistency. Two constraints include (1) benefits from using the information should be greater than costs of providing it and (2) materiality.

If accounting information is to be useful to the users of the information, it must be understandable. The quality of *understandability* is essential to decision usefulness. Information

Figure 1-3
Qualitative Characteristics of Accounting Information

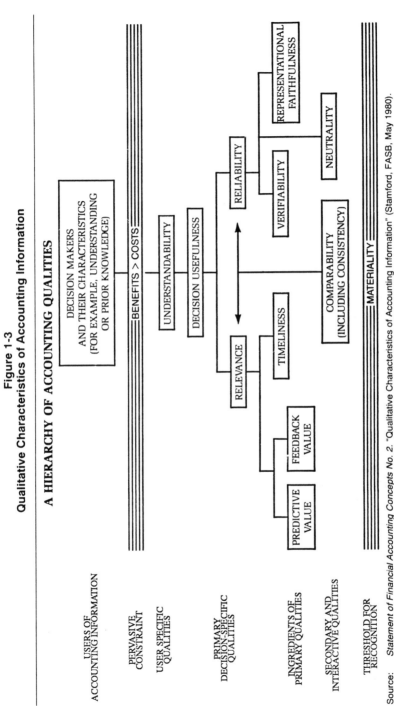

A HIERARCHY OF ACCOUNTING QUALITIES

USERS OF
ACCOUNTING INFORMATION

DECISION MAKERS
AND THEIR CHARACTERISTICS
(FOR EXAMPLE, UNDERSTANDING
OR PRIOR KNOWLEDGE)

PERVASIVE
CONSTRAINT

BENEFITS > COSTS

USER SPECIFIC
QUALITIES

UNDERSTANDABILITY

DECISION USEFULNESS

PRIMARY
DECISION-SPECIFIC
QUALITIES

RELEVANCE

RELIABILITY

INGREDIENTS OF
PRIMARY QUALITIES

PREDICTIVE
VALUE

FEEDBACK
VALUE

TIMELINESS

VERIFIABILITY

REPRESENTATIONAL
FAITHFULNESS

SECONDARY AND
INTERACTIVE QUALITIES

COMPARABILITY
(INCLUDING CONSISTENCY)

NEUTRALITY

THRESHOLD FOR
RECOGNITION

MATERIALITY

Source: *Statement of Financial Accounting Concepts No. 2.* "Qualitative Characteristics of Accounting Information" (Stamford, FASB, May 1980).
Copyright by Financial Accounting Standards Board, High Ridge Park, Stamford, Connecticut 06905, U.S.A. Reprinted with permission.

cannot be useful to decision makers if it is not understood. The understandability of information depends on the background of users, e.g., their prior knowledge, a reasonable understanding of business and economic activities, and a willingness to study the information provided with reasonable diligence. Therefore, information should be understandable, so as to allow users to perceive its significance.

The overriding objective of financial reporting is to provide information that is useful to making rational economic decisions. All other qualities must be viewed in terms of their contribution to decision usefulness. Decision making plays a central role in financial reporting.

The qualitative characteristics of accounting information as defined by the Financial Accounting Standards Board are shown in Figure 1-3. *Relevance* and *reliability* are the primary qualitative characteristics of useful accounting information. Primary characteristics distinguish "better" (more useful) information from "inferior" (less useful) information. If either relevance or reliability is completely missing, the information will not be useful. Relevance means the capacity of information to make a difference in a decision by helping users to form predictions about the outcome of past, present, and future events or to confirm or correct prior expectations in a timely manner. To be relevant, information must have *predictive value* or *feedback value* or both. Reliability is the quality of information that assures that information is reasonably free from error and bias and faithfully represents what it purports to represent. Verifiability, neutrality, and representational faithfulness are the three major characteristics of reliability:

1. *Verifiability* The ability through consensus among measurers to ensure that information represents what it purports to represent or that the chosen method of measurement has been used without error or bias (objectivity). Verifiability can be demonstrated by securing a high degree of consensus among independent measurers using the same measurement methods.

2. *Neutrality* The absence in reported information of bias intended to attain a predetermined result or to induce a particular mode of behavior. The objectives of financial reporting serve many different information users who have diverse interests; no one predetermined result is likely to suit all interests.

3. *Representational faithfulness* Correspondence or agreement between a measure or description and the phenomenon that it purports to represent (validity).

Timeliness is another quality of relevance. Timeliness refers to having information available to a decision maker before it loses its capacity to influence decisions.

Secondary qualities of accounting information include *comparability* and *consistency.* Information that is measured, recognized, and reported in a similar manner for different enterprises is considered comparable. The essence of comparability is that information becomes more useful when it can be related to a benchmark or standards. Consistency requires that an accounting entity apply the same accounting policies and procedures from period to period for similar accounting events. Companies can change accounting principles if it can be demonstrated that the newly adopted method is preferable to the former method. The nature and effect of the accounting change must be disclosed in the financial statements for the period in which the change is made.

There are two pervasive constraints underlying the qualitative characteristics of accounting information: a *cost-benefit relationship* (cost effectiveness) and *materiality*. To be useful and worth providing, the benefits of information should exceed its costs. Materiality refers to the magnitude of an omission or misstatement of accounting information that, in the light of surrounding circumstances, makes it probable that the judgment of a reasonable person relying on the information would have been changed or influenced by the omission or misstatement. Materiality judgments are primarily quantitative in nature. Questions of materiality pose this question: Is this item large enough for users of the information to be influenced by it?

The rate at which one quality of information can be sacrificed in return for a gain in another quality without making the information less useful overall will differ in different situations. *Tradeoffs* are sometimes necessary and beneficial if they increase the overall usefulness of the information provided.

DEVELOPMENT OF GENERALLY ACCEPTED ACCOUNTING PRINCIPLES—THE AICPA'S ROLE

Currently the American Institute of Certified Public Accountants (AICPA), the Financial Accounting Standards Board (FASB), and the Securities and Exchange Commission (SEC) are the major entities associated with developing generally accepted accounting principles (GAAP) in the United States. The contributions made by each of these entities will now be discussed.

AICPA's Organization and Structure

The AICPA is the national professional organization of Certified Public Accountants (CPA). Membership in the AICPA is limited to certified public accountants. The AICPA has had a major impact on financial accounting theory and practice primarily through committees and boards. In 1930 the AICPA appointed a special committee to cooperate with the New York Stock Exchange on matters of common interest to accountants, investors, and the Exchange. An outgrowth of this special committee was the Committee on Accounting Procedures.

Committee on Accounting Procedures

The AICPA became involved in developing accounting principles in 1938 when it established the Committee on Accounting Procedure (CAP). The purpose of CAP was to develop accounting principles, primarily by reducing the number of alternatives available for use in accounting practice. The committee addressed accounting problems on a problem-by-problem basis. Membership in CAP consisted of 21 volunteer members, primarily practicing accountants.

CAP issued *Accounting Research Bulletins* (ARBs), which summarized proper accounting treatment for specific problems. The ARBs were advisory only. A two-third vote of the members was required for the adoption of ARBs. CAP also published *Accounting Terminology Bulletins*, which explained accounting terminology.

CAP was criticized and ultimately replaced on the grounds that it failed to develop a framework of objectives and basic principles for accounting, on its piecemeal approach to dealing with issues, its lack of research in supporting conclusions, and inconsistent guidance.

Accounting Principles Board

Because of certain inconsistencies in the CAP's pronouncements, and for other reasons, the AICPA established a new committee charged with developing accounting principles in 1959. The Accounting Principles Board (APB) operated from 1959 to 1973. Membership consisted of from 18 to 21 members with various accounting backgrounds.

A two-thirds vote of the Board was required for passage of an *Opinion*. The Board issued 31 *Opinions*, which reflected the board's view on authoritative accounting for specific areas of accounting. It also issued four *Statements* containing broad principles, which were also considered authoritative, *Accounting Interpretations* (of an APB Opinion) to provide additional guidance to accountants, and 15 *Accounting Research Studies*.

Similar criticisms to CAP plagued the APB, along with the concern that large accounting firms had too much influence over the establishment of accounting principles. As a result, the AICPA appointed a seven-person committee (the Wheat Committee) to study the process of establishing accounting principles and to recommend ways for improving the process. In 1973, the APB was replaced by the Financial Accounting Standards Board (FASB). FASB is discussed later in this chapter.

Accounting Standards Executive Committee

The AICPA's Accounting Standards Executive Committee (AcSec) issues *Statements of Position* (SOPs) that are designed to influence the development of accounting principles in specialized areas not treated in FASB pronouncements. The AcSec also provides *Issues Papers*, which identify financial accounting and reporting issues. In addition, the AICPA publishes *Industry Audit Guides* and *Industry Accounting Guides*, which contain guidance for specialized industry questions. The guides are prepared by committees or task forces and typically deal with specialized financial reporting issues that pertain to particular industries (including banks). Banking guides were among those developed and are widely used in banking practice, including the AICPA audit and accounting guides *Audits of Banks, Savings and Loan Associations and Credit Unions*.

The AICPA has also organized an Auditing Standards Board (ASB) which is the senior technical body of the AICPA. The purpose of the ASB is to develop auditing standards and enforce the application of professional ethics. Auditors are required to comply with these standards.

THE FINANCIAL ACCOUNTING STANDARDS BOARD

The Wheat Committee's recommendations resulted in the elimination of the APB and the creation of a new standard setting structure composed of three organizations—the Financial Accounting Foundation (FAF), the Financial Accounting Standards Advisory Council (FASAC), and the Financial Accounting Standards Board (FASB).

The Financial Accounting Foundation (FAF) is an independent entity governed by a 16-member board of trustees appointed from the memberships of organizations with knowledge of corporate financial reporting:

- The American Institute of Certified Public Accountants,
- Financial Executives Institute,
- Institute of Management Accountants (formerly National Association of Accountants),
- Financial Analysts Federation,
- American Accounting Association,
- Securities Industry Association,
- Government Finance Officers Association, and
- National Association of State Auditors, Comptrollers, and Treasurers

The major responsibilities of the FAF are to raise funds for the organization, appoint the members of the Financial Accounting Standards Advisory Council and the FASB, and provide oversight to FASB's activities. The FASAC consists of about 30 members responsible for advising the FASB about major policy issues, the priority of topics, the selection of task forces, the advisability of tentative decisions, and other matters.

Standard Setting

Beginning in July 1973, the Financial Accounting Standards Board has been the official private sector entity assigned the responsibility of establishing and improving generally accepted accounting principles in the United States. The FASB consists of seven members who are fully remunerated and serve full time. Members of the board are not required to be CPAs. A five to three vote (referred to as a "super majority") is required for the adoption of a FASB standard to minimize compromises and close votes. The FASB is organized as a part of the Financial Accounting Foundation, as shown in Figure 1-4. Advantages claimed for FASB include smaller membership; full-time, renumerated membership; greater autonomy (not a senior committee of the AICPA); increased independence (ties severed with firms); broader representation (non-accountants can serve).

Pronouncements

The FASB ruled at its outset that ARBs and APB *Opinions* should remain in force until superseded by the FASB. The FASB currently issues four types of pronouncements:

1. *Statements of Financial Accounting Concepts* Concept statements establish a theoretical foundation for financial accounting and reporting standards. They do not create generally accepted accounting principles. Collectively they are referred to as the FASB's conceptual framework project.
2. *Statements of Financial Accounting Standards* Standards establish generally accepted accounting principles and describe the methods and procedures required on specific accounting issues and transactions.
3. *Interpretations* Interpretations clarify previously issued official pronouncements. They can also establish accounting principles.

Figure 1-4
Organizational Structure for Establishing Accounting Standards

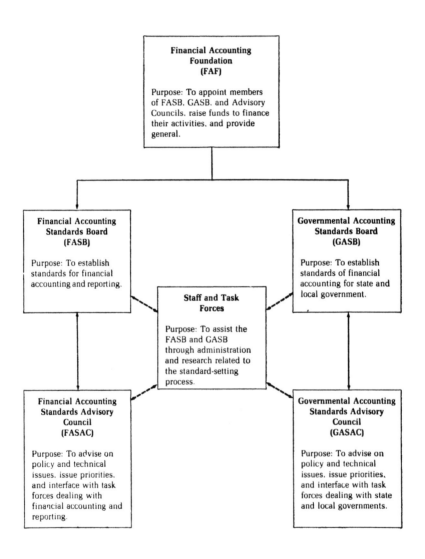

4. *Technical Bulletins* Technical bulletins are issued by the staff of the FASB and provide clarification, and elaboration on accounting and reporting issues related to Statements of Standards or Interpretations.

Due Process

The FASB follows a due process system when developing Statements of Financial Accounting Standards. The process typically involves the following major steps:

1. The board identifies an accounting problem and places the problem on its agenda.

2. The board appoints a task force of technical experts, which conducts extensive research on the problem.

3. The board issues a *Discussion Memorandum*, which summarizes the issues involved and suggests possible solutions.

4. The board conducts a public hearing, at which interested parties can present their views.

5. The board issues an *Exposure Draft* of a standard, which is being proposed for public comment.

6. The board issues an *Standard* after considering the responses to the Exposure Draft and obtaining a positive vote from the board.

Appendix B presents a List of Official Pronouncements of the AICPA and FASB.

Emerging Issues Task Force

In 1984 the FASB established an Emerging Issues Task Force (EITF) to resolve on a timely basis accounting problems that are associated with new and innovative types of transactions. The task force is composed of approximately 18 persons who come from CPA firms, major companies, the FASB, and the SEC. A consensus exists if no more than two of the voting members object to a suggested accounting approach. The task force publishes minutes of its deliberations and decisions.

GOVERNMENTAL ACCOUNTING STANDARDS BOARD

In 1984 the Governmental Accounting Standards Board was established under the oversight of the Financial Accounting Foundation to deal with state and local governmental reporting issues. The GASB has five members. The operational structure of the GASB is similar to that of the FASB (See Exhibit 1-4). It has its own advisory council, staff, and task forces. The GASB establishes generally accepted accounting principles for state and local governments. It issues authoritative pronouncements including *Statements, Interpretations,* and *Technical Bulletins.*

FEDERAL GOVERNMENT ACCOUNTING

The major financial management responsibilities of the federal legislative and executive branches include the following:

Legislative Branch
    Congress
    General Accounting Office (Comptroller General)
    Congressional Budget Office
Executive Branch
    President
    Office of Management and Budget
    Secretary of the Treasury
    Federal Agencies
Joint Financial Management Improvement Program (overall Federal complex)

The accounting principles and standards for federal agencies are prescribed by the Comptroller General. These principles and standards are contained in Appendix I, "Accounting Principles and Standards," of Title 2—"Accounting," of the *GAO Policy and Procedures Manual for Guidance of Federal Agencies*. A portion of Title 2 is published separately as *Accounting Principles and Standards for Federal Agencies*.

INTERNATIONAL ACCOUNTING STANDARDS

The European Economic Community (EEC) has developed directives that identify basic financial reporting requirements. The member countries are in the process of conforming their laws to the EEC's directives. The accounting profession has also undertaken a major project to encourage voluntary uniformity in the application of accounting principles and practices. Professional groups in the major industrial countries of the world formed the International Accounting Standards Committee (IASC) in 1973 and gave it the responsibility for articulating international standards. This body now represents more than 100 accountancy bodies from 75 countries. Member countries' professional organizations agreed to use their efforts to bring about compliance with the standards adopted by the IASC. The development and enforcement of international accounting standards can only increase in importance as banks and other entities extend their operations globally.

THE AMERICAN ACCOUNTING ASSOCIATION

The American Accounting Association (AAA) is an organization for accounting academicians. Practicing professional accountants also belong to the AAA. An AAA representative serves on a panel that selects the trustees of the Financial Accounting Foundation and an AAA committee reacts to FASB pronouncements. The impact of the AAA on the development of accounting standards has been considered by some accounting educators to have been minimal. The AAA serves at times as a critic of standard setters by appraising accounting practice and recommending improvements. The AAA publishes *The Accounting Review, Accounting Horizons*, and *Issues in Accounting Education*.

THE SECURITIES AND EXCHANGE COMMISSION

The Securities and Exchange Commission (SEC) is an independent regulatory agency of the United States government which administers the Securities Act of 1933, the Securities Exchange Act of 1934, and other legislation. The SEC has broad statutory powers to prescribe the accounting practices and standards to be used by companies that come within its jurisdiction. When the Commission was formed, Congress gave it power to establish accounting principles as stated in the following excerpt from the Securities Exchange Act of 1934, Section 13(b):

> The Commission may prescribe, in regard to reports made pursuant to this title, the form or forms in which the required information shall be set forth, the items or details to be shown in the balance sheet and the earning statements, and the methods to be followed in the preparation of reports, in the appraisal or valuation of assets and liabilities.

The SEC has affirmed its support for the FASB, indicating that financial statements conforming to standards set by the FASB will be presumed to have authoritative support. The SEC requires registrants to adhere to GAAP. The SEC in its reports to Congress has indicated "that it continues to believe that the initiative for establishing and improving accounting standards should remain in the private sector, subject to Commission oversight."

The most important corporate reports of the SEC include the following:

1. *Registration statement* A detailed report required when a company makes a public offering of its securities.

2. *10-K* A report including audited financial statements that companies file annually.

3. *10-Q* A quarterly report that includes financial information relating to the activities of the entity reporting.

4. *8-K report* A report that explains a material event that investors should know about (such as a major acquisition or lawsuit).

The Commission has issued statements pertaining to accounting and auditing issues. These statements are usually specific in nature and deal with a particular company or a specific situation. Presently, SEC statements are referred to as either *Financial Reporting Releases* (FRRs) or *Accounting and Auditing Enforcement Releases* (AAERs).

The SEC is discussed more thoroughly in Chapter 2.

THE INTERNAL REVENUE SERVICE (IRS)

The Internal Revenue Service has exercised an influence on accounting practice. Firms often adopt accounting procedures that minimize taxable income. Tax laws also exert a pervasive influence on business decision making and financial reporting. When preparing financial statements, tax principles and procedures must conform to the requirements of generally accepted accounting principles.

GENERALLY ACCEPTED ACCOUNTING PRINCIPLES (GAAP)

Generally accepted accounting principles are those accounting guidelines or standards that have substantial authoritative support. GAAP describe accepted accounting practice at a particular time. The objective of GAAP is to reduce the differences and inconsistencies in accounting practice, thereby improving the comparability and credibility of financial reports. The Accounting Principles Board of the American Institute of Certified Public Accountants (AICPA) stated that

> Generally accepted accounting principles incorporate the consensus at a particular time as to which economic resources and obligations should be recorded as assets and liabilities . . . which changes in assets and liabilities should be recorded, when these changes should be recorded, how the recorded assets and liabilities and changes in them should be measured, what information should be disclosed, and which financial statements should be prepared.

Statement on Auditing Standards No. 69, "The Meaning of Present Fairly in Conformity with Generally Accepted Accounting Principles in the Independent Auditor's Report" explains the meaning of the phrase "present fairly . . . in conformity with generally accepted accounting principles" in the independent auditor's report. Statement No. 69 classifies generally accepted accounting principles in five categories arranged in a GAAP hierarchy for business (nongovernmental) entities:

1. Pronouncements of the Financial Accounting Standards Board (FASB) and its predecessors, the Accounting Principles Board (APB), and AICPA Research Bulletins
    These pronouncements include FASB statements of Standards and Interpretations, APB Opinions, and AICPA Accounting Research Bulletins (ARB).

2. FASB Technical Bulletins and AICPA's Interpretations, AICPA Industry Audit and Accounting Guides, and AICPA Statements of Position

3. Consensus positions of the FASB Emerging Issues Task Force and AICPA Practice Bulletins

4. AICPA accounting interpretations, "Qs and As" published by the FASB staff, as well as industry practices widely recognized and prevalent

5. Other accounting literature, including FASB Concepts Statements; APB Statements; AICPA Issue Papers; International Accounting Standards Committee Statements; GASB Statements, Interpretations, and Technical Bulletins; pronouncements of other professional associations or regulatory agencies; AICPA *Technical Practice Aids;* and accounting textbooks, handbooks, and articles

Categories 1 through 4 represent established accounting principles. Category 5 represents other accounting literature. In the absence of established accounting principles, the auditor may consider other accounting literature, depending on its relevance in the circumstances.

If an established accounting principle from one or more sources in categories 2, 3, or 4 is relevant to the circumstances, the auditor should be prepared to justify a conclusion that another treatment is generally accepted. If there is a conflict between accounting principles relevant to the circumstances from one or more sources in category 2, 3, 4, the auditor should follow the treatment specified by the source in the higher category—for example, follow category 2 treatment over category 3, or be prepared to justify a conclusion that a treatment specified by a source in the lower category better presents the substance of the transaction in the circumstances.

Rules and interpretative releases of the Securities and Exchange Commission have an authority similar to category (1) pronouncements for SEC registrants. In addition, the SEC staff issues Staff Accounting Bulletins that represent practices followed by the staff in administering SEC disclosure requirements.

The auditor is aware that the accounting requirements adopted by regulatory agencies for reports filed with them may differ from generally accepted accounting principles in certain respects. Paragraph .04 of AU section 544, *Lack of Conformity With Generally Accepted Accounting Principles (AICPA, Professional Standards,* Vol. 1 and SAS No. 62, *Special Reports,* Vol. 1, (AICPA, *Professional Standards,* Vol. 1, AU sec. 623) provide guidance if the auditor is reporting on financial statements prepared in conformity with a comprehensive basis of accounting other than generally accepted accounting principles.

Because of developments such as new legislation or the evolution of a new type of business transaction, there sometimes are no established accounting principles for reporting a specific transaction or event. In those instances, it might be possible to report the event or transaction on the basis of its substance by selecting an accounting principle that appears appropriate when applied in a manner similar to the application of an established principle to an analogous transaction or event.

Source: *Statement of Auditing Standards No. 69.*

MAJOR ACCOUNTING ASSUMPTIONS, PRINCIPLES, AND CONVENTIONS

The accounting profession has developed a number of significant accounting assumptions and conventions which underlie financial statements. Several of these assumptions and conventions are described here:

1. *Economic entity assumption* Information is recorded and reported about each separate economic entity that is a particular unit of accountability, e.g., The First National Bank.

2. *Continuity (Going concern) assumption* A company is assumed to continue operations, unless substantial evidence to the contrary exists.

3. *Timely and periodic reporting assumption* Information is reported in the financial statements at least on an annual basis. This assumption is also referred to as the "periodicity assumption."

4. *Monetary unit assumption* The national currency of a company is used as a stable unit of measure in preparing financial reports. The purchasing power of money is not reported in the financial statements.

There are three basic principles used to record transactions:

1. *Historical cost principle* Generally, the exchange price at the time of an acquisition of an asset or liability is retained in the accounting records as the value of an item until it is consumed, sold, or liquidated, and removed from the accounting records. The acquisition cost of the asset or liability is its historical cost. The historical cost is objective and verifiable.

2. *Revenue realization principle* Accrual accounting realizes (recognizes) revenue when (1) it is earned and (2) an exchange has taken place (not when cash is received). Revenue is considered earned when the entity has substantially accomplished what it must do to be entitled to the benefits represented by the revenues. Recognition of an item in the financial statement is made only after the following criteria are met:

    (a) *Definition* The item must meet the definition of an element of financial statements.

    (b) *Measurability* The item must have a relevant attribute measurable with sufficient reliability.

    (c) *Relevant* The information must be capable of making a difference in decision making.

    (d) *Reliability* The information must be representationally faithful, verifiable, and neutral.

3. *Matching principle (expense recognition).* The practice of letting the expense follow (match; associate with) the revenue is sometimes referred to as the matching principle. Expenses are to be matched—directly or indirectly—with revenues whenever it is reasonable and practicable to do so.

Additional significant concepts or conventions are also applicable to financial reporting:

1. *Accrual accounting* Accrual accounting recognizes the financial effects of transactions, events, and circumstances having cash consequences to the period in which they occur rather than when the cash receipt or payment occurs.

2. *Conservatism* Conservatism requires that uncertainties and risks related to a company are reflected in its accounting reports. APB *Statement 4* had this to say about conservatism:

    Frequently, assets and liabilities are measured in a context of significant uncertainties. Historically, managers, investors, and accountants have generally preferred that possible errors in measurement be in the direction of understatement rather than overstatement of net income and net assets. This has led to the convention of conservation.

3. *Full disclosure principle* The full disclosure principle requires that circumstances and events that make a difference to financial statement users be disclosed.

4. *Substance over form* Financial accounting is concerned with the legal as well as the economic effect of transactions. When an apparent conflict exists between the economic substance and the legal form of a business transaction, accountants tend to

emphasize economic substance. For example, current accounting principles require a lessee to report certain kinds of leases as assets and liabilities even though the lessee does not actually own the leased property.

BANK SPECIFIC: GAAP vs. RAP

Bank regulators have promulgated specific reporting practices and procedures referred to as regulatory accounting principles (RAP), which can differ from GAAP. This difference is due to the different objectives of regulators (to monitor the soundness and safety of banks) and accounting authorities (to provide relevant decision-making information). The Financial Institutions Reform, Recovery and Enforcement Act of 1989 (FIRREA) directed federal banking regulators to adopt a single comprehensive accounting framework to deal with the problem.

The four federal regulatory agencies that regulate banks and thrift institutions—the Federal Reserve System, the Office of the Comptroller of the Currency, the Federal Deposit Insurance Corporation, and the Office of Thrift Supervision—do require special purpose financial statements from the financial institutions they regulate. Each of the agencies, while requiring that regulated entities generally follow GAAP, has set forth a relatively small number of reporting rules and regulations which depart from GAAP. They are sometimes referred to as regulatory accounting procedures or regulatory accounting principles (RAP).

Regulatory accounting principles usually arise because the financial services industry must deal with a specific type of accounting issue not fully covered by GGAP, or to obtain more consistent or comparable financial information for oversight purposes. Regulators believe that specific, limited departures from GAAP are sometimes necessary to adequately monitor and evaluate the safety and soundness of financial institutions.

A regulatory accounting principle may deviate from its GAAP counterpart in either of two ways. Difference can occur when RAP specific accounting methods—some of which are mandatory and some of which are optional—are contrary to GAAP. Extensions of GAAP exist when GAAP allows flexibility in the accounting treatment of a particular transaction but RAP limit or restrict the accounting treatment to one or more particular GAAP methods. The differences cited in the first example produce financial information that does not conform with GAAP, while the extensions cited in the second example result in financial information that does conform with GAAP.

It has been suggested that the term "regulatory accounting principles" is somewhat misleading. For some regulatory agencies, RAP is not a comprehensive basis of accounting and arguably should not be considered as an "accounting principle."

Figure 1-5 specifies the accounting treatment required by regulatory agencies for accounting issues where at least one federal regulator required RAP.

Figure 1-5
Accounting Treatment Required by Regulatory Agencies
for Accounting Issues Where at Least One Federal Regulator Requires
RAP Be Followed

Accounting issue	Accounting treatment(a) prescribed for regulatory reports submitted to			
	FHLBB	FRS	FDIC	OCC
Basis of Accounting-Cash versus Accrual	RAP-D[b]	GAAP	GAAP	GAAP
Intangibles-Goodwill	RAP-X	RAP-X	RAP-X	RAP-X
Sale of Receivables with Recourse	GAAP	RAP-D	RAP-D	RAP-D
Securities Transactions-Trading Account	GAAP	RAP-D	RAP-D	RAP-D
Subordinated Debt Securities	RAP-D	GAAP	GAAP	GAAP
Sale and Leaseback	GAAP	RAP-D	RAP-D	RAP-X
Future Contracts	RAP-D	RAP-D	RAP-D	RAP-D
Gains/Losses on Sales of Loans and Certain Securities	RAP-D[c]	GAAP	GAAP	GAAP
Acquisition, Development, and Construction Loan Transactions	RAP-D	GAAP	GAAP	GAAP
Appraised Equity Capital	RAP-D[d]	GAAP	GAAP	GAAP
Loan Origination Charges and Credits	RAP-D	GAAP	GAAP	GAAP
Premium/Discount on Purchase of Mortgage Loans	RAP-D	GAAP	GAAP	GAAP
Loan Commitment Fees	RAP-D	GAAP	GAAP	GAAP
Convertible Debt Securities	RAP-D[e]	GAAP	GAAP	RAP-D[e]
Recordation of Loss Reserves	RAP-D	GAAP	GAAP	GAAP
Sale of Real Estate Developed by the Association	RAP-D	GAAP	GAAP	GAAP
Wash Sales	RAP-D	GAAP	GAAP	GAAP
Net Worth Certificates	RAP-D	N/A	RAP-D	N/A
Participation in Bankers Acceptances	N/A[f]	RAP-D[f]	RAP-D[f]	RAP-D[f]
In-Substance Defeasance	GAAP	RAP-D	RAP-D	RAP-D
Net Deferred Tax Charges	GAAP	GAAP	RAP-X	RAP-X

[a]GAAP indicates a generally accepted accounting principle for that accounting issue.

RAP-D indicates a regulatory accounting principle which differs from its GAAP counterpart for that accounting issue. For some issues, use of the principle is optional, for other issues, use of the principle is mandatory.

RAP-X indicates a regulatory accounting principle which is an extension of its GAAP counterpart for that accounting issue.

N/A indicates not applicable. Financial institutions reporting to that federal regulatory agency do not encounter that particular accounting issue.

KEY DEFINITIONS

Accounting An information system developing information, primarily financial, about a specific entity. The AICPA defines accounting as a service activity whose "function is to provide quantitative information, primarily financial in nature, about economic entities that is intended to be useful in making economic decisions."

Accounting conventions Methods or procedures used in accounting.

Accounting policies Accounting principles used by a specific entity.

Accounting principles The methods or procedures used in accounting for events, transactions, and circumstances reported in the financial statements. The term is generally used when a method or procedure has received official authoritative sanctions by a pronouncement of a group, e.g., the APB, EITF, FASB, or SEC.

Accounting procedures The methods used for implementing accounting principles.

Accounting standards Accounting principles.

Accrual accounting A basic accounting assumption that revenues are recognized when earned and expenses are recognized when incurred, without regard to when cash is received or paid.

Annual report A report to shareholders and others prepared annually. The report includes a balance sheet, an income statement, a statement of cash flows, a reconciliation of changes in owners' equity, a summary of significant accounting principles and other explanatory notes, the auditor's report, and comments from management relating to the current year's activities.

Conceptual framework of accounting Broad qualitative standards for financial reporting developed by the FASB. The concepts serve to guide the selection of economic events to be recognized and measured for financial reporting and their display in financial statements or related means of communicating information to those who are interested. The concepts do not represent GAAP.

   1   Objectives of Financial Reporting by Business Enterprises (discussed in this chapter)

   2   Qualitative Characteristics of Accounting Information (discussed in this chapter)

   3   Elements of Financial Statements by Business Enterprises was replaced by Concepts Statement No. 6.

4   Objectives of Financial Reporting by Nonbusiness Organizations

5   Recognition and Measurement in Financial Statements of Business Enterprises (discussed in this chapter)

6   Elements of Financial Statements (discussed in next chapter)

Conservatism A constraint underlying the reporting of accounting information that assumes when doubt exists concerning two or more reporting alternatives, one should select that alternative with the least favorable impact on owners' equity.

Consistency A quality of useful accounting information requiring that accounting methods be followed consistently from one period to the next unless conditions indicate that changing to another method would provide more useful information.

Elements of Financial Statements The building blocks with which financial statements are constructed—the classes of items that financial statements comprise:

Assets	Expenses
Liabilities	Losses
Equity	Investments by owners
Revenues	Distribution to owners
Gains	Comprehensive income (earnings)

FASB Financial Accounting Standards Board An independent board that establishes generally accepted accounting principles. The official pronouncements of the board are called Statements of Financial Accounting Concepts, Statements of Financial Accounting Standards, and Interpretations.

Financial accounting The activity associated with the development of financial information for external users that produce general-purpose financial statements.

Generally accepted accounting principles (GAAP). The conventions, rules, and procedures that define accepted accounting practice at a particular time, including general guidelines and detailed practices and procedures.

Going concern An entity that is expected to continue in existence for the foreseeable future.

Historical cost The cash equivalent price of goods or services at the date of acquisition; the acquisition cost.

Income statement A statement that reports a firm's net income for a time period. The statement summarizes revenues, expenses, gains, and losses.

Management accounting The activity related to financial reporting for internal users.

Materiality A constraint underlying for the reporting of accounting information that determines a threshold for recognition of an item in the financial statements.

Normal operating cycle The time required for cash to be converted to inventories, inventories into receivables, and receivables into cash.

Objectives of Financial Reporting FASB *Statement of Financial Accounting Concepts No. 1* establishes the broad objectives of financial reporting that guide the development of accounting standards:

1. To provide information useful in investment, credit, and similar decisions.

2. To provide information useful in assessing cash flow prospects.

3. To provide information about enterprise resources, claims to those resources, and changes in them.

Qualitative Characteristics of Accounting Information (FASB) *Statement of Accounting Concepts No. 1* presents a hierarchy of qualities, with usefulness for decision making of most importance.

RAP Regulatory accounting practices (principles).

Registration statement A report the SEC requires when a regulated company makes a public offering of its securities.

10-K The annual report required by the SEC of most publicly held corporations.

10-Q A quarterly report required by the SEC.

Chapter 2

Bank Regulation and Reporting

B anking regulation and reporting has deep historical roots and is considered essential to the concept of banking as a public trust. Regulation, deregulation, and reregulation reflect the evolutionary nature of commercial banking. Banking is interconnected and confidence-sensitive in relation to the nation's economy and well-being so that some form of regulation is deemed desirable, if not necessary. Bank regulation involves the formulation and issuance by authorized agencies of specific rules or regulations, under governing law, for the conduct and structure of banking. Bank supervision relates to the concerns of financial regulators with the safety and soundness of individual banks, involving the general and continuous oversight of the activities of this industry to ensure that banks are operated prudently and in accordance with applicable statutes and regulations. This chapter deals with the current status of bank regulation and reporting in the United States.

OBJECTIVES OF BANKING REGULATION

Banking regulation has three basic objectives: safety, stability, and structure. The specific aims of banking regulation are to protect (1) depositors and the deposit-insurance fund, (2) the economy from inappropriate influence of the financial system, and (3) bank customers from the arbitrary control of banks.

REGULATORY AGENCIES—AN OVERVIEW

Various governmental bodies are responsible for supervising and regulating depository institutions. This supervisory structure has evolved as a result of the complexity of the U.S. financial system. It reflects a wide variety of federal and state laws and regulations designed to remedy problems that U.S. commercial banks and nonbank depository institutions have encountered over the past century. The Federal Reserve System (Fed), the Office of the Comptroller of the Currency (OCC), the Securities and Exchange Commission (SEC), the Federal Deposit Insurance Corporation (FDIC), and the Office of Thrift Supervision (OTS) currently share authority with bank and thrift supervisors of the fifty states. This dual banking system provides for the chartering, supervision, and regulation of commercial banking organizations at the federal and state levels. The current regulatory and supervisory structure for depository institutions is shown here:

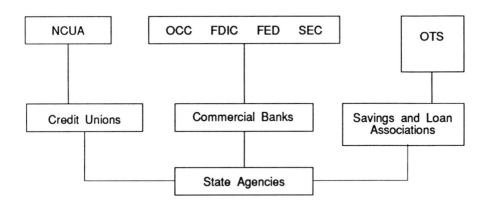

The National Credit Union Association (NCUA) charters, supervises, examines, and provides share insurance for all federally-chartered credit unions and has the authority to examine and supervise those state-chartered credit unions that apply and are accepted for NCUA insurance. Commercial banks are subject to oversight by the OCC, FDIC, Fed and the SEC and, where appropriate, by state banking agencies.

The Office of Thrift Supervision supervises the thrifts, including federally chartered savings and loans associations and federally chartered savings banks. It also supervises savings and loan holding companies, and shares with the states the supervision of federally insured, state-chartered savings and loan associations.

The Financial Institutions Reform, Recovery and Enforcement Act of 1989 (FIRREA) is major legislation that changed the banking structure and its regulation in the United States. FIRREA created the OTS and the Savings Association Insurance Fund (SAIF) as the thrift institutions' insurer (to replace the Federal Savings and Loan Insurance Corporation) to be administered by the FDIC.

The Federal Financial Institutions Examination Council (FFIEC), an interagency body, was established by statute to prescribe uniform principles, standards, and report forms for the federal examination of depository institutions and to promote coordination in other areas of supervision. The council is composed of the chairs of the Office of Thrift Supervision, National Credit Union Administration, and the Federal Deposit Insurance Corporation, the Comptroller of the Currency and a governor of the Federal Reserve Board appointed by the chair of that board.

It is the intention of the banking agencies to follow GAAP wherever appropriate. However, call reports that are supervisory and regulatory documents and the FFIEC call report instructions do not follow GAAP in all cases. Banks are expected to follow GAAP in reporting transactions not covered by the FFIEC call report instructions. Where neither GAAP nor the FFIEC instructions are clear, a specific ruling should be sought from a bank's primary federal bank supervisory agency.

FEDERAL RESERVE SYSTEM

The Federal Reserve System is the central banking system of the United States, created by the Federal Reserve Act, approved December 23, 1913. The Federal Reserve System was created to provide for safer and more flexible credit and monetary systems.

Central banks typically perform additional functions, including the transfer of funds, handling government deposits and debt issues, supervising and regulating banks, and acting as lender of last resort and as a bank for banks. The Federal Reserve System grew out of the defects and insufficiencies of the former decentralized national-state banking system.

The System consists of six parts: the Board of Governors in Washington, DC; the 12 Federal Reserve Banks and their 25 branches and other facilities situated throughout the country (37 automated clearinghouses, 46 regional check processing centers, and the Culpeper Communications and Record Center); the Federal Open Market Committee; the Federal Advisory Council; the Consumer Advisory Council; the Thrift Institutions Advisory Council; and the nation's financial institutions, including commercial banks, savings and loan associations, mutual savings banks, and credit unions. A graphic description of the Federal Reserve System and its operations are presented in Figure 2-1.

The Board of Governors is composed of seven members appointed by the President with the advice and consent of the Senate. The Chairman of the Board is a member of the National Advisory Council on International Monetary and Financial Policies. The Board determines general monetary, credit, and operating policies for the System as a whole and formulates the rules and regulations necessary to carry out the purposes of the Federal Reserve Act. The Board monitors credit conditions; supervises the Federal Reserve Banks, member banks, and bank holding companies; and regulates the implementation of various consumer credit protection laws.

The Federal Open Market Committee is composed of the Board of Governors and five of the presidents of the Reserve Banks. Open market operations of the Reserve Banks are conducted under regulations adopted by the Committee and pursuant to specific policy directives issued by the Committee. Operations are carried out principally in U.S. Government obligations, Federal agency obligations, and bankers' acceptances. All operations are conducted in New York. The Federal Reserve Bank of New York executes the transactions.

Figure 2-1
The Federal Reserve System: Relationship to Credit Policy Instruments

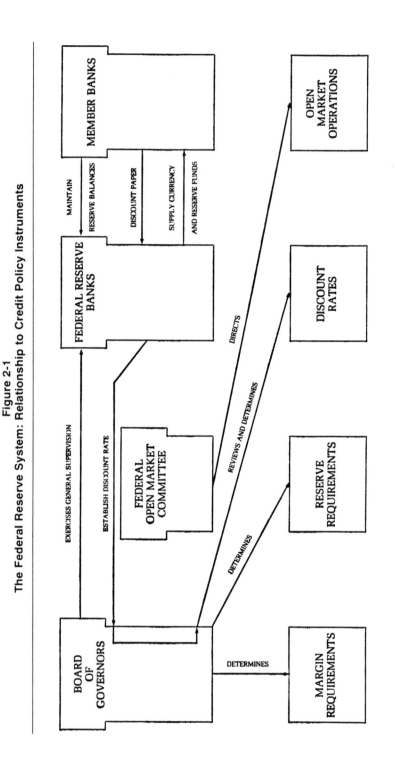

Source: Board of Governors, *The Federal Reserve System: Purposes and Functions.*

The Reserve Banks issue Federal reserve notes, which constitute the bulk of money in circulation. These notes are obligations of the United States and are a prior lien upon the assets of the issuing Federal Reserve Bank. They are issued against a pledge by the Reserve Bank with the Federal Reserve agent of collateral security, including gold certificates, paper discounted or purchased by the Bank, and direct obligations of the United States. The reserve banks also receive and hold on deposit the reserve or clearing account deposits of depository institutions. The Reserve Banks assist in the extensions of credit to depository institutions subject to Federal Reserve requirements on transaction accounts or nonpersonal time deposits. Reserve Banks act as clearinghouses and as collection agents for depository institutions in the collection of checks and other instruments. They also act as depositories and fiscal agents of the United States and exercise other banking functions specified in the Federal Reserve Act.

The Federal Advisory Council acts in an advisory capacity, conferring with the Board of Governors on general business conditions. The Consumer Advisory Council confers with the Board of Governors on the Board's responsibilities in the field of consumer credit protection. The Thrift Institutions Advisory Council is an advisory group made up of representatives from nonbank depository thrift institutions, which includes savings and loans, mutual savings bankers, and credit unions. The Council meets with the Board to discuss developments relating to thrift institutions, the housing industry and mortgage finance, and certain regulatory issues.

The more important activities of the Fed can be grouped under the following main areas:

1. Fiscal and monetary activities:
   - Acting as fiscal agent for the U.S. government
   - Regulating money supply
2. Banking services:
   - Maintaining legal resources of banks
   - Transferring funds (FedWire)
   - Clearing and collecting checks
   - Issuing loans to members and other depository institutions
   - Supplying currency when needed
3. Examination and supervision:
   - State-chartered member banks
   - Federal Reserve banks, bank holding companies, and new banking affiliates
   - Regulating foreign transactions of its member banks and the transactions of foreign banks doing business in the United States
   - Enforcing legislation and issuing rules and regulations dealing with "truth in lending" and deceptive and unfair bank practices
4. Research and publication

Under federal statute, the examination of member banks falls under the Federal Reserve System. As a practical matter, the Fed accepts the results of examinations of national banks conducted by the OCC. The Fed primarily regulates and supervises member state banks, including the registration and reporting requirements of the Securities Exchange Act of 1934.

Monetary Policy

A primary function of the Federal Reserve System is to promote a flow of credit and money that will facilitate economic growth, a stable dollar, and long-term balance in intentional payments. The principal means available to the System to influence monetary policy include open market purchases and sales, primarily of U.S. Government securities but also of foreign currencies, discount operations (lending to commercial banks), and changes in bank reserve requirements. Bank reserves constitute the legally required basis of bank deposits. Changes in the reserve position of banks can directly affect the flow of bank credit and money throughout the economy.

The Federal Reserve System can influence interest rates by exerting pressure on the nation's saving and investments, market expectations, and the flow of bank credit and money as they affect decisions to lend, spend, and save. Operations by the System in foreign exchange markets also have an impact on the international balance of payments.

Supervisory Function

Specific and detailed supervisory powers of the Fed through its Board include prescribing rules and regulations governing

- Examination of Federal reserve banks, state member banks, bankholding companies, and their nonbank subsidiaries
- Requiring periodic reports of member banks
- Approving or denying FRS membership applications and applications for branches, merger, or the creation of bank holding companies
- Advances and discounts by Federal Reserve banks to member banks
- Open market purchases of bills of exchange, trade acceptances, and bankers' acceptances by Federal Reserve banks
- Acceptance by member banks of drafts or bills of exchange; legal reserve requirements of member and nonmember banks and other depository institutions
- Purchase of warrants by Federal Reserve banks
- Accounting and disclosure requirements for equity securities of state member banks; extension of securities credit by lenders other than banks, brokers, or dealers
- Eligibility requirements and conditions for membership in the Federal Reserve System by state-chartered banking institutions
- Issuance and cancellation of stock of Federal Reserve banks
- Collection of checks and other items by Federal Reserve banks
- Regulation of corporations engaged in foreign banking and financing
- Regulation of interlocking bank relationships under the Clayton Act

- Regulation of foreign branches of national banks
- Relationships with foreign banks and bankers
- Loans to executive officers of member banks
- Prescription of minimum security devices and procedures for Federal Reserve banks and state member banks
- Regulation of interest on time and savings deposits
- Relationships with dealers in securities
- Bank service arrangements
- Extension of securities credit by brokers and dealers and by banks for the purpose of purchasing or carrying securities on margin
- Loan guarantees for defense production
- Regulation of bank holding companies: prescription of disclosure and computation requirements on consumer credit charges (the Truth in Lending Act), as well as a variety of other functions under other consumer-oriented legislation
- Other supervisory powers include the following: to fix upon affirmative vote of not less than six of its members, for each Federal Reserve district, the percentage of individual bank capital and surplus which may be represented by security loans; to direct any member bank to refrain from further increases in loans secured by stock and bonds collateral for any period up to one year; to suspend at its discretion any member bank from use of Federal Reserve credit facilities when in the board's judgment such member bank is making undue use of such credit, to remove any bank officer or director of a member bank who continues to violate any law relating to such bank or continues unsafe and unsound practices in conducting the bank's business, after receiving warning by the Comptroller of the Currency; to suspend or remove any officer, director, or employee of Federal Reserve banks for cause; to suspend any Federal Reserve bank, to operate it, and, if necessary, to reorganize it.

Central Banking Activities

The Federal Reserve banks perform a variety of central banking functions, which can be summarized as follows:

1. To serve as a depository for reserve and clearing balances of depository institutions
2. To furnish an elastic currency and credit
3. To provide efficient system of collecting out-of-town cash items
4. To engage in open market operations, to deal in gold, and to establish foreign correspondents and agencies
5. To serve as depository and fiscal agent for the Treasury and to carry on subtreasury operations
6. To develop and maintain the U.S. money market

7. To apply federal criminal conflict-of-interest provisions for federal employees to Federal Reserve bank directors, officers, and employees

8. To provide for expedited board approval of bank and bank holding company acquisitions, consolidations, and mergers in emergency situations or when immediate action is necessary to prevent the probable failure of the bank or bank holding company involved in the transaction (Section 3(b) of the Bank Holding Company Act)

9. To disapprove changes in control of insured banks and bank holding companies

10. To enhance and maintain public confidence in the banking system by preventing serious adverse effects from anticompetitive combinations of interests, inadequate financial support, and unsuitable management

Depository Institutions

The Federal Reserve's responsibilities for supervising and regulating the activities of depository institutions in the United States include (1) supervision and regulation of state-chartered banks that are members of the Federal Reserve System, all Edge act and agreement corporations, and all bank holding companies; (2) supervision and regulation of the U.S. activities of foreign banking organizations under the International Banking Act of 1978; (3) regulation of the U.S. commercial banking structure through administration of the Bank Holding Company Act of 1956 as amended and, along with other federal agencies, the Bank Merger Act of 1960 and the Change in Bank Control Act of 1978; and (4) regulation of the foreign activities of all U.S. commercial banking organizations that are members of the Federal Reserve System or that conduct their foreign activities through an Edge corporation. The Federal Reserve System is also responsible for several consumer protection statutes, such as the Truth in Lending Act, the Fair Credit Billing Act, the Equal Credit Opportunity Act, The Fair Credit Reporting Act, the Consumer Leading Act, the Real Estate Settlement Procedures Act, the Electronic Fund Transfer Act, and the Federal Trade Commission Improvement Act.

Bank Specific

The Federal Reserve has supervision and on-site examination responsibilities over domestic and international operations of all member banks, Edge act and agreement corporations, and U.S. bank holding companies, as well as over many of the U.S. activities of foreign banking organizations. The Comptroller of the Currency has primary responsibility for supervising and examining member banks that are nationally chartered. The Federal Reserve System exercises primary supervisory responsibility for and examines only those member banks that are charted by the states, and share this responsibility with state supervisory agencies. The Federal Reserve conducts joint examinations with state agencies, or alternates annual examinations with those agencies.

According to Federal Reserve System regulations, the System's examination involves (1) an appraisal of the soundness of the institution's assets; (2) an evaluation of internal operations, policies, and management; (3) an analysis of key financial factors such as capital, earnings, liquidity, and interest rate sensitivity; (4) a review for compliance that all banking laws and regulations; and (5) an overall determination of the institution's solvency. The Federal Reserve also conducts special examinations of state member banks in certain areas such as consumer affairs; activities of trust departments, stock transfer agents, and municipal securities dealers; and electronic data processing.

The Federal Reserve is the primary supervisor for bank holding companies under the Bank Holding Company Act of 1956, as amended. The Federal Reserve conducts on-site inspections of parent bank holding companies and their significant nonbank subsidiaries. These inspections include a review of nonbank assets and funding activities, an evaluation of policies and procedures for managing the holding company and its subsidiaries, and a review for compliance with the Bank Holding Company Act and other relevant banking statues. The Federal Reserve is responsible for requiring a bank or a bank holding company that is not considered in satisfactory condition to take steps to correct the situation. Typically the Federal Reserve will enter into an informal agreement or memorandum of understanding with the bank and its directors concerning the appropriate actions to be taken. In more serious cases, a written agreement or cease and desist order is issued to direct the bank to take the necessary corrective measures.

Should a bank's condition become critical, the Federal Reserve may assume a significant role in the design of a plan to provide financial and managerial assistance. The Board of Governors can approve the immediate acquisition of a failed or problem bank by a bank holding company or a state member bank. Occasionally, liquidity assistance can be provided through the discount window to problem institutions before the reacquisition by another depository institution or liquidation by the insurance authority.

Fed and International Operations of U.S. Banks

The Federal Reserve has four principal statutory responsibilities related to the supervision and regulation of the international operations of U.S. banking organizations that are members of the Federal Reserve System. These responsibilities include (1) authorizing the establishment of foreign branches of member banks and regulating the scope of their activities; (2) chartering and regulating the activities of Edge act corporations; (3) authorizing overseas investments by member banks, Edge act and agreement corporations, and bank holding companies, and regulating the activities of foreign firms acquired by such investments; and (4) establishing supervisory policies with respect to foreign lending of member banks.

The Fed and U.S. Activities of Foreign Banks

The International Banking Act of 1978 (IBA) provided for federal regulation of the U.S. operations of foreign banks and granted important responsibilities to the Federal Reserve for the supervision and regulation of such operations. The IBA created a federal regulatory and supervisory structure for U.S. branches and agencies of foreign banks similar to that applicable to U.S. banks to promote equality between domestic and foreign banking institutions in the United States. The IBA limited expansion of interstate deposit-taking and domestic nonbanking activities of foreign banks, and required FDIC insurance for branches that engage in retail deposit-taking. The Federal Reserve has statutory authority to examine on site the assets and liabilities of all branches and agencies of foreign banks, but it typically relies upon examinations that state and other federal banking authorities conduct.

Regulation of the Banking Structure

The Federal Reserve System has statutory responsibility for the administration of the Bank Holding Company Act of 1956 as amended, the Bank Merger Act of 1960, and the Change in Bank Control Act of 1978. Under these acts the Board approves or denies the acquisition of banks and closely regulates nonbanking activities by bank holding companies and allows or rejects certain other changes of control and mergers of bank and bank holding companies.

Under the Bank Holding Company Act as amended in 1970, a bank holding company is defined as any company that (1) directly or indirectly owns, controls, or has power to vote 25 percent or more of any class of the voting shares of a bank; (2) controls in any manner the election of a majority of the directors or trustees of a bank; or (3) exercises a controlling influence over the management or policies of a bank. Prior approval of the Federal Reserve is required of a company that seeks to become a bank holding company. In considering applications to acquire a bank or a bank holding company, the Board must take into account the likely effects of the acquisition on banking competition, the convenience and needs for baking services of the community to be served, and the financial and managerial resources and prospects of the holding company and the bank.

The Bank Holding Company Act of 1956 intended that holding companies be prevented from engaging in nonbanking activities or from acquiring nonbanking companies but did not completely prohibit a holding company from becoming involved in nonbanking activities that might be in the public interest. Congress provided some exceptions to the prohibition against bank holding companies engaging in nonbanking activities, and the 1970 amendments to the act broadened the exceptions. The current trends appear to be in the direction of broadening the exceptions. Examples of activities that a bank holding company might engage in include the following: making and servicing loans and other extensions of credit; operating as an industrial bank; performing trust activities; acting as an investment or financial adviser; leasing real or personal property on a full-payout basis; make equity and debt investments in corporations or projects designed primarily to promote community welfare; providing financially related bookkeeping and data processing services; acting as an agent or broker for credit-related insurance and certain other limited forms of insurance; acting as an underwriter for credit life insurance and for credit accident and health insurance directly related to extensions of consumer credit by the bank holding company system; providing financially related courier services; providing management consulting advice to nonaffiliated bank and nonbank depository institutions; acting as an agent or broker for the sale at retail of money orders, U.S. savings bonds, and the issuance and sale of travelers checks; performing real estate appraisals; arranging equity financing for commercial real estate; underwriting and dealing in government obligations; providing foreign exchange advisory and transaction services; acting as a futures commission merchant; providing discount securities brokerage services; and investing in export trading companies.

Bank Holding Companies Reports

Bank holding companies with consolidated assets of $140 million or more or with more than one subsidiary bank must file form FR Y-6 Annual Report of Bank Holding Companies with the

Federal Reserve. Multitiered holding companies can comply, with each indirectly or directly owned subsidiary submitting the requested information to the top-tier bank holding company. FR Y-6 requires that the following information be filed:

Form	Report Title	When Filed
FR Y-6	Annual Report of Bank Holding Companies	Annually
FR Y-9C	Consolidated Financial Statements	Quarterly
FR Y-9LP	Parent Company Only Financial Statements	Quarterly
FR Y-110	Combined Financial Statement of Nonbank Subsidiaries	Quarterly
FR Y-111	Annual Report of Selected Financial Data for Nonbank Subsidiaries	Quarterly

The first three forms are filed for quarters on March 31, June 30, September 30, and December 31. Banks are given until the fifteenth day of the second month in the following quarter to comply with the filing dates—May 15, August 15, November 15, and February 15.

Form FR Y-6 must be submitted to the appropriate Federal Reserve District Bank. The filing consists of the following eight items:

1. Two-year comparative financial statements (if assets exceed $150 million, statements must be certified by independent public accountant)

2. Nonbank subsidiary financial statements

3. Organization chart for bank holding company's direct and indirect ownership of subsidiaries

4. Amendments to organizational documents (charters) not yet filed with the Federal Reserve System

5. List of shareholders of record that directly or indirectly own, control or hold 5 percent or more

6. List of principal share holders, directors, executive officers with some biographical data

7. Loans to insiders or his/her interests (an executive officer of any person acting as such regardless of title, or any shareholder owning in excess of 10 percent of total outstanding shares. His/her interests are those companies, partnerships or businesses in which the insider holds in excess of a 25 percent interest).

8. Confirm that all changes in investments and activities required in FR Y-6A were reported.

The Annual Report of Bank Holding Companies—FR Y-6 must be signed by one director of the bank holding company. The report must be prepared in accordance with the instructions provided by the Federal Reserve System. The original report and three copies of the FR Y-6 should be submitted to the appropriate Federal Reserve Bank. The information submitted by bank holding companies in the FR Y-6 is available to the public upon request. A bank holding company may request confidential treatment for certain items in the report. The financial statement should be prepared in accordance with generally accepted accounting principles.

Bank holding companies that are registered with the SEC must submit a copy of the most recent Form 10-K filed with the SEC.

Consolidated Reports of Condition and Income, Form No. FFIEC 031, 032, 033, and 034, must be filed with the Federal Deposit Insurance Corporation, which publishes the *Call Reports* under the auspices of the FFIEC. Agencies responsible for the reports are the Federal Reserve Bank, Comptroller of the Currency, and Federal Deposit Insurance Corporation. Officials of these agencies form the Federal Financial Institutions Examination Council (FFIEC). The filings are made quarterly, and submitted no later than 30 calendar days after the report date. The reports must be completed and signed by a duly authorized officer of the bank.

The filing includes the Report of Condition and the Report of Income, including several supplementary schedules and memoranda items. Extensive instructions are contained in FFIEC books. In this reporting, differences between regulatory reporting requirements and generally accepted accounting principles can occur.

State banks that are members of the Federal Reserve System are required to file a report of condition annually within 20 days of a call by the Federal Reserve Board.The report must also appear in a newspaper published where the bank is located. State banks that are FDIC-insured but not members of the Federal Reserve System are required to prepare an annual disclosure statement and must make it available on request no later than March 31 of the following year.

The Monetary Control Act of 1980 and the International Banking Act of 1978 impose reserve requirements on depository institutions. Depository institutions with total reserveable liabilities that exceed the Federal Reserve's deposit exemption amount ($3.2 million) and with total deposits of $40 million or more must submit the report of Transaction Accounts, Other Deposits and Vault Cash (FR 2900) weekly. Banks with smaller deposits can file FR 2900 quarterly or FR 291q, Quarterly Report of Selected Deposits, Vault Cash, and Reserveable Liabilities.

Federal Reserve Regulations

The Federal Reserve is directly involved in the regulation of the banking system. Regulations are published in the Federal Register. A list of its principal regulations follows:

Regulation	Subject Matter
A	Loans by the Fed to depository institutions
B	Implements the Equal Credit Opportunity Act
C	Implements the Home Mortgage Disclosure Act
D	Reserve requirements
E	Implements the Electronic Funds Transfer Act
F	Registration and filing of securities statements by state-chartered member banks
G	Extension of credit to finance securities transactions
H	Membership requirements
I	Member stock in federal reserve banks
J	Check collection and funds transfer
K	International banking operations

Regulation	Subject Matter
L	Interlocking bank relationships
M	Consumer leasing
N	Relationships with foreign banks
O	Loans to executive officers of member banks
P	Member bank protection standards
Q	Interest on deposits (As of 1986, the only remaining restriction was on the payment of interest on commercial demand deposits.)
R	Interlocking relationships between securities dealers and member banks
S	Reimbursement for providing financial records
T	Margin credit extended by brokers and dealers
U	Margin credit extended by banks
V	Guarantee of loans for national defense work
W	Extensions of consumer credit (revoked)
X	Borrowers who obtain margin credit
Y	Bank holding companies
Z	Implements the Truth in Lending and Fair Credit Billings Acts
AA	Consumer complaint procedures
BB	Implements the Community Reinvestment Act
CC	Implements the Expedited Funds Availability Act

Source: Board of Governors of the Federal Reserve System

COMPTROLLER OF THE CURRENCY

The Office of the Comptroller of the Currency dates back to the Civil War. Its functions were primarily to provide the country with a safe and uniform currency system. Currently the OCC serves as a chartering and regulatory agency for national banks. Its regulatory functions consist of (1) entry/exit regulation, and (2) bank examination. The Office is an integral part of the national banking system.

Historical Background

American banking originated in the colonial period and developed as a source of short-term credit to shippers and merchants in the post-Revolutionary War period. Banks issued their own notes when making loans, with an expressed or implied requirement that the notes be redeemable in gold and silver. This practice led to the appearance of a currency as varied as the banks that issued them. Beginning in the 1830s, private firms compiled periodical directories of bank notes showing which notes were good, which bad, and which counterfeit. After the independent Treasury Act of 1846, the Treasury insisted on payments of its obligations in specie. When the United States negotiated a huge bank loan in 1861 to help pay for the war, the payment-in-specie policy so drained the reserves of commercial banks as to precipitate a general suspension of specie payments.

In 1861 Secretary Chase recommended a system of federally chartered national banks. Each would have power to issue standardized national bank notes based on United States bonds held by the bank. Opposition arose to federal bank chartering, reminiscent of the antagonism during the Jacksonian period to a central federal bank. This antagonism had finally destroyed both the First Bank of the United States and the Second Bank of the United States, which ceased doing business as a government agency in 1832.

Substantial public concern with the state of the currency and the press of financing the Civil War overcame this opposition. Under the guidance of Representatives E. G. Spaulding of New York and Samuel Hooper of Massachusetts and Senator John Sherman of Ohio, the National Currency Act was passed by Congress and signed into law by the President on February 25, 1863. The administration of the new national banking system was vested in the newly created currency bureau and its chief administrator, the Comptroller of the Currency. The National Banking Act of 1864 made major changes in the banking legislation. The original National Banking Act gave the Comptroller of the Currency authority to examine national banks periodically and to enforce provisions of the act. The act also empowered the Comptroller to regulate lending and investing activities of national banks. Other responsibilities were added to the Office subsequent to the original establishment of the Office.

The national banking system was instituted in the crisis atmosphere of the Civil War. President Lincoln's administration was concerned with long-term financing of the war effort. Secretary of the Treasury Salmon P. Chase, later Chief Justice of the Supreme Court, believed a bond-secured currency, provided in the Currency Act of 1863, would stimulate the sale of government bonds and assure a homogeneous national currency.

The Office of the Comptroller

The Office of the Comptroller of the Currency was created by an act of Congress approved February 25, 1863, as a part of the National Banking System. The OCC is the federal agency responsible for regulating all national banks. The comptroller serves at the pleasure of the president, with Senate approval, for a five-year term. The comptroller is required by law to report directly to Congress annually. The OCC is funded through assessments on the assets of national banks.

By statute, the comptroller serves a concurrent term as a Director of the Federal Deposit Insurance Corporation and the Resolution Trust Corporation, and as a member of the Federal Financial Institutions Examination Council. At one time, the comptroller was a member of the Board of Governors of the Federal Reserve System.

The comptroller, as the administrator of national banks, is responsible for the execution of laws relating to national banks and promulgates rules and regulations governing the operations of approximately 4,000 national and District of Columbia banks. Approval of the comptroller is required for the organization of new national banks, conversion of state-chartered banks into national banks, consolidations or mergers of banks where the surviving institution is a national bank, and the establishment of branches by national banks.

The comptroller exercises general supervision over the operations of national banks, including trust activities and overseas operations. Each bank is examined periodically through a nationwide staff of approximately 2,000 bank examiners under the immediate supervision of six district deputy comptroller and six district administrators. These examinations operate in the public interest by assisting the comptroller in appraising the financial condition of the banks, the soundness of their operations, the quality of their management, and their compliance with laws, rules, and regulations.

Organization of the Office

The OCC divides the United States into six geographical districts, with each headed by a deputy comptroller. The deputy comptroller functions as chief executive officer of the district. A district administrator manages day-to-day operations of the district. Each district office has a district counsel, directors of administration, bank supervision, analysis, and field office directors.

Regulatory and Supervisory Functions

The major, specific regulatory and supervisory functions of the OCC include:

- Approving or denying applications for new charters, branches, capital or other changes in corporate or banking structure
- Examining national banks as required
- Overseeing the organization, conversion, merger, establishment of branches, relocation, and dissolution of national banks
- Taking supervisory actions against banks that do not conform to laws and regulations or that otherwise engage in unsound banking practices, including removal of officers, negotiation of agreements to change existing banking practices, and issuance of cease and desist orders
- Issuing rules and regulations concerning banking practices and governing bank lending and investment practices and corporate structure
- Determining insolvency and referring insolvent banks to the FDIC
- Administering the registration and reporting requirement of the 1934 Act as it applies to national banks

Bank Examinations

The specific purposes of an external bank examination are to ascertain (1) whether the bank is solvent as shown by a verification of its assets and liabilities; (2) whether the management is conforming to the restrictions imposed by law; and (3) whether the bank, although conforming to the legal restrictions, is adopting policies that may lead to serious problems. An external bank examination is not a complete audit and is not so intended. It does not result in a certification that no defalcations have occurred nor that the bank statements purport to be a true and correct report of the bank's financial condition. Further discussion of bank examinations can be found in Chapter 15.

After the examination is completed, a comprehensive report is prepared and submitted in writing by the chief bank examiner to the board of directors. The board of directors is required to adopt the recommendations of the bank examiner who may, for example, require writing off all overdue notes. The report of a national bank examiner is required to be read at the next succeeding meeting of the board of directors and noted in the minutes. The report of examination is the property of the Comptroller of the Currency, and is loaned to the bank or holding company for its confidential use only.

The authority to correct problems varies according to federal and state banking regulations. Typically a letter of agreement or an informal memorandum of understanding is written to the bank, requesting it to take action against any questionable or illegal practice. Regulatory agencies are also legally empowered to issue cease and desist orders, especially where there is a finding that an offender is engaging, has engaged, or may engage in unsafe and unsound banking practices. If a bank examination reveals severe cases of illegal action, the FDIC can deny insurance, or a state or federal banking agency may remove bank officers or directors from the bank. Judicial reviews are provided for under various statutes once the bank examination is completed.

Regulatory Functions

The most important functions of the Comptroller of the Currency relate to the organization, operation, and liquidation of national banks. The comptroller's approval is required by law in connection with the organization of new national banks, the conversion of state-chartered banks into national banks, and the consolidation or merger of national banks with national banks or of state banks with national banks where the continuing institution is a national bank. The establishment of branches by national banks also requires approval by the comptroller.

The office of comptroller exercises general supervision over the operations of national banks. Each national bank is required to publish and file reports of condition not less than four times a year. National bank examiners, under the immediate supervision of the regional administrators of national banks, examine each national bank at least three times each two years. Such examinations are for the purpose of determining the financial condition of national banks, the soundness of their operations, and their compliance with the requirements of the National Bank Act and other applicable statutes.

In accordance with statutory direction, the Comptroller of the Currency promulgates regulations governing the operations of national banks, contained in the *Comptroller's Manual for National Banks* and the *Comptroller's Manual for Representatives in Trusts*. The office also publishes authoritative compilations of banking statistics, particularly in connection with the comptroller's annual report to Congress.

Financial Reports

Every national bank shall, in accordance with Section 5211 of the Revised Statues (12 U.S.C. 161), make to the Comptroller of the Currency not less than four reports during each year, according to the form prescribed by the comptroller. These reports shall be verified by the declaration of the president, vice president, cashier, or any other officer designated by the board of directors of the bank to make such declaration that the report is true and correct to the best of his knowledge and belief. The correctness of the report of condition shall be attested by the signatures of at least three of the directors of the bank other than the officer making such declaration, with the declaration that the report has been examined by them and to the best of their knowledge and belief is true and correct.

Each such call report of condition shall exhibit in detail and under appropriate heads the resources and liabilities of the bank. The chart of accounts and instructions for their preparation are furnished to the reporting banks by the office of the comptroller. Reported condition shall be as of the close of business on any past day specified by the comptroller in his call (mid-year and year-end calls are in practice as of the calendar dates, for statistical purposes), but the intervening first quarter and third quarter are more likely to involve surprise calls, i.e., as of varying dates. Report shall be transmitted to the comptroller within 10 days after the receipt of call therefor. In addition, the report of condition in the same form in which it is made to the comptroller shall be published at the expense of the bank in a newspaper published in the place where the national bank is established, or if there is no newspaper in the place, then in the one published nearest thereto in the same county. Proof of publication shall be furnished to the comptroller as specified by him.

The comptroller may call for additional reports of condition, in such form and containing such information as he may prescribe, on dates to be fixed by him, and may call for special reports from any particular national bank whenever, in his judgment, the same are necessary for his use in the performance of his supervisory duties. The same requirements also apply to each of the national bank's affiliates other than member banks, to the end that the comptroller be able to inform himself as to the effect of such affiliates upon the affairs of the national bank. However, reports of affiliates are no longer required of national banks unless specifically requested by the comptroller.

Although they serve a legal reporting purpose, call reports of condition, as published, do not contain the detail for analytical purposes that the required annual report of national banks contains, nor are they intended to serve in place of the reports of examination for regulator purposes.

Source: Office of the Comptroller of the Currency

THE SECURITIES AND EXCHANGE COMMISSION

The Securities and Exchange Commission (SEC) is an independent, quasi-judicial agency of the U.S. government. The SEC was created by the Securities Exchange Act of 1934 to administer and enforce the federal security laws, which includes:

- The Securities Act of 1933
- The Securities Exchange Act of 1934
- Securities Investor Protection Act of 1970
- The Public Utility Holding Company Act of 1935
- The Trust Indenture Act of 1939
- The Investment Company Act of 1940
- The Investment Advisor Act of 1940
- Foreign Corrupt Practices Act of 1977
- Insider Trading Sanctions Act of 1984

These federal securities laws seek to provide protection for investors; to ensure that securities markets are fair and honest; and, when necessary, to provide the means to enforce securities laws through sanctions. Banks are not exempt from requirements imposed by the Securities Exchange Act of 1934. The registration and reporting provisions of the Act relating to banks are administered by federal bank regulatory agencies instead of the SEC.

The commission also serves as adviser to the United States district courts in connection with reorganization proceedings for debtor corporations in which there is a substantial public interest. The commission also has certain responsibilities under the Bretton Woods Agreements Act of 1945 (22 U.S.C. 286k-1) and the Internal Revenue Code of 1954 (26 U.S.C. 851(e)).

The commission is vested with quasijudicial functions. Persons aggrieved by its decisions in the exercise of those functions have a right to review by the United States courts of appeals.

Organization of the SEC

The SEC is composed of five commissioners appointed by the president with the approval of the U.S. Senate. No more than three of the commissioners may be of the same political party. The SEC maintains nine regional offices. There are four operating divisions in the SEC:

- Division of Corporation Finance
- Division of Market Regulation
- Division of Enforcement
- Division of Investment Management

The Division of Corporation Finance has the basic responsibility to determine that the financial information presented to the general public related to security offerings is appropriate and complete. The division also examines and reviews the information included in registration statements, proxy materials and periodic reports. The division is authorized to draft rules, regulations, and forms for registration and reporting. It also offers guidance on the application and interpretation of SEC rules, regulations, and forms to accountants, attorneys, underwriters, and others associated with the various filings. It reviews reports concerning insider trading by officers and directors of registered companies. The division has been responsible for overseeing the development of the Electronic Data Gathering, Analysis, and Retrieval (EDGAR), which is a computerized filing and retrieval system. This division has had an impact on the accounting profession.

The Division of Market Regulation regulates security exchanges and over-the-counter markets. The Division of Investment Management administers the Investment Company Act of 1940 and the Investment Advisers Act of 1940 and oversees the Public Utility Holding Company Act of 1935. The Division of Enforcement is responsible for enforcing the various acts administered by the Commission.

An organization chart of the SEC is presented in Figure 2-2.

The more important offices having a banking and accounting connection include

- Office of the Chief Accountant
- Office of the Chief Economist
- Office of the General Counsel

Figure 2-2
The Organization of the SEC

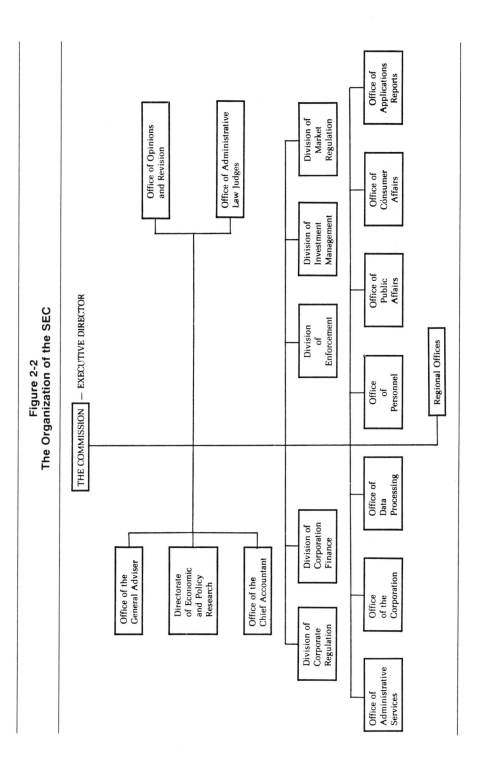

The Office of Chief Accountant serves as the principal adviser on accounting and auditing. The office serves as a link with the accounting profession and independent public accountants. The chief accountant is in a position to exert considerable influence on the development of generally accepted accounting principles and auditing standards. The chief accountant carries out SEC policy on accounting principles and on matter relating to the form and content of financial statements filed with the SEC. The chief accountant also consults and rules on accounting questions from registrants and independent accountants. He or she establishes and maintains relationships with accounting authorities. He or she also prepares Financial Reporting Releases (FRRs) and issues Accounting and Auditing Enforcement Releases (AAERs) and Staff Accounting Bulletins (SABs).

Powers and Functions

Activities of the SEC relate primarily to full and fair disclosure in financial reporting; regulation of securities markets, mutual funds, investment companies, companies controlling utilities, and investment advisers; rehabilitation of failing corporations; representation of debt securities holders; and enforcement activities.The SEC has powers and functions related to rule making associated with the legislation it supervises, administrative interpretations of the Acts, investigations of practices within the securities market, and enforcement activities required to investigate potential violations and to provide remedies for violations of the Acts. Remedies allow the SEC to suspend or revoke the registration of persons, exchanges, or securities, as required by the 1933 and 1934 Acts and to seek preliminary and final injunctions to prevent violations of the Acts or rules.

Full and fair disclosure requirements are specified under the Securities Act of 1933 (15 U.S.C. 77a). The Act requires issuers of securities and their controlling persons making public offerings of securities in interstate commerce or through the mails, directly or by others on their behalf, to file with the commission registration statements containing financial and other pertinent data about the issue and the securities being offered. It is unlawful to sell such securities unless a registrations statement is in effect (with limited exceptions).

The SEC guarantees investors access to information for their investment decisions. It does not provide evaluations of different investments or protect investors from losses.

The SEC and the Accounting Profession

The SEC has influenced the development of accounting and auditing principles. The SEC can prescribe accounting principles to be used in filings under the 1933 and 1934 Acts and other acts for all companies whose securities are publicly traded. The SEC usually exercises its authority through Regulation S-X, staff accounting bulletins, and financial reporting releases.

The SEC has had a profound influence on the accounting profession. The SEC has worked with the accounting profession in developing generally accepted accounting principles and auditing standards. The agency's position is that the balance sheet should be presented with full market value accounting for all marketable securities. Marketable securities exclude real estate, plant and equipment, intangible assets, and loans. The SEC would prefer to see securities portfolio of all firms, including commercial banks, marked to market. Likewise, related liabilities, would be marked to market. Changes in the value of these assets and liabilities would be recorded either as gains or losses in the income statement, or as changes in retained earnings.

The SEC has authority to establish auditing standards and procedures as it relates to brokers, dealers, and investment companies. Regulation S-X requires auditors to state whether examinations were in accordance with generally accepted auditing standards. Regulation X-X established the qualifications of public accountants necessary to practice before the SEC.

Regulation S-X

The SEC is authorized to establish accounting standards. Regulation S-X contains the SEC's principal guidelines for accounting regulation. The SEC adopted Regulation S-X Form and Content of and Requirements for Financial Statements in 1940. Regulation S-X outlines SEC reporting requirements and standards of financial statement disclosure. These requirements specify the form and content of all financial statements, their notes, and any schedules that are filed as part of registration statements accompanying the provisions of (1) the Securities Act of 1933; (2) The Securities Exchange Act of 1934, including annual or other reports, proxy statements (any authorization given to someone by security holders to act on their behalf at a stockholders' meeting), and information statements; (3) the Public Utility Holding Company Act of 1935 and related annual reports; and (4) Investment Company Act of 1940 and related annual reports. Regulation S-X is organized into twelve articles by subject matter:

Regulation S-X Contents

Article	Subject
1	Application and scope of Regulation S-X (Specifies the registration statements and reports to which Regulation S-X applies and defines terminology used in the Regulation)
2	Qualifications and Reports of Accountants (Sets professional standards and types of audit's opinions accepted by the SEC)
3	General Information for Financial Statements (Sets of instructions for financial statements and the persons, dates, and periods they must cover and which interim financial statements are required to be included in registration and proxy statements)
3A	Consolidated and Combined Financial Statements (Contains requirements for these statements)
4	Rules of General Application (Contains the rules for form, order, terminology, materiality, and completeness)
5	Commercial and Industrial Companies
5A	Companies in the Development Stage
6	Registered Investment Companies
6A	Unit Investment Trusts
6B	Face-Amount Certificate Investment Companies

Article	Subject
6C	Employee Stock Purchase, Savings, and Similar Plans
7	Insurance Companies Other than Life Insurance Companies
7A	Life Insurance Companies
8	Committees Issuing Certificates of Deposit
9	Bank Holding Companies and Banks
10	Interim Financial Statements
11	Pro forma Financial Information
11A	Statement of Cash Flows
12	Form and Content of Supporting Schedules

Regulation S-X also specifies certain footnote items and financial schedules required for SEC reports.

Regulation S-X establishes the standards of reporting for accountant's reports.Technical requirements prescribe that the accountant's report (1) shall be dated, (2) shall be signed manually, (3) shall indicate the city and state where issued, and (4) shall identify the financial statements covered by the report. The requirements also extend the representations as to the audit, the opinion to be expressed, and exceptions reflected in the opinion.

Regulation S-K

Regulation S-K is a comprehensive set of integrated disclosure rules outlining the requirements for nonfinancial statement data to be included in 1933 and 1934 securities laws filings. Regulation S-X prescribes the requirements for financial statements as indicated in the preceding section.

Regulation S-K Table of Contents

General
Item
100   General

    (a) Application of Regulation S-X

    (b) Commission Policy on Projections

    (c) Commission Policy on Security Ratings

101   Description of Business
102   Description of Property
103   Legal Proceedings
      Securities of the Registrant
201   Market Price and Dividends on Registrant's Common Stock and Related Stockholders Matter
202   Description of Registrant's Securities
      Financial Information
301   Selected Financial Data

Item 304 is of special interest to accountants. The content of the disclosure reflects concerns of statement users:

(a) State the date of such resignation (or declination to stand for reelection), dismissal, or engagement.

(b) State whether in connection with the audits of the two most recent fiscal years and any subsequent interim period preceding such resignation, dismissal, or engagement there were any disagreements with the former accountant on any matter of accounting principles or practices, financial statement disclosure, or auditing scope or procedure, which disagreements if not resolved to the satisfaction of the former accountant would have caused him to make reference in connection with his report to the subject matter of the disagreement(s); also describes each such disagreement.The disagreements required to be reported in response to the preceding sentence include both those resolved to the former accountant's satisfaction and those not resolved to the former accountant's satisfaction. Disagreements contemplated by this rule are those which occur at the decision-making level (i.e., between personnel of the registrant responsible for presentation of its financial statements and personnel of the accounting firm responsible for rendering its report).

(c) State whether the principal accountant's report on the financial statements for any of the past two years contained an adverse opinion or a disclaimer of opinion or was qualified as to uncertainty, audit scope, or accounting principles; also describe the nature of each adverse opinion, disclaimer of opinion, or qualification.

(d) The registrant shall request the former accountant to furnish the registrant with a letter addressed to the Commission stating whether she agrees with the statements made by the registrant in response to this item and, if not, stating the respects in which she does not agree.The registrant shall file a copy of the former accountant's letter as an exhibit to the report on this form. If the former accountant's letter is unavailable at the time of filing, it shall be filed within thirty days thereafter.

(e) State whether the decision to change accountants was recommended or approved by

   (1) Any audit or similar committee of the Board of Directors, if the issuer has such a committee; or

   (2) The Board of Directors, if the issuer has no such committee

In 1988, the SEC expanded the disclosure requirement of Item 4 to include the following information:

■ Certain "reportable events." These include situations in which the former accountant had expressed concerns about the adequacy of the company's internal controls, the reliability of management's representations, or an unwillingness to be associated with the financial statements. Such reportable events are to be reported in a manner similar to disagreements.

■ Certain prior consultations with the newly engaged accountant within two years prior to the change. Disclosure is required in either of two situations. In the first, the consultation is such that the consulted accountant must deal with it in accordance with the requirements of Statement on Auditing Standards No. 50, "Reports on the Application of Accounting Principles." That covers situations in which the accountant believes the advice is important to the company's decision on an accounting, auditing, or financial reporting issue. In the second situation requiring disclosure, the consultation is related to a disagreement or a reportable event between the company and the former accountant. In either of these two situations, the Form 8-K must describe the newly engaged accountant's views, state whether the former accountant was consulted and, if so, state his views.

■ Whether any disagreement or reportable event was discussed with the company's audit committee.

■ Whether the company authorized the former accountant to respond fully to questions the newly engaged accountant asked about disagreements with the company.

■ Whether the former accountant resigned, declined to stand reelection, or was dismissed.

SEC Reporting Requirements

In 1980 the SEC adopted new requirements for reporting financial information by publicly held companies. This system is referred to as the *integrated disclosure system*. The integrated disclosure system prescribes a standard set of information including

- Audited consolidated financial statements consisting of balance sheets in the latest two years, and statements of income, retained earnings, and cash flows for the most recent three fiscal years
- A five-year summary of selected financial data
- A management discussion and analysis of the company's financial condition and results of operations
- Market price and dividend information on the company's common stock
- Major accounting reports required by the SEC related to the Securities Exchange Act of 1934 for the purpose of updating information contained in the original registration include

1. Form 10-K   The annual report that includes certified financial statements. The report is filed within 90 days after the end of the registrant's year-end. Form 10-K calls for information about the corporation's management, outstanding securities, and business operations. Annual reports to security holders may be combined with the required information of Form 10-K and will be suitable for filing with the SEC if the following conditions are met:
    (a)   The combined report contains answers to all items required by Form 10-K
    (b)   The cover page and required signatures are included

2. Form 10-Q   The quarterly report with financial statements required for the first three quarters of the fiscal year to be filed within 45 days of each quarter's end. The interim financial reports are condensed and consolidated. The report consists of a financial report and a special events report. The report is arranged as follows:

Part I Financial information
    A.   Financial statements (unaudited)
    B.   Management's discussion and Analysis

Part II Other information
    A.   Legal Proceedings
    B.   Changes in securities
    C.   Defaults on senior securities
    D.   Submission of matters to a vote of security holders
    E.   Other information
    F.   Exhibits and reports on Form 8-K

3.   Form 8-K   A report filed after the occurrence of a significant event, such as major charges or credits made to net income, including gains or losses from the early extinguishment of debt or the tax benefits of loss carryforwards, significant asset changes, or important legal proceedings. The form has seven items:

1.   Changes in control of registrant
2.   Acquisition or disposition of assets
3.   Bankruptcy or receivership
4.   Change in registrant's certifying accountant
5.   Other events (information that is considered to be important to the stockholders but that is not specifically required to be reported on Form 8-K.
6.   Resignations of Registrant's directors
7.   Financial statements and exhibit Form 8-K must be filed whenever appropriate within 15 days of such a significant event.

4.   Form 11-K   Annual Report of employee stock purchase, savings, and similar plans
5.   Form 14-K   Annual report of certificates of deposit issued by a committee
6.   Form 10   Securities for which no other form is prescribed; generally used for registration under the 1934 act
7.   Form 12   Securities of issuers who file reports with certain other federal agencies (e.g., Federal Communications Commission, Interstate Commerce Commission, or Federal Power Commission
8.   Form 20-F   Securities of certain foreign private issuers

The above periodic reports must be filed by corporations with 500 or more shareholders and assets exceeding $3,000,000.

Form 10-K

Form 10-K is the most common SEC annual report form. It must be filed with the SEC within 90 days of a company's fiscal year-end. Detailed information relating to the contents of Form 10-K is provided here:

Form 10-K

Summary of operations and management's discussion and analysis:

■ Description of business (industry segments, product sales, foreign and domestic operations and export sales for the three most recent years)

■ Properties (location and general characteristics)

■ Legal proceedings (pending lawsuits including details)

■ Voting matters (listing and description of matters submitted to a vote of security holders)

■ Market for the registrant's common stock and related security holder matters (identification of market)

- Selected financial data (five-year summary of net sales, income (loss) from continuing operations (and EPS), total assets, long-term debt, and cash dividends, including adjustments for changing prices)
- Management's discussion and analysis of financial condition and results of operations (including liquidity, capital resources, and results of operations)
- Financial statements and supplementary data (audited financial statements)
- Balance Sheets as of the end of each of the two latest fiscal years
- Statements of Income for each of the three latest fiscal years
- Statement of Cash Flows for each of the three latest fiscal years
- Statement of Changes in Stockholders' Equity for each of the three latest years
- Disagreements on accounting and disclosure (If accountants were changed due to disagreements on accounting principles, details of the disagreement must be provided.)
- Directors and executive owners of the registrant (names, ages, and positions)
- Management renumeration and transactions (listing of names, positions, salaries, stock options, and other benefits)
- Security ownership (listing of beneficial owners and management owners of corporation's securities)
- Certain relationships (listing of related parties)
- Figures, financial statement schedules, and reports (detailed supporting schedules on a variety of financial statement elements)
- Signatures (Chief executive, financial, and accounting officers, and board of directors)

Annual Report to Stockholders

SEC registrants may use their discretion in preparing the format of a bank's annual stockholders' report unless there are specific SEC requirements. Items usually required for an annual report to shareholders include the following information:

- Summary of operations and management's discussion and analysis
- Identity of directors and executive officers
- Identity of principal market where voting securities are traded and high/low sales prices and dividends paid for past eight quarters
- Statement that Form 10-K is provided without charge
- Audited financial statements. Audited balance sheets for the latest 2 years and statements of income and cash flows for the latest 3 years are required
- Footnote disclosure required by Regulation S-X
- Reconciliation of differences between 10-K and financial statements
- Schedule XVI, Supplementary Earnings Statement Information
- Opinion letter

■ Other voluntarily disclosed information (including letter to shareholders: announcement of annual meeting and the year in brief)

■ While a letter from the bank's president is not required in the annual report, it is usually presented voluntarily. The contents should be accurate and not misleading. The president's letter typically provides:
An explanation to the stockholders of the results of operations,
A description of any new products or divisions, or other significant operating matters, and
A discussion of the future impact of current developments.

Nonfinancial information is often discussed in the annual report and is presented at the company's discretion.

The National Commission on Fraudulent Financial Reporting, headed by former SEC Commissioner James C. Treadway, recommended that public companies include in their annual report a management report signed by the CEO and the chief accounting officer. This report should acknowledge management's responsibilities for the financial statements and internal control, describe how these responsibilities were fulfilled, and include management's assessment of the effectiveness of the company's internal controls. The commission also recommends that annual reports of public companies include a letter from the chair of the audit committee, describing the committee's responsibilities and activities during the period.

SEC Financial Reporting Releases

The SEC issues *Accounting Series Releases (ASRs)* and *Financial Reporting Releases (FRRs)*. Beginning in 1937, the SEC began to issue opinions related to major accounting and auditing issues in the form of ASRs. ASRs contain new policy statements and amendments to existing SEC rules. In 1982 the SEC began to issue FRR, which codified all previously issued ASRs that were still applicable and related to financial matters. They reflect the SEC's current views and interpretations. In 1975 the SEC staff began to issue Staff Accounting Bulletins (SABs), which were interpretations and practices followed by the staff of the SEC's Division of Corporation Finance and the Office of the Chief Accountant in administering the disclosure requirements of federal securities laws. SABs do not carry official Commission approval.

The SEC also issues Auditing Enforcement Releases (AAERs).

AAERs present SEC enforcement actions against accountants related to accounting and/or auditing issues. They typically report unacceptable practice before the SEC.

Electronic Data Gathering Analysis and Retrival System

The SEC implemented its pilot Electronic Data Gathering, Analysis, and Retrieval (EDGAR) system in 1984. This system automated the receipt, internal processing, and public dissemination of reports filed with the SEC. Banks may volunteer to participate in this program.

Source: Securities and Exchange Commission.

Foreign Corrupt Practices Act (FCPA)

Congress passed the Foreign Corrupt Practices Act in 1977 to discourage an American corporation from bribing a foreign official as a means to secure or promote business for itself. The act
established a legal requirement that publicly held companies must maintain internal accounting
controls sufficient to provide reasonable assurances as to the achievement of the accuracy of
accounting records. Two major provisions of the act are:

1. It is a criminal offense to offer a bribe to a foreign official, foreign political party, party
    official, or candidate for foreign political office for the purpose of obtaining, retaining,
    or directing business to any person.

2. Every public company must devise, document, and maintain a system of internal
    accounting records to ascertain that the objectives of internal control are attained.

The act requires corporations to disclose in their reports to SEC any illegal or questionable
corporate practices related to corrupting foreign officials. The SEC has responsibility to enforce
the accounting, record keeping, and internal control provisions. Corporate officers, directors,
accountants, insiders, and other persons can be subjected to civil and criminal penalties.
Violations of the antibribery provisions can result in fines of up to $1,000,000 for companies.
Individuals can be fined up to $10,000 and imprisoned up to five years, or both. The SEC can
also sue violators civilly for violations of the antibribery provisions.

FEDERAL DEPOSIT INSURANCE CORPORATION (FDIC)

The Federal Deposit Insurance Corporation was established in 1933, under Section 12B of the
Federal Reserve Act (12 U.S.C. 264), as an independent executive agency to promote and
preserve public confidence in banks and to protect the money supply through provision of
insurance coverage for bank deposits and periodic examinations of insured state-chartered
banks that are not members of the Federal Reserve System.

The Corporation insures deposits under two separate funds: the Bank Insurance Fund
(BIF) and the Savings Association Insurance Fund (SAIF). The Bank Insurance Fund is available
for insuring national and state banks that are members of the Federal Reserve System, which
are required to be insured, and for state nonmember banks and branches of foreign banks,
which are not required to be insured by the FDIC. The Savings Association Insurance Fund was
established under the authority of the Financial Institutions Reform, Recovery, and Enforcement Act of 1989. The SAIF replaces the Federal Savings and Loan Insurance Corporation
(FSLIC) as the insurer of deposits in federal savings and loan associations and federal savings
banks. State thrift institutions are also insured by this fund.

The Federal Deposit Insurance Corporation (FDIC) is an independent agency of the
executive branch of the federal government. It is headed by a five-member board of directors:
The Comptroller of the Currency, the Director of the Office of Thrift Supervision, and three
members appointed by the president with the advice and consent of the Senate. The headquar-
ters office is located in Washington, D.C., and there are Division of Liquidation and Division of

Figure 2-3
Federal Deposit Insurance Corporation

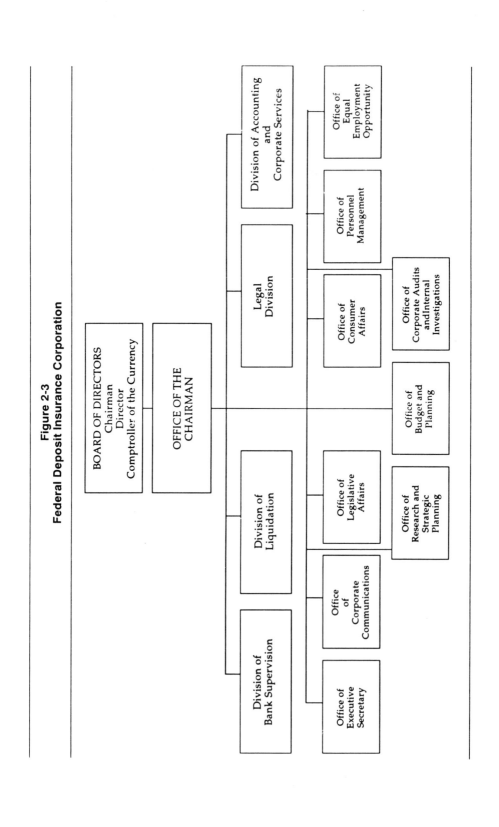

Supervision regional offices in the field with directors in charge of each. Most FDIC field employees are bank examiners or liquidators.

The FDIC is self-sustaining. Its income consists of (1) assessments on insured banks and (2) income from investments. An FDIC organization chart is presented in Figure 2-3.

FDIC's Functions and Activities

The Corporation insures, up to the statutory limitation, the deposits in national banks, in state banks that are members of the Federal Reserve System, in state banks that apply for Federal deposit insurance and meet certain prescribed qualifications, and in savings and loans that are members of the SAIF. In the event of a bank failure, the claim of each depositor (up to $100,000) is promptly paid upon assignment to the Corporation of the depositor's rights to recoveries to the extent of his or her insured deposits.

The Corporation may make loans to or purchase assets from insured depository institutions to facilitate mergers or consolidations, when such action for the protection of depositors will reduce risk or avert threatened loss to the agency. It may reopen a closed insured depository institution or prevent the closing of an insured depository institution when it considers the continued operation of such institution essential to providing adequate banking services in the community (but this power has been restricted).

The Federal Deposit Insurance Act authorizes the Corporation to terminate the insured status of a depository institution that continues, after notice and a hearing, to engage in unsafe and unsound banking practices or in violation of law or regulations, publish notice of such termination, and regulate the manner in which the depository institution can give the required notice of such termination to depositors (whose deposits in the bank at the time of termination continue to be insured for two years).

The Corporation acts as receiver for all national banks placed in receivership and for state banks placed in receivership when it is appointed by state authorities.

Federal Bank Deposit Insurance

The FDIC was created by the Banking Act of 1933 (Glass-Steagall Act) to administer the federal bank deposit insurance program. All nationally chartered banks and all state-chartered banks that are members of the Fed are required to have FDIC insurance. FDIC insurance is funded by a flat tax on total domestic deposits (currently 1/12 of 1 percent [.000825] of their total assessable deposits). Banks typically pass on the costs of deposit insurance to their customers or owners.

The Deposit Insurance Fund represents the Corporation's accumulated net income since inception. The fund is available to meet future deposit insurance claims and related losses. Its adequacy to meet these requirements is dependent upon the soundness of the financial condition of insured banks and the ability to maintain solvency despite adverse factors such as unfavorable economic conditions generally and individual bank difficulties specifically. The size of the fund is not a measure of the deposit insurance risk. The insurance covers deposits including individual and commercial deposits, time deposits, savings deposits, and trust funds awaiting investment. No distinction is made between public and private deposits. Currently the maximum insurance is $100,000 upon funds maintained in each different right and capacity.

After FDIC-insured banks submit their June and December quarterly call reports, they must also complete a semiannual Certified Statement using data from the call reports. Certified Statements are used for FDIC insurance assessments.

Source: Federal Deposit Insurance Corporation.

OFFICE OF THRIFT SUPERVISION

In 1989 the Office of Thrift Supervision (OTS) was created as a bureau within the Department of the Treasury by the Financial Institutions Reform, Recovery, and Enforcement Act of 1990 (FIRREA). FIRREA brought about a major reorganization of the thrift regulatory structure. In that act Congress gave OTS authority to charter Federal thrift institutions, and to serve as the primary regulator of approximately 2,000 federal- and state-chartered thrifts belonging to the Savings Association Insurance Fund (SAIF). OTS carries out this responsibility by adopting regulations governing the savings and loan industry, by examining and supervising thrift institutions and their affiliates, and by taking whatever action necessary to enforce their compliance with federal law and regulations. The OTS has primary regulatory authority to approve branching applications and allow mutual-to-thrift charter conversions. In addition to overseeing thrift institutions, OTS also regulates, examines, and supervises companies that own thrifts and controls the acquisition of thrifts by such holding companies.

OTS is headed by a director appointed by the president and confirmed by the Senate to serve a five-year term. The director also serves on the boards of the Federal Deposit Insurance Corporation, the Resolution Trust Corporation, and the Thrift Depositor Protection Oversight Board, and is a director of the Neighborhood Reinvestment Corporation.

OTS is organized into five main divisions:

Washington operations includes supervisory operations, policy, information resources management, and the administration program areas of OTS. This division develops national policy guidelines to clarify and implement statutes and regulations; establishes programs to implement new policies and laws; develops and maintains surveillance systems that monitor the condition of the industry and assist in identifying emerging supervisory problem areas; develops and maintains financial management and information systems; maintains human resources programs; processes thrift institution applications; provides special supervision of selected thrift institutions; and performs other related functions.

Regional operations examines and supervises thrift institutions in the five OTS regions to ensure the safety and soundness of the industry. It also oversees the training and development of Federal thrift regulators through accredited programs. The regional offices are headquartered in Jersey City, Atlanta, Chicago, Dallas, and San Francisco.

Chief Counsel provides a full range of legal services to the agency, including drafting regulations, representing the agency in court, and taking enforcement actions against savings institutions that violate laws or regulations. This office also processes corporate filings required by the Securities and Exchange Act of 1934.

Congressional Affairs interacts with members of Congress, congressional staff, and committee members on behalf of OTS.

Public Affairs oversees dissemination of information concerning OTS regulations, policies, and key developments within the agency. The Resolution Trust Corporation (RTC) is a federal agency established by Congress to oversee the disposal of the assets of failed S&Ls in the wake of the thrift crisis of the 1980s by December 31, 1996. The RTC was given a portfolio of $104 billion assets from the failing S&Ls that federal regulators had seized since February 1989. The RTC has become the largest financial institution in the world.

Source: Office of Thrift Supervision

BANK SPECIFIC: RECOMMENDATIONS

The financial reporting required by banks for Federal regulatory authorities would be improved if banks were required to send audited financial prepared by independent public accountants as a part of the package. Management's report should include annual financial statements prepared in accordance with generally accepted accounting principles and disclosure requirements prescribed by the appropriate Federal banking agency.

The report should include a statement of management's responsibilities for preparing financial statements, for establishing and maintaining an adequate internal control structure and procedures over financial reporting, and for complying with laws and regulations related to safety and soundness or designated by the appropriate federal banking agency. The report should also contain an assessment, as of the end of the institution's most recent fiscal year, of

- The effectiveness of such internal control structure and procedures
- The institution's compliance with laws and regulations related to safety and soundness as prescribed by the appropriate banking agency

The independent accountants should report separately on management's assertions regarding (1) the effectiveness of internal controls and (2) compliance with the laws and regulations designated by federal banking agencies.

Each depository institution should be required to maintain an independent audit committee consisting of outside directors who are independent of management. For large institutions, the audit committee should be comprised of members with banking expertise who would have access to their own outside counsel, and the members would not include any large customers of the institution. For large institutions, the banking regulators should require the independent public accountants to review the institution's quarterly financial reports.

In late 1991 the House Banking Committee was considering some of these recommendations for fiscal years beginning January 1, 1993.

KEY DEFINITIONS

Automated clearinghouse A computer-based clearing and settlement operation, often operated by a Federal Reserve Bank, established for the exchange of electronic transactions among participating depository institutions.

Bank holding company A company that owns or controls one or more banks. The Board of Governors of the Fed has responsibility for regulating and supervising bank holding companies, such as approving acquisitions and mergers and inspecting the operations of such companies.

Bank regulation The formulation and issuance by authorized agencies of specific rules or regulations, under governing law, for the conduct and structure of banking.

Bank supervision Concerns of financial regulators with the safety and soundness of individual banks, involving the general and continuous oversight of the activities of this industry to ensure that banks are operated prudently and in accordance with applicable statutes and regulations.

Bankwire An electronic communications network owed by an association of banks and used to transfer messages between subscribing banks.

Cease-and-desist order An order issued after notice and opportunity for hearing, requiring a depository institution, a holding company, or a depository institution official to terminate unlawful, unsafe, or unsound banking practices.

Commercial banks Banks which are allowed to engage in varied lending activities and to offer more financial services than are other depository institutions. Commercial banks owned by stockholders and operate for profit.

Comptroller of the Currency An officer of the Treasury department responsible for chartering national banks and who has primary supervisory authority over them.

Credit unions Financial institution organized as a cooperative of individuals with a common affiliation. Credit unions accept deposits of members, pay interest, and primarily provide consumer installment credit to members.

Discount rate Rate charges for borrowing from the Fed.

Discount window A bank is said to be going to the discount window when it borrows from the Fed.

Edge Act Corporation An organization chartered by the Federal Reserve to engage in international banking operations. The Edge corporation gets its name from Senator Walter Edge of New Jersey, the sponsor of the original legislation.

8-K Report A report required in the Securities Exchange Act of 1934 that explains a material event that investors want to know about.

Electronic Fund Transfer Systems A variety of systems and technologies for transferring funds electronically rather than by check. Includes Fedwire, Bankwire, automated clearinghouses, and other automated systems.

Fed Federal Reserve Banks.

Federal Advisory Council A group consisting of one member from each Federal Reserve District elected annually by the Board of Directors of each of the 12 Federal Reserve Banks. They meet with the board to discuss business and financial conditions and make advisory recommendations.

Federal Deposit Insurance Corporation An agency of the federal government that insures accounts at various banks coming under its jurisdiction.

Federal funds Reserve balances that depository institutions lend each other, usually on an over-night basis. Federal funds also include certain other kinds of borrowings by depository institutions from each other and from federal agencies.

Federal Open Market Committee A major policy-making body of the Federal Reserve System.

Federal Reserve Banks The 12 banks that make up the central bank of the United States.

Federal Reserve float Checkbook money that for a period of time appears on the books of both the payor and payee due to the lag in the collection process. It often arises during the Federal Reserve's check collection process.

Federal Reserve System The central bank of the United States.

Fiscal policy The coordinated policy of a government with respect to taxation, the public debt, public expenditures, and fiscal management, with an objective—for example, attempting to stabilize national income of the economy.

Fractional reserve banking Banking in which only a fraction of a bank's deposits is held in the form of liquid reserve, with the balance lent to earn interest.

Lender of last resort A nation's central bank which extends credit to depository institutions or to other entities in unusual circumstances involving a national or regional emergency, where failure to obtain credit would have a severe adverse impact on the economy.

M1 A narrow definition of money, consisting only of means of payment. M1 is the most liquid measure of money.

M2 A definition of money that includes both means of payment and time deposits.

M3 A broad definition of money consisting of M2 money plus large-denomination time deposits and specialized money market funds for institutional investors. M3 is the least liquid measure of money.

Monetary policy Any policy relating to the supply or use of money in the economy. The coordinated adaptation of the credit control powers of the monetary authorities of a country exercised through the central bank upon the banking system, pursuant to a policy.

Money Anything that serves as a generally accepted medium of exchange, a standard of value, and a means to save or store purchasing power.

Mutual savings bank A financial institution that accepts deposits primarily from individuals, and places a large portion of their funds into mortgage loans.

National Credit Union Administration The federal government agency that supervises, charters, and insures federal credit unions. The NCUA also insures state-chartered credit unions that apply and qualify for insurance.

Regulation S-X The regulation which prescribes the form and content of financial statements filed with the SEC.

Reserves Funds set aside by depository institutions to meet reserve requirements.

Required reserves Reserves designated by the Fed that member banks must hold against demand deposits.

Reserve requirements Reserves that must be held against customer deposits of banks and other depository institutions. The reserve requirement ratio affects the expansion of deposits that can be supported by each additional dollar of reserves.

Savings and loan association A financial institution which accepts deposits primarily from individuals, and have historically channeled their funds primarily into residential mortgage loans until most recently.

Securities and Exchange Commission An independent agency of the U.S. government that administers comprehensive legislation governing the securities industry.

Self-regulatory organizations Nongovernment organizations that have statutory responsibility to regulate their own members such as the NYSE, AMEX, and NASD.

Surplus reserves Reserves over and above required reserves that a bank may have.

10-K Report A detailed report filed annually under the Securities Exchange Act of 1934 that includes a description of various corporate activities as well as audited financial statements.

10-Q Report A quarterly report filed under the Securities Exchange Act of 1934. It is less detailed than the 10-K report and includes financial information that has been reviewed but not audited by an independent CPA.

Treadway Commission The National Commission on Fraudulent Financial Reporting. The commission, named after its chair, former SEC Commissioner James C. Treadway, was organized in 1985 to develop recommendations for fraudulent financial reporting. In its final report in 1987, the committee recommended that all public companies establish audit commission consisting of independent directors, that the independent auditor's responsibility for the detection of fraudulent financial reporting should be increased, that auditors should use analytical procedures in all audit engagements to detect fraudulent financial reporting, and that auditor's should clarify the role and responsibilities of the independent auditor and describe the extent to which the auditor has reviewed and evaluated the internal control structure.

The report recommended that public companies should maintain an effective internal audit function. Also, the SEC should mandate audit committees composed solely of independent directors and should mandate management reports on internal controls, including management's assessment of the effectiveness of those controls. Management should advise the audit committee when it seeks a second opinion on significant accounting issues.

For regulators and others, the report recommended that the SEC should increase criminal prosecution of fraudulent financial reporting and should be given increased resources to help prevent, detect, and deter fraudulent financial reporting. The SEC should require all public accounting firms that audit public companies to be members of an organization that has a peer review function and independent public oversight.

For educators the report recommended that curricula be revised to foster knowledge and understanding of factors that may cause fraudulent financial reporting and of strategies that can lead to its reduction. Continuing education courses should include a review of the techniques and procedures that contribute to fraudulent financial reporting and a discussion of the relevant ethical and technical standards.

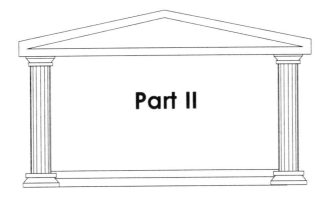

Part II

Bank Accounting: Theory and Practice

Chapter 3

The Controllership Function

The role of the controller is constantly changing. The controller acts as an advisor to management and supervises all accounting and reporting activities. In recent years the controllership function has expanded so that the controller is called upon more frequently to participate more actively in the management decision process.

CONTROLLER

The controller (or comptroller) is the chief accounting executive in most business organizations. Functions performed by the controller include internal auditing, general accounting, tax planning, cost accounting, and budgeting. The treasurer is responsible for assuring that the firm has the financial resources required to conduct its activities. In addition, the treasurer usually has responsibilities relating to the custody of cash, banking, investments, and insurance. The treasurer's function is basically custodial; the controller's function is basically an information and reporting function. The Financial Executive Institute is the association of corporate treasurers and controllers.

Controllership Functions

The following functions are usually assigned to controllers and treasurers:

Controller:

1. Planning for control
2. Overseeing the general accounting function (especially accounting entries and general ledger monitoring)
3. Reporting and interpreting reports and statements
4. Evaluating and consulting on financial matters
5. Tax administration
6. Protection of assets
7. Economic appraisal
8. Regulatory compliance (selected areas)
9. Internal controls
10. Managerial accounting responsibilities (e.g., budgets, forecasts, reports to management, inventory management computer usage, capital expenditures, government contracts, and others)
11. Risk management
12. Internal and operational auditing responsibilities
13. Real estate planning and control

Treasurer:

1. Provision of capital
2. Investor relations
3. Short-term financing
4. Banking and custody
5. Credit and collections
6. Investments (including hedging financial risks including foreign exchange risk and interest risk)
7. Insurance

The list of responsibilities associated with the controllership function is comprehensive and complex. Extensive education and training is required to perform these functions efficiently, effectively, and responsibly. In addition, controllers must be able to communicate effectively orally and in writing and to work in harmony with others within and outside of the organization. Controllers must also be able to utilize the capabilities associated with computer hardware and software. Continuing professional education in carrying out the controllership functions is absolutely necessary.

Reporting Responsibilities

The controller's role in monitoring and evaluating financial and operating results is critical to the success of a bank. The controller must understand, develop, analyze, and interpret the needs of a bank as they relate to the controller's role and functions. The controller must provide the required data or information in a usable format on a timely basis. Bank controllers report to various constituencies including

The Bank's CEO

Board of Directors

Federal and state regulators:

    Federal Reserve Board

    Office of the Comptroller of the Currency

    Federal Deposit Insurance Corporation

    Office of Thrift Supervision

    Securities and Exchange Commission

    Internal Revenue Service

    State banking and thrifts regulatory commissions

Shareholders and the investment community

Management teams, project leaders, and employees

Professional associations

Controllers must develop systematic methods for accumulating relevant, reliable, and timely data and information. The financial accounting system, including the general ledger, serves as a major source of information. Data and information must be accessible if it is to be useful. On-line computer terminals, advanced networking systems, electronic spreadsheets, desktop and laptop computers, and similar computer-related software and hardware are available commercially.

Major accounting related responsibilities include preparing the bank's operating and capital budgets, compiling the bank's consolidated financial statements, various corporate reports (for profit, cost and investment centers), and compiling regulatory reports (see Chapter 2). If a holding company is involved, the holding company's controller is responsible for preparing consolidated financial statements.

Planning Function

Planning is a major function of management. Planning is a process that establishes goals and objectives and that develops a decision model for selecting the means of attaining those goals and objectives. Planning requires that the organization make choices regarding

1. Goals and objectives   What it wants to do and why it wants to do it
2. The means of attaining the   When, where, and how to do it
   goals and objectives

Strategic planning involves establishing the basic philosophy and direction of the organization. The strategic planning model consists of four components:

1. Basic research and analysis of internal and external environments and identification of macro- and micro-level trends

2. Identification and analysis of alternative goals and objectives

3. Statement of goals and objectives

4. Development of policy alternatives and resource utilization

Short-run planning (forecasting and budgeting) involves deciding how the organization will utilize its resources during a period of time (usually one year or less). Short-run planning identifies the results expected to be achieved during this time frame.

Project and situation planning involves decision making that relates to specific projects or situations. Project and situation planning involves specific actions that usually have long-term implications for the bank.

A hierarchy of planning showing types of planning, levels, and scope follows:

Planning	Level	Scope
Goals and objectives	Top management of the organization	Broad, company wide, and long term
Policies, departmental	Middle management	Narrow, variable term, tactical, flexible
Procedures and methods	Line and supervisory	Narrow, variable term, detailed

Control Function

Control is a managerial function that provides a degree of assurance that the organization's activities are being performed effectively and efficiently. Control is defined as follows:

> Control consists of verifying whether everything occurs in conformity with the plan adopted, the instructions issued, and principles established. It has for an object to point out weaknesses and errors in order to rectify and prevent recurrence.

The control function consists of setting standards, measuring performance, evaluating results, and taking appropriate action. There is a direct linkage between controlling and planning. Planning provides the institution's goals and objectives; control provides one of the means for achieving those goals and objectives. The planning and control cycle is illustrated in Figure 3-1.

Control consists primarily of the following activities:

1. Determining that actions undertaken are in accordance with plans

2. Using feedback to assure that goals and objectives are being attained

Control techniques include both financial and nonfinancial controls. Financial controls focus on monitoring costs, assessing profits or benefits attained, and evaluating asset utilization.

Figure 3-1
Steps in Planning and Control Cycle

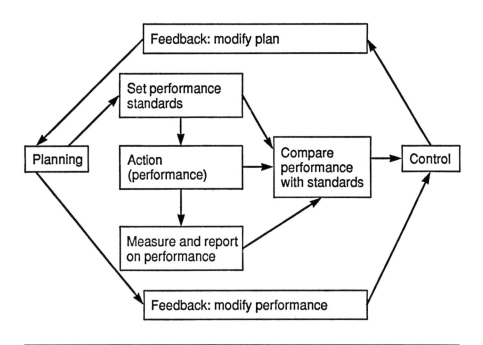

Nonfinancial controls monitor important activities and programs as they relate to nonfinancial aspects of efficiency, economy, and effectiveness.

Organizational controls are used to evaluate overall performance, often in terms of profitability, goal attainment, changes in organizational structure, plans, and objectives. Operational controls are used to measure the period-to-period performance by establishing standards which can be used to monitor the performance. Operational controls include such tools and techniques as productivity ratios, unit costs, and workload measures.

Supervisory control relates primarily to control at the operational level. Two generally recognized supervisory controls include output controls and behavior controls. Output controls are usually based on formal measurement records of outputs and productivity. Behavior controls are based upon personal observations of employees and their performance.

The information managers ordinarily need to control effectively can be classified as (1) score-card information, (2) attention-directing information, and (3) problem-solving information. Score-card information responds to the question: How well or poorly are we doing? Attention-directing information answers such questions as: Is the company performing according to plans? What problems or opportunities exist? What areas of the enterprise need to be changed, if any? Problem-solving information helps management resolve a particular problem:

What is the problem or concern? What are the alternatives? Which alternative is preferable? Reporting and analysis of data developed through a control system is communicated to concerned parties through formal and informal reports.

Communication Function

Communication is the reporting of pertinent information to management and others for internal and external uses. Communication can also be considered as the process of transmitting and receiving information that is relevant to the management of an enterprise. Communication is a function of the organizational structure and relationships. Major managerial functions of planning, organizing, directing, and controlling are carried out through communication. The controller should be skilled in oral and written communications and with group interactions. Figure 3-2 shows the major elements of a communication model.

Primary organizational issues associated with communication include the following:

1. What should be communicated?
2. Who should communicate?
3. When should information be communicated?
4. Where should information be communicated?
5. How should information be communicated?

The human element in communication is affected by cognitive and affective factors. Cognitive factors relate to content and rational thought contained in the message; affective factors relate to values, emotions, and feelings. For communication to be effective, both the cognitive and affective factors must be in harmony. To reduce or eliminate error in communicating, communication models provide for repetition and verification. For example, repetition may involve the use of both written and oral forms of the same message. Verification involves procedures for independent feedback.

Communication models include one-way and two-way communication. The difference between these two models can be summarized as follows:

	One-way (without feedback)	Two-way (with feedback)
Speed	Faster	Slower
Accuracy	Less	More
Noise	Relatively quiet	Relatively noisy
Order	Relatively orderly	Relatively disorderly
Feelings of receiver	Anxiety, insecurity	More confident, less anxious
Feelings of communicator	More confident, secure	Threatened, attacked, less secure

In interpersonal communication communicating is generally improved if both parties understand that communication has both cognitive and affective components and verify to each other (provide feedback of) their understanding of what the other party means.

Figure 3-2
Communication Flows

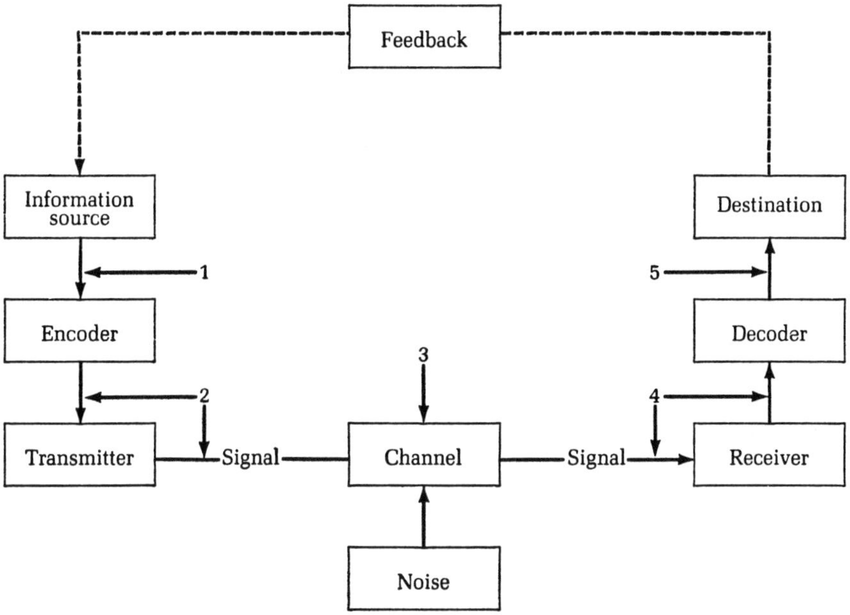

Source: Robert N. Blakeney and Eugene C. Bell, Advanced Leadership (Houston, Human Resources
           Center, College of Business Administration, University of Houston).

In formal communication the organizational structure of the entity establishes the channels of communication. In informal communication networking and the grapevine supplement the formal structure provided by the enterprise. In the formal structure communication occurs in four directions: downward, upward, horizontally (across boundaries on the same organizational level), and diagonally (across both a horizontal and a vertical boundary). Horizontal and diagonal directions are commonly referred to as cross communication. Some organizational behaviorists maintain that where cross communication is allowed, all parties should obtain advance permission from their superiors and should inform their superiors of any significant developments resulting from the communication. Formal communication systems involve policies (principles or rules of action), standards (for conformity and evaluation), and procedures (detailed instructions, usually provided for in procedural manuals).

Research in organizational communication suggests that

1.   As information flows through an organization, it is frequently translated, altered, filtered, sharpened (highlighted) or leveled (selectivity), and evaluated. These transformations can either facilitate or distort communication.

2. Downward communication is more easily accomplished than is upward communication. Downward communication tends to be unfavorable and important, while upward communication tends to be favorable and unimportant.

3. Trust and accuracy are essential in interpersonal and organizational communication. Trust is reflected in the openness and honesty of the communication; accuracy is reflected in the content of the communication. Trust is established by a communicator who is trustworthy (believable, ethical) and informed (experienced, competent).

4. Performance is improved when subordinates are provided with information required to improve performance along with accurate information about their performance.

Performance Evaluation Function

Performance evaluation is based upon the application of guidelines against which the organization's efforts and accomplishments can be measured. Evaluation implies the existence of a bench mark against which actual performance can be compared. Evaluation can result in the identification of both successes and failures. Comparing actual performance with standard performance is commonly referred to as feedback. Feedback provides a basis for interpreting the results of the evaluation and reinforces the successes and eliminates the failures.

Performance evaluation of profit centers typically focuses upon either net income or contribution toward the firm's income. Performance evaluation can reflect this relationship:

$$\text{Operation ratio} = \frac{\text{Income}}{\text{Sales}}$$

Performance evaluation of an investment center typically focuses on both the return on investment (ROI) and the residual income. ROI is conceptualized as follows:

$$\text{ROI} = \frac{\text{Income}}{\text{Investment (or Capital employed)}}$$

The residual income approach charges an investment center with an interest charge for the assets employed. The interest charge is usually the company's cost of capital. Performance is evaluated in terms of income earned in excess of the minimum desired rate of return:

$$\text{Residual income} = \text{Investment center income} - \text{Interest charge}$$

Leadership Function

Leadership is a major function of management. Basic functions of leadership include providing structure and ensuring motivation and compliance. Leadership is required if organizational goals and objectives are to be achieved. Leadership influences persons to act for a common objective. It is a quality of managers that involves getting subordinates (followers) to assist in the attainment of organizational ends.

The skill of a leader relates to traits of the leader, the leader's knowledge of the personality, character, and needs/wants of followers, behavior patterns and interrelationships, situational dimensions (position power, task structure, leader-member relations), organizational requirements, and other factors. More specifically, successful leadership depends on

1. The confidence subordinates have in their leader

2. The nature of the subordinates' jobs (routine, nonroutine)

3. The authority or power placed in the leadership position (rewards, punishments)

To be successful, a leader should

1. Have expertise in the planning, organizing, control, and performance evaluation functions of management

2. Have confidence in his or her ability to lead

3. Possess communication skills

4. Understand persons, tasks, organizational structure, motivation, personalities, and the art of persuasion

Leadership theories are many and varied. Older forms of leadership theory are based on an understanding of the traits of a leader: maturity, character, decisiveness, intelligence, and others. Research generally confirms that no single trait or set of traits can assure effective leadership. Behavioral theories of leadership styles have been proposed to explain leadership. Leadership styles include the following:

1. Autocratic model

2. Participative model

3. Hands-on model

4. Two-dimensional model

The autocratic style of leadership is essentially leadership centered in the manager. The manager makes and announces the decision. The area of freedom for subordinates is limited, and the use of authority by the manager is considerable. The participative leadership style is primarily subordinate-centered leadership where subordinates have considerable freedom and the use of authority by the manager is limited.

A hands-on management style requires a high degree of involvement in operations by a manager. Two-dimensional models of leadership are behavior oriented. In two-dimensional models, one dimension focuses on people, and the other dimension focuses on tasks (assignments; production). For example, a leadership style could be one in which the manager had a high concern for people and a low concern for tasks. Another style would be the opposite. A third style could be a moderate concern for people and tasks. A fourth could be high concern for both people and tasks. Other combinations are possible.

Robert Blake and Jane Mouton provided a structure for leadership in *The New Managerial Grid* (see Figure 3-3). The two-dimensional grid identifies combinations of concern for production and concern for people. Concern for people is represented on the vertical axis of the grid; concern for production (tasks) is represented on the horizontal axis. The four corners of the grid and the center describe various management styles:

Corner	Leadership Style
1.1	Low concern for both people and production

Corner	Leadership Style
1.9	High concern for people and low concern for production; democratic leadership
9.1	High concern for production and low concern for people; autocratic leadership
9.9	High concern for both people and production; Blake and Mouton believe that this style is the most effective leadership style
5.5	Equal concern for people and production (that is, a balanced approach to leadership).

ORGANIZATIONAL STRUCTURE

Organizations can be organized in two ways: centralized or decentralized. From an organizational perspective, centralization and decentralization are issues of how authority is delegated

Figure 3-3
The Managerial Grid

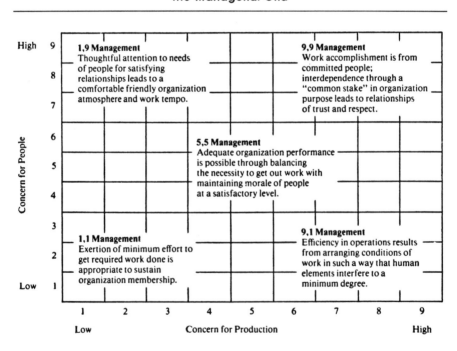

Source: Robert R. Blake and Jane S. Mouton, The Managerial Grid, Houston, Gulf Publishers

to the different organizational levels. Centralization refers to the organizational level that has authority to make a decision. When decisions are delegated to lower organizational levels, the organization is decentralized.

Decentralization gives greater autonomy to subunits of the organization. In a decentralized firm decision-making authority is pushed downward through the organizational levels to enable effective planning and activities at the most appropriate level. Decentralized operations enable the firm to fulfill its objectives, while providing sufficient autonomy to managers to enable them to test their ideas and skills, and to develop their potential. Communication and coordination are more effective, and decisions can be made more quickly in a decentralized organization. In a decentralized organization, the risk exists that managers will promote their decentralized unit at the expense of the company as a whole. The extent to which a firm centralizes its operations depends upon the firm's environment (for example, competitive situation, market characteristics), the size and growth rate of the firm, and the firm's characteristics (for example, costs and risks involved, top management's preference; available managerial skills, the history of the entity, and cost-benefit considerations). Delegation of authority requires that authority, responsibility, and accountability be coextensive.

In a centralized organization structure decision making and coordinating functions are concentrated at the higher levels of the organization structure. Operational activities and responsibilities remain at the lower levels. Centralized operations are usually used by a firm that wants to provide greater uniformity of actions or integration of organizational effort.

THE COMPUTER REVOLUTION

The information revolution has brought about the growth and development of the computer in banking operations. The computer enables the controller to be not only a provider of information but also a decision maker. This contribution that the computer can make to controllership should not be underestimated.

The controller should be skilled in evaluating and selecting computer software and hardware capable of performing banking functions efficiently and effectively. The controller should be knowledgeable concerning security and internal control procedures, operational manuals, network computer system, and trends in computer applications. Continuing professional education in this functional area should be a priority item for the experienced controller.

The volume and velocity of banking transactions that require processing has made the use of electronic data processing a prerequisite to successful banking. State-of-the-art banks are capable of initiating, processing, and executing most banking functions and transactions efficiently with minimal disruption. Electronic record keeping provides an adequate substitute for paper trails of transactions in most situations.

INTERNAL CONTROL SYSTEM

Banks and other financial institutions have major risks associated with their operations. High volume and high value transactions associated with money and money equivalents are common to such institutions. Well-developed control systems can be used to manage and control these risks to a considerable extent.

The controller should have a high level of understanding of internal control structures including the control environment, the accounting system, and control procedures. Policies and procedures should be developed and be operational to ensure that adequate internal controls are in place.

The control environment represents the effect of various factors on establishing, enhancing, or mitigating the effectiveness of specific policies and procedures. Such factors include the following:

- Management's philosophy and operating style
- The entity's organizational structure
- The functioning of the board of directors and its committees
- Methods of assigning authority and responsibility
- Management's control methods for monitoring and following up on performance, including internal auditing
- Personnel policies and practices
- External influences that affect an entity's operations and practices

The control environment should reflect the overall attitude, awareness, and actions of the board of directors, management, and personnel as they relate to internal control.

Control procedures have specific objectives. Generally, they can be categorized as procedures that pertain to proper authorization of transactions and activities; segregation of duties that reduce the opportunities to allow any person to be in a position to both perpetrate and conceal errors or irregularities in the normal course of his or her duties; design and use of adequate documents and records to ensure the proper recording of transactions and events; adequate safeguards over access to and use of assets and records; and independent checks on performance and proper valuation of recorded amounts, such as reconciliations, computer-programmed controls, management review of reports, comparison of assets with recorded records, and many others.

The proof function in banking is a significant factor in an effective control environment. Strict controls should be maintained to ensure that transactions and entries are subjected to the proof process by individuals and departments to ensure that the records of the bank are in balance.

Internal auditing departments can be a very effective component of a systematic internal control system. This department has a major responsibility for reviewing compliance with the control system. External and regulatory auditors will devote considerable attention to the internal control system of an institution as a routine part of its audit program.

Bank controllers should be aware of the Foreign Corrupt Practices Act of 1977, which requires public companies to " ... devise and maintain a system of internal accounting controls."

KEY DEFINITIONS

Control Actions that support the planning decision and performance evaluation; the possession, direct or indirect, of the power to direct or cause the direction of the management and policies of a specified party whether through ownership, by contract, or otherwise.

Controllability The degree of influence that a specific manager has over the costs, revenues, or other items.

Controller The title used for the chief accountant of an organization. Sometimes spelled comptroller.

Effectiveness The degree to which an objective or target is met.

Efficiency The degree to which inputs are used in relation to a given level of outputs.

Effort Exertion toward a goal or target.

Goal congruence Goal sharing by managers and their subordinates.

Management by objectives Procedures under which jointly formulated goals and plans for attaining those goals for a subsequent period are designed.

Motivation Desire, drive, or pursuit related to attaining a goal.

Organizational culture Beliefs and values shared by members of an organization or entity.

Organizational goals Objectives that an organization attempts to accomplish.

Performance reports Measurements of results, which are usually compared with budgeted or standard amounts.

Planning Establishing goals, forecasts, and budgets to achieve goals and objectives. Generally involves decision making, evaluation, and feedback.

Productivity The input/output ratio within a time period.

Quality Conformance of a product or service with a standard.

Short-run planning Forecasting and budgeting.

Strategic planning Establishing the basic philosophy and direction of the organization. Factors considered in strategic planning include the mission, goals, and objectives of the organization, resources available to the entity, competition, technological changes, and the marketplace.

Treasurer A name associated with the chief financial officer of a business.

Utility The value assigned to a specific outcome by a decision maker.

Waste Inputs that do not become a part of outputs.

Chapter 4

The Accounting Model for Banks

A major objective of accounting is to communicate relevant and reliable information to individuals and organizations. Financial reporting standards require that timely financial reporting be performed. To meet this requirement, most banks produce (1) daily summaries, (2) monthly financial reports for the board of directors, management, and others, (3) quarterly financial reports to regulatory authorities (call reports) and to stockholders, and (4) annual financial statements to stockholders and regulatory authorities. This chapter will examine the process by which accounting achieves this reporting objective within the banking environment.

THE ACCOUNTING CYCLE

The accounting cycle is a sequence of activities that records, summarizes, and reports economic events and transactions. The steps in the cycle include journalizing transactions, posting to a ledger, taking a trial balance adjusting the accounts, preparing financial statements, closing the accounts, and taking a post closing trial balance. The cycle is repeated each accounting period. The operations of the cycle can be conceptualized as shown in Figure 4-1.

Accounting Equation

The accounting equation expresses the relationship that exists among assets, liabilities, and owners' equity. In its simplest form, the accounting equation can be represented as follows:

Exhibit 4-1
Normal Operating Cycle of a Business

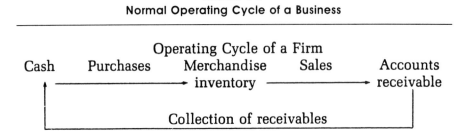

Assets − Liabilities = Owners' Equity (or Capital)

The equation states an equality and establishes a relationship among the three major accounting elements. Assets are the economic resources a business owns that are expected to be of benefit in the future. Liabilities are economic obligations payable to outsiders. Owners' equity is shown as the residual of assets over liabilities. The Accounting equation can also be stated in this form:

Assets = Liabilities + Owners' Equity (or Capital)

This formulation of the accounting equation shows that owners and creditors have claims against the assets of the enterprise.

Accounting Functions

Accounting deals with numbers and measurable quantities. The accounting system accumulates, measures, and communicates numbers and measurable quantities of economic information about an enterprise. These three functions can be represented as a flow of information from source to destination as follows:

Accounting Period

An accounting period is the time period for which financial statements are prepared. Custom, as well as income tax and other legal considerations, have focused on annual reporting periods and an annual accounting cycle. If the reporting period begins on January 1 and ends on December 31, it is referred to as a calendar year accounting period. Any other beginning and ending period of one year is called a fiscal year. The accounting period is identified on the financial statements.

Financial reports for periods shorter than one year, such as quarterly reports, are referred to as interim reports or interim statements.

For income tax purposes, the accounting period is usually a year. Unless a fiscal year is chosen, taxpayers must determine their tax liability by using the calendar year as the period of measurement. A change in the accounting period requires approval of the IRS.

Regulatory reporting periods are specified by the regulatory agencies according to their needs. These should be complied with.

Accounting Policies and Procedures

The accounting principles of a reporting entity are the specific accounting principles and the methods of applying those principles that are judged by the management of the business to be the most appropriate in the circumstances to present fairly a financial position, results of operations, and cash flow in accordance with generally accepted accounting principles.

Information about the accounting policies adopted by a reporting enterprise is essential for financial statement users, and should be disclosed adequately. Accounting principles and their methods of application in the following areas are important:

1. A selection from among existing alternatives (e.g., lifo or fifo inventory procedures; straight line or accelerated depreciation).

2. Areas that are peculiar to a particular industry in which the company operates (e.g., applying market value to securities in certain industries).

3. Unusual and innovative applications of generally accepted accounting principles.

The preferred place to disclose accounting policies is under the caption "Summary of Significant Accounting Policies" or as the initial note to the financial statements.

Accounting System

An accounting system is a management information system that is responsible for the collection and processing of data to produce information useful to decision makers in planning and controlling the activities of an organization. An accounting system deals primarily with one category of information, namely financial information that concerns the flow of financial resources through the organization.

The data processing cycle of an accounting system can be conceptualized as the total structure of records and procedures associated with five activities: collection or recording; classifying; processing, including calculating and summarizing; maintenance or storage; and output or reporting. The process of data in a typical accounting system can be illustrated as follows:

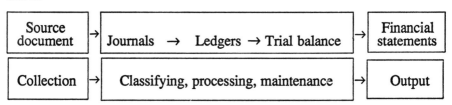

The development of accounting information involves the following stages: analysis, design, implementation, and operations. During the analysis stage, the analyst determines information needs of the system, the sources of information, and the strengths and deficiencies of the current system. The design stage involves an evaluation of different kinds of data processing equipment, processing methods, and procedures suitable to the proposed project. During the design stage, the detailed system is completed. After the system is designed, the implementation of the system commences. During the implementation stage, the system becomes operational. Modifications of the system may be required as problems arise or as needs or technology develop.

Accounting Basis

Accounting basis refers to methods for recognizing revenues, expenses, assets, and liabilities in accounting statements. Major bases of accounting include the accrual, cash, and modified cash bases.

In accrual accounting revenue and gains are recognized in the period when they are earned. Expenses and losses are recognized in periods when they are incurred. Accrual basis accounting is concerned with the economic consequences of events and transactions rather than with only cash receipts and cash payments. Under accrual accounting, net income does not necessarily reflect cash receipts and cash payments for a particular time period. Accrual accounting generally provides the most accurate measure of earning, earning power, managerial performance, future cash flows, and stewardship.

Cash-basis accounting recognizes only transactions involving actual cash receipts and disbursements occurring in a given period. Cash-basis accounting recognizes revenues and gains when cash is received and expenses and losses when cash is paid. No attempt is made to record unpaid bills or amounts owed to or by the unit. Cash basis accounting is generally deficient as an accounting model that attempts to produce a statement of financial position and an income statement. Nevertheless, cash-basis accounting is widely used for income tax purposes.

Under a modified cash basis of accounting, certain expenditures but not necessarily all, are capitalized and amortized in the future. Some revenues are recognized as earned, while others await cash receipts before the revenue is recognized. The modified cash basis of accounting is essentially part cash basis and part accrual basis accounting.

Net income from operations computed according to generally accepted accounting principles (accrual basis) can be converted to cash flow from operations according to the following general procedures:

Net income from operations

+   Items reducing income but not using cash, such as depreciation, depletion, and amortization expenses
    Decreases in current assets other than cash
    Increases in current liabilities

−   Increases in current assets other than cash
    Decreases in current liabilities

=   Cash flow from operations

Accounting Controls

Accounting controls include the plan of organization and the procedures and records dealing with the broad objectives, and safeguarding assets and improving the reliability of financial records required for the preparation of financial statements. Accounting controls are concerned primarily with systems authorization and approval, controls over assets, internal auditing procedures, and other financial matters. It is management's responsibility to establish and maintain an appropriate system of internal accounting control. The operative objectives of accounting controls is designed to provide reasonable assurance that

1. Transactions are executed in accordance with management's general or specific authorization.

2. Transactions are recorded as necessary (a) to permit the preparation of financial statements in conformity with generally accepted accounting principles or any other criteria applicable to such statements, and (b) to maintain accountability for assets.

3. Access to assets is permitted only in accordance with management's authorization.

4. The recorded accountability for assets is compared with the existing assets at reasonable intervals and appropriate action is taken with respect to any difference.

Accounting control systems provide reasonable, not absolute, assurance that the accounting control objectives are met. The concept of reasonable assurance recognizes that accounting control systems are subject to cost-benefit constraints.

Administrative Controls

Administrative controls include the plan of organization and the procedures and records associated with the decision processes involved in management's authorization of transactions. Administrative controls are designed to facilitate management's responsibility for achieving the objectives of the organization and to improve operational efficiency and compliance with management's and regulatory agency's policies. Administrative controls are the basis for establishing the accounting control over transaction.

Administrative controls can be contrasted with accounting controls. Examples contrasting administrative and accounting controls include the following:

Accounting Controls	Administrative Controls
Cash	
Cash receipts are to be deposited daily; all cash disbursements are to be made by check.	Use cash forecast to determine short-term borrowing requirements.
Inventory	
The perpetual inventory method account for property	Inventory modeling techniques are to be used to determine the quantity of inventory to order and the timing of orders.

Internal Control

Internal control refers to the systems, procedures, and policies employed by an enterprise to assure that transactions are properly authorized, executed, and recorded. Internal control applies to both administrative controls and accounting controls. Administrative (operating) controls include a plan of organization, procedures and records that lead up to management's authorization of transactions. Accounting (financial) controls deal with the plans, procedures, and records required for safeguarding assets and producing reliable financial records.

Broad categories of control procedures that apply in both financial and administrative controls include the following:

1. Organizational:

    (a) Separation of duties

    (b) Clear lines of authority and responsibility

    (c) Formal policies

2. Procedures:

    (a) Accounting checks and balances

    (b) Proper documents and records

    (c) Error detection and correction procedures

    (d) Physical control over assets and records

3. Competent, trustworthy personnel (bonded where appropriate)

The topic of internal controls is covered extensively in Chapter 15, Bank Examinations and Audits.

THE GENERAL LEDGER

An *account* is a systematic arrangement that shows the effect of transactions and other events on a specific asset, liability, or equity. A separate account is kept for each asset, liability, revenue, gain, expense, loss, and capital (owners' equity). A book, file, or electronic tape or disks contain all or groups of the bank's accounts arranged according to a chart of accounts. This is called a *ledger.*

A *chart of accounts* is a list of a bank's general and subsidiary ledger accounts and numbers systematically organized. The *general ledger* is a summary accounting record of all the subsidiary ledgers. Separate or *subsidiary ledgers* are kept for a variety of transactions: loans, deposits, investments, and other transactions. Subsidiary ledgers are used to collect, analyze, and produce schedules associated with their purpose. The general ledger is used to collect and code all transactions, posting all accounting entries; develop trial balances, balance sheets, and income statements; and provide the information required for statements of cash flow, retained earnings, and changes in owners' capital. An account-numbering system is usually designed as a code that indicates classifications and relationships of accounts. The classification, grouping, and description of accounts should be sufficiently complete to achieve clarity of presentation.

Certain regulatory agencies have rules as to disclosures and financial statement presentation of specific items. The Securities and Exchange Commission has rules as to disclosures in and presentation of financial statements. Familiarity with the rules in Regulation S-X is essential to the proper preparation of such financial statements. SEC rules with regard to annual reports to shareholders are contained in Rule 14a-3 of the proxy rules, which refers to Regulation S-X. The financial statements, including the notes thereto, are to be identical in the annual report to shareholders and the Form 10-K filed with the SEC. This should be kept in mind when constructing or reviewing general ledger accounts.

Generally ledger accounts are usually arranged in the order in which they appear on the financial statements. First the asset, liabilities, and permanent owners's equity accounts appear in the order of their listing on the statement of financial position. Then revenue and expense accounts are listed in the order of their listing on the income statement. This arrangement facilitates the preparation of financial statements.

Charts of account numbers are assigned to bank accounts according to major categories (for illustration purposes only):

Category	Account Number Range
Assets	1000–1999
Liabilities	2000–2999
Capital	3000–3999
Interest and Fee Income	5000–5999
Interest Expense and Provision for Loan Losses	6000–6999
Noninterest Income	7000–7999
Noninterest Expenses	8000–8999
Taxes	9000–9999
Extraordinary Items	9500–9599

General ledger accounts should be limited to those accounts required to meet financial and managerial reporting requirements. Titles used for general ledger accounts should be consistent with titles used in other ledgers, reports, and financial statements.

The general ledger should provide methods and procedures for

1. Preparing, processing, and monitoring general ledger entries
2. Preparing reports and financial statements required by the board of directors, management, and regulatory authorities
3. Supporting and confirming various compliance requirements
4. Preparing cost accounting studies and profit-center reports

5. Maintaining and developing the computer hardware and software associated with the system

6. Recruiting, selecting, and training personnel capable of operating the system at an acceptable level

RECONCILIATION AND EVALUATING PROCEDURES

Balance sheet accounts should be reconciled where the book balance and the financial statement balances are adjusted for such items as deposits in transit, outstanding checks, bank charges, notes collected, and similar items. Since there are no open items for income and expense accounts, such accounts must be verified according to the nature of the accounts. Many expense account transactions can be verified during the accounts payable process. Fees and service charges accounts can use listings by customer to compare with the general ledger.

Controllers frequently use reviews of historical trends, ratios, normal balances, accruals, and activity, budget variances and similar analytical tools to evaluate financial reports and statements before they are published (see Chapter 12). Judgment and experience are required to perform this review function satisfactorily.

Bank Specific

Responsibility for preparing, balancing, and processing daily general ledger entries is typically placed at a bank's department or branch office. These entries provide the basis for additional processing and posting at the operational center.

Control over cash is accomplished by a variety of means, including a daily reconciliation of the cash pool by tellers, daily balance sheets and cash reports by management, and the separation of duties to include individuals responsible for handling cash versus those who have access to the recording process or accounting records. Similar procedures are used for other general ledger accounts in addition to cash.

A bank typically generates reports that assist management in the performance of their operations, including

1. Daily trial balance containing the chart of accounts numbers, the current balance, and a total of all account activity for the day

2. Daily new account report, which shows the bank's new business connections for the day

3. Daily overdraft report that reports the overdraft position of all accounts accepted by the bank

4. Daily significant balance change, which shows material changes in an account that is reported to management

The financial statements of banks are discussed in detail in Chapters 5, 6, and 7.

THE MINICOMPUTER ENVIRONMENT

System analysts are aware of the risks and relevant control policies and procedures associated with the minicomputer environment. An understanding of risks and controls would include the following considerations:

- *Segregation of Functions Between the EDP Department and Users* (Personnel in the user department initiate and authorize source documents, enter data into the system, operate the computer, and use the output reports.)

  Risks

  Perpetration and concealment of errors or irregularities

  Unauthorized changes to master files

  Inaccurate and incomplete processing of data

  Processing errors

  Incomplete or erroneous data

  Uncorrected errors

  Relevant Control Policies and Procedures

  Maintenance of transaction logs and batch controls by user departments

  Independent review of processing logs, transaction logs, and batch control information

  Management supervision

  Passwords to control access to files and libraries

  Required vacations and rotation of duties

  Reconciliation of record counts or hash totals

  Use of application programs to make changes in master files

  Independent reconciliation of transaction totals recorded in batch control or with input and output totals. Comparison of system manufacturer's utility program with authorized application version

  Lost, added, or altered data

- *Location of the Computer* (The computer is located in the same area as the user department.)

  Risk

  Improper use or manipulation of data files

  Unauthorized use or modification of computer programs

  Improper use of computer resources

Relevant and Control Policies and Procedures

Menus and procedures to control processing access

Management review of usage reports (history logs)

Periodic comparison of usage reports with processing schedule

Physical control over data entry devices

■ *Segregation of Functions Within the EDP Department* (Segregation between programmers and operators imposed)

Risks

Unauthorized access to information and programs

Perpetration and concealment of errors or irregularities

Errors caused by improper use or manipulation of data files or unauthorized or incorrect use of computer program

Application programs that do not meet management's objectives

Relevant Control Policies and Procedures

Use of a compiler to convert source code into object code

Comparison of library directories with manual records

■ *Training of EDP personnel* (Supervisors responsible for data processing have extensive knowledge of EDP.)

Risks

Failure of systems to meet management objectives or operate according to management specifications

Lack of adequate application controls

Inadequate testing and review of system

Relevant Control Policies and Procedures

Operations documentation

Program documentation

System documentation

Use of third party to review new and modified programs and systems

■ *Utility Programs* (Used extensively to enter and to change data)

Risk

Unauthorized access and changes to data

Undetected errors in file manipulation

Lack of adequate application controls

Processing of unauthorized transactions and omitting of authorized transactions

Perpetration and concealment of errors or irregularities

Relevant Control Policies and Procedures

Use of passwords to control access to data files

Use of application programs to update files

Independent control over transaction and master file changes, such as item count, control total, and hash totals

Limited access to utilities

Removal of utilities from system when practical to do so

■ *Diskettes* (Used extensively for file storage)

Risks

Processing of wrong file

Inability to detect errors in file changes

Inability to highlight operator errors

Relevant Control Policies and Procedures

Control over access to diskettes

Storage of data in format not readable by key entry device

Use of manual logs to control diskette library

■ *Terminals* (Used for transaction data entry, inquiry, and other interactive functions)

Risks

Unauthorized input

Erroneous or fraudulent data

Errors caused by improper use or manipulation of data files or computer programs

Erroneous or incomplete data

Relevant Control Policies and Procedures

Use of software that will allow only certain terminals to be used for specific functions

Use of physical controls to limit access to data files

Use of passwords to control access to data files

Encryption of data and programs

On-line computer edit procedures

Record counts, batch controls, run-to-run controls, verification

Error handling control procedures and error logs

Use of menus and procedures

■ *Software Packages* (Purchased software packages used extensively, rather than internally developed applications)

Risks

Failure of systems to meet management and user objectives

Lack of adequate applicator controls

Inadequate testing of systems

Relevant Control Policies and Procedures

Use of third party to review and evaluate proposed software packages

■ *Documentation* (Available system program, operator, and user documentation may be limited or nonexistent.)

Risk

Undetected errors during processing and system maintenance

Relevant Control Policies and Procedures

User-based controls

Comparison of program in use with an authorized version

Use of interpretative language programs

Passwords to control access to libraries and files

Software controls to limit system access capabilities according to employee functions

Test libraries

Management review of usage reports (history logs)

System of transaction logs, batch controls, processing logs and run-to-run controls
Source: American Institute of Certified Public Accountants.

KEY DEFINITIONS

Account A systematic arrangement that shows the effect of transactions and events on a specific asset, liability, or equity.

Accounting A service activity the function of which is to provide quantitative information, primarily financial in nature, about economic entities that is intended to be useful in making economic decisions—in making reasoned choices among alternative courses of action.

Accounting basis The method of recognizing revenue and expenses. The accrual basis of accounting recognizes revenues as goods or services that are sold or performed. Expenses are recognized in the period when the associated revenue is recognized. The cash basis of accounting recognizes revenue and expenses as cash received or disbursed.

Accounting controls A system of controls to provide reasonable assurances that (1) transactions are executed in accordance with management's authorizations, (2) transactions are recorded to allow preparation of financial statements and to maintain accountability for assets, (3) access to assets is permitted only with management's authorization, and (4) recorded accountability for assets is compared with the existing assets at reasonable intervals.

Accounting cycle The sequence of accounting procedures used during a period of time commencing with journal entries and ending with financial statements.

Accounting equation Assets – Liabilities = Residual equity (capital; owners' equity).

Accounting periods The time intervals used for financial reporting.

Accounting system The procedures used for collecting, processing, and summarizing financial data in an organization.

Adjusting entries A journal entry made at the end of an accounting period that records a transaction or event which has not been recorded during the accounting period to update the accounts.

Administrative controls The plan of organization and the procedures and records that relate to the decision processes leading to management's authorization of transactions.

Arm's length transactions Exchanges between parties who are independent of each other and who act in their own best economic interest.

Balance sheet A financial statement that reports as of a given point in time the assets, obligations, and residual ownership claims; a statement of financial position.

Chart of accounts A list of names and numbers of ledger accounts systematically arranged.

Closing entries A journal entry that transfers the balances in temporary ledger accounts to a zero balance to prepare the accounts for the next financial period.

Control account An account with a balance that equals the sum of the balances in a group of related accounts in a subsidiary ledger.

Credit An entry on the right side of an account.

Current assets Cash and resources that are reasonably expected to be converted into cash during the normal operating cycle of a business or within one year, whichever period is longer.

Current liabilities Obligations that are reasonably expected to be paid using current assets or by creating other current liabilities during the normal operating cycle of a business or within one year, whichever period is longer.

Debit An entry on the left side of an account.

Economic entity A specific reporting unit.

Entity An organization or a section of an organization for accounting purposes.

Event A happening of consequence to an entity. An event is often the source or cause of changes in assets, liabilities, and equity. Events are either external or internal.

Financial statements Reports that reflect the final summation of accounting data for a period or as of a specific date.

General journal A book of original entry in which a transaction is recorded.

General ledger A record where similar transactions are recorded in financial statement accounts; a book of final entry.

Internal control Procedures used to ensure that a company's plans, policies, and actions are carried out or to safeguard assets.

Journal The chronological accounting record of transactions.

Journalizing Recording a transaction in a journal.

Nominal account See *Real and nominal accounts.*

Postclosing trial balance A list of ledger accounts and balances remaining after the journalizing and posting of the closing entries.

Posting Transferring of amounts from the journal to the ledger.

Real and nominal accounts Real or permanent accounts are asset, liability, and equity accounts that appear on the balance sheet. Nominal or temporary accounts are revenue and expense accounts that appear on the income statement. Nominal accounts are periodically closed at the end of an accounting period. Real accounts are also referred to as permanent accounts; nominal accounts are also referred to as temporary accounts.

Reversing entries A journal entry that can be made at the beginning of an accounting period to reverse a previous adjusting entry to simplify the accounting process in a subsequent accounting period.

Special purpose journal A journal used to record a single type of transaction.

Subsidiary ledger A book of accounts that provides supporting details on individual account balances, the total of which is reported in a general ledger account.

Transaction An external event involving the transfer or exchange of something of value between two or more entities.

T account A form of account that has a physical resemblance to the letter T.

Trial balance A statement that shows the name and balance of all ledger accounts arranged according to whether they are debits or credits. The total of the debits must equal the total of the credits.

Voucher A written authorization prepared for an expenditure used in a voucher system.

Voucher check A check designed for use in a voucher system.

Voucher register A special-purpose journal in which vouchers are recorded after they have been approved.

Voucher system An accounting system providing documentary evidence of and written authorization for business transactions typically associated with expenditures.

Working capital The amount by which total current assets exceed total current liabilities.

Work sheet A working paper that is used to assist in the preparation and support of financial statements and other documentation.

Chapter 5

The Statement of Condition

Financial statements are the most widely used and the most comprehensive way of communicating financial information. Different users of financial statements have different informational needs. General purpose financial statements have been developed to meet the needs of external users of financial statements, primarily the needs of investors and creditors.

INFORMATION CONTENT

Financial statements are affected not only by the environment in which financial reporting takes place but also by the characteristics and limitations of the kind of information that financial statements provide. The information provided by financial statements

- Is primarily financial in nature, quantified and expressed in units of money
- Is summarized information and merely one source of information needed by those who make economic decisions about business enterprises

- Relates to specific enterprises and not to industries
- Includes estimates and approximations and not exact measurements
- Requires judgments and interpretations
- Reflects the financial effects of transactions and events that have already occurred
- Is provided and used at a cost; the benefits derived from the information provided are expected to at least equal the costs incurred in producing the information

External financial statements prepared by banks are governed by two different authorities: The Financial Accounting Standards Board and regulatory authorities. The FASB's standards reflect generally accepted accounting principles (GAAP). Regulator's accounting rules are commonly referred to as RAP. Statements prepared for general external distribution and for the Securities and Exchange Commission are required to use GAAP; statements prepared for regulatory authorities must use RAP. Fortunately, many of the differences between GAAP and RAP are being reconciled.

Banks typically prepare three major external reports: a report of condition (or balance sheet), income statement, and statement of cash flows. These statements are described in this chapter and the two following chapters. The statement of condition (or balance sheet) will now be discussed in some detail.

THE STATEMENT OF CONDITION

The statement of condition, or balance sheet, is a report that shows the financial position of the enterprise at a specific time, including the bank's economic resources (assets), economic obligations (liabilities) and the residual claims of owners (owners' equity). Notes to financial statements are considered an integral part of the statement. The statement of condition is also referred to as the balance sheet and the statement of financial position.

Assets

Assets are probably future economic benefits obtained or controlled by a particular entity as a result of past transactions or events. The future economic benefit of assets usually result in net cash inflows to the bank. Assets are recognized in the financial statements when (1) the item meets the definition of an asset, (2) it can be measured with sufficient reliability, (3) the information is capable of making a difference in user decisions, and (4) the information about the item is reliable and verifiable. The intrinsic attributes of assets can be conceptualized as follows:

Attribute	Description	Time
Historical cost	The acquisition cost of an asset	Past
Current cost (or fair value)	The amount that has to be paid today to acquire an asset. Fair value of a financial instrument is the amount at which the instrument could be exchanged in a current transaction between willing parties, other than in a forced or liquidation sale. The quoted price for a single trading unit in the most active market is the basis for determining market price and reporting fair value (SFAS No. 107, Disclosure about Fair Value of Financial Instruments, December 1991).	Present
Current exit value	The amount that could be obtained today if an asset were sold in orderly liquidation	Present
Expected exit value	The amount expected to be received in the normal course of business	Future
Present value of expected cash flows	The amount of discounted net cash inflows that an asset is expected to produce	Future

The historical cost and fair value attributes are currently emphasized when accounting for assets. The reliability and verifiability of historical cost are considered relevant when choosing a device for measuring an asset. However, fair value has been recommended for financial instruments because it is especially relevant and reliable when reporting on financial instruments (effective December 15, 1995). Financial instruments represent significant assets for banks and thrifts. The other attributes are occasionally used when reporting assets in financial statements.

The valuation of assets has come under increasing question in recent years. The question of whether historical cost or market value is the more appropriate method of valuing assets has not been resolved. Regulators and the accounting profession have brought increasing pressure to move toward market value accounting. Banks have typically employed the historical cost basis of accounting, which reflects the nontrading aspect of most of their activities. This will now change with the adoption of SFAS 107.

The breakdown of financial assets for all U.S. banks in 1991 demonstrates the wide variety of such assets held by commercial banks as a percentage of total assets:

Cash	1.4%
Investment securities	20.8
Loan portfolio	58.2

Business loans represented 21.1 percent of assets. Consumer loans represented 12.4 percent of assets. Mortgage-backed securities and direct mortgages represented 34.6 percent in 1991.

Liabilities

Liabilities are the economic obligations of a particular entity to transfer assets or provide services to other entities in the future as a result of past transactions or events. Liabilities have three major characteristics: (1) a duty or obligation to pay exists, (2) the duty is virtually unavoidable by a particular entity, and (3) the event obligating the enterprise has occurred. The chief liabilities of banks are deposits, borrowings from the Federal Reserve bank or other banks, liabilities on account of letters of credit, and acceptances.

Most liabilities arise from agreements between parties. However, some liabilities are imposed by government or courts or are accepted by an entity to avoid legal costs. Other liabilities are discretional actions by management, such as donations. While most liabilities are legally enforceable, some arise from the acceptance of an equitable or constructive obligation. The uncertainty of events and transactions have made it difficult to measure specific liabilities.

Liabilities reported on the statement of condition are measured by different attributes, i.e., historical cost, current cost (fair value), current exit value, expected exit value, and present value of future cash flows, depending upon the nature of the item and the relevance and reliability of the attribute measured. SFAS No. 107 applies to liabilities as well as to assets.

At one time commercial banks accepted large amounts of noninterest-bearing demand deposits and relatively low-yielding savings and time deposits. As treasurers of nonfinancial corporations became more sophisticated, they sought higher yielding, short-term investments to replace demand deposits. The negotiable CD was banks' response to this deposit drain. In 1991 checkable deposits represented 16.6 percent of total liabilities; a share of these were interest-bearing NOW accounts. Small time and savings accounts represented 40.6 percent, and large time deposits were 13.5 percent. Short-term and long-term borrowed funds were 2.9 percent of total liabilities. Both the interest rates and the instruments themselves that are a part of the industry's liability portfolio are very sensitive to market conditions.

Equity

Equity (or capital) is the residual interest in the assets of an entity that remains after deducting its liabilities. Equity is increased or decreased by operations, investments by owners, distribution to owners, and other events and circumstances that affect an entity.

An entity may have various classes of equity, with different risks, rights, and obligations. It is generally recognized that no class of equity carries an unconditional right to receive future transfers of assets from an enterprise except in liquidation, subject to liabilities that must be settled.

Usefulness of the Statement

The statement of condition assists external users in evaluating the bank's liquidity, financial flexibility, operating capabilities and the earning performance for the period. Liquidity describes the amount of time that is expected to elapse until an asset is realized or otherwise converted into cash or until a liability has to be paid. Financial flexibility is the ability of an enterprise to take effective actions to alter the amounts and timing of cash flows so it can respond to unexpected needs and opportunities.

Bank Specific: A Sample Statement

The statement of conditions in Figure 5-1 reports the bank's assets, liabilities and stockholders equity. Observe that the statement is unclassified; it does not make a distinction between current and noncurrent assets and liabilities. Those distinctions have generally been considered inappropriate for banks owing to the nature of a bank's assets and liabilities. Investment securities appearing as assets on a bank's statement are primarily debt instruments. Also note that bank assets are classified as either earning or nonearning as follows:

1. *Earning assets*
    a. Interest-bearing deposits in other financial institutions
    b. Federal funds sold and securities purchased under resale agreements
    c. Investment securities
    d. Loans
    e. Due from customers on acceptances

2. *Nonearning assets*
    a. Cash and due from banks
    b. Premises and equipment
    c. Accrued interest receivable
    d. Other assets

Statements of condition are usually presented in comparative form. Comparative statements include the current year's statement and statements of one or more of the preceding accounting periods. Comparative statements are useful in evaluating and analyzing trends and relationships. Figure 5-1 illustrates a comparative bank balance sheet.

CASH AND CASH ITEMS

Cash and cash items include highly liquid assets including vault cash, due from banks, due from Federal Reserve, and cash items in collection. This category of assets is sometimes referred to as primary reserves. Essentially, these cash categories are available on a same-day or next-day basis at the carrying value. There are virtually no factors that will cause the market value of these assets to differ from book value.

TEMPORARY INVESTMENTS

Temporary investments include interest-bearing time deposits in other banks, federal funds sold, term federal funds sold, and securities purchased under agreement to resell. These investments are expected to earn a reasonable rate of return. These funds are considered secondary reserves.

Figure 5-1

FIRST SAMPLE BANK
BALANCE SHEETS
December 31, 19X2 and 19X1

	19X2	19X1
ASSETS		
Cash and due from banks	$11,820,189	$15,009,846
Investment securities (Approximate market value $50,405,000 and $39,162,000 respectively)(Note 2)	51,172,385	41,284,011
Federal funds sold	2,040,000	5,000,000
Loans, net (Notes 3 and 5)	73,983,971	68,475,492
Direct lease financing (Note 4)	1,897,025	1,113,423
Bank premises and equipment, net (Note 6)	3,663,495	3,565,867
Accrued income receivable	1,378,072	1,121,050
Other real estate owned	95,000	50,000
Prepaid expenses and other assets	180,270	148,200
	$146,230,407	$135,797,889
LIABILITIES AND STOCKHOLDERS' EQUITY		
Liabilities		
Deposits:		
Demand	$ 35,694,104	$ 36,304,092
NOW Accounts	25,957,283	18,763,947
Savings	29,346,911	29,569,682
Time, $100,000 and over (Note 7)	8,304,600	6,488,800
Other time	28,460,224	27,001,136
	$127,763,122	$118,127,637
Federal funds purchased	1,000,000	1,000,000
Notes payable (Note 7)	5,000,000	5,000,000
Accrued expenses and other liabilities	511,401	728,339
Deferred income tax credits (Note 9)	884,000	726,000
Subordinated debentures (Note 8)	1,196,000	1,196,000
	$136,354,523	$126,777,996
Commitments and contingencies (Note 11)		
Stockholders' equity:		
Capital stock:		
Preferred, no par value; authorized 20,000 shares; issued none	$ —	$ —
Common, $5 par value; authorized and issued 600,000 shares	3,000,000	3,000,000
Surplus	3,000,000	2,000,000
Retained earnings (Notes 7 and 14)	3,875,884	3,989,893
	$ 9,875,884	$ 8,989,893
	$146,230,407	$135,767,889

INVESTMENT SECURITIES

Investment securities are an important component of a bank's balance sheet. A bank's investing activities are engaged in for many reasons: liquidity, risk diversification, income, regulatory requirements, and others. Investment securities include U.S. Treasury securities, U.S. government agency securities (Fannie Mae, Ginnie Mae, Freddie Mac, Sallie Mae, and Farmer Mac), tax-exempt securities, and other investment securities (CMO, foreign government bonds, and others).

Generally, commercial banks may invest only in those securities that are rated as "investment grade," or have bond ratings in the top four categories. Banks may invest no more than 10 percent of capital and surplus in this category of bonds. Investments in equity securities other than Federal reserve stock are prohibited.

Investment securities are typically recorded at cost, with any difference from the face amount recorded as a discount or premium. Discounts and premiums are amortized to income using the interest method over the period held.

BOND TRADING ACTIVITIES

A bank's trading activity is related to speculation with the expectations of profiting from price movements. The bond trading account contains securities that are managed by commercial banks that buy or underwrite U.S. government securities and other securities for resale to other banks and to the general public. The bank's profit is derived from the difference between the price the bank pays for the bonds and the price at which they are later sold. Trading account securities are marked to market. Interest income on investment and trading securities are segregated as a component of interest income; gains and losses are recorded as a separate component of noninterest income or loss. Trading gains and losses include realized and unrealized gains and losses.

Investment and trading portfolios are shown separately in the financial statements. Transfers between the portfolios must be marked to market.

LOANS

Loans constitute the largest and most important earning asset in a bank's balance sheet. Loans provide the most revenue to a bank and provide the greatest risk to a bank. Legal limits are imposed on bank lending activities:

- *Financing limits* Loans to one borrower based on a percentage (generally 15 percent) of the bank's capital position.
- *Loans to officers* National banks may only make loans to executive officers on an arm's-length basis in accordance with specific criteria.
- *Stock purchase* Federal Reserve Board Regulation U limits amounts that may be loaned for purchasing or financing securities.

- *Consumer financing* Many Federal Reserve Board Regulations and laws place restrictions on loans to consumers.

Article 9 of the SEC Industry Guide deals with loans and the lending function. Article 9 describes in considerable detail loans and related disclosure requirements including the following.

Accounting for Loans

Commercial loans are made to business enterprises for many reasons and in several forms. Business clients typically need loans for working capital (short-term) and long-term purposes. The forms of commercial loans include the following:

- Bullet loan (a one-time payment at termination)
- Working capital line of credit (pre-approved credit)
- Term loan (for a specified period of time)
- Revolving line of credit (A form of credit replenishment in which funds are advanced as needed as provided by the line of credit.)
- Asset-based loan (A loan secured by assets directly related to the loan repayment.)

The market value of these loans is related to the loan maturity, cash flows, interest rate structure, and other factors.

Real estate loans are primarily residential mortgage loans, commercial mortgage loans, and construction loans and land development loans. These loans can be fixed or variable rate loans.

Consumer loans are made to individuals and households for many reasons: durable goods purchases, vacations, medical expenses, education, and others. Consumer loans include installment loans and credit card loans, such as Mastercard and Visa.

Securities loans are collateralized by marketable securities. Securities loans enable bank customers to purchase securities on credit. The Federal Reserve regulates these transactions through Regulation U when the loans are made by banks.

Overdrafts are checks written by bank clients that exceed the available balance in the clients' accounts. If a bank pays them, they amount to temporary loans.

Loans are typically recorded at their face value or at a discounted basis (i.e., interest and certain other payments are added to the amount advanced). Unearned income is recorded as a contra asset to the loan balance. The loan portfolio is disclosed net of a reserve for uncollectible accounts. Interest is accrued on the principal amount, usually daily. Unearned income on discounted loans is amortized to income of the life of the loan using the interest method to achieve a level yield on the loan balance. Interest accrual is usually suspended on loans that are in excess of 90 days past due, unless the loan is adequately secured and in the process of collection. Certain consumer loans are not placed on a nonaccrual basis because they are charged off within a relatively short period after delinquency, often within 180 days. Interest received on loans placed on a nonaccrual status is recorded on a cash basis or used to reduce the principal balance as related to the loan's collectibility.

Loan commitments are recorded in memorandum accounts and are disclosed in notes to the financial statements.

Loans and Related Disclosures

Banks must disclose total loans, related unearned income, and allowance for loan losses separately, on the face of the balance sheet. Also on the face of the balance sheet or in a related note, the bank must disclose loan categories:

Commercial, financial, and agricultural
Real estate—construction
Real estate—mortgages
Installment loans to individuals
Lease financing
Foreign loans
Significant geographic areas
Other (including any unusual risk concentration)

SEC Guide 3 defines various statistical disclosures required by banks and bank holding companies, including the following:

1. Types of loans as of the end of each of the last five fiscal years.

2. Maturities and sensitivity to changes in interest rates

    a. Maturity: distribution (due in one year or less; due after one year but before five; due after five years)

    b. Interest sensitivity: Total loan due after one year—breakdowns as follows:
        Predetermined interest rate
        Floating or adjustable rate

3. Risk element:

    a. Nonaccrual, past due, and restructured loans

    b. Potential problem loans

    c. Foreign outstanding

    d. Loan concentrations

4. Loan Loss experience (analysis for loan losses that shows the amounts of charge-offs for each loan category)

Allowance (Reserve) for Loan Losses

The Allowance for Loan Losses account represents the excess of accumulated provision for loan losses over the net loan losses charged. This reserve is intended to be sufficient to cover losses that may arise from the loan portfolio and related interest on receivable accounts. The Allowance for Loan Losses account is a contra asset account with a normal credit balance. The allowance is increased by provisions that are charged to the income statement and decreased by charge-offs of loans considered uncollectible. Recoveries of write-offs are usually applied to the allowance account. Serving as a contra-asset account or valuation account, the reserve reduces the carrying value of the loan portfolio to an approximation of loans thought to be collectible.

The adequacy of the allowance account is assessed by different methods, including a review of delinquent loans, past experience of the bank, and the quality of the portfolio. A typical entry to record the allowance for loan losses would be as follows:

Account No. xx Provision for Loan Losses (debit)	XXX
Account No. xx Allowance for Loan Losses (credit)	XXX

To record the write-off of a commercial loan:

Account No. xx Allowance for Loan Losses (debit)	XXX
Account No. xx Commercial Loans (credit)	XXX

The Board of Directors authorizes the charge-off of unpaid balances of loans considered uncollectible. Internal auditors are expected to determine that

1. Charges to the account are authorized by the Board.

2. Adequate collection procedures are provided.

3. The reserve for loan losses is adequate (reasonable).

Conceptually, the reserve account is divided into three parts: the valuation portion, the contingency portion, and the deferred tax portion. The valuation portion is available to absorb loan losses. The contingency portion reflects the cumulative amount of transfers from undivided profits. The deferred income tax portion reflects the tax effect on the temporary differences between the deduction for loan losses claimed on the income tax return and the provision for possible loan losses claimed for financial reporting purposes.

When evaluating the adequacy of the Allowance for Bank Loan Losses, the auditor should consider those factors which may cause loans to develop credit risk problems: improper credit extension procedures, changes in the economy, changes in the status of a particular industry or geographic area, undue loan concentrations, insider transactions and deterioration in the credit worthiness of the borrower. Management must maintain reasonable records in support of their evaluations and entries.

The Allowance for Loan Losses must not have a debit balance. If losses charged off exceed the amount of the allowance, a provision sufficient to restore the allowance to an adequate level must be charged to expense on the income statement immediately.

The amount of the loss to be recognized on a loan includes the difference between the current fair value of the assets received in a foreclosure or similar settlement and the carrying value of the loan on the balance sheet. The loss would be charged to the allowance at the time of foreclosure or repossession.

Accounting Policies for Nonperforming Loans

Asset quality is a major risk factors of great concern to banks, bank investors, and bank regulators. In recent years nonperforming loans have become of increasing importance when evaluating asset quality.

Rules for reporting troubled assets are prescribed in sources such as the glossary to the Call Report instructions, the *Handbook for National Bank Examiners*, and SEC Guide 3. The prescribed principles and procedures are broad in scope and allow for diverse practices. In terms of increasing risk of default, bank examiners, adverse classifications are *substantial, doubtful, and loss.* Examiners also have a category for loans that have minor problems. In the CAMEL rating system,

C = Capital adequacy
A = Asset quality
M = Management/Administration
E = Earnings
L = Liquidity

The asset quality rating is based on the examiners, classification of assets—substandard, doubtful, and loss. Weights of 20 percent, 50 percent, and 100 percent are applied to these classes, respectively. This weighted dollar amount is compared to the sum of a bank's loan-loss reserve and equity capital to determine the bank's ability to absorb potential losses related to the adversely classified assets. CAMEL ratings and dollar amounts of bank's classified assets are considered confidential information by the banking agencies.

Loans past due 90 days (180 days for consumer loans) or more are described as nonperforming loans by banks and bank examiners. Nonaccrual loans are loans switched to a cash basis—unless payments are received before they are not recorded. Bank regulators usually allow a 29-day grace period before a loan is required to be classified as past due.

Survey of Nonperforming Loan Practices

The Bank Administration Institute conducted a survey of accounting policies for nonperforming Loans and reported the results of the survey in a *Report on an Industry Survey* (1990).

Results of the survey are summarized here in part, with the permission of the Institute:

1. The survey supports the premise that there is wide diversity in practice for accounting for nonperforming loans.

2. The largest banks (banks over $20 billion) were significantly more likely to place loans on nonaccrual by management discretion. This can probably be attributed to their active and well-established loan review processes.

3. Commercial loans less than 90 days past due are about as likely to be part of the nonaccrual totals at a smaller bank as at a large one. Loans less than 90 days past due comprise between 10 percent and 50 percent of total nonaccrual loans at 40 percent of total nonaccrual loans at 40 percent of the larger banks and 35 percent of the smaller banks.

4. Thirty-seven percent of the respondents indicated that at least some portion of their Other Real Estate Owned (OREO) consisted of insubstance foreclosures, with 15 percent indicating that they exceed 25 percent of their OREO balance. In-substance foreclosures are expected to be an issue for an increasing number of banks of all sizes.

5. A restructuring occurs when, in view of a borrower's financial condition and in an attempt to maximize recovery of its investment, a lender allows a borrower concessions it would not normally consider. Among the larger banks responding, only one in three reverses interest on residential mortgages going on nonaccrual, compared to

three of every four among the smaller banks. Similarly, nearly half of the smaller banks responding consider the circumstances before deciding whether to place a delinquent consumer loan on nonaccrual or to charge it off, compared to only 7 percent of the larger banks. Over half of the smaller banks responding always consider the value of consumer loan collateral in determining the amount of a loan charge-off, compared to one in six of the larger banks.

Sale of Loans

Loans held for resale are reported at the lower of cost or current market value. Loans sold to other institutions are referred to as participations.

When recourse provisions are involved, the provisions must be examined according to SFAS No. 77, "Reporting by Transferors for Transfers of Receivables with Recourse." If the following provisions are met, the transaction must be recorded as a sale and not as a financing:

- The selling bank transfers the future economic benefits associated with the receivables and has no option to repurchase them.
- A reasonable estimate can be made of the recourse obligation.
- The selling bank cannot be required to repurchase the receivable except under the recourse arrangement.

If any of the conditions are not met, the amount of the proceeds from the transfer of receivables is reported as a liability.

SFAS No. 77 also applies to specified interests in particular receivables or pool of receivables that provide for recourse (participation agreements). If a transfer qualifies to be recognized as a sale, all probable adjustments in connection with the recourse obligations to the transferor must be accrued in accordance with SFAS Statement No. 5, "Accounting for Contingencies." The difference between (a) the sale price (adjusted for the accrual for probable adjustments) and (b) the net receivables shall be recognized as a gain or loss on the sale of receivables.

For transfers of receivables with recourse reported as sales, the transferor's financial statements must disclose (a) the proceeds to the transferor during each period for which an income statement is presented and (b) if the information is available, the balance of the receivables transferred that remain uncollected at the date of each balance sheet presented.

Recourse is the right of a transferee of receivables to receive payment from the transferor of those receivables for (a) failure of the debtors to pay when due, (b) the effects of prepayments, or (c) adjustments resulting from defects in the eligibility of the transferred receivables.

Sale and Repurchase Agreements

Sale and repurchase agreements are considered short-term loans secured by securities that are expected to be repurchased. The difference between the purchase and sale of the securities represents the interest charge that is recorded for the use of funds borrowed or lent.

Troubled debt restructuring.

Banks routinely restructure loans to allow the debtor certain concessions that would not normally be considered. The concessions must be made in light of the debtor's financial difficulty, and the objective of the creditor must be to maximize recovery of the investment. Troubled debt restructuring is often the result of legal proceedings or negotiation between the parties. A creditor accounts for a troubled debit restructuring by the type of restructuring:

1. Transfer of assets in full settlement

2. Granting an equity interest in full settlement

3. Modification of terms of the debt (reducing or extending interest rates or dates, the face or maturity amounts, and accrued interest)

When a creditor receives either assets or equity as full settlement of a receivable, the bank will account for these at fair value at the time of the restructuring if it is more clearly determinable than the fair value of the asset or equity acquired. In partial payments the creditor must use the fair value of the asset or equity received. The excess of the recorded receivable over the fair value of the asset received is recognized as a loss.

When the bank creditor accepts a modification of terms, the bank accounts for the restructuring prospectively and does not change the recorded investment unless it exceeds the total future cash payments provided for in the new agreement. The creditor bank recognizes interest income at a constant rate of effective interest. If the total future cash receipts are less than the recorded investment, the investment should be reduced and a loss recognized. All subsequent cash received is applied to reduce the balance of the recorded investment. None is interest.

The creditor bank must disclose restructured receivables by major category and the amount(s) of any commitment(s) to lend additional funds to any debtor who is a party to a restructuring.

Securitization

Collateralized mortgage obligations are securitized investment products formed by the pooling of assets, specifically, mortgage-backed securities or mortgage loans. Collaterized mortgage obligations (CMOs) are dealt with in FASB's Technical Bulletin 85-2, "Accounting for Collateralized Mortgage Obligations," and SFAS No. 77, "Reporting by Transfers of Receivables with Recourse."

Certain types of bonds secured by mortgage-backed securities or mortgage loans are structured so that all or substantially all of the collections of principal and interest from the underlying collateral are paid through to the holders of the bonds. The bonds are typically issued with two or more maturity classes; the actual maturity of each bond class will vary depending upon the timing of the cash receipts from the underlying collateral. These bonds are issued by a minimally capitalized special-purpose corporation (issuer) established by a sponsoring parent corporation and are commonly referred to as CMOs. The mortgage-backed securities or mortgage loans securing the obligation are acquired by the special-purpose corporation and then pledged to an independent trustee until the issuer's obligation under the bond indenture has been fully satisfied. The investor can look only to the issuer's assets or third parties for repayment of the obligations.

In a CMO the regular principal and interest payments made by borrowers are separated into different streams, creating several bonds that repay invested capital at different rates, or in different tranches, to meet the needs of investors. There are often four tranches:

- The first, which pays off interest and principal rapidly

- The second, which pays interest only until the earlier tranches are repaid completely, then pays both interest and principal

- The third, which pays variable interest based on an index, typically the London Interbank Offered Rate (LIBOR), even though the underlying mortgages are fixed-rate loans

- The fourth, called an accrual bond or Z-bond, which pays no interest or principal until all other tranches have been retired

According to FASB Technical Bulletin 85-2, CMOs should be presumed to be borrowings that are reported as liabilities in the financial statements of the issuer unless all but a nominal portion of the future economic benefits inherent in the associated collateral have been irrevocably passed to the investor and no affiliate of the issuer can be required to make future payments with respect to the obligation.

The existence of all of the following conditions at the date of issuance of the CMO would generally indicate that the borrowing presumption has been overcome, that the associated collateral should be eliminated from the issuer's financial statements, and that gain or loss should be recognized:

1. The future economic benefits from the collaterized assets are surrendered by the issuer of the obligation and its affiliates.

2. The investor can look only to the collaterized assets or third-party guarantees for repayment of interest and principal on the instruments.

3. The issuer and affiliated entities are not secondarily liable.

If the associated collateral is eliminated from the financial statements because all of the above conditions are met, any expected residual interest in the collateral should not be recognized as an asset.

Collateralized loan obligations (CLOs) are securitized investment products which are formed by pooling of assets, specifically, senior bank loans. The collateral is financed by liabilities structured and tranched to produce a customized security to fit the particular needs of institutional investors. The concept of cash flow tranching is equivalent to that used in the mortgage-backed securities market in CMOs. Securitization usually involves some form of recourse. SFAS No. 77 applies in accounting for these transactions. Any gain or loss on the sale of the loans is computed as the difference between the recorded cost and the sales price, adjusted for estimated recourse costs, normal servicing fees, and costs of securitization.

FINANCIAL INSTRUMENTS

Financial instruments are complex and diversified. They also represent significant assets for commercial banks and thrifts. The major accounting and reporting issues associated with financial instruments can be grouped into five categories:

1. *Recognition* What financial assets or liabilities should be recognized in the statement of financial position: When should they be recognized?

2. *Display* How should recognized financial assets and liabilities, gains and losses, and other items be reported in statements of financial position, income statements, and other financial statements?

3. *Initial Measurement* At what amount should financial assets and liabilities be measured initially?

4. *Subsequent Measurement* At what amount should financial assets and liabilities be measured after recognition, that is, at each later reporting date? How should any unrealized gain or loss resulting from subsequent measurement be reported?

5. *Derecognition* When should a financial asset or liability be removed from the statement of financial position? How should the realized gain or loss resulting from derecognition be reported?

A financial instrument is cash, evidence of an ownership interest in an entity, or a contract that has both of the following characteristics that place emphasis on the future receipts, payments or exchange of cash or other financial instruments that ultimately result in cash:

1. The contract imposes on one entity a contractual obligation (a) to deliver cash or another financial instrument to a second entity or (b) to exchange financial instruments on potentially unfavorable terms with the second entity.

2. The contract conveys to the second entity a contractual right (a) to receive cash or another financial instrument from the first entity or (b) to exchange other financial instruments on potentially favorable terms with the first entity. (Source: SFAS No. 105, "Disclosure of Information about Financial Instruments with Off-Balance-Sheet Risk and Financial Instruments with Concentrations of Credit Risk")

This definition of financial instruments includes trade receivables and payables, debt securities and common stock, many insurance contracts, financial futures and forward contracts, interest rate swaps and caps, collateralized mortgage obligations and financial guarantees.

Financial instruments may also include contracts that may not be recognized in financial statements at present—off-balance-sheet—such as financial guarantees, letters of credit, loan commitments, and obligations under operating leases. The definition excludes items such as prepaid expenses and deferred revenues, advances to supplies, and most warranty obligations, which involve the receipt or delivery of goods or services. It also excludes contracts to be settled by delivery of a commodity, such as ounces of gold or barrels of oil rather than in cash.

Accounts payable and accounts receivable meet the contractual obligation/right to deliver/receive cash and so are clearly liabilities and assets. Convertible bonds are an example of "potentially unfavorable" features referred to in the definition. Future contracts, options, and financial swaps are contracts referenced in Parts a and b in the definition.

Financial instruments have raised difficult accounting problems, such as the following: off-balance-sheet financing; unjustifiable deferral of losses; premature recognition of gains; inadequate disclosure about risks. Off-balance-sheet (OBS) risk exposes a company to a risk of accounting loss that exceeds the amount recognized for the instrument in the balance sheet.

SFAS No. 105 DISCLOSURE OF INFORMATION ABOUT FINANCIAL INSTRUMENTS WITH OFF-BALANCE-SHEET RISK AND FINANCIAL INSTRUMENTS WITH CONCENTRATION OF CREDIT RISK

SFAS No. 105 requires that financial statements should provide significant information relating to all financial instruments with or without off-balance-sheet risk: credit risk (maximum credit risk, probable and reasonably possible credit losses, and individual, industry, or geographic concentration); market risk, including interest rate and foreign exchange risks (effective interest rates and contractual repricing or maturity dates); liquidity risk (contractual future cash receipts and payments); and current market values if they could be determined or estimated.

If a bank has a concentration of credit risk with one firm or a group of entities, disclosures of the concentration must be provided. Guidelines as to what constitutes significant concentration of credit risk is not described in SFAS No. 5. A bank is allowed to use judgment in making the decision.

Figure 5-2 outlines disclosure requirements of SFAS No. 105 for financial instruments with off-balance sheet risk and with a concentration of credit risk.

The disclosures required by SFAS No. 105 should help users assess a company's risk of accounting loss: credit risk; market risk; risk of theft or physical loss, and the risk from a concentration of credit risk.

SFAS NO. 107, DISCLOSURE ABOUT FAIR VALUE OF FINANCIAL INSTRUMENTS

In December 1991 the FASB issued *Statement of Financial Accounting Standards No. 107*, "Disclosures about Fair Value of Financial Instruments." SFAS No. 107 requires disclosure about fair value of all financial instruments, both assets and liabilities recognized and not recognized in the statement of financial positions of all firms, including commercial banks.

The Board decided to use the term *fair value* instead of *market value* to avoid confusion and to be consistent with the terminology used in similar disclosure by various national and international standard-setting organizations.

Figure 5-2
Disclosure Requirements for Financial Instruments [a]

Disclosures for Financial Instruments with Off-Balance-Sheet Risk

Extent, Nature and Terms:

(1) The contract, face or notional amount of the financial instrument.

(2) A description of the financial instrument's nature and terms with disclosure of market and credit risks, cash requirements, and disclosures required under APB Opinion No. 22, as a minimum. [b]

Financial Instruments with Credit Risk:

(3) The company's Policy for financial instrument collateral, nature and description of such collateral and company access to the collateral. [c]

(4) The Amount of accounting loss assuming that the counterparty to the contract defaults and any collateral related to the contract is of no value to the company.

Disclosures for All Financial Instruments with Concentration of Credit Risk

(1) All significant concentrations of credit risk including both individual and group concentrations.

(2) For each significant concentration of credit risk, disclose the economic characteristics, region or activity that identifies the concentration.

(3) For ech significant concentration of credit risk, disclose company policy for financial instrument collateral, nature and description of such collateral and company access to the collateral.

(4) For each significant concentration of credit risk, the best estimate or the amount of accounting loss assuming that counterparties to the contracts making up the concentration default and any collateral related to the contracts is of no value to the company.

---

a The disclosures are by class of instrument and can be presented directly in the statement of financial position or related notes.

b APB Opinion No. 22 requires the disclosure of all significant accounting policies used in the preparation of the financial statements.

c An enterprise may wish to disclose additional information about collateral underlying financial instruments, especially if the additional disclosures mitigate the credit risk.

Definition

According to SFAS No. 107, a financial instrument is defined as cash, evidence of an ownership interest in an entity, or a contract that both

1. Imposes on one entity a contractual obligation (a) to deliver cash or another financial instrument to a second entity or (b) to exchange other financial instruments on potentially unfavorable terms with the second entity.

2. Conveys to that second entity a contractual right (a) to receive cash or another financial instrument from the first entity or (b) to exchange other financial instruments on potentially favorable terms with the first entity.

Fair Value

The fair value of a financial instrument is the amount at which the instrument could be exchanged in a current transaction between willing parties, other than in forced or liquidation sale. If a quoted market price is available for an instrument, the fair value to be disclosed for that instrument is the product of the number of trading units of the instrument times that market price. The quoted price for a single trading unit in the most active market is the basis for determining market price and reporting fair value.

If the quoted market price of a financial instrument is not available, management can base its best estimate of fair value on either of the following:

■ The quoted market price of a financial instrument with similar characteristics

■ Valuation techniques, such as present value of estimated future cash flows using a discount rate commensurate with the risk involved, option pricing models, or matrix pricing models

Management's best estimate of fair value involves judgments about the methods and assumptions to be used. According to SFAS No. 107, some short-term financial instruments and liabilities may be valued at the carrying amount in the financial statements (book value). For other financial instruments (e.g., interest rate swaps and foreign currency contracts), the fair market value might be based on the quoted market price of a similar financial instrument. Market valuation models are often related to future cash flows, time to maturity, the expected rate of return, and an appropriate discount rate. Option pricing models have been developed to value options, such as the Black-Scholes model and binomial models.

Certain factors may give rise to a difference between book value and market value: time to maturity; contractually fixed interest rates (coupon, loan, deposit, or borrowing rates); call provisions in bond indentures; possible loan prepayments; interest rate caps and floors; interest rate changes; off-balance-sheet treatment.

SFAS No. 107 identifies four kinds of markets in which financial instruments can be both sold or originated:

1. *Exchange market* An "auction" market that provides high visibility and order to the trading of financial instruments

2. *Dealer market* A market in which dealers stand ready to trade for their own account

3. *Brokered market* A market in which brokers attempt to match buyers with sellers but do not stand ready to trade for their own account

4. *Principal-to-principal market* A market in which transactions are negotiated independently, with no intermediary

Where prices are quoted in several markets, the price in the most active market will generally be considered the best indicator of the fair value.

For banks, loans receivables are significant financial instruments. If no quoted market price exists for a category of loans, an estimate of fair value may be based on (a) the market prices of similar traded loans with similar credit ratings, interest rates, and maturity dates, (b) current prices (interest rates) offered for similar loans in the entity's own lending activities, or (c) valuations obtained from loan pricing services offered by various specialist firms or from other sources. An estimate of the fair value of a loan or group of loans may be based on the discounted value of the future cash flows expected to be received from the loan or group of loans. Judgment should be used in selecting an appropriate current discount rate that reflects the relative credit, interest rate, and prepayment risks involved. In some circumstances, a single discount rate could be used to estimate the fair value of a homogeneous category of loans.

The fair value of financial liabilities for which quoted market prices are not available can generally be estimated using techniques used for estimating the fair value of financial assets. For example, a loan payable to a bank could be valued at the discounted amount of future cash flows using the bank's current incremental rate of borrowing for a similar liability. For deposit liabilities with defined maturities, including certificates of deposit, an estimate of fair value might be based on the discounted value of the future cash flows expected to be paid on the deposits. The rate could be the current rate for similar deposits with the same remaining maturities. For deposit liabilities with no defined maturities, SFAS No. 107 requires that the fair value to be disclosed be the amount payable on demand at the reporting date.

SFAS No. 107 does not allow a financial entity such as a commercial bank to take into account the value of its long-term relationships with depositors when estimating the fair value of deposit liabilities, referred to as core deposit intangibles.

Excluded Items

The following items are excluded from disclosure requirements imposed by SFAS No. 107:

■ Employers' and plans' obligations for pension benefits, other postretirement benefits, employee stock option and stock purchase plans, and other forms of deferred compensation arrangements, as defined by SFAS Statements Nos. 35, 87, 43 and APB Opinions Nos. 25 and 12

■ Substantively extinguished debt (SFAS No. 76) and assets held in trust in connection with an in-substance defeasance of that debt

■ Insurance contracts, other than financial guarantees and investment contracts, as discussed in SFAS 3, Nos. 60 and 97

■ Lease contracts, as discussed in SFAS No. 13

■ Warranty obligations and rights

- Unconditional purchase obligations, as discussed in SFAS No.47
- Investments accounted for under the equity method, as discussed in APB Opinion No. 18
- Minority interests in consolidated subsidiaries
- Equity investments in consolidated subsidiaries
- Equity instruments issued by the entity and classified in stockholders' equity in the statement of financial position

Financial Statement Disclosure

An entity must disclose either in the body of the statements or in the accompanying notes, the fair value of financial instruments and liabilities for which it is practicable to estimate fair value. An entity must also disclose the method(s) and significant assumptions used to estimate the fair value of its financial instruments and liabilities.

For trade receivables and payables, no disclosure is required under SFAS No. 107 when the carrying amount approximates fair value.

Where it is not practicable for an entity to estimate the fair value of a financial instrument or a class of financial instruments, the following shall be disclosed:

- Information pertinent to estimating the fair value of that financial instrument or class of financial instruments, such as the carrying amount, effective interest rate, and maturity
- The reasons why it is not practicable (e.g., an estimate cannot be made without incurring excessive costs) to estimate fair value

In the context of SFAS No. 107, *practicable* means that an estimate of fair value can be made without incurring excessive costs. What is practicable for one entity might not be for another; what is not practicable in one year might be in another. Practicability refers to cost considerations and the required precision of the estimate.

SFAS No. 107 Disclosures Illustrated

Appendix B to SFAS No. 107 provides illustrations of disclosure requirements about fair value of financial instruments. Alternative ways of disclosing the information are permissible if they satisfy the disclosure requirements of the statement. The disclosures provide descriptions, measures, and help in assessing risks and potentials. The disclosures should be included within the basic financial statements. Summarized interim financial information need not include the disclosures required by Statement No. 107.

The guide of disclosure requirements provided in SFAS No. 107, Appendix B, for a financial entity such as a commercial bank is provided here:

Note C: Disclosure about Fair Value of Financial Instruments

The following methods and assumptions were used to estimate the fair value of each class of financial instruments for which it is practicable to estimate that value:

Cash and short-term investments

For those short-term instruments, the carrying amount is a reasonable estimate of fair value.

Investment securities and trading account assets

For securities and derivative instruments held for trading purposes (which include bonds, interest rate futures, options, interest rate swaps, securities sold not owned, caps and floors, foreign currency contracts, and forward contacts) and marketable equity securities held for investment purposes, fair values are based on quote market prices or dealer quotes. For other securities held as investments, fair value equals quoted market price, if available. If a quoted market price is not available, fair value is estimated using quoted market prices for similar securities.

Loan receivables

For certain homogeneous categories of loans, such as some residential mortgages, credit card receivables, and other consumer loans, fair value is estimated using the quoted market prices for securities backed by similar loans, adjusted for differences in loan characteristics. The fair value of other types of loans is estimated by discounting the future cash flows using the current rates at which similar loans would be made to borrowers with similar credit ratings and for the same remaining maturities.

Deposit liabilities

The fair value of demand deposits, savings accounts, and certain money market deposits is the amount payable on demand at the reporting date. The fair value of fixed-maturity certificates of deposit is estimated using the rates currently offered for deposits of similar remaining maturities.

Long-term debt

Rates currently available to the bank for debt with similar terms and remaining maturities are used to estimate fair value of existing debt.

Interest rate swap agreements

The fair value of interest rate swaps (used for hedging purposes) is the estimated amount that the bank would receive or try to terminate the swap agreements at the reporting date, taking into account current interest rates and the current creditworthiness of the swap counterparties.

Commitments to extend credit, standby letters of credit, and financial guarantees written

The fair value of commitments is estimated using the fees currently charged to enter into similar agreements, taking into account the remaining terms of the agreements and the present creditworthiness of the counterparties. For fixed-rate loan commitments, fair value also considers the difference between current levels of interest rates and the omitted rates. The fair value of guarantees and letters of credit is based on fees currently charged for similar agreements or on the estimated cost to terminate them or otherwise settle the obligations with the counterparties at the reporting date.

The estimated fair values of the bank's financial instruments can be disclosed as follows (data omitted for this illustration):

	19X9		19X8	
	Carrying Amount	Fair Value	Carrying Amount	Fair Value
Financial Assets:				
Cash and short-term investments	$XX	$XX	$XX	$XX
Trading account assets	XX	XX	XX	XX
Investment securities	XX	XX	XX	XX
Loans	XX		XX	
Less: allowance for loan losses	(XX)		$(XX)	
Financial liabilities:				
Deposits	XX	XX	XX	XX
Securities sold not owned	XX	XX	XX	XX
Long-term debt	XX	XX	XX	XX
Unrecognized financial instruments:				
Interest rate swaps:				
In a net receivable position	XX	XX	XX	XX
In a net payable position	(XX)	(XX)	(XX)	(XX)
Commitments to extend credit	(XX)	(XX)	(XX)	(XX)
Standby letters of credit	(XX)	(XX)	(XX)	(XX)
Financial guarantees written	(XX)	(XX)	(XX)	(XX)

The amounts shown under "carrying amount" for unrecognized financial instruments represent accruals or deferred income (fees) arising from those unrecognized financial instruments. Interest rate swaps and other derivative instruments entered into as trading activities are included in "trading account assets" or "securities sold not owned."

Effective Date

SFAS No. 107 shall be effective for financial statements issued for fiscal years ending after December 15, 1992, except for entities with less than $150 million in total assets in the current statement of financial position. For such entities, the effective date shall be for financial statements issued for fiscal years ending after December 15, 1995. Earlier application is encouraged.

Pros and Cons

Proponents of fair value disclosure maintain that such disclosures

- Are useful for predictive purposes and for evaluating management's performance
- Reflect valuations of a company's resources and liabilities
- Result in a better estimate of the true value of bank equity
- Discourage transactions intended solely to improve accounting returns. Market value accounting discourages "gains trading," i.e., selling appreciated assets while retaining depreciated assets merely to increase reported earnings.
- Assist investors, creditors, and other users to assess the consequences of an entity's investment and financing strategies as reflected in a bank's performance record
- Assist regulators to more easily identify those banks with impaired capital and to begin necessary corrective action sooner
- The expected benefits of the resulting information exceeds the perceived costs.

Major arguments against fair value accounting relate primarily to the subjectivity and unreliability of the data. The cost of providing the information can also be considerable.

Robert Clark, Comptroller of the Currency, sums up the arguments for and against market-value accounting:

The argument in favor of a mark-to-market standard is simple: It assumes that the mark-to-market standard would provide the best possible information to users of financial data—investors, depositors, the market place, even regulators.

In opposing the mark-to-market standard, bankers argue that it would create too much volatility in bank earnings and capital. They also object to applying a mark-to-market standard to assets without taking into account the other side of the balance sheet.

Alan Greenspan, Chairman of the Federal Reserve Board, urged caution and questioned the relevance of market values of loans in measuring the success of commercial banking. Chairman Greenspan objected to a partial valuation that could result in volatility and a measure of capital that is not indicative of the bank's true financial condition. In addition Greenspan noted, "the adoption of market value according for investment securities . . . might also affect the amount of securities that banks are willing to hold . . . thereby having the undesired effect of reducing the liquidity of banking organizations."

In December 1990 SEC General Counsel James Doty testified before the Senate Judiciary Antitrust Subcommittee as follows:

Market-value accounting for debt securities is a reflection of a simple but important principle: no publicly held entity should knowingly misstate the value of its assets to its creditors and public shareholders.

The current historical-cost accounting convention was established in 1938. The economic environment in which financial institutions now operate, which has resulted in sophisticated asset-liability management strategies, has undermined whatever original strength there may have been in the 50-year-old presumption that investment securities will be held to maturity.

The U.S. Treasury's position of the mark-to-market controversy is consistent with the views of the bank regulators (1991):

> Despite the theoretical appeal, comprehensive MVA has a number of problems that argue against its adoption at this time. Because active trading markets do not exist for the bulk of the assets and liabilities of depository institutions . . . fair market values would have to be estimated. . . . The subjectivity inherent in such procedures would reduce . . . comparability . . . and render it difficult to verify valuations. . . . Such reliability problems would make financial statements more prone to manipulation. . . . Although it is possible that reasonably specific standards could be developed to provide the basis for appropriate accounting and auditing practices in this area, such a process is likely to require considerable time.

> A second concern is the cost of developing and implementing a comprehensive MVA system. Such cost could be substantial, and would likely fall disproportionately on smaller banks and thrifts.

The SEC's position is that the balance sheet should be presented with full market value accounting for all marketable securities. "Marketable securities" excludes real estate, plant and equipment, intangible assets, and loans. Likewise, related liabilities would be market to market. Changes in the value of these assets and liabilities would be recorded either as gains or losses in the firm's income statement, or as changes in retained earnings. The SEC's position remains that a more accurate statement of financial position can be achieved at little or no cost by marking-to-market debt securities that are held as investments. It desires to eliminate from the income statement the benefit of "gains' trading," i.e., selling profitable and holding losing positions, but has declared neutrality on whether the unrealized gains and losses from marking-to-market are to be included in net income or directly in equity.

FINANCIAL FUTURES

A financial futures contract is a contract to make or take delivery of a financial instrument at a future date. Banks often use futures for trading and hedging purposes, including speculation, and as an instrument for protection from price or interest rate risks. Futures contracts are traded on the Chicago Board of Trade, the New York Mercantile Exchange, the London International Financial Futures Exchange, and other exchanges. Financial futures include interest rate instruments, currency, stock indices and others.

SFAS No. 80, "Accounting for Futures Contracts," established the basic accounting for financial futures. To qualify under Statement No. 80, the contract must be traded either on an exchange in the United States or a foreign country and must meet the following criteria:

1.   The contract requires the buyer/seller to receive or deliver a specified quantity of an item on a specified date or period of time, or to provide for a cash settlement in lieu of the commodity.

2. The contract may be canceled prior to delivery date by entering into an offsetting contract for the same item.

3. Changes in the contract's market value are settled on a regular basis.

The initial margin deposit paid to a broker is recorded as an asset on the bank's books. As the market value of the futures contract changes, the change is reflected in the enterprise's accounts with the broker on a regular basis. When market changes increase the broker account, the enterprise may be able to withdraw cash from the account, and when market changes decrease the account, the bank may be required to pay additional cash to the broker to maintain a specified minimum balance. The contract may be closed out by either delivering or receiving the item, paying or receiving cash, or by entering into an offsetting contract. When the contract is closed out, the margin deposit is returned to the bank with the cash from the gains on the contract. If a loss is suffered, the margin deposit is offset against the amounts to be paid by the enterprise to the broker. The accounting differs for a contract entered into as a speculation and one entered into as a hedge (of an existing asset or liability, of a firm commitment, to an anticipated transaction).

SFAS No. 80, "Accounting for Futures Contracts," requires that all contracts that do not meet specified criteria for hedge accounting must be market to market with realized and unrealized gains and losses recorded in other income, unless the contract qualifies as a hedge of certain exposures to price or interest rate risk. Immediate gain or loss recognition is also required if the futures contract is intended to hedge an item that is reported at fair value. Otherwise, deferral accounting is appropriate if the transaction can be classified as a hedge transaction. In these cases a change in the market value of the futures contract is either reported as an adjustment of the carrying amount of the hedged item or included in the measurement of a qualifying subsequent transaction.

SFAS No. 80 specified the conditions that qualify a transaction as a hedge:

1. The item to be hedged exposes the enterprise to price or interest rate risk.

2. The futures contract reduced that exposure and is designated as a hedge. There must be a high correlation between changes in the value of the hedged item and the type of futures contract used for hedging.

Banks and money managers with diversified portfolios can use futures to attempt to reduce risk. To illustrate the accounting for such a situation, assume that the Standard & Poor Index futures contract sells for 500 times the value of the Index. Assume that a contract maturing in March 199X sells for $130,000 in September 1990. The bank invests $260,00 in such contracts. Two contracts are acquired (130,000 × 2) = 260,000). The bank must place a 15 percent margin requirement of $39,000 (= 2 × .15 × $130,000). The balance of the $260,000 is invested in Treasury bills yielding 7 percent annually to reduce variations in its $260,000 investment. The accounting for the initial transaction is as follows:

Margin Deposit	39,000	
Investment in Treasury Bills	221,000	
Cash		260,000

At December 199X, the S&P Index futures price declined by 1 percent, and the contracts are closed out at $257,400, a loss of $2,600 or 1 percent of $260,000. Cash in the amount of $2,600 is deposited.

Loss on Futures Contracts	2,600	
Cash		2,600
To record the loss on the futures contracts		
Cash	39,000	
Margin Deposit		39,000
To record receipt of initial margin		
Investment in Treasury Bills	3,867	
Interest Income		3,867
To record accrued interest income (.07 X $221,000/4)		

The bank has a net gain ($3,867 income minus $2,600 loss).

Regulators are essentially consistent with the accounting profession's position on accounting for futures contracts.

See Chapter 10 for a discussion of foreign currency futures and contracts.

SWAPS

Swaps are contracts between parties to exchange sets of cash flows based on a predetermined notional principal. Only the cash flows are exchanged. The major types of swaps are interest rate swaps and currency swaps. Accounting practice requires that trading swaps be marked to market. Hedge swaps are accounted for on an accrual basis over the life of the swap (net cash inflow or outflow is recorded as a component of net interest income on the accrual basis).

Accounting for currency swaps is prescribed in SFAS No. 52 for foreign currency forward contracts (see Chapter 10). Currency swaps are equivalent to a series of foreign currency forward contracts.

Interest rate swaps involve an exchange of interest payment obligations on existing or new debt. The principal amount of the debt is not exchanged. Such swaps typically involve exchanging a floating rate interest obligation for a fixed rate interest obligation on debt denominated in the same currency. In effect, the floating rate debt is converted to fixed rate debt, and vice versa. Certain swaps involve combined interest rate and currency swaps (circus). Hedging and speculation are the basic motives for interest rate swaps. Interest rate swaps are off-balance-sheet items.

Interest rate swaps create a disclosure problem for lenders such as banks. Origination or other fees paid by a counterparty to an intermediary are usually amortized to interest income or interest expense over the swap's life (paragraph 5 of SFAS No. 91). This procedure adjusts the yield on the loan over its life (paragraph 37 of SFAS No. 91). Effective-interest amortization is required; the straight line amortization method could be used if the result is not materially different.

The swap does not create or extinguish the underlying debt although it does modify the effective periodic interest revenue and expense recorded by all of the parties to the swap. Currently, the only asset or liability effects of swaps on the counterparties refer to the incremental interest receivable or payable that accrues under the terms of the swap and the deferral of unamortized fees. Swaps are considered synthetic instruments and are not given accounting recognition in that they are executory contracts.

According to SFAS No. 105, disclosure in notes to financial statements include

Notional amounts and terms of swaps

Summary of impact of fixed and floating rates involved

The Floating-rate indices used

Identification of whether swaps are hedges or speculative

Instruments including an assessment of the credit and market risk

OPTIONS

Options contracts give the purchases the right but not the obligation to purchase a specified instrument. The seller has the obligation to deliver the instrument to the buyer at the buyer's option. Option contracts are made on such items as currency, interest rate products, and financial futures.

Accounting for options is evolving. According to the AICPA issues paper, "Accounting for Options," trading options that do not qualify for hedge accounting should be marked to market and any unrealized gain or loss included currently in trading income. Premiums paid or received are recorded on the balance sheet as trading account assets and other liabilities. When options are exercised, liquidated, or expire, the premium paid or received remaining on the balance sheet is considered when computing the gain or loss on the option position. If specified criteria are met, hedge accounting can be used to the extent of the premium received on the option sold. According to the AICPA issue paper, hedge accounting cannot be used if the hedged item is an asset carried at cost.

Premiums paid on purchased (written) options are initially recorded as assets (liabilities). Generally, the time value of a purchased option qualifying as a hedge should be accounted for separately through amortization to income over the life of the option from the option's intrinsic value. The intrinsic value is adjusted as the option's market value changes. The time value component of a premium paid or received on a speculative transaction is not accounted for separately. The entire premium is considered the point for subsequent gain and loss realization from changes in the option's market value.

Gains and losses on options are recognized (1) currently if the option is not serving as a hedge or if the option is hedging an existing asset or liability exposure being carried at market, and (2) deferred for all other hedge options. Deferred gains and losses adjust the carrying amount of hedged assets and liabilities carried at other than market at reporting dates.

COUPON STRIPPING, TREASURY RECEIPTS, AND STRIPS

Coupon stripping occurs when a security holder physically detaches unmatured coupons from the principal portion of a security and sells either the detached coupons or the ex-coupon security separately. (Such transactions are generally considered by federal bank supervisory agencies to represent improper investment practices for banks.) In accounting for such transactions, the original cost, including any unamortized premium or discount, must be allocated between the ex-coupon security and the detached coupons at the time the security is divided in order to establish a basis for determining the carrying value of the portion retained and the gain or loss on the portion sold. This allocation shall be based upon the yield to maturity of the security at the time it was originally purchased and must establish the same yield to maturity for each portion.

Under a program called Separate Trading of registered Interest and Principal of Securities (STRIPS), the U.S. Treasury has issued certain long-term note and bond issues that are maintained in the book-entry system operated by the Federal Reserve Banks in a manner that permits separate trading and ownership of the interest and principal payments on these issues. STRIPS held in the reporting bank's securities portfolio are reported as U.S. Treasury securities. The discount on separately traded portions of STRIPS must be accreted. Net gains or losses from the sale of STRIPS shall be reported in gains (losses) on securities not held in trading accounts.

Detached coupons, ex-coupon securities, Treasury receipts, and U.S. Treasury STRIPS held in a trading account shall be valued on a basis consistent with the valuation of other trading account assets.

MISCELLANEOUS FINANCIAL AND MONEY MARKET INSTRUMENTS

Certificates of deposits are considered negotiable instruments issued by a bank for a fixed period of time. CDs are recorded at par value; interest is accrued as provided for in the agreement.

Federal funds are recorded as lending or borrowings; interest income or expense is recorded as provided for in the agreement. Certificates of deposit are usually recorded at par. Interest is accrued as determined with the terms of the contract.

Commercial paper is typically issued and recorded on a discount basis.

Time and savings deposits are recorded at the amounts deposited and interest is accrued.

Banker's acceptances are recorded as a receivable from the bank's customer and as the bank's liability under the agreement.

An extensive glossary of recent innovations in financial instruments is presented at the end of this chapter.

EITF REFERENCES TO FINANCIAL INSTRUMENTS

The Emerging Issues Task Force (EITF) of the Financial Accounting Standards Board has dealt with the following matters related to financial instruments:

BANK PREMISES AND EQUIPMENT

Bank premises and equipment includes the bank building, the furnishings and equipment in the bank offices, and automated teller machines. The book value is original cost less accumulated depreciation.

OTHER REAL ESTATE OWNED

When real estate loans are foreclosed, the property is recorded in this account. With foreclosure, the collateral property is auctioned. The lending bank often bids the amount owed. If no other bidders place higher bids, the bank retains the property and records the asset in its other real estate owned (OREO). Professional appraisal of the value of the property is required.

LIABILITY ACCOUNTS

A bank's major liabilities include deposits and borrowed funds. Deposit accounts are essentially funds or checking and savings accounts held by a bank for another party. Deposit accounts can be interest bearing or noninterest bearing, payable on demand or payable at an agreed upon date. Noninterest-bearing accounts are demand deposit accounts that can be withdrawn without notice and which pay no interest.

Noninterest-bearing accounts include the following: due from banks, commercial deposits, consumer deposits (checking accounts other than NOW accounts and money market deposit accounts), public funds, trust deposits, official checks (cashier's checks or treasurer's checks). Interest-bearing transactions accounts include negotiable order of withdrawal (NOW) accounts and the Super NOW account. A NOW account is a combination of checking and savings account. The Super NOW account is a checking account and a money market deposit account.

Small time and savings accounts contain all deposit accounts excluding transactions accounts and time deposits of $100,000 or more. These accounts are held primarily by individuals. Savings accounts are interest bearing and are nonnegotiable. The typical savings account pays either a fixed or variable rate of interest. The two forms of savings account are passbook savings (evidenced by a passbook) and statement savings (evidenced by a periodic statement showing the account's activities).

Money market deposit accounts are savings accounts that allow commercial banks to compete with money market mutual funds that pay market interest rates and allow withdrawals by check. A money market certificate pays an interest rate tied to the yield on six-month U.S. Treasury bills.

Individual retirement accounts (IRAs) allow individuals to invest up to a specified amount on a tax-deferred basis. They are a popular form of investing for many investors/savers.

Large time deposits include nonnegotiable time deposits equal to or greater than $100,000, negotiable CDs, and foreign deposits. Nonnegotiable time deposits are usually evidenced by certificates of deposits (CDs) or Jumbo CDs. Negotiable CDs are Jumbo CDs that can be traded on secondary markets. Foreign deposits are classified as an international banking facility (IBF) or Eurodollar time deposits. An IBF is similar to an offshore banking facility within a domestic bank. Eurodollar time deposits are held in banks outside the United States, either foreign banks or overseas affiliates of U.S. banks. Large time deposits can reflect a difference between book value and market value.

Deposit accounts are recorded at the amount deposited. These accounts are valued at book value. Interest expense is accrued according to the agreement.

Borrowed funds include federal funds purchased, term federal funds purchased, securities sold under agreement to repurchase, commercial paper, Treasury tax and loan accounts, and other short-term borrowed funds. Book value and market value of these short-term borrowed funds are usually identical. Long-term borrowed funds include subordinated notes and debentures and other long-term borrowings. Market values of long-term borrowed funds can differ from book value because the debt is often traded on secondary markets.

Major liabilities discussed in future chapters include bonds payable, leases, pensions, post-retirement benefits other than pensions, and compensated absences, which are discussed in Chapter 8. Income taxes are treated in Chapter 9.

OFF-BALANCE-SHEET ITEMS

Off-balance sheet items refers to assets and liabilities related to financing and investing activities that are not disclosed on the balance sheet. Off-balance-sheet items relate to certain leasing and pension transactions, sales of receivables with recourse, sophisticated financial instruments, unconsolidated entities, research and development arrangements, project financing arrangements, and others. Off-balance-sheet items are sometimes used to avoid including debt on the balance sheet. It may allow a company to borrow more than it otherwise could due to debt-limit restrictions and at a lower cost.

For banks, major categories of off-balance-sheet items include

- Commitments to extend credit
- Standby letters of credit
- Financial guarantees written

Commitments to extend credit, standby letters of credit, and financial guarantees written are off-balance-sheet items that are not reflected directly in the balance sheet. A loan commitment is an agreement to make a loan at a quoted rate during a specified future period. A standby letter of credit is a form of guarantee to back up an obligation of a bank client. Financial guarantees written are noncancellable indemnity bonds guaranteeing the timely payment of interest and principal due on securities issued by bank clients. These items are recorded as a memorandum entry and are disclosed in the financial statements as contingent liabilities.

Serious accounting problems relate to off-balance-sheet items. The disclosure of information relating to such items and accompanying risks are often difficult to identify. The recognition and measurement of these items is not an easy task. Certain of these items contain characteristics of both debt and equity, making it difficult to distinguish between liability and equity interests.

CAPITAL ACCOUNTS

In its most generic meaning, capital refers to a bank or bank holding company's funds resulting from the sale of stock, bonds, or notes issued by the bank or bank holding company, and also its retained earnings.

Regulation H, 12 CFR 208.1 (f) refers to capital as "Common stock, preferred stock, and legally issued capital notes and debentures purchased by the Reconstruction Finance Corporation, which may be considered capital and capital stock for purposes of membership in the Federal Reserve System under the provisions of Section 9 of the Federal Reserve Act." For purposes of other regulatory agencies, capital includes the amount of common stock outstanding and unimpaired, plus the amount of preferred stock outstanding and unimpaired.

Capital and surplus is referred to as "Paid-in and unimpaired capital and surplus, which includes undivided profits but does not include the proceeds of capital notes or debentures" (Regulation K, 12 CFR 211.1 [b]).

In reporting on stockholders' equity, the various elements of stockholders' equity are generally accumulated in an account structure designed to meet the statutory and corporate charter requirements. In general, the equity accounts should be classified and presented by source of capital rather than by the respective rights of each class of shareholders. Each authorized class of stock should be disclosed, preferably on the face of the balance sheet, whether or not any of the shares is outstanding. Pertinent facts concerning capital stock reserved for use under stock option or stock purchase plans, warrants, or rights should be disclosed. Pertinent facts concerning any stock repurchase agreements or other commitments and agreements affecting the capital stock or other capital accounts should be disclosed. Both the Securities and Exchange Commission and the New York Stock Exchange have specific requirements for reporting on stockholders' equity, which should be referenced when drafting financial statements to be filed with such agencies. These requirements are useful guidelines in drafting other financial statements.

Capital and surplus accounts found in the stockholders' equity section of a bank balance sheets can include the following:

- *Preferred stock* The par value of preferred stock outstanding

- *Common stock* The par value of common stock outstanding of shares (multiplied by par value per share)

- *Surplus* (or capital surplus) The portion of net income transferred from undivided profits plus paid-in surplus from the sale of stock when stock is sold at a price that exceeds the par value. Regulatory requirements affect the minimum amount of such surplus that banks must maintain.

- *Undivided profits* The accumulation of current and prior year's profits and losses. In nonfinancial corporations, this account is called retained earnings.

Preferred stock represents a class of stock that has rights or privileges ranking ahead of those assigned to common stock. In reporting on the preferred stock, the description of preferred stock should be the same as it appears in the articles of incorporation and should include disclosure of par value, the number of shares authorized, issued, and outstanding, and the total amount related to each class of preferred stock. Dividend and liquidation preferences should be disclosed. Call or conversion features should also be disclosed. The amount of any accumulated dividends in arrears should be shown.

Generally, common stock represents the residual ownership of a corporation's assets after liabilities and preferred shareholder and other proprietary claims have been satisfied. In reporting on common stock, the terms capital stock and common stock are synonymous where there is only one class of stock. The statements should preferably use the term designated in the corporate charter. The par or stated value per share, the number of shares authorized, issued, and outstanding, and the total dollar amount related to each class of stock should be disclosed, preferably on the face of the balance sheet. No-par-value stock may be recorded at the fair value of the consideration received or at a stated or assigned amount, usually at the discretion of the board of directors.

Treasury stock generally represents any class of capital stock that had been issued and reacquired by purchase or by donation, but not retired by appropriate corporate action. Treasury stock should ordinarily be recorded at acquisition cost. The class and number of shares held as treasury stock should be disclosed. Ordinarily, treasury stock is presented in the stockholders' section of the balance sheet as an unallocated deduction from contributed capital and retained earnings (or surplus and undivided profit) (the cost method). In some instances, treasury stock is presented in the stockholders' equity section of the balance sheet as a deduction from the issued stock of the same class (the par value method). Retained earnings or surplus may be restricted as to the payment of dividends to the extent of the cost of treasury stock. If material, such restrictions should be disclosed.

Additional paid-in capital (or surplus) is used to indicate capital contributions by shareholders or others in excess of amounts credited to the capital stock accounts. Sources of paid-in-capital include

premiums collected on sales of par-value stock,

excess of sales price over stated value of no-par value capital stock,

donated assets by stockholders and others,

reduction of the par or stated value per share of outstanding capital stock,

retirement of capital stock at a price less than that at which it was originally sold,

sale of treasury stock at a price in excess of its cost, conversion of capital stock into stock with a smaller par or stated value, and

declaration of a stock dividend that is recorded on the basis of fair market value

Surplus (or retained earnings) indicates the accumulated net earnings or losses after deducting dividends paid to stockholders and transfers to capital stock and additional capital accounts. Surplus should be shown separately in the equity section of the balance sheet. Restrictions of surplus should be indicated in a note or parenthetically on the face of the balance sheet.

Net unrealized losses due to temporary market fluctuations in the valuation of the noncurrent marketable equity securities portfolio should be shown as reductions of stockholders' equity. Accumulated changes in the valuation allowance for noncurrent marketable equity securities (or in a bank's unclassified balance sheet) should be shown as a separate item in the equity section.

Cumulative translation adjustments from translations of foreign financial statements into U.S. dollars, when the functional currency is determined to be the local country's currency, should be recorded as a separate item of stockholders' equity. This is discussed further in Chapter 10, "International Transactions and Operations."

Equity is the difference between assets and liabilities (Assets − Liabilities = Equity). The market value of equity is the residual of the market value of assets less the market value of liabilities.

RISK-BASED CAPITAL

Within the framework for risk-based capital presented by the Basle Supervisors' Committee, the Federal Reserve Board, the Comptroller of the Currency, and the FDIC have adopted risk-based capital guidelines for banks. The Federal Reserve has issued similar guidelines covering bank holding companies with assets over $150 million. On January 19, 1989, the Board issued the final version of its risk-based capital guidelines. The OCC rule appeared on January 27, 1989, and the FDIC's on March 21, 1989. The guidelines define capital and establish a system for assigning risk categories for assets and off-balance-sheet items.

The 1992 risk-based capital standards establish two forms of capital:

- *Tier 1 (core) capital* Elements of capital comprised of stockholders' equity (common stock, surplus, and retained earnings); any goodwill is deducted from Tier 1 capital. Banks can include noncumulative preferred stock as Tier 1 capital. Bank holding companies can include preferred stock, both cumulative and noncumulative, up to 25 percent of Tier 1 capital. It must represent at least 50 percent of the qualifying total capital base.

- *Tier 2 (supplementary) capital* Elements of capital that bank regulators view as limited in one or more respects from participating in losses of the bank or holding company. Tier 2 capital includes general loan loss reserves, cumulative perpetual preferred stock, long-term preferred stock, hybrid capital instruments, subordinated debt, and intermediate preferred stock within limits. The allowance for loan losses is included up to a limit of 1.25 percent of risk-weighted assets. Tier 2 capital is limited to 100 percent of Tier 1 capital, net of goodwill.

The guidelines bring the full range of on- and off-balance sheet assets into the risk-based system. A risk-weighting system has been developed to assess the different degrees of risk associated with each category of assets. The risk assessed is generally credit risk, i.e., risk of loss. Specific percentages are assigned to assets and off-balance sheet activities ranging from 0 percent for low risk assets (cash and U.S. government securities) to 100 percent for most of the loan portfolio. Off-balance-sheet activities are converted to a balance sheet credit equivalent amount and then are assigned a percentage based on collateral, guarantor, or obligor.

An institution's risk-adjusted capital ratio is the sum of its total Tier 1 and Tier 2 capital divided by the sum of its risk-adjusted on-balance-sheet assets and risk-adjusted off-balance sheet assets.

Risk-based capital requirements are discussed at some length in Chapter 12, "Financial Statement Analysis."

SUMMARY OF SIGNIFICANT ACCOUNTING POLICIES

Accounting policies of a bank are the specific accounting principles and the methods of applying these principles that have been adopted by the bank. The accounting policies can significantly influence the information reported in the financial statements. Generally accepted accounting principles require that when financial statements are presented, a description of all significant accounting policies be included as an integral part of the statements.

The disclosures should encompass a discussion of the principles relating to revenue recognition and asset cost allocation, particularly when these principles and methods involve (1) a selection from existing acceptable alternatives, (2) principles and methods peculiar to the industry in which the company operates, and (3) unusual or innovative applications of generally accepted accounting principles.

It is recommended that the disclosure is particularly useful when made in a separate *Summary of accounting policies* preceding the notes to the financial statements or as the initial note.

Examples include those policies related to the following items:

- investment securities
- bank premises and equipment
- depreciation methods
- amortization of intangibles
- inventory pricing
- trading account securities
- foreign currency transactions
- loan and lease financing
- recognition of profits on long-term contracts
- revenue recognition from franchise and leasing operations
- consolidation policy
- loans and leasing financing reporting
- income taxes
- pension plans
- provision for loan losses
- foreign currency translation

LEVERAGE IN BANK STATEMENTS

Bank statements of condition are highly leveraged. Bank liabilities greatly exceed bank capital. Such a situation is fundamental to a bank's operations and performance. Having a solid base of quality assets enhance the earning potential of banks. However, being highly leveraged, the bank is vulnerable to losses. To cope with this problem, regulators have imposed minimum capital requirements to assure a degree of capital adequacy. See Chapter 13 for a fuller discussion of leverage.

PERSONAL FINANCIAL STATEMENTS

The reporting entity of personal financial statements is an individual, a husband and wife, or a group of related individuals. Personal financial statements are often prepared to deal with obtaining bank loans, income tax planning, retirement planning, gift and estate planning, and the public disclosure of financial affairs.

For each reporting entity, a statement of financial position is required. The statement presents assets at estimated current values, liabilities at the lesser of the discounted amount of cash to be paid or the current cash settlement amount, and net worth. A provision should also be made for estimated income taxes on the differences between the estimate current values of assets. Comparative statements for one or more period should be presented. A statement of changes in net worth is optional. AICPA Statement of Position 82-1, "Personal Financial Statements," deals with the preparation and presentation of personal financial statements.

Personal financial statements should be presented on the accrual basis. A classified balance sheet is not used. Assets and liabilities are presented in the order of their liquidity and maturity, respectively (not on a current/noncurrent basis). A business interest that constitutes a large part of an individual's total assets should be shown separate from other assets. Such an interest would be presented as a net amount and not as a pro rata allocation of the business's assets and liabilities.

A statement of changes in net worth presents the major sources of increases (decreases) in net worth.

Extensive financial statement disclosures are suggested for personal financial statements including

- An indication of the individuals covered therein
- The measurement of assets and liabilities
- The nature of joint ownership of assets
- Concentrations of investments, names of the companies or industries, and estimated current values of securities
- Description of intangible assets
- Face amount of life insurance owned
- Basic tax information
- Maturities, interest rates, collateral, and other details relating to receivables and debt

Statements of financial condition and net worth could contain the following accounts:

Statement of Financial Position

Assets

Cash

Securities

Loans receivable

Partnership and venture interests

Real estate interest

XYZ Corporation

Cash surrender value of life insurance

Personal residence

Personal jewelry and furnishings

Liabilities

Mortgage payable

Income taxes payable

Estimated income taxes on difference between estimated current values of assets and estimated current amounts of liabilities and their tax bases

Net worth

Statement of Net Worth

Realized increases in net worth:

    Salary and bonus

    Dividend and interest income

    Distribution from partnerships

    Gain on sale of marketable securities

Realized decreases in net worth

    Income taxes

    Interest expense

    Real estate taxes

    Personal expenditure

Unrealized increases in net worth

    Marketable securities

    Benefit plans

    Personal jewelry and furnishings

Unrealized decreases in net worth

Estimate income taxes on the difference between the estimated current values of assets and the estimated current amounts of liabilities and their tax bases

Net increase (decrease in net worth)

Net worth at the beginning of year

Net worth at the end of the year

KEY DEFINITIONS

Accounting loss The loss that may have to be recognized due to credit and market risk as a direct result of the rights and obligations of a financial instrument.

Assets Probable future economic benefits obtained or controlled by an entity as a result of past transactions or events.

Balance sheet See Statement of Financial Position.

Bankers Acceptance A draft or bill of exchange that has been drawn on and accepted by a banking institution (the accepting bank) or its agent for payment by that institution at a future date specified in the instrument.

Capital Common stock, preferred stock, and legally issued capital notes and debentures purchased by the Reconstruction Finance Corporation, which may be considered capital and capital stock for purposes of membership in the Federal Reserve system under provisions of Section 9 of the Federal Reserve Act. For purposes of other regulatory agencies, capital includes the amount of common stock outstanding and unimpaired, plus the amount of preferred stock outstanding and unimpaired (Regulation H, 12 CFR 208.1 [f]).

Capital and surplus Paid-in and unimpaired capital and surplus, which includes undivided profits but does not include the proceeds of capital or debentures (Regulation K, 12 CFR 211.1 [b]).

Credit risk The possibility that a loss may occur from the failure of another party to perform according to the terms of a contract.

Current assets Cash and other assets which are reasonably expected to be realized in cash or sold or consumed during the normal operating cycle of the business or within one year from the balance sheet date, whichever is longer.

Current liabilities Obligations whose liquidation is reasonably expected to require the use of existing resources properly classifiable as current as assets.

Distribution to owners Decreases in equity of a particular business enterprise resulting from transferring assets, rendering services, or incurring liabilities by the enterprise to owners. Distributions to owners decrease ownership interests in an enterprise.

Elements of financial statements The building blocks with which financial statements are constructed; the classes of items that financial statements comprise.

Equity Net assets, or the residual interest in the assets of an entity that remains after deducting its liabilities.

Financial instrument Cash, evidence of an ownership interest in an entity, or a contract that both (a) imposes on one entity a contractual obligation (1) to deliver cash or another financial instrument to a second entity or (2) to exchange financial instruments or potentially unfavorable terms with the second entity; (b) conveys to that second entity a contractual right (1) to receive cash or another financial instrument from the first entity or (2) to exchange other financial instruments on potentially favorable terms with the first entity.

Financial statements A central feature of financial reporting and a principal means of communicating financial information to those outside an entity.

Forward contract An agreement between two parties to exchange specific items at a specified future date and at a specified price.

Futures contract A legal agreement between a buyer or seller and the clearing-house of a futures exchange. Futures contracts obligate the purchaser (seller) to accept (make) delivery of a standardized quantity of a commodity or financial instrument at a specified date or during a specified period, or they provide for cash settlement rather than delivery. Futures contracts can be canceled before the delivery date by entering into an offsetting contract for the same commodity or financial instrument.

Interest rate swap An agreement between two parties to exchange one interest stream for another based on a contractual or notional amount. No principal changes hands.

Intrinsic value The gain that would be realized by exercise of an option rather than buying or selling the security or commodity in the cash market.

Investments by owners Increases in equity of a particular business enterprise resulting from transfers to it from other entities of something valuable to obtain or increase ownership interest in it. Assets are most commonly received as investments by owners, but services or satisfaction or conversion of liabilities of the enterprise also reflect investments by owners.

Liabilities Probable future sacrifices of economic benefits arising from present obligations of an entity to transfer assets or provide services to other entities in the future as a result of past transactions or events.

Market risk The possibility that future changes in market prices may make a financial instrument less valuable or more onerous.

Measurability A relevant attribute that can be quantified in monetary units with sufficient reliability. Items reported in financial statements are measured by different attributes.

Net assets Total assets minus total liabilities.

Off-balance-financing The ability to borrow without having to report the liability on the statements. Off-balance-sheet risk relates to the following major financial instruments: transfer of receivables where the investor has recourse to the issuer; certain repurchase agreements; covered and naked put option on stock; put options on interest rate contracts; call option on stock, foreign currency, or interest rate contracts; fixed and variable loan commitments; interest rate caps; interest rate floors; financial guarantees; note issuance facilities at floating rates; letter of credit at floating rates; interest rate swaps; currency swaps; financial futures contracts; forward contracts.

Operating cycle The average time it takes for the enterprise to spend cash for inventory, sell the inventory in exchange for a receivable, and collect the receivable in cash.

Owners' equity A measure of the owners' interest in the assets of a business.

Risk Sensitivity of income associated with a change in market price or yields of existing assets, liabilities, firm commitments, or anticipated transactions.

Statement of financial position A financial statement that provides information about an entity's assets, liabilities, and equity and their relationships to each other at a moment in time. The statement delineates the entity's resource structure—major classes and amounts of assets—and its financing structure—major classes and amounts of liabilities and equity.

Time value of a purchased option The cost to the purchaser of obtaining protection against the risk of loss over the option's exercise period. The difference between the total value at the inception of the position of an option and the option's intrinsic value.

Working capital The difference between total current assets and total current liabilities.

GLOSSARY OF FINANCIAL INSTRUMENTS: RECENT INNOVATIONS

Wall Street has developed numerous innovative financial instruments in recent years. These new financial instruments are difficult to classify according to traditional categories: debt, equity, and hedging instruments. Frequently they are hybrid instruments. The following glossary was previously published in the *Journal of Accountancy*. The terms are divided into four categories: debt instruments, asset-backed securities, equity instruments, hedging instruments.

Debt Instruments

Bull and bear bonds Bonds linked to upward and downward movements in a designated index. Bulls yield more in a rising market; bears yield more in a falling market.

Capped floater An FRN with an interest rate ceiling.

Carrot and stick bonds Carrots have a low conversion premium to encourage early conversion, and sticks allow the issuer to call the bond at a specified premium if the common stock is trading at a specified percentage above the strike price.

CATS Certificates of accrual on Treasury certificates.

Commercial paper Unsecured short-term (up to 270 days) obligations issued through brokers or directly. The interest is usually discounted.

Convertible bonds with a premium put Convertible bonds issued at face value with a put entitling the bondholder to redeem the bonds for more than their face value.

Convertible bonds Debt securities that are convertible into the stock of the issuer at a specified price at the option of the holder.

Convertible FRNs The issuer can convert the FRNs into long-term fixed-rate bonds.

COPS (covered option securities) Short-term debt that gives the issuer an option to repay the principal and interest in U.S. dollars or in a mutually acceptable foreign currency.

COUGRs Certificates of government receipts.

Debt with equity warrants Bonds issued with warrants for the purchase of shares. The warrants are separately tradeable.

Drop-lock FRNs The FRNs automatically convert to fixed-rate bonds when short-term interest rates fall below a specified level.

Dual-currency bonds Bonds that are denominated and pay interest in one currency and are redeemable in another currency, thus allowing interest rate arbitrage between two markets.

ECU bonds (European currency unit bonds) A Eurobond denominated in a basket of currencies of the 10 countries that constitute the European Community. The bonds pay interest and principal in ECUs or in any of the 10 currencies at the option of the holder.

Flip-flop notes An instrument that allows investors to switch between two types of securities—for example, to switch from a long-term bond to a short-term fixed-rate note.

FRNs (floating rate notes) Debt instruments that feature periodic interest rate adjustments.

ICONs (indexed currency option notes) A bond denominated and paying interest in one currency with redemption value linked to the exchange rate of another currency.

Indexed debt instruments Instruments with guaranteed and contingent payments, the latter being linked to an index or prices of certain commodities (oil or gold, for example).

LYONs (liquid yield option notes): Zero-coupon bonds that are convertible into the issuer's common stock.

Minimax FRNs FRNs with upper and lower interest limits—that is, a ceiling and a floor.

PERLS (principal exchange-rate-linked securities) Securities paying interest and principal in dollars but with principal payments linked to the exchange rate between the dollar and a second currency.

Put bonds Bonds that the investor can put (or tender) back to the issuer after a specified period.

SPINs (Standard & Poor's indexed notes) A debt instrument featuring interest payments linked to the performance of the Standard & Poor's stock indexes.

STAGs Sterling transferrable accruing government securities.

Stripped government securities A type of zero coupon bond, these securities represent long-term Treasury bonds "stripped" of semiannual interest coupons by an investment banker who resells these coupons and an interest in the principal payments. Investment banks market these stripped securities under such registered acronyms as

CATs certificates of accrual on Treasury Certificates.

COUGRs certificates of government receipts.

LYONs (liquid yield option notes): zero-coupon bonds that are convertible into the issuer's common stock.

STAGs sterling transferrable accruing government securities.

STRIPs separate trading of registered interest and principal of securities.

TIGRs treasury investment growth certificates.

ZEBRAs zero coupon eurosterling bearer or registered accruing certificates.

Universal commercial paper Foreign currency denominated commercial paper that trades and settles in the United States.

Asset-Backed Securities

CARDs (certificates of amortizing revolving debts) Debts backed by credit card debt.

CARs (certificates of automobile receivables) Receivables backed by automobile loans.

CLEOs (collateralized lease equipment obligations) Obligations backed by leasing receivables.

CMOs (collateralized mortgage obligations) Debt obligations that are backed by a pool of whole mortgages or mortgage-backed securities such as Ginnie Maes.

FRENDS (floating rate enhanced debt securities) Debt securities backed by LBO loan participations.

Mortgage backed Securities A participation in an organized pool of residential mortgages, including Ginnie Maes (Government National Mortgage Association), Fannie Maes (Federal National Mortgage Asssociation) and Freddie Macs (Federal Home Loan Mortgage Corporation).

Securitized receivables Debt securities collateralized by a pool of receivables.

Equity Instruments

MMP (money market preferred stock or dutch auction preferred stock) Preferred stock featuring dividends that are reset at a dutch auction—that is, an auction in which the securities are sold at the lowest yield necessary to sell the entire issue. Several investment banks have issued these instruments under such registered names as

CAMPS Cumulative auction market preferred stock.

CMPS Capital market preferred stock.

Convertible MMP stock MMPs that can be converted into common stock.

DARTS Dutch-auction rate transferable securities.

Exchangeable PIK preferred stock The issuer can convert the PIK stock into debt.

FRAPS Fixed rate auction preferred stock.

MAPS Market auction preferred stock.

PIK (pay in kind) preferred stock Dividends are paid in additional shares of preferred stock.

STARS Short-term auction rate cumulative preferred stock.

STRAPS Stated rate auction preferred stock.

Hedging Instruments

Butterfly spread Options strategy involving two calls and two puts in the same or different markets, with several maturity dates.

Calendar spread Options strategy that involves buying and selling options on the same security with different maturities.

Cancelable forward exchange contracts The holder has the unilateral right to cancel the contract at maturity.

CIRCUS Combined currency and interest rate swap.

Convertible option contracts A foreign currency option that converts to a forward contract if the forward exchange rate falls below a trigger price.

Cross-hedging Hedging one exposure with an instrument pegged to another market or index.

Cylinder options A combined option and put option on currency.

OPPOSSMS Options to purchase or sell specified mortgage-backed securities.

Perpendicular spread Options strategy using options with the same maturities but different strike prices.

Range Forwards A forward exchange contract specifying a range of exchange rates within which currencies will be exchanged at maturity.

Swaption An option to enter or be forced to enter a swap.

Synthetic instruments Two or more transactions that have the effect of a financial instrument. For example, a fixed-rate bond combined with an interest rate swap can result in a synthetic floating rate instrument.

ZCRO (zero cost ratio option) A cylinder option with a put written in an amount offsetting the call premiums.

Zero-coupon bonds A bond that's sold at a deep discount from its face value. It carries no interest coupon, but investors receive the gradual appreciation to face value.

Zero-coupon swap A swap of zero-coupon debt into floating rate debt.

Chapter 6

The Income Statement

A bank's income statement reports its earnings over a period of time. The statement also serves as an important link between successive balance sheets and indicates that the financial statements are related (or articulate).

Net income reported on the income statement is an important measure of a bank's management's past performance. It is also a relatively reliable predictor of cash flows. Net income is a measure of the change in net assets of an enterprise for a period of time, assuming no new capital contributions by the owners or dividend distributions by the bank.

CONTENTS OF THE INCOME STATEMENT

The income statement provides information concerning return on investment, risk, financial flexibility, and overall operating capabilities. Return on investment is a measure of a bank's overall performance. Risk is the uncertainty associated with the future of the enterprise. Financial flexibility is the firm's ability to adapt to problems and opportunities. Operating capability is related to the firm's ability to maintain a given level of operations.

Components of Net Income

SEC Article and the AICPA amendment to its *Bank Industry Audit Guide* require a one-step approach to reporting the results of bank operations by including securities gains and losses as another line item in the basic income statement.

The components of net income are revenues, gains, expenses, and losses. The components are defined in reference to assets and liabilities. The Financial Accounting Standards Board provides the following definitions:

- *Revenues* Inflows or other enhancements of assets of an entity or settlement of its liabilities (or both) during a period, based on production and delivery of goods, provisions of services, and other activities that constitute the entity's major operations. Examples are sale revenue, interest revenue, and rent revenue.

- *Expenses* Outflows or other use of assets or incurrences of liabilities (or both) during a period as a result of delivering or producing goods, rendering services, or carrying out other activities that constitute the entity's ongoing major or central operations. Examples are cost of goods sold, salaries expense, and interest expense.

- *Gains* Increases in owners' equity (net assets) from peripheral or incidental transactions of an entity and from all other transactions and events affecting the entity during a period, except those that result from revenues or investments by owners. Examples are a gain on the sale of bank building and a gain on the early retirement of long-term debt.

- *Losses* Decreases in owners' equity (net assets) from peripheral or incidental transactions of an entity and from all other transactions and events affecting the entity during a period except those that result from expenses or distributions to owners. Examples are losses on the sale of investments and from litigations.

Revenue and Expense Recognition

The revenue recognition principle generally requires that revenue be recognized in the financial statements when (1) realized or realizable and (2) earned. Revenues are realized when products or other assets are exchanged for cash or claims to cash or when services are rendered. Revenues are realizable when assets received or held are readily convertible into cash or claims to cash. Revenues are considered earned when the entity has substantially accomplished what it must do to be entitled to the benefits represented by the revenues. Recognition through sales or the providing of services provides a uniform and reasonable test of realization.

In recognizing expenses, accountants rely on the matching principle because it requires that efforts (expenses) be matched with accomplishment (revenues) whenever it is reasonable and practical to do so. Direct labor and direct material are costs that can be matched against the revenues that they helped to generate. For costs for which it is difficult to adopt some association with revenue, accountants use a rational and systematic allocation policy that will approximate the matching principle. Depreciation, goodwill amortization, bond premium/discount amortization, and the inventory method (FIFO, LIFO) used to allocate inventory costs to cost of goods sold are matched against revenue based on the rational and systematic allocation policy justification. Finally, some costs are charged to the current period as expenses (or losses) merely because no future benefit is anticipated or no connection with revenue is apparent or no allocation is rational and systematic. Officers' salaries and advertising expenses usually reflect these costs.

Extraordinary Items

Income statements also report extraordinary items, unusual gains and losses, changes in accounting principles, and discontinued operations. Extraordinary items are material items of a character significantly different from the typical or customary business activity of the entity. Extraordinary items are both unusual in nature *and* infrequent in occurrence, considering the environment in which an entity operates, defined by the Accounting Principles Board as follows:

Unusual nature The underlying event or transaction should possess a high degree of abnormality and be of a type clearly unrelated to, or only incidentally related to, the ordinary and typical activities of the entity, taking into account the environment in which the entity operates.

Infrequency of occurrence The underlying event or transaction should be of a type that would not reasonably be expected to recur in the foreseeable future, taking into account the environment in which the entity operates.

The accountant must also consider the characteristics of the company when determining how to handle an event or transaction. Extraordinary items must be material.

Extraordinary items can include the direct result of a major casualty, an expropriation, or a prohibition under a newly enacted law or regulation that meets the criteria of unusual and infrequent. A material gain or loss from the extinguishment of debt ordinarily should be reported as extraordinary even though these gains or losses do not meet the criteria mentioned for extraordinary items. Extraordinary items are shown net of taxes in a separate section in the income statement, usually just before net income.

Unusual Gains and Losses

Unusual gains and losses refer to items which are unusual *or* infrequent but not both, if material. They must be disclosed separately above "income (loss) before extraordinary items." They would not be reported net of taxes.

Accounting Changes

Accounting changes can significantly affect the financial statements for an accounting period, trends in comparative statements, and historical summaries as well as the confidence and relevance that financial statements have for statement users. Consistency in the application of accounting principles is assumed to enhance the usefulness and understandability of financial statements.

An accounting change is understood to be a change in

1. *Accounting principles or methods:* a change from one generally accepted accounting principle to another generally accepted accounting principle, including the methods of applying these principles.

2. *Estimate:* a revision of an accounting measurement based on new information and experience (normal, recurring adjustments).

3.   *Reporting entity:* a change in principle that results in the reporting of an entity that is different from the one reported on in previous financial statements.

Accounting principles describe three methods of reporting accounting changes and the type of changes for which each should be used. These methods include

1.   *Retroactive:* Restating all previous financial statements that are presented with the current financial statements for comparative purposes.

2.   *Current:* Recording the cumulative effect of the event as an adjustment to the current year's income.

3.   *Prospective:* Spreading the cumulative effect of the change over current and future reporting periods.

The effect on net income of adopting a new accounting principle should be disclosed as a separate item following extraordinary items in the income statement. A change in accounting principles occurs when a company selects a generally accepted accounting principle that differs from the generally accepted accounting principle used in a prior reporting period. The cumulative effect of a change in accounting principle is computed as the effect of a change on retained earnings at the beginning of the period of change on retained earnings.

A change in accounting principle includes a change in the method of inventory pricing from FIFO to average cost or a change in depreciation from the double-declining to the straight line method. A cumulative change in accounting principles is reported after extraordinary items and before net income on a net-of-tax basis. Prior financial statements are not restated. Income before extraordinary items and net income computed on a pro forma (as if) basis is shown for all periods presented as if the newly adopted principle was applied in those previous years.

There are certain exceptions to this basic treatment of accounting changes. Some special exceptions require that the change be handled retroactively; that is, prior years' financial statements are restated on a basis consistent with the newly adopted principle, and the effect of the change attributable to years prior to those be presented as an adjustment of the earliest retained earnings presented. A change from the LIFO inventory valuation method to another method is such a change. Such changes are considered so significant that they require a retroactive presentation in the financial statements of all prior periods presented.

Certain accounting changes are handled prospectively; that is, only the current and future periods affected by the change are adjusted. No change should be made in previously reported periods. Changes in accounting estimates are such changes. Changes in estimate are handled prospectively. Examples of changes in estimate could include uncollectible receivables, obsolescence of inventory, and changes in the lives and salvage values of assets.

A change in reporting entity would be an accounting change that results in financial statements that are the statements of a different entity. Presenting consolidated statements in place of statements of individual companies would be a change in entity. Changes in the reporting entity are disclosed by restating the financial statements of all prior periods presented. The effect is that financial information is reported as if the new reporting entity had existed for all periods reported. The effect of the change would be described, and the nature of and reasons for the change would be disclosed. The effect of the change on income before extraordinary, items, net income, and corresponding per share amounts would also be disclosed for all periods.

The nature of and justification for each accounting change must be disclosed in the financial statements along with the monetary effects of each change.

Prior period adjustments are (1) the correction of an error in the financial statements of a prior period, and (2) adjustments that result from realization of income tax benefits of pre-acquisition operating loss carryforwards of purchased subsidiary. Errors are not accounting changes but rather the result of mistakes or oversights such as the use of incorrect accounting methods or mathematical miscalculations. The effect of the error is not reported on the income statement but as an adjustment of the opening balance on the statement of retained earnings. All prior period statements currently presented are restated to show the correct amounts.

Materiality should be considered for each correction individually, as well as for all corrections in total. Correction of errors requires the retroactive restatement of financial statements. The adjustment to the beginning balance of retained earnings in the retained earnings statement is made as follows:

Retained earnings, beginning balance	$XXX
PRIOR PERIOD ADJUSTMENT (+ or −)	XX
Retained earnings, beginning balance, adjusted	XXX
Add: Net income (or Less: Net loss)	XX
Less: Dividends	XX
Retained earnings, ending balance	$XXX

Discontinued Operations

Discontinued operations refer to the operations of a segment of a business that has been sold, abandoned, spun off, or otherwise disposed of or, although still operating, is the subject of a formal plan for disposal. Discontinued operations can result in gains or losses from the disposal of a segment of a business. An industry segment is a component of an enterprise engaged in providing a product or service or group of related products and services primarily to unaffiliated customers for a profit. A reportable segment is an industry segment for which information is required to be reported by this segment. To qualify as a segment, the assets and results of operations of the discontinued segment should be physically, operationally, and for financial reporting purposes distinct.

The effect of discontinued operations is shown net of tax as a separate category in the income statement after continuing operations but before extraordinary items. If a loss is expected from the discontinuance of a business segment, the estimated loss shall be provided for as of the measurement date. The measurement date is the date on which management commits itself to a formal plan to dispose of a segment of the business, whether by sale or abandonment. If a gain is expected, it should be recognized when realized. Earnings per share data should be presented on the face of the income statement.

The following information should be presented for each of the reportable segments: revenue, profitability, identifiable assets, depreciation, depletion, and amortization for each segment, capital expenditures for each segment, equity method investees that are vertically related and the geographic location of such investees, and changes in accounting principles that relate to the industry segments. Disclosure of segmental information is allowed (1) within the body of the financial statements, (2) in the footnotes to the financial statements, or (3) in a separate schedule.

Earnings per Share

Generally accepted accounting principles require disclosing earnings per share amounts on the income statement of all public reporting entities. Earnings per share is a significant summary indicator used in financial analysis. It offers a single item that communicates considerable information about and enterprises financial position and performance. Earnings per share data provide a measure of the bank's management and past performance and enables users of the statements to evaluate future prospects of the bank and assess dividend distributions to shareholders. Earnings per share data is especially useful in (1) establishing the value of a firm, and (2) estimating expected future dividends.

Earnings (or loss) per share data should be disclosed on the face of the earnings statement for

- Earnings or loss from continuing operations
- Earnings or loss before extraordinary items
- The cumulative effect of a change in accounting principle
- Net earnings or loss

Earnings per share should be computed based on the weighted average number of shares outstanding or considered outstanding. The computation gives recognition to the effect of stock dividends, splits, or reverse splits. Many corporations issue convertible securities, options, warrants or other rights that upon exercise or conversion can dilute the earnings per common share. In these cases, it is necessary to compute primary earnings per share and fully diluted earnings per share to give effect to the contingent issuance of common stock upon exercise or conversion.

The basic calculation of earnings per share (EPS) is to divide income available to common stockholders, after deducting required payments to senior security holders, by the weighted average number of common shares outstanding during the accounting period.

$$EPS = \frac{\text{Net income}}{\text{Number of shares of common stock outstanding}}$$

A company that has convertible securities, options, warrants, or other rights that on conversion or exercise could (in the aggregate) dilute earnings per share by 3 percent or more is defined as having a complex capital structure. Two earnings per share computations are required for a company with a complex capital structure: (1) primary earnings per share and (2) fully diluted earnings per share.

The numerator to use in computing primary earnings per share is determined by summing net income and the net of tax earnings accruing to securities properly classified as common stock equivalents. The denominator consists of the weighted average number of common shares outstanding during the period plus the weighted average number of shares that would be issued if all securities classified as common stock equivalents were assumed to have been exchanged at the beginning of the period or when they become exchangeable during the period.

Primary EPS =

$$\frac{\text{Net income after taxes – preferred dividends (if declared or on cumulative preferred if not declared for nonconvertible preferred stock or convertible preferred stock that is not a common stock equivalent) + interest and dividends (net of tax effect) on securities considered to be common stock equivalents}}{\text{Weighted average of common shares outstanding + shares issuable from common stock equivalents}}$$

The fully diluted computation adds all contingent issuances of shares available during the period to the denominator and adds the earnings (net of tax) that accrued to these additional securities to the numerator. Common stock equivalents are defined as securities that are not common stock but that contain provisions that enable the holders of such securities to become common stockholders and to participate in any value appreciation of the common stock. Common stock equivalents include stock warrants and options, participating securities, and convertible securities subject to the 66 2/3 percent Aa bond rating test. When a convertible security has an effective yield to maturity of less than 66 2/3 percent of the Aa bond effective interest rate at the date of issuance, it is assumed to be purchased for its conversion feature and is included in computing EPS.

Options, warrants, and stock rights are considered common stock equivalents. Dilution is computed by applying the treasury stock method for computing primary earnings per share. Under this method, earnings per share data are computed as if the options and warrants were exercised at the beginning of the period (or at the time of issuance, if later) and as if the funds obtained thereby were used to purchase common stock at the average market price during the period. The higher of the market price at the close of the period or the average price is used in fully diluted computations.

Fully diluted EPS =

$$\frac{\text{The numerator for primary EPS + interest and dividends (net of tax effect) on securities assumed converted for fully diluted purposes}}{\text{The denominator for primary EPS + all other contingently issuable shares}}$$

Antidilutive securities are ignored in all calculations and should not be considered in computing either primary or fully diluted EPS.

Sample Bank Income Statement

A bank's income statement can be summarized as follows:

Interest income (by source)
– Interest expense (by source)
Net interest income
– Provision for loan losses
Net interest income after provision for loan losses

+ Other income (by source)
– Other expenses by source)
Income before income taxes
– Income tax expense
Net income
Net income per common share

A bank's income statement is organized so as to report net interest income (interest income minus interest expense). This format focuses attention on the bank's role as a financial intermediary (the business of banking). The spread or difference between interest income and interest expense is a key performance and profitability measurement for banks.

Interest income is the primary source of revenue for a bank. It represents the return a bank receives on its earning assets (loans, investment securities, and interest-earning deposits). Interest income is reported in categories of interest on loans, federal funds sold and securities purchased under resale agreement, etc., which relate directly to balance sheet categories of earning assets (loans, federal funds sold and securities purchased under agreement to resell, etc.).

Income Statement Items	*Balance Sheet Items*
Interest income:	Earning assets:
Loans	Loans
Federal funds sold and securities purchased under agreement to resell	Federal funds sold and securities provided under agreement to resell
Investment securities	Investment securities
Deposits in other banks	Interest-bearing deposits in other banks
Trading account securities	Trading account securities

Security gains or losses (excluding those from trading-account securities) are shown at the bottom of the income statement and shown net of tax. Bank income statements provide a basic division between operating and nonoperating revenues and expenses. Figure 6-1 presents a typical bank's income statement.

Interest expense is the largest expense of a bank. It reflects the expense a bank pays for the right to use other entities, funds in conducting banking business. Interest expense on the income statement can be associated with related balance sheet items:

Income Statement Item	*Balance Sheet Item*
Interest expense on:	Earning assets: loans
Deposits	Interest-bearing deposits
Short-term borrowings	Federal Funds and securities sold under agreement to repurchase
	Other short-term borrowing
Long-term debt	Long-term debt

Figure 6-1
A Bank's Income Statement

	19X2	19X1
Interest income:	$6,182,453	$5,822,016
Interest and fees on loans	125,204	74,599
Lease financing income		
Interest on investment securities		
U.S. Treasury	693,253	596,179
U.S. Government agencies and corporations	501,479	451,738
States and political subdivisions	1,157,170	959,094
Other	351,959	355,042
Interest on federal funds sold	382,895	537,412
	$9,394,413	$8,796,080
Interest expense:		
Interest on deposits	$4,381,893	$3,780,690
Interest on securities sold under agreement to repurchase and federal funds purchased	405,992	549,745
Interest on capital notes	89,700	89,700
	$4,877,585	$4,420,135
Net interest income	$4,516,828	$4,375,945
Provision for possible loan losses (Note 5)	89,000	96,000
Net interest income after provision for possible loan losses	$4,427,828	$4,279,945
Other income:		
Trust department income	$147,270	$236,583
Service fees	410,584	412,110
Other	154,441	115,843
Securities gains (losses)	105,827	(16,998)
	$ 818,122	$ 747,538
Other expenses:		
Salaries and wages	$1,668,093	$1,539,427
Pensions and other employee benefits (Note 10)	291,373	237,997
Occupancy expenses	198,374	166,868
Equipment rentals, depreciation, and maintenance	243,487	301,255
Other operating expenses	954,632	775,333
	$3,355,959	$3,020,880
Income before income taxes	$1,889,991	$2,006,603
Applicable income taxes (Note 9)	332,000	520,500
Net income	$1,557,991	$1,486,103
Net income per share of common stock	$ 2.60	$ 2.48

Provision for Loan Losses

The provision for loan losses is an estimated amount charged to earnings to maintain the level of the related allowance for loan losses at a level estimated by management to be sufficient to absorb estimated losses associated with the bank's loan portfolio. This amount tends to be a highly subjective estimate. The bank's loan mix, loss experience, state of the economy, and other factors enter into the determination of the provision for loan losses. Auditors, regulators, and the financial community are advisedly concerned over the adequacy of this provision.

The loan loss reserve on the balance sheet should reflect the estimated amount of losses in a bank's loan portfolio. If loan losses deplete this account, the account should be adjusted to the required level.

Nonaccrual of Interest on Loans

A bank should not accrue interest on any asset that (1) is recorded on a cash basis due to the weakening of a borrower's financial condition, (2) is in default for in excess of 90 days (except consumer loans secured by one- to four-family residential properties), and (3) is not expected to make payments on interest or principal. Any interest receivable recorded on nonaccrual loans should ordinarily be eliminated.

Loan Fees, Direct Origination Costs, and Other Fees

SFAS No. 91, "Accounting for Nonrefundable Fees and Costs Associated with Originating or Acquiring Loans and Initial Direct Costs of Leases," specifies the accounting and reporting requirements for loan origination, commitment, and syndication fees and costs. It also covers fees and costs in refinancing or restructuring and the accounting requirements when a loan or group of loans are purchased.

Loan fees and associated *direct origination costs* are offset. The net amount is deferred as part of the loan and reported as a component of loans in the balance sheet and recognized over the life of the loan or loan commitment period as an adjustment of the yield on the loan. Loan fees and costs for loans originated or purchased for resale are deferred and recognized when the related loan is sold.

Commitment fees received by the lender to originate or purchase a loan are usually deferred until the commitment is either exercised or expires. If the commitment is exercised and the loan acquired, the commitment fee is amortized over the life of the loan as an adjustment to the loan yield. If the loan commitment is not exercised, the commitment fee is recognized as income when the commitment expires. There are two exceptions to this general rule:

1. If past experience indicates that the extension of a loan is not likely, the fee is recognized over the commitment period.

2. Nominal fees on a commitment may be recognized in income at the determination date.

Costs may be deferred for the following activities: evaluating the borrower, guarantees, collateral, and other security; preparation and processing of loan documentation for loan origination; and negotiating and closing the loan. Costs which cannot be deferred include advertising and solicitation, credit supervision and administration, and similar indirect costs.

Refinancing and restructuring fees and costs associated with a new loan, and unrecognized items related to the old loan, such as costs, fees, or prepaid penalties, should be taken to interest income in the accounting period that the new loan is granted. When the restructuring or refinancing is not classified as a new loan, the refinancing is accounted for as a continuation of the loans. In such cases any unamortized net costs or fees and any prepayment penalties are included as part of the net investment in the loan.

When an enterprise *purchases a loan or a group of loans in a lump-sum purchase*, the investment in the loan(s) includes the purchase price less any fees received by the buyer plus any fees paid by the buyer. If there is a difference between the investment in the loan and the loan's principal, the difference is accounted for as an adjustment to the loan yield over the life of the loan. All other costs incurred in completing the loan purchase are expenses as incurred.

Loan syndication fees are recognized when received, unless the yield on the portion of the loan retained by the syndicating bank is not at least equal to the yield received by the other members of the syndicate. In such cases, a portion of the fee must be deferred and amortized to income to obtain a yield equal to the average yield of the other banks in the syndicate. Securitization where loans are sold to a separate entity that then finances the purchase through the issuance of debt securities or undivided interests in the loan are subject to SFAS No. 77.

Assets and liabilities of the trust department of a bank are held in an agency or fiduciary capacity. Such trust items are not recorded on the balance sheet of the bank. *Fees earned from fiduciary services* are recorded in the bank's income statement when earned.

Banks also generate *other fee income* from a broad variety of activities: underwriting, brokerage, advisory services, private placement of securities, and private banking activities including tax, investment, and credit planning. Generally, fee income from such activities is recognized as income when earned.

Fees and costs that are adjustments to the loan yield over the life of the loan generally should be amortized using the interest method. The interest method involves the application of a constant rate against the net investment in the receivable.

All unamortized loan items, including origination fees, commitment fees and costs, purchase discounts and premiums, are included in the related loan balance and reported on the balance sheet. All amortization of fees and costs recognized as an adjustment to the loan yield is reported on the income statement as interest income. Other fees amortized using a straight-line method, such as commitment fees, or fees that are written off at the end of the commitment period, are charged to service fee income.

BANK SPECIFIC SFASs

A number of bank specific FASB Statements that affect the balance sheet or income statement are briefly discussed here.

SFAS No. 65, "Accounting for Certain Mortgage Banking Activities." SFAS No. 65 establishes accounting and reporting standards for the sales, financing, and servicing activities of a mortgage banking enterprise.

SFAS No. 72, "Accounting for Certain Acquisitions of Banking or Thrift Institutions." SFAS No. 72 provides guidance concerning the valuation and amortization of intangible assets resulting from an acquisition. The statement also sets forth guidelines for accounting for acquisitions when assistance is received from regulatory agencies.

SFAS No. 83, "Designation of AICPA Guides and Statement of Position on Accounting by Brokers and Dealers in Securities, by Employee Benefit Plans, and by Banks as Preferable for Purposes of Applying APB Opinion No. 20." SFAS No. 83 specifies that specialized accounting and reporting principles and practices contained in revised AICPA guides for banks, brokers, dealers in securities, and employee benefit plans and AICPA Statement of Position of reporting of investment securities gains (loss) by banks are preferable accounting principles for purposes of justifying a change in accounting principles under APB No. 20.

SFAS No. 77, "Reporting by Transferors for Transfers of Receivables with Recourse," applies to sale of loans under specific conditions. Loans held for resale are recorded at the lower of cost or current market value. The bank records a gain or loss based on the difference between the sale proceeds and the recorded value of the loan. If there are any recourse provisions, SFAS No. 77 establishes financial accounting reporting standards by transferors for transfers of receivables with recourse that purport to be sales of receivables applies. Transfers of receivables with recourse is recognized as a sale if all three of the following provisions are met:

1. The selling bank transfers control of future economic benefits embodied in receivables.

2. Transferor's obligation under recourse provisions can be reasonably estimated.

3. Transferee cannot require transferor to repurchase receivables except pursuant to recourse provisions.

If these provisions are not met, the transaction must be recorded as a financing (the amount of proceeds from the transfer shall be reported as a liability). If transfer qualifies as a recognizable sale, gain (loss) shall be recognized, measured by the difference between (a) sales price, adjusted for accrual for probable adjustments, and (b) net receivables. If receivables are sold with servicing retained by transferor, the sales price must be adjusted to provide for normal servicing fees in each subsequent period in cases in which either (1) the stated servicing fee rate differs materially from the normal servicing fee rate, or (2) no servicing fee is specified. For transfers of receivables with recourse reported as a sale, the transferor shall disclose (1) the proceeds received during each period for which income statements are presented and (2) the balance of receivables transferred that remain uncollected at date of each balance sheet presented.

INTERIM FINANCIAL REPORTS

Interim reports are financial statements that cover periods of less than on year. Interim reports are considered an integral part of the annual reporting period and are not viewed as an independent time period.

Interim reports are essential in providing investors, creditors, and others with more timely information as to the financial position and operating results of an enterprise. In general, the results for each interim period should be based on the generally accepted accounting principles and reporting practices used in the annual report.

Major uses and objectives of interim reporting include the following:

1. To estimate annual earnings
2. To make projections and predictions
3. To identify turning points in operations and financial position
4. To evaluate management performance for a period of time shorter than a year
5. To supplement information presented in the annual report

Publicly traded companies usually report the following summarized financial information at interim dates:

1. Gross revenues, provision for income taxes, extraordinary items, effects of accounting changes, and net income
2. Primary and fully diluted earnings-per-share data
3. Material seasonal variations of revenues, costs, and expenses
4. Contingent items, unusual or infrequently occurring items, and effects of the disposal of a segment of a business
5. Material changes in financial position

Interim data are usually less reliable than annual data as a measure of a company's operations and financial position because of the shortness of the period. Also, disclosures on interim reports are usually very limited as compared with annual reports. Interim reports are frequently unaudited.

With few exceptions, revenues and expenses are recognized for interim periods on the same basis as for the annual period. Interim period income tax expense should reflect the concepts of interperiod and intraperiod income tax allocation. At the end of each interim period, an estimate is made of the effective income tax rate expected to be applicable for the annual period. This rate is then applied to income earned to date for that year. Any income tax recognized in previous interim periods is subtracted from the amount resulting from the above computation, and the difference is recognized as income tax expense in the current period.

STATEMENT OF CHANGES IN STOCKHOLDERS' EQUITY

To inform external users of financial statements about capital activities in the annual report, APB Opinion No. 12 states:

> . . . disclosure of changes in the separate accounts comprising stockholders' equity (in addition to retained earnings) and of the changes in the number of shares of equity securities during at least the most recent annual fiscal period . . . is required to make the financial statements sufficiently informative.

The statement of changes in stockholders' equity typically discloses the different classes of common stock, treasury stock, surplus, net income, dividends, retained earnings, and other changes in equity. Such disclosures are helpful in assessing a company's financial flexibility, profitability, and risk. This statement reconciles stockholders' equity at the beginning of the period and at the end of the period. The ending amount on this statement can be traced to the stockholders' equity in the balance sheet. Figure 6-2 illustrates a statement of changes in stockholders' equity for a bank.

KEY DEFINITIONS

Commitment fees Bank charges associated with an agreement that obligates the bank to make a loan under specific conditions.

Common stock equivalent A security that, because of its terms or the circumstances under which it was issued, is in substance equivalent to common stock.

Comprehensive income The change in equity of a business enterprise during a period from transactions and other events and circumstances from nonowner sources. It includes all changes in owners' equity during a period except those resulting from investments by owners and distributions to owners.

Dilution A reduction in earnings per share resulting from the assumption that convertible securities have been converted or that options and warrants have been exercised or other shares have been issued upon the fulfillment of certain conditions.

Figure 6-2

FIRST SAMPLE BANK
STATEMENTS OF STOCKHOLDERS' EQUITY
Years Ended December 31, 19X2 and 19X1

	Preferred Stock	Common Stock	Surplus	Retained Earnings	Total
Balance, December 31, 19X0	$—	$3,000,000	$2,000,000	$3,103,790	$8,103,790
Net Income	—	—	—	1,486,103	1,486,103
Cash dividends declared	—	—	—	(600,000)	(600,000)
Balance, December 31, 19X1	—	$3,000,000	$2,000,000	$3,989,893	$8,989,893
Net income	—	—	—	1,557,991	1,557,991
Cash dividends declared	—	—	—	(672,000)	(672,000)
Transfer to surplus	—	—	$1,000,000	(1,000,000)	—
Balance, December 31, 19X2	$—	$3,000,000	$3,000,000	$3,875,884	$9,875,884

Discontinued operations The operations of a segment of a business that has been sold, abandoned, spun off, or otherwise disposed of or, although still operating, is the subject of a formal plan for disposal.

Disposal date The date of closing the sale, if the disposal is by sale, or the date that operations cease, if the disposal is by abandonment.

Dual presentation The presentation with equal prominence of two types of earnings per share amounts on the face of the income statement: one is primary earnings per share; the other is fully diluted earnings per share.

Earnings per share The amount of earnings attributable to each share of common stock.

Expenses Outflows or other uses of assets or incurrences of liabilities (or both) during a period as a result of delivering or producing goods, rendering services, and carrying out other activities that constitute the entity's major operations.

Expired cost An expense or a loss.

Extraordinary items A material event or transaction that is both unusual in nature and infrequent in occurrence.

Fully diluted earnings per share The amount of current earnings per share reflecting the maximum dilution that would have resulted from conversion, exercises, and other contingent issuances that individually would have decreased earnings per share and in the aggregate would have had a dilutive effect.

Gains Increases in equity (net assets) from peripheral or incidental transactions of an entity and from all other transactions and other events and circumstances affecting the entity except those that result from revenues or investments by owners.

Income statement A statement that reflects the extent to which and the ways in which the equity of an entity increased or decreased from all sources other than transactions with owners during a period.

Losses Decreases in equity (net assets) from peripheral or incidental transactions of an entity and from all other transactions and other events and circumstances affecting the entity except those that result from expenses or distributions to owners.

Measurement date The date on which the management having authority to approve the action commits itself to a formal plan to dispose of a segment of the business, whether by sale or abandonment.

Net income The excess of all revenues and gains for a period over all expenses and losses of the period.

Origination fees Bank charges associated with originating, refinancing, or restructuring loans.

Primary earnings per share The amount of earnings attributable to each share of common stock outstanding, including common stock equivalents.

Prior period adjustments Adjustments related to prior periods and excluded in the determination of net income for the current period.

Revenue recognition principle An accounting principle that is used to determine when revenue should be recognized (recorded). As a general rule, the revenue recognition principle requires that revenues are recognized when the earning process is substantially complete and the revenues are realized or realizable.

Revenues Inflows or other enhancements of assets of an entity or settlement of its liabilities (or both) during a period, based on production and delivery of goods, provision of services, and other activities that constitute the entity's major operations.

Segment of business A segment of business is a component of an enterprise whose activities represent a separate major line of business or a separate class of customer.

Statement of owners' equity A statement of investments by and distributions to owners that reflects the extent to which and in what ways the equity of an entity increased or decreased from transactions with owners during a period. It reflects the capital transactions of the entity.

Statement of retained earnings A financial statement which reconciles the balance of the retained earnings account from the beginning to the end of the period.

Chapter 7

Statement of Cash Flows

Assessing the amounts, timing, and uncertainty of cash flows is one of the basic objectives of financial reporting. The statement that provides information needed to meet this objective is a statement of cash flows. The statement of cash flows presents a detailed summary of all the cash inflows and outflows, or the sources and uses of cash, during the period.

THE STATEMENT OF CASH FLOWS

The Financial Accounting Standards Board issued SFAS, "Statement of Cash Flows," (November 1987) which requires that a statement of cash flows be reported as a basic financial statement when a business enterprise issues financial statements that report both financial position and results of operations. A statement of cash flows shall be presented for each accounting period for which results of operations are presented. The statement of cash flows replaces the statement of changes in financial position required by APB Opinion No. 19, "Reporting Changes in Financial Position." The statement is prepared on a cash basis and not on the accrual basis of accounting as are the balance sheet and the income statement.

Objectives of the Statement

The statement's value is that it helps meet the informational needs of users including the needs for

- *Liquidity* The nearness to cash of its assets and liabilities
- *Financial flexibility* The ability to take effective actions to alter the amount and timing of future cash flows so the company can respond to unexpected needs and opportunities
- *Operating capability* The ability to maintain a given level of operations

The statement of cash flows can also help external users to assess a bank's

1. Ability to generate positive future cash flows
2. Ability to meet its obligations and pay dividends
3. Needs for external financing
4. Differences between its net income and associated cash receipts and payments
5. The cash and noncash aspects of its investing and financing transactions during the accounting period

Cash flows are important indicators of a bank's profitability and viability. To be profitable and viable, a bank must have sufficient cash flows to make loans and investments, meet withdrawals, satisfy loan commitments, and meet other cash requirements. Cash basis information provides critical support to accrual basis accounting (but does not replace the need for accrual basis accounting).

Cash and Cash Equivalents

In the cash flow statement, cash flows include "cash and cash equivalents." Cash equivalents are short-term, highly liquid investments, such as treasury bills, commercial paper, money market funds, and, for an enterprise with banking operations, federal funds sold. They must be readily convertible to known amounts of cash, and so near their maturity that they present insignificant risk of changes in value because of changes in interest rates. Generally, cash equivalents only include investments with original maturities of three months or less. An enterprise shall establish a policy concerning which of these investments shall be treated as cash equivalents. This policy shall be disclosed. A change to this policy is a change in accounting principle that shall be effected by restatement of all comparative financial statements presented. The total amounts of cash and cash equivalents at the beginning and end of the period shown in the statement of cash flows shall be the same amount as similarly titled line items or subtotals shown in the statement of financial position as of those dates.

Contents of the Statement

The statement of cash flows reports cash flows relating to operating financing, and investing activities of a company:

1. Operating activities include all transactions and events that are not investing and financing activities. Such activities include revenues and expense transactions associated with the sale of products or the delivery of services, e.g., all activities that enter into the determination of net income. Operating activities for a bank could include cash flows from:

Cash receipts:

Interest income

Dividend income

Fees for services

Sale of trading securities and loans acquired specifically for resale

Other receipts not classified as investing or financing activities

Cash payments:

Salaries and wages

Interest

Taxes

Purchase of trading securities and loans acquired specifically for resale

Other payments not classified as investing or financing activities

2. Investing activities include (a) lending money and collecting on those loans and (b) acquiring and disposing of investment and productive long-lived assets. Bank lending activities are included in this section and not as operating activities (although bank lending is a major operating activity of banks). A bank's investing activities could include cash flows from:

Cash receipts:

Collection of loans

Sale of loans other than those acquired specifically for resale

Sale or maturity of investments

Sales of property, plant, and equipment

Cash payments:

Loans to customers

Purchase of loans other than those acquired specifically for resale

Purchase of investments securities

Purchase of property, plant, and equipment

3. Financing activities involve liability and owner's equity items and include (a) obtaining cash from creditors and repaying the amounts borrowed and (b) obtaining capital from owners and providing them with a return on their investment (dividends) or other distributions to owners, including outlays to reacquire the enterprise's equity instruments (purchase of treasury stock). Bank deposit transactions are financing activities, not operating activities (although they are a major operating activity of banks). Cash flows from financing activities include:

Cash receipts:

Receiving deposits

Issuance of equity securities (capital stock)

Issuance of debt securities (bonds, notes, mortgages)

Cash payments:

Withdrawals of deposits

Redemption of debt

Payment of dividends

Purchase of treasury stock by a bank holding company

The statement must also clearly show (1) the net increase or decrease in cash and (2) a reconciliation of the beginning cash balance to the ending cash balance.

In the statement the inflows and outflows for each category should be shown separately, and the net cash flows (the difference between the inflows and outflows) should be reported. A comprehensive illustration of a bank's statement of cash flows is presented in Figure 7-1.

The Direct and Indirect Methods

SFAS No. 95 allows two ways to calculate and report a company's cash from operating activities on its statement of cash flows. Cash flows from operating activities can be computed under either the direct method or the indirect method. The direct method shows cash receipts from revenues are compared with cash payments for expenses. When the direct method is used, the statement of cash flows reports cash inflows and outflows from operating activities as follows:

Cash inflows:

Collections from customers

Interest and dividends collected

Other operating receipts

Cash outflows:

Payment to suppliers and employees

Payment of interest

Other operating payments

Payment of income taxes

When the indirect method of reporting operating activities is used, net income is adjusted for items included in the income statement that do not result in an inflow or outflow of cash from operating activities. The effect is to eliminate from net income any noncash transaction to determine the net cash flow from operating activities. The indirect method provides a link between the statement of cash flows and the income statement and balance sheet. In effect the indirect method is a reconciliation method. The indirect method of reporting net cash flow from operating activities is illustrated as follows:

Net income	$100,000
Adjustments for differences between income flows and cash	10,000
flows from operating activities:	
Depreciation expense	
Increase in accounts receivable	(4,000)
Decrease in inventory	15,000
Increase in accounts payable	12,000
Decrease in taxes payable	(3,000)
Amortization of bond premium	(1,000)
Net cash flow from operating activities	$129,000

The following diagram shows the more common types of adjustments that are made to net income to compute net cash flow from operating activities under the indirect method:

Net Income

Additions	**Deductions**
Depreciation expense	
Amortization of intangible assets	
Amortization of bond discount	Amortization of bond premium
Increase in deferred income tax liability	Decrease in deferred income tax liability
Loss on investment in common stock using the equity method	Increase on investment in common stock using the equity method
Loss on sale of plant assets	Gain on sale of plant assets
Decrease in receivables	Increase in receivables
Decrease in inventories	Increase in inventories
Decrease in prepaid expense	Increase in prepaid expense
Increase in accounts payable	Decrease in accounts payable
Increase in accrued liabilities	Decrease in accrued liabilities

=

Net cash flow from operating activities

To summarize the direct and indirect method, when the indirect method is used for operating activities, convert net income from accrual basis income to cash basis of accounting. When the direct method is used, convert revenues and expenses from accrual basis of accounting to cash basis of accounting.

If the indirect method is used, amounts of interest paid (net of amounts capitalized) and income taxes paid must be provided in related disclosures.

Regardless of whether the direct or the indirect method is used, the amount reported as net cash flow provided (used) from operating activities will be identical. The direct method of

Figure 7-1

FIRST SAMPLE BANK
STATEMENTS OF CASH FLOWS
Years Ended December 31, 19X2 and 19X1

	19X2	19X1
Cash flows from operating activities:		
Interest received from:		
Loans and leases	$ 6,125,042	$ 6,030,871
Investment securities	2,509,887	2,290,103
Federal funds sold	383,462	537,412
Trust department income	147,270	236,583
Service fees	410,584	412,110
Other income	154,441	115,843
Interest paid to depositors	(4,598,831)	(3,589,933)
Interest paid on federal funds purchased	(405,992)	(549,745)
Interest paid on capital notes	(89,700)	(89,700)
Cash paid to suppliers and employees	(3,193,922)	2,806,158)
Income taxes paid	(174,000)	(430,500)
Net cash provided by operating activities	$ 1,268,241	$2,156,887
Cash flows from investing activities:		
Proceeds from sales of investment securities	$ 10,610,000	$ 9,321,000
Purchase of investment securities	(20,273,547)	7,996,125)
Federal funds sold, net	2,960,000	(2,150,000
Principal collected on loans	25,316,540	13,695,098
Loans made to customers	—	(30,959,019)
Purchase of assets to be leased	(1,457,204)	(568,520)
Principal payments received under leases	673,602	278,356
Capital expenditures	(914,041)	(697,315)
Proceeds from sale of capital items	622,306	—
Net cash used in investing activities	$(13,421,363)	$(3,094,540)
Cash flows from financing activities:		
Net increase in demand deposits, NOW accounts and savings accounts	$ 6,360,577	$ 858,770
Proceeds from sales of time deposits	40,218,400	39,857,412
Payments for maturing time deposits	(36,943,512)	(33,942,480)
Dividends paid	(672,000)	(600,000)
Net cash provided by financing activities	$ 8,963,465	$ 6,173,702
Net increase (decrease) in cash and cash equivalents	$ (3,189,657)	$ 5,236,049
Cash and cash equivalents, beginning	15,009,846	9,773,797
Cash and cash equivalents, ending	$ 11,820,189	$15,009,846

reporting net cash flows from operating activities is preferred by the FASB. (A survey by KPMG Peat Marwick of 100 bank financial statements in 1989 indicated that 96 percent used the indirect method). When the direct method is used, a reconciliation of net income to net cash flow from operating activities must be provided.

Bank Specific

Several of the guidelines provided in SFAS No. 95 for businesses in general were not appropriate for banks. The FASB subsequently made several modifications, which were designed especially for banks.

In 1989 the Financial Accounting Standards Board issued *SFAS No. 104,* "Statement of Cash Flows—Net Reporting of Certain Cash Receipts and Cash Payments and Classification of Cash Flows From Hedging Transactions," that amends SFAS No. 95. The amendment affects bank reporting. Bankers requested the reconsideration of how certain gross data required under SFAS No. 95 were to be reported by banks. Bankers maintained that certain gross data required under SFAS No. 95 were of little value and were difficult and costly to accumulate.

The Board concluded that for banks, savings institutions, and credit unions, the cost of providing information about certain gross cash receipts and payments generally exceeds the benefit to users of their statements of cash flows. Banks, savings institutions, and credit unions are not required to report gross amounts of cash receipts and cash payments for (a) deposits placed with other financial institutions and withdrawals of deposits, (b) time deposits accepted and repayment of deposits, and (c) loans made to customer and principal collections of loans. When those enterprises constitute part of a consolidated enterprise, net amounts of cash receipts and cash payments for deposit or lending activities of those enterprises shall be reported separate from gross amounts of cash receipts and cash payments for other investing and financing activities of the consolidated enterprise.

In general the information about cash receipts and cash payments shall be presented as gross amounts (debit and credit transactions are reported separately). However, net amounts of related cash receipts and payments may be presented for certain classes of cash flows, which greatly simplifies recordkeeping and reporting (source: SFAF No. 104):

1. Cash purchases and sales of investments classified as cash equivalents (less than three months) need not be reported as gross amounts.

2. Net reporting is also appropriate for items for which the turnover is quick, the items are large, and the maturities are short (e.g., loans with maturities of three months or less).

According to SFAS No. 104, banks can net such items as

1. Deposits placed with and withdrawn from other financial institutions

2. Time deposits accepted and repaid

3. Loans made to customers and principal collected from such loans

4. Futures contracts, forward contracts, option contracts, or swap contracts that are accounted for as hedges of identifiable transactions or events to be classified in the

same category as the cash flows from the item being hedged, provided that this accounting policy is disclosed

SFAS No. 102, "Statement of Cash Flows—Exemption of Certain Enterprises and Classification of Cash Flows from Certain Securities Acquired for Resale," requires that cash receipts and cash payments resulting from acquisitions and sales of (a) securities and other assets that are acquired specifically for resale and are carried at market value in a trading account and (b) loans that are acquired specifically for resale and are carried at market value or the lower of cost or market value be classified as operating cash flows in a statement of cash flows.

It should be noted that cash flows associated with interest expense, interest revenue, and dividends earned are included in computing net cash flow from operating activities (determinants of net income), not financing or investing activities. Cash flows associated with dividends paid are included in financing activities.

Significant Noncash Transactions

Some significant noncash transactions and other events that are investing or financing activities are omitted from the body of the statement of cash flows. Such items are presented in either a separate schedule or a narrative description. Such items include the following: the acquisition of assets by assuming liabilities by issuance of equity securities, exchanges of nonmonetary assets, conversion of debt or preferred stock to common stock, the issuance of equity securities to retire debt. Stock dividends, stock splits, and appropriations of retained earnings are generally not reported as significant noncash transactions.

Cash Flow Per Share

A cash flow per share amount shall not be reported in the statement of cash flows. This avoids confusing cash flow per share with the significant earnings per share amount reported in the income statement. Net income is generally a better measure of performance than cash flows. The statement of cash flows is not an alternative for the income statement.

Foreign Operations

An entity with foreign operations shall report the reporting currency equivalent of local currency cash flows, using the current exchange rate at the time of the cash flows. The effect of exchange rate changes on cash balances held in local currencies shall be separately identified in the statement of cash flows and reported as part of the reconciliation of the change in cash and cash equivalents during the period.

Worksheet for Preparation of the Statement

Information for the preparation of a statement of cash flows comes primarily from comparative balance sheets, the current income and retained earnings statements, and selected transaction data from the general ledger. The basic steps involved in preparing a statement of cash flows include the following:

1.   Determine the change in cash for the period.
2.   Identify sources and uses of cash by transaction analysis.

3. Prepare a formal statement in accordance with standards required by the FASB.

When preparing a worksheet for a statement of cash flows, it is necessary to obtain the following:

1. The beginning and ending balance sheets (in the work sheet)

2. The income statement

3. The statement of retained earnings

In addition, supplemental information is usually required to explain the changes in the balance sheet accounts (other than cash). A review of the bank's books and other records could provide this information.

The worksheet could be set up in three major sections (Figure 7-2):

1. Balance sheet accounts columns showing debit and credit; Balances at the beginning and end of the year are copied into the worksheet.

2. A debit and credit column for reconciling items (The accounts in the comparative balance sheet are analyzed to determine each cash inflow and cash outflow.)

3. A section to show the effect of transactions of cash flows (which provides the information for the formal statement of cash flows) in terms of operating, investing, and financing activities

The steps followed in developing this worksheet are the following:

1. Enter the balance sheet accounts and their beginning and ending balances in the balance sheet accounts section.

2. Enter the data that explains the changes in the balance sheet accounts (other than cash) and their effects on the statement of cash flows in the reconciling columns (change) of the work sheet:

    (a) Move net income (accrual basis, $19,000) to the operating section of the statement of cash flows (entry a).

    (b) Work down the balance sheet debit and credit column to explain all the changes in the accounts.

3. Enter the increase or decrease in cash on the cash line and at the bottom of the work sheet (entry v).

Using the Statement

Each section of the statement can be examined to determine if important changes have occurred. A comparison with other banks can also reveal whether the bank is obtaining or using a greater proportion of its cash from financing or investing activities instead of from operations. This could be important in evaluating relative risk.

The statement helps assess future cash flows, to identify the relationship between net income and net cash flows from operating activities, and provides information about the quality of earnings (e.g., the extent to which income has been turned into cash). The statement is also useful in understanding (1) the level of capital expenditures required to support ongoing and

Figure 7-2
Worksheet for the Preparation of Statement of Cash Flows

Balance sheet:

Debit accounts	Balance 12/31/90	Change Debits	Change Credits	Balance 12/31/91
Cash	$ 10,000	10,000 (v)		$ 20,000
Trading securities	20,000	10,000 (b)		30.000
Investment securities	40,000	13,000 (c)	3,000 (d)	50,000
Loans	80,000	15,000 (e)	5,000 (f)	90,000
Interest receivable	1,000	1,000 (g)		2,000
Fees receivable	2,000	1,000 (h)		1,000
Premises & equipment	10,000	12,000 (i)	10,000 (j)	11,000
			1,000 (k)	
Total	$163,000			$204,000
Credit accounts				
Allowance for credit losses	$ 3,000	5,000 (f)	4,000 (l)	2,000
Deposits	80,000		20,000 (m)	100,000
Short-term borrowing	14,000	11,000 (o)		3,000
Interest payable	2,000	1,000 (n)		1,000
Expenses payable	5,000		1,000 (p)	6,000
Taxes payable	2,000		1,000 (q)	3,000
Long-term debt	20,000	2,000 (r)	7,000 (s)	25,000
Common stock	20,000		10,000 (y)	30,000
Retained earnings	17,000	2,000 (u)	19,000 (a)	34,000
Total	$163,000			$204,000

Cash flows statement:

Operating activities	Inflows	Outflows
Net income	19,000 (a)	
Increase in trading securities		10,000 (b)
Increase interests receivable		1,000 (g)
Decrease fees receivable	1,000 (h)	
Decrease interest payable		1,000 (o)
Increase expenses payable	1,000 (p)	
Increase taxes payable	1,000 (q)	
Gain on sale investment securities		1,000 (d)
Gain on sale premises and equipment		2,000 (j)
Depreciation expense	1,000 (k)	
Provision for credit losses	4,000 (l)	

Figure continues

Figure 7-2
Continued

Operating activities	Inflows	Outflows
<u>Investing activities</u>		
Sale investing securities	4,000 (d)	
Purchase investing securities		13,000 (c)
Increase loans to customers		15,000 (e)
Purchase equipment		12,000 (i)
Proceeds sale of equipment	12,000 (j)	
<u>Financing activities</u>		
Increase in deposits	20,000 (m)	
Payment on short-term note		11,000 (n)
Proceeds from long-term note	7,000 (s)	
Payment on long-term note		2,000 (r)
Proceeds sale common stock	10,000 (t)	
Payment cash dividend		2,000 (u)
	$80,000	$70,000
Increase in cash		10,000 (v)
Total	$80,000	$80,000

growing levels of activity, (2) the major changes in the financing of a firm, and (3) the ability of the bank to distribute future cash dividends.

FINANCIAL RATIOS

Useful ratios using data from the statement of cash flows statement, the income statement, and the balance sheet can be constructed:

1. Quality of Earnings (to support current level of operations and to generate future earnings):

    (a) Net income to cash provided by operating income: Net income/Cash provided by operating activities

    (b) Reinvestment activities: Capital investments/Depreciation + Proceeds from sale of assets

    (c) Cash flow for adequacy:
    Cash provided by operating activities/Cash investments + Inventory additions + Dividends + Debt uses

2. Financial Management (reliance on outside financing for growth):

 (a)   Cash provided by sources:
        (i)   Cash provided by operating activities/Total sources of cash
        (ii)   Cash provided by investing activities/Total sources of cash
        (iii) Cash provided from financing activities/Total sources of cash

 (b)   Productivity ratio: Cash from operating activities/Capital investments

 (c)   Cash flow per share of outstanding common stock: Net increase in cash/number of common shares outstanding

 3. Mandatory Cash Flows (primarily interest and repayment of principal):

 (a)   Long-term debt payment ratio: Cash applied to long-term debt/Funds supplied by long-term debt

 (b)   Total fund sources required for long-term debt: Cash applied to long-term debt/Total cash sources

 4. Discretionary Cash Flows (e.g., for dividends, to acquire other companies, to invest in short-term securities):

 (a)   Discretionary cash uses/Total sources of cash

 (b)   Individual discretionary use (e.g., dividends)/Total discretionary uses

 (c)   Dividend payout of cash from operating activities/Cash from operating activities

KEY DEFINITIONS

Cash equivalents Cash equivalents are short-term, highly liquid investments that are both (a) readily convertible to cash and (b) near their maturity so that they present insignificant risk of changes in interest rates. Generally, only investments with original maturities of three months or less qualify. Examples include treasury bills, commercial paper, and money market funds, purchased with cash that is in excess of money needs.

Direct approach A method of determining "net cash provided by operating activities" whereby cash receipts from revenues are compared with cash payments for expenses.

Financial flexibility The capacity to adapt to favorable and unfavorable changes in operating conditions.

Financing activities Cash flow activities that are associated with liability and stockholders' equity items and include (a) obtaining cash from creditors and repaying amounts borrowed and (b) obtaining capital from owners and providing them with a return on their investment (dividends).

Indirect approach A method for determining "net cash provided by operating activities," whereby net income is adjusted for items that did not affect cash to reconcile to net cash provided by operating activities.

Investing activities Cash flows that include (a) lending and collecting loans and (b) acquiring and disposing investments and productive long-lived assets.

Liquidity An indication of the nearness to cash of the assets and liabilities of an enterprise.

Operating activities Cash flows that include the cash impacts of transactions that are related to net income for the period.

Statement of cash flows A basic financial statement that provides information about the cash receipts and cash payments of a bank or other enterprise during a period, classified as operating, investing, and financing activities. The statement reconciles the beginning and ending cash balances.

Chapter 8

Liabilities: Recognition and Measurement

I n this chapter a selection of major liabilities that are encountered by banks and other entities are presented to provide an understanding of complexities associated with accounting for liabilities. The basic nature of liabilities was discussed in Chapter 5, "The Statement of Condition." In this chapter specific liabilities are discussed at some length: bonds payable, troubled-debt restructures, leases, pensions, post-retirement employee benefits, contingencies, and compensated absences. Deferred income tax liability is discussed in Chapter 9.

BONDS PAYABLE

A bond is a written, unconditional promise made under corporate seal in which the borrower promises to pay a specific sum at a determinable future date, together with interest at a fixed rate and at fixed dates. If bonds are sold above face value, they are sold at a premium, i.e., the effect interest rate is less than the nominal rate since the issuer received more than the face amount of the bonds but is required to pay interest only the face amount. If bonds are sold below face value, they are sold at a discount, i.e., the effective interest rate paid is more than the nominal rate since the issuer received less than the face amount of the bonds but is required to pay interest on the face amount.

The price of a bond can be determined by mathematical computation or from bond tables. The price of a bond is conceptualized as follows:

1. The present value at the effective rate of a series of interest payments, i.e., an annuity, and

2. The present value of the maturity value of the bond

Under the effective (market) interest rate method interest expense for any interest period is equal to the effective rate at the date of issuance times the carrying value of the bonds at the beginning of that interest period (effective interest rate × net book value).

To determine the price of a $1,000 four-year bond having a 7 percent nominal interest rate with interest payable semiannually purchased to yield 6 percent, use the following procedure:

Present value of maturity value at effective rate (3 %) for eight periods:	$ 789.41
$1,000 × .789409	
Present value of an annuity of eight interest payments of $35 each at effective interest rate of 3%:	245.69
$35 × 7.01969	
Price of the bond	$1,035.10

Now assume that a $10,000 bond, semiannual interest at 6 percent contract rate, maturing in six years, and the market rate of 5 percent, is issued for $10,514. The amortization table which follows presents the effective interest amounts and premium amortization for the first four periods:

Period	3% Cash Interest	2.5% Effective Interest	Decrease in Book Value	Book Value of Bond
0				$10,514.00
1	$ 300(a)	$ 262.85(b)	$ 37.15(c)	10,476.85(d)
2	300	261.92	38.08	10,438.77
3	300	260.97	39.03	10,399.74
4	300	259.99	40.01	10,359.73
	$1,200	$1,045.73	$154.27	

(a) 3% × $10,000
(b) 2.5% × $10,514.00
(c) $300 − $262.85
(d) $10,514.00 − $37.15

To illustrate bond discounts, assume that a company issued 12 percent bonds with a face value of $100,000 sold to yield 14 percent, for $95,233 (at a discount of $4,767). Interest is paid semiannually for three years. A partial discount accumulation schedule is presented here:

Period	6% Cash	7% Effective	Increase in Book Value	Book Value of Bonds
0				$ 95,233
1	$ 6,000(a)	$ 6,666(b)	$ 666(c)	95,899(d)
2	6,000	6,718	713	96,612
3	6,000	6,763	763	97,375
4	6,000	6,816	816	98,191
5	6,000	6,873	873	99,064
6	6,000	6,936	936	100,000
	$36,000	$40,767	$4,767	

(a) 6% × $100,000
(b) 7% × $95,233
(c) $6,666 − $6,000
(d) $95,233 + $666

Note that a discount increases and a premium decreases the amount of interest expense reported in the financial statements. Interest expense is recorded at a constant rate under the interest method.

Bond issue costs include certain costs incurred in preparing and selling a bond issue. Bond issue costs include legal, accounting, underwriting, commission, engraving, printing, registration, and promotion costs. These costs reduce the net proceeds from the bond issue, thus increasing the effective interest rate for the issuer. Bond issue costs are classified as a deferred charge (long-term asset) and not as a reduction of the premium or increase in the discount (APB Opinion No. 21, par. 16). Bond issue costs are expensed against revenues during the bond term.

Disclosure requirements relating to bond payable typically include interest rates, maturity dates, debt restrictions, call provisions and conversion privileges. Any assets pledged as collateral for debt also are disclosed. In addition, SFAS No. 47, "Disclosure of Long-Term Obligations," requires disclosure of the aggregate amount of maturities and sinking fund requirements for all long-term debt for each of the five years following the balance sheet date.

TROUBLED DEBT RESTRUCTURING

A troubled debt restructuring is a debt restructuring if the creditor, for economic or legal reasons related to the debtor's financial difficulties, grants a concession to the debtor that it would not otherwise consider at a point earlier than the scheduled maturity date. For a debt structuring to be troubled, the creditor must accept new debt or assets with an economic value less than the book value of the original debt. A restructuring consummated under reorganization, arrangement, or other provisions of the Federal bankruptcy act or other Federal statues related thereto is considered a troubled debt restructuring. Major creditors, including banks, supported the development of SFAS No. 15, "Accounting for Debtors and Creditors for Troubled Debt Restructuring," which became the official document for debt restructuring.

Generally, a debtor who can obtain funds from other than his or her existing creditor at an interest rate near the current rate for nontroubled debt is not a troubled debt restructuring even though the debtor may be experiencing difficulty.

The principal types of debt restructuring include a transfer of assets or equity interest from a debtor to a creditor in full settlement of a debt and a modification of terms. Modification of terms include such arrangements as interest-rate reductions, maturity-date extensions, reduction of the face amount or maturity amount of the debt as stated in the instrument or other agreement, and reduction of accrued interest. Debtors experience gains and creditors recognize losses on troubled debt restructurings.

Accounting Procedures

The accounting procedures for troubled debt restructurings involving a *settlement* can be summarized as follows for the debtor and creditor (Source: SFAS Statement No. 15):
Debtor:

1. The debtor recognizes an extraordinary gain equal to the difference between debt book value and market value of consideration paid.

2. The accounts related to the debt are removed.

3. A gain or loss on disposal is recognized equaling the difference between the market value and book value of consideration transferred (no gain or loss is recognized if the debtor issues stock).

Creditor:

1. The creditor records the consideration received at market value and recognizes an ordinary, unusual or infrequent, or extraordinary loss. The loss equals the difference between the recorded value of the investment or receivable less the market value of considerations received.

2. The accounts related to the investment or receivable are removed.

Accounting for a debt restructuing involving a *modification of terms* where the total restructured payments are less than the book value of the debt or receivable follows:
Debtor:

1. The debtor recognizes an extraordinary gain equal to the difference between debt book value and the sum of restructured cash flows.

2. The liability is reduced to the sum of the restructured cash flows.

3. All prestructure payments reduce the restructured debt; no further interest expense is recognized.

Creditor.

1. The creditor recognizes an ordinary, unusual or infrequent, or extraordinary loss. The loss equals the difference between investment or receivable book value and the sum of restructured cash flows.

2. The investment in receivable is reduced to the sum of the restructured cash flows.

3. All postrestructure receipts reduce the restructured investment; no further interest revenue is recognized.

When the total restructured flows exceed the book value of debt, the accounting by the debtor and creditor is as follows:

1. For both debtor and creditor, no entry is required at restructure date and no gain or loss is recognized.

2. No change is made to the book value of the old debt (receivable).

3. The rate of interest equating the old book value and present value of restructured cash flows is used to measure interest expense (revenue). This interest rate must be less than the prestructure effective rate (the creditor's concession).

4. Every restructured flow includes principal and interest except for those which immediately follow the restructure. The excess of restructured flows over the old book value represents interest recognized over the term of the restructured debt.

When only a portion of a debt is settled, the terms of the remaining portion may be modified. The amount of original debt settled is treated as a settlement at the market value of consideration transferred. No gain or loss is recognized on the settlement, and the remaining portion is treated as a modification of terms.

Financial Statement Disclosures

SFAS No. 15 requires extensive footnote disclosures for troubled debt restructures. These disclosures include a description of the restructure, amount of gain and loss and any tax effects, amounts contingently payable under the agreement, per share amount of gain or loss on debt extinguishment, and commitments to lend additional funds to debtors owing receivables whose terms were modified in the restructuring.

LEASES

A lease is a contract whereby real or personal property is provided by a lessor/owner to a lessee/renter for a specified period of time in exchange for compensation in the form of rent. Leases are usually entered into by a lessee primarily to acquire the right to use or control an asset. Leasing is popular because it can conserve cash, protect against obsolescence and interest rate changes.

In SFAS No. 13 as Amended and Interpreted through January 1990, a lease is defined "as an agreement conveying the right to use property, plant, or equipment usually for a stated period of time." A lessee is the party who acquires the right to use the property, plant, and equipment; a lessor is the party giving up the right.

Lease Classification

The basic objective of lease accounting is to recognize the economic substance of leases rather than their legal form. Lease classifications for financial accounting and reporting purposes can be summarized as to type and accounting method by lessee and lessor:

Type	Lessee	Lessor
Noncapitalized (no sale or purchase of asset assumed lease assumed)	Operating lease	Operating lease
Capitalized (sale and purchase of asset)	Capital lease	Sales-type lease Direct-financing lease Leveraged lease

The lessee classifies a lease as a capital lease if it meets any one of the following criteria:

1. The lease transfers ownership of the property to the lessee by the end of the lease term.

2. The lease contains an option to purchase the leased property at a bargain price.

3. The lease term is equal to or greater than 75 percent of the estimated economic life of the leased property.

4. The present value of rental and other minimum lease payments equals or exceeds 90 percent of the fair value of the leased property less any investment tax credit retained by the lessor.

If none of these criteria is met, the lease is an operating lease.

For the lessor, a lease must meet one of the four criteria specified for the lessee and both of the following criteria:

1. Collectibility of the minimum lease payments is reasonably predictable.

2. No important uncertainties surround the amount of nonreimbursable costs yet to be incurred by the lessor under the lease.

If none of these criteria are met, the lease is an operating lease. An operating lease is merely a rental agreement. An operating lease merely requires the recognition of the rental agreement requiring periodic payments for the use of an asset during that period. Rent expense or rent income is recognized on the income statement of the lessee and lessor, respectively. No new assets or liabilities are recorded.

Capital Lease

A capital lease for a lessee is, in substance, the purchase of an asset and the incurrence of a liability. A capital lease transfers substantially all of the ownership privileges, including the benefits and risks of property ownership, and represents in economic substance but not in legal form a purchase or sale of an asset. Such leases should be accounted for by the lessee as the acquisition of an asset and the incurrence of a liability.

A sales-type lease involves a transaction giving rise to a manufacturer's or dealer's profit (or loss) to the lessor. A profit exists when the fair value of the leased property at the inception of the lease is greater than its cost or carrying value. A direct financing lease does not involve a transaction giving rise to a manufacturer's or dealer's profit (or loss) to the lessor. In a direct financing lease, the fair value of the lease property at the inception of the lease equals its cost or carrying value.

A direct financing lease can be illustrated as follows:

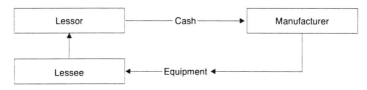

A sales-type lease is illustrated below:

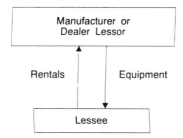

Lease disclosure requirements for both lessees and lessors are extensive and include data on payments to be made and descriptions of lease agreements for both capital and operating leases. When a lessor has lease receivables (and the lessee has lease payables) extending beyond one year (or the operating cycle of the business, if longer), the amount of the lease to be reported as a current asset by the lessor and as a current liability by the lessee must be determined. The lessor's total lease receivable, as well as the lessee's payable, should be reported at their present values using the interest rate applied to the lease. This also involves a separation of the current and long-term portion. A widely used approach recognizes the present value of the next year's payment as the current portion.

Leveraged Lease

A leveraged lease is a three-party lease involving a lessor, a lessee, and a long-term creditor, usually a bank or other financial institution. The long-term creditor provides nonrecourse financing to the lessor. The financing provides the lessor with substantial leverage in the transaction. For example, a contractor might agree to build an office building and lease it to a company. To finance the construction of the building, a bank lends money to the contractor (lessor). The contractor uses a relatively small amount of his or her own funds. The lessor-owner's return on the investment comes from lease rentals, investment tax credit, and income tax benefit from depreciation on the total cost of the property and interest expense deductions on the debt, and other expenses. The lessor classifies the leveraged lease as a direct financing lease. A leveraged lease is shown here:

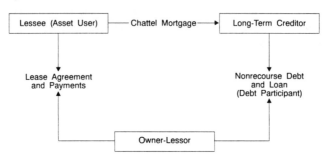

Sale-Leaseback

A sale-leaseback occurs when an owner sells property and then leases the same property back. The seller-lessee usually has a tax advantage in that the entire lease payment can be deducted, which can include interest and amortization of the cost of land and partially depreciated other real property. The sale-leaseback is often used when financing is a problem. From an accounting point of view, any profit or loss incurred by the seller-lessee from the sale of the asset under a capital lease is deferred and amortized over the lease term or the economic life of the asset. If the lease is an operating lease, any profit or loss on the sale should be deferred and amortized in proportion to the rental payments over the period the asset is used by the lessee.

Accounting for a Capital Lease

To illustrate the accounting for a capital lease, assume that Lessee Bank Company leases a piece of machinery for six years with an annual rental of $10,000 payable on December 31, 1990. The current market value of the asset is $50,000. The life of the leased asset is nine years, and the residual value is estimated to be $7,800. The company uses the straight-line method of depreciation.

This is a capital lease because the lease term of six years is less than 75 percent of the asset's nine-year life. The lessee makes the following entries:

Lessee's Entries

Dec. 31, 1990	Leasehold Rights	47,908	
	Liability Under Lease		47,908
	$10,000 × 4.79079 (PV of an annuity due in six payments at 10%)		
Dec. 31, 1990	Liability Under Lease	10,000	
	Cash		10,000
Dec. 31, 1991	Interest Expense	3,791	
	Liability Under Lease	6,209	
	Cash		10,000

	1990: ($50,000 − $12,092 discount) × 10% = $3,791		
	1991: ($40,000 − $8,301 discount) × 10% = $3,170		
Dec. 31, 1991	Amortization Expense	7,985	
	Accumulated Amortization		7,985
	1990: $47,908/6 years = 7,985		

From the lessor's viewpoint, this is a direct financing lease because the fair market value of the asset ($50,000) equals its cost. It is assumed that the lease meets the necessary requirements specified for a direct financing lease and that the investor's rate of return on the lease is 12 percent.

Lessor's Entries

Dec. 31, 1990	Investment in Lease	67,800	
	Equipment		50,000
	Unearned Interest		17,800
Dec. 31, 1990	Cash	10,000	
	Investment in lease		10,000
Dec. 31, 1991	Unearned Income	4,800	
	Interest Revenue		4,800

	1991:	Gross investment in lease	$67,800
		Deduct first rental	10,000
			$57,800
		Minus unearned interest	17,800
		Net investment	$40,000 × 12 =
		Interest revenue	$ 4,800

Real Estate Leases

Special accounting problems are associated with leases that include land, either alone or in combination with buildings or equipment. If a lease involves land only, it is classified as a capital lease if title to the land is certain to be transferred in the future or if transfer is reasonably based on a bargain purchase option. On the lessor's books, the lease must also meet both of the lessor's additional criteria to be classified as a capital lease.

If a lease includes both real estate and equipment, the equipment is accounted for separately in determining the classification by the lessee and lessor and is accounted for separately over the term of the lease. The real estate portion of the lease is classified and accounted for in accordance with the basic applicable real estate lease criteria.

Real Estate Duration

Duration analysis, or the sensitivity of an asset's value to changes in interest rates, has implications for real estate and lease transactions. Real estate can be diversified and leasing contract can be designed to accommodate different maturities and bond-like cash flows by altering the terms of the portfolio of leases. Further, leasing transactions can be indexed to inflation to provide investors with rates of return indexed to inflation. Duration analysis is relevant in the measurement of total portfolio duration for portfolios with a significant real estate content. Real estate investors own annuities with a claim on a residual (which is inflation sensitive). Investors have some control over the duration of the asset through the contracting negotiations. Investors should also realize that market conditions influence the duration of real estate.

PENSIONS

A pension is an allowance, annuity, or subsidy. A pension plan is an arrangement whereby an employer agrees to provide benefits to retired employees. A pension plan may be either contributory or noncontributory. In a contributory plan both employer and employee contribute to the fund from which benefits are to be paid. In a noncontributory plan only the employer makes contributions to the fund (Source: *SFAS No. 87,* "Employers Accounting for Pensions," and SFAS No. 88, "Employers' Accounting for Settlements and Curtailments of Defined Benefit Pension Plans and for Termination Benefits").

Pension Features

A *single-employer plan* is a pension plan established unilaterally by an employer. *Multi-employer plans* are sometimes established within an industry.

The *funding* aspect of pension plans are important features of any plan. Funding means to pay to a funding agency. Funding also refers to assets accumulated by a funding agency to provide retirement benefits when they come due. Pension costs that have been paid over to a funding agency are said to have been funded. A funding agency is an organization or individual, such as an insurance company or a trustee, who accumulates assets which will be used for the payments of benefits under the plan and who administers the program. Terminal funding occurs when the benefits payable to a retired employee are funded in full at the time the employee retires; there is no funding for active employees. Pay-as-you-go funding does not provide any prior funding for retirement benefits but provides resources for the pensions as they come due after retirement.

In an insured pension plan, annuities are purchased for employees under individual or group annuity contracts between an employer and an insurance company. The insurance company guarantees the payment of benefits. Noninsured plans are generally funded by a trust agreement between an employer and a trust company.

When pension benefits are no longer contingent on an employee's continued employment, the employee's benefits under the plan are said to be *vested benefits.* When benefits vest, an employee's pension rights cannot be reduced or taken away.

A *defined benefit plan* is a plan that states the benefits to be received by employees after retirement or the method of determining such benefits. A *defined contribution plan* is one in which the employer's contribution is determined based on a specified formula. Future benefits are limited to those that the plan can provide. A defined contribution plan specifies the amount of the periodic contributions to be paid by the plan's sponsor (not the benefits to be received by a participant). Benefits are usually based on amount credited to an individual's account.

Determination of Pension Cost

Pension cost is a net amount computed by adding six facts:

1. *Service Cost* The actuarial present value of benefits attributed by the pension benefit formula to employee service during the current period.

2. *Interest on Projected Benefit Obligation* The increase in the amount of the projected benefit obligation due to the passage of time. The projected benefit obligation is the actuarial present value as of a date of all benefits attributed by the pension benefit formula to employee service rendered prior to that date. The projected benefit obligation is measured using assumptions as to future compensation levels.

3. *Actual Return on Plan Assets* The difference in the fair value of plan assets at the beginning and the end of the period adjusted for contributions made to the plan and benefit payments made by the plan during the period.

4. *Prior Service Cost* Retroactive adjustments that are granted to recognize services rendered in the previous period. These costs are caused by either an amendment to an existing plan or the initiation of a new plan where a retroactive allowance is made for past services rendered.

5. *Gain or loss* The change in the amount of the projected benefit obligation as well as the change in the value of an assets resulting from experience being different from that assumed or from a change in an actuarial assumption.

Pension plan settlements, curtailments, and termination benefits are events that require immediate recognition of gains or losses.

Minimum Pension Liability

A *minimum liability* must be recognized to the extent that the accumulated benefit obligation at year end exceeds the fair value of plan assets at year end. The accumulated benefit obligation is the actuarial present value of benefits attributed by the pension benefit formula to employee services rendered before a specific date and based on employee services and compensation prior to that date. The amount of the additional liability should take into consideration any existing balance in the Accrued/Prepaid Pension Cost account. The account that offsets the Additional Liability account when an adjustment is required is an intangible asset referred to as a Deferred Pension Cost. When the value assigned to the Deferred Pension Cost account would exceed the amount of unrecognized prior service cost, the excess should be charged to a contra-equity account reported as a deduction from total stockholders' equity referred to as Net Loss Not Recognized as Pension Expense.

Pension Disclosures

An employer's financial statements shall include the following disclosures concerning defined benefit pension plans:

1. A description of the plan including employee groups covered, type of benefit formula, funding policy, types of assets held, significant nonbenefit liabilities, and the effect of significant matters affecting comparability of information for all periods presented.

2. The amount of net periodic pension cost for the period, showing separately the service cost component, the interest cost component, the return on plan assets for the period, and the net total of all other components.

3. A schedule reconciling the funded status of the plan with amounts reported in the employer's statement of financial position.

Pension plans, an accounting entity distinct from the employer, are subject to separate accounting and reporting guidelines. The major objective of plan financial statements is to provide information useful in assessing the present and future ability of the plan to pay benefits when due. Information about assets and benefits of the plan must appear in the plan financial statements. The value of accumulated benefits of participants is treated as the equity of the pension plan, and equals the plan assets at fair value less plan liabilities.

Pension Fund Management

Pension funds have both assets and liabilities to manage. Pension fund managers typically focus only or mainly on the assets associated with pension funds. The allocation of assets within the fund is usually determined by considering the trade-off between risk and return. Optimizing a portfolio's expected return within defined risk parameters is the objective to be attained for the asset side of the equation. The pension fund portfolio is expected to settle specific pension fund liabilities that are difficult to measure and extremely long term. To ignore the liability side of the issue is to take undue risks. The fund managers must focus on managing the difference between the fair value of the assets and the book value of the liabilities at current market interest rates, i.e., surplus management. The problem becomes increasingly complex as the company or bank grows and matures. SFAS No. 87 gives little or no guidance regarding this management problem.

The analysis of duration, or the sensitivity of an asset's value to changes in interest rates, has applications to pension fund management. Fund managers should place some emphasis on duration matching and define risk as including liabilities. This is especially important where matching focuses on the interest-rate sensitivity of assets and liabilities. Also, short-term and long-term benefit streams should be provided in funds that are denominated in real purchasing power (adjusted for changing general price levels). These additional dimensions can make the portfolio asset allocation between equities versus bonds more significant.

POSTRETIREMENT BENEFITS OTHER THAN PENSIONS

SFAS No. 106, "Employers' Accounting for Postretirement Benefits Other Than Pensions," establishes standards for all forms of postretirement benefits, including health care benefits. Prior to SFAS No. 106, postretirement benefits were usually accounted for on a pay-as-you-go (cash) basis. According to SFAS No. 106, the amount recognized in an employer's financial statements as the cost of postretirement benefit plan for a period consists of the following: service cost, interest cost, actual return on plan assets, gain or loss, amortization of unrecognized prior service cost, and amortization of the unrecognized transition obligation or asset.

The disclosure requirements include the following:

1. Description of substantive plan (basis for accounting)

2. Amount of net periodic postretirement benefit cost

3. Schedule, reconciling funded status of plan with amounts reported in employer's statement of financial position

4. Weighted-average discount rate and rate of compensation increase used to measure the accumulated postretirement benefit obligation and the weighted average expected long-term rate of return on plan assets

5. Assumed health care cost trend rates used to measure expected cost of benefits for next year and any patterns of change in the trend rates, thereafter

6. Approximate amount of annual benefits of employees and retirees covered by annuity contracts issued by employer and related parties

7. Alternative amortization method used

8. Effect of a one-percentage-point increase in assumed health care cost trend rated on (a) aggregate of service and interest cost components of net periodic postretirement health care benefit cost and (b) accumulated postretirement benefit obligation for health care benefits

CONTINGENCIES

A contingency is an existing condition, situation, or set of circumstances involving uncertainty as to possible gain or loss to an enterprise that will ultimately be resolved when one or more future events occurs or fails to occur (SFAS No. 5). Gain contingencies do not receive accounting recognition. Loss contingencies are related to the possible incurrence of liabilities or the impairment of assets. Examples of loss contingencies include collectibility of receivables, obligations related to warranties, litigation, claims and assessments, and the guarantee of indebtedness of others.

Three terms are used to describe the range of possibilities of an event occurring: probable, reasonably possible, and remote. Different accounting is prescribed for contingencies which fall within these ranges:

Term	Definition	Accounting
Probable	The future event is likely to occur.	Record the probable event in the accounts if the amount can be reasonably estimated. If not estimable, disclose in a note.

Term	Definition	Accounting
Reasonably possible	The chance of the future event occurring is more than remote but less than likely.	Report the contingency in a note.
Remote	The change of the future event occurring is slight.	No recording or reporting unless contingency represents a guarantee. Then disclose in a note.

Loss contingencies related to general or unspecified business risks, such as losses related to a strike or recession, are not disclosed in the financial statements because they are public matters.

COMPENSATED ABSENCES

Compensated absences are absences from employment for which it is expected that employees will be paid. Compensated absences include vacations, illness, holidays, and others. SFAS No. 43, "Accounting for Compensated Absences," requires that a liability be accrued for the cost of compensation for future absences if all of the following conditions are met:

1. The employer's obligation relating to employees' rights to receive compensation for future absences is attributable to employee's services already rendered.
2. The obligation relates to the rights that vest or accumulate.
3. Payment of the compensation is probable.
4. The amount can be reasonably estimated.

A modification of the general rules relates to sick pay. If sick pay benefits vest, accrual is required. If they accumulate but do not vest, accrual is allowed.

The expense and the related liability for compensated absences should be recognized in the period in which they are earned by employees.

KEY DEFINITIONS

Bonds Payable

Amortization The process of allocating an amount to expense over the periods benefitted.

Bond issue costs Costs related to issuing a bond.

Carrying value The face amount of a debt issue increased or decreased by the related unamortized premium or discount and issue costs.

Debenture Long-term debt not secured by collateral.

Defeasance Extinguishment of debt.

Effective interest method The method of amortizing the discount or premium to interest expense so as to result in a constant rate of interest when applied to the amount of debt outstanding at the beginning of any period.

Face value The stated amount due on the maturity date.

In-substance defeasance The irrevocable placement of assets into a trust for the sole purpose of paying interest and principal on the debt. The debtor does not actually pay the creditor.

Market rate The current rate of interest available for obligations issued under the same terms and conditions.

Maturity value See face value.

Principal See face value.

Refunding A bond issue is replaced with another bond issue.

Stated rate The interest rate written on the face of a debt instrument.

Straight-line method The method of amortizing the premium or discount to interest expense such that there is an even allocation of interest expense over the life of the debt.

Troubled Debt Restructure

Troubled debt restructure Occurs when the creditor, for economic or legal reasons related to the debtor's financial difficulties, grants a concession to the debtor (deferment or reduction of interest or principal obligation) that it would not otherwise consider.

Leases

Bargain purchase option A provision allowing the lessee to purchase property at the end of the life of the lease at a price so favorable that the exercise of the option appears to be reasonably assured.

Bargain renewal option A provision allowing the lessee to renew the lease for a rental that is so favorable that the exercise of the option appears to be reasonably assured.

Capital lease A lease treated by the lessee as both the borrowing of funds and the acquisition of an asset to be amortized. Both the liability and the asset are recognized on the balance sheet.

Direct financing lease A lease in which the lessor "sells" the asset at a fair market value equal to its cost or carrying value and records a receivable. No manufacturer's or dealer's profit (or loss) arises out of a direct financing lease. Expenses consist of interest on the debt and amortization of the asset. The lessor treats the lease as a sale of the asset in return for a series of future cash receipts.

Executory costs Ownership-type costs, such as insurance, maintenance, and property taxes.

Guarantee residual value The portion of the estimated residual value of the leased property that is guaranteed by the lessee or by a third party unrelated to the lessor.

Initial direct costs Costs incurred by the lessor to originate a lease that result directly from and are essential to acquiring that lease and would not have been incurred had that leasing transaction not occurred.

Interest rate implicit in the lease The interest (discount) rate that, when applied on a present value basis to the sum of the minimum lease payments and any unguaranteed residual value accruing to the lessor, causes the resulting aggregate present value to be equal to the fair value of the leased property to the lessor.

Lease A contract requiring the lessee to pay the lessor for the use of an asset for a specific period of time in return for stipulated cash payments.

Lease term The duration of the lease, which may be from a brief period to the full economic life of the leased property.

Lessee's incremental borrowing rate The rate that, at the inception of the lease, the lessee, over a similiar term, would have incurred to borrow the funds necessary to purchase the leased property.

Leveraged lease A direct-financing lease in which a long-term creditor advances funds to the lessor for the purpose of purchasing an asset for lease. The leverage lease can provides the lessor with significant tax advantages.

Manufacturer's or dealer's profit or loss The difference between the fair value of the property at the inception of the lease and the cost or carrying amount of the leased asset.

Minimum lease payments The payments that are required or that may be required to be paid by the lessee to the lessor over the life of the lease.

Operating lease A lease accounted for by the lessee without showing an asset for the lease rights or a liability for the lease payment obligations. Rental payments are reported as expenses of the period. The asset remains on the lessor's books where rental collections are reported as revenues.

Sale-leaseback An arrangement whereby one party sells an asset, then leases the asset from the buyer. The seller retains the use of the asset in a sale-leaseback arrangement. Any profit on the sale should be amortized over the lease term.

Sales-type lease A capital lease in which the lessor "sells" the asset and records an investment in a lease or a receivable. In sales-type leases the fair market value of the asset that is "sold" differs from its cost or carrying value. A dealer's or manufacturer's profit or loss occurs in a sales-type lease.

Sublease The leasing of property by a lessee (the sublessor) to a new lessee (the sublessee). The general lease classification rules apply to the sublease arrangement.

Unguaranteed residual value That portion of the estimated residual value of the lease property that is not guaranteed by the lessee or by a third party unrelated to the lessor.

Pensions and Postretirement Benefits

Accumulated benefit obligations The actuarial present value of all the benefits attributed by the pension benefit formula to employee service rendered before a specified date. The amount is based on current and past compensation levels of the employees and therefore includes no assumptions about future pay increases.

Actual return on plan assets The difference between the fair value of the plan assets at the end of the period and the fair value at the beginning of the period, adjusted for contributions and payments of benefits during the period.

Actuarial funding method Any of several techniques that actuaries use in determining the amounts and timing of employer contributions to provide for pension benefits.

Additional pension liability An additional pension liability that may have to be recognized if the accumulated benefit obligation is greater than the fair value of the plan assets at the end of the period.

Contributory plan A pension plan where employees bear part of the cost of the plan and make contributions from their salary into the pension fund. Under noncontributory plans, the employee pays the entire cost of the plan.

Defined benefit plan A pension plan that either specifically states the benefits to be received by employees after retirement or the method of determining such benefits.

Defined contribution plan A pension plan where the employer's contribution is determined based on a specified formula, and any future benefits are limited to those contributions and the returns earned on the investment of those contributions.

Discount rate The rate at which the pension benefits can be effectively settled.

Employee Retirement Income Security Act of 1974 (ERISA) The Pension Reform Act of 1974 that attempted to correct standards for operation and maintenance of pension funds in an effort to correct reported abuses in pension funds. The Act provides guidelines for employee participation in pension plans, vesting provisions, minimum funding requirements, financial statement disclosure, and the administration of the plan. The Act requires the filing of annual reports with the Department of Labor that include a description of the plan and copies of the relevant financial statements. The Act created the Pension Benefit Guaranty Corporation (PBGC) that provides benefits to employees covered by plans that have been terminated. The PBGC is funded by an annual fee from every employee covered by the plan that is subject to the PBGC. The PBGC can also impose a lien against the net assets of the company.

Expected return on plan assets An amount calculated by applying the expected long-term rate of return on plan assets to the fair market value of the plan assets at the beginning of the period.

Gain or loss A change in the value of either the projected benefit obligation or the plan assets resulting from experience different from that assumed or from a change in an actuarial assumption.

Interest cost The increase in the projected benefit obligation due to the passage of time.

Multi-employer plan A pension plan that involves two or more unrelated companies in which assets contributed by each company are available to pay benefits to the employees of all the involved companies.

Net periodic pension expense The pension expense recognized by a company including five elements: service cost, interest cost, actual return on plan assets, amortization of unrecognized prior service cost, and gain or loss.

Pension A plan providing employee retirement benefits after they retire for services provided while employed.

Pension benefit formula The basis for determining payments to which employees will be entitled during retirement.

Postretirement benefit plans Pensions, health care services, life insurance, tuition assistance, legal and tax services, day care, housing subsidies, and other benefits provided to employees after retirement.

Prior service cost The cost of retroactive benefits granted in a plan amendment or at the initial adoption of the plan. The cost is the present value of the additional benefits attributed by the pension benefit formula.

Projected benefit obligation The actuarial present value, at a specified date, of all the benefits attributed by the pension benefit formula to employee service rendered prior to that date. The amount includes future increases in compensation that the company projects that it will pay to employees during the remainder of their employment, if the pension benefit formula is based on those future compensation levels. The projected benefit obligation differs from the accumulated benefit obligation in that it includes anticipated future pay increases.

Service cost The actuarial present value of benefits attributed by the pension benefit formula to services rendered by employees during the current period.

Vested benefits Benefits for which the employee's right to receive a present or future pension benefit is no longer contingent on remaining in the service of the employer.

Contingencies

Contingency An existing condition, situation, or set of circumstances involving uncertainty as to possible gain or loss to an enterprise that will ultimately be resolved when one or more future events occur or fail to occur.

Gain contingency An existing condition or set of circumstances involving uncertainty as to possible gain.

Loss contingency An existing condition or set of circumstances involving uncertainty as to possible loss.

Probable The future event is likely to occur.

Reasonably possible The chance of occurrence of the future event is more than remote but less than likely.

Remote The chance of occurrence of the future event is slight.

Compensated Absences

Compensated absence Vacations, holidays, sick days, and other absences away from work during which time the regular salary or wage of an employee is continued.

Nonvesting Accumulated rights employees are not entitled to if employment ceases.

Vesting Accumulated rights employees are entitled to if employment ceases.

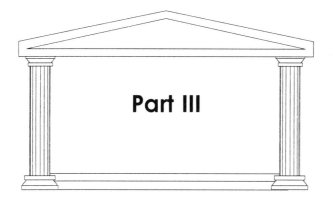

Part III

Topics in Federal Income Taxes

Chapter 9

Income Taxes and Interperiod Tax Allocation

Part I INCOME TAXES

The income tax system in the United States is a progressive tax reflecting the ability-to-pay principle of taxation. With a progressive tax the percentage of income paid in taxes increases with income. The marginal tax rate is the rate at which the last dollar of income of taxable income is taxed. Under a progressive tax the marginal tax increases as income increases. The average tax rate is the ratio of an individual's total taxes to total earned income. Average tax rates are lower than marginal tax rates because federal income taxes are levied only on a portion of income.

The Constitution of the United States and the Internal Revenue Code are the foundation of tax law. The Treasury department issues *regulations* as interpretations of the statute. Regulations can be classified as interpretative or statutory. Congress has delegated its rule-making authority to the Treasury.

THE LEGISLATIVE PROCESS

The legislative process begins in the House of Representatives. The Ways and Means Committee of the House is the committee responsible for initiating statutory changes related to tax legislation. The committee reports proposed legislation to the floor of the House for consideration. Legislation approved by a majority vote in the House goes to the Senate to be considered by the Senate Finance Committee. The proposed legislation then moves to the full Senate. Upon approval by the Senate, the bill goes to the President for approval or veto, provided the House and Senate versions of the legislation are in agreement. Should the president sign the bill, it becomes law. Congress can override a presidential veto by a vote of at least two-thirds of the members of each house of Congress.

TAX COURTS

The court system proves three tax trial courts: the U.S. Tax Court, the U.S. Claims Court, and U.S. District Courts. A taxpayer can begin litigation in any of these courts. If the taxpayer wants to litigate either in a U.S. District Court or in the U.S. Claims Court, he or she must first pay the additional tax that the IRS claims is due. The taxpayer would then file a claim for refunds which the IRS will deny. The tax suit would usually follow. If a taxpayer starts litigation in the Tax Court, payment of the deficiency need not take place until the case has been decided.

Appeals from Tax Court and U.S. District Court decisions are made to the Court of Appeals for the taxpayer's circuit. Decisions of the U.S. Claims Court can be appealed to the Court of Appeals for the Federal Circuit. The Federal Circuit hears cases that originate in the Claims Court. The party losing at the Court of Appeals level can appeal to the Supreme Court (see Figure 9-1).

BUSINESS ENTITIES SUBJECT TO TAXATION

Congress has the power to levy and collect taxes on incomes. Because the purposes and policies of tax accounting (for example, related to revenue-producing activities) and financial accounting (for example, related to investment and credit needs) frequently differ, accounting practices also differ. As a general rule, the Internal Revenue Service accepts any accounting method that clearly reflects income as long as the tax statutes and regulations are followed.

Figure 9-1

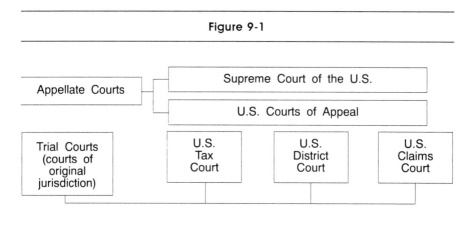

Sole proprietors are not separate taxable entities. The owner of the business reports business transactions on his or her individual income tax return. Partnerships are not subject to the income tax. The results of partnership operations flow through to the individual partners. Estates and trusts have similarities to the partnership in that income is taxed only once. However, the tax may be imposed on the estate or trust. Whether the income of an estate or trust is taxed to the estate or trust or to the beneficiary generally depends on whether the income is retained by the entity or distributed to the beneficiary. The corporation is taxed as a separate taxpaying entity. Corporate income is taxed again to the shareholder when distributed as dividends, subject to certain limitations. Subchapter S corporations are usually treated as partnerships and so frequently can avoid taxes at the corporate level.

Corporations, including banks, can select a calendar year or a fiscal year for reporting purposes, as can individuals. A change in accounting period generally requires the approval of the IRS. Corporations can use a variety of accounting methods depending upon the surrounding circumstances: the cash or accrual method, the installment method, or the percentage of completion and the completed contract method when long-term contracts are involved. Corporations that are members of a parent-subsidiary group can file a consolidated income tax return for a taxable year. The affiliated group is considered to constitute a single taxable entity, although the members of the group are legally separate entities. Corporate income taxes are computed for the 1990 tax year according to the following schedule:

If taxable income is:	The tax rate is:
$0 to $50,000	15%
50,000 to 75,000	25%
75,000 to 100,000	34%
100,000 to 335,000	39%
335,000 and above	34%

A trust is an arrangement created either by will or by an inter vivos declaration whereby trustees take title to property for the purpose of protecting it or conserving it for the beneficiaries. A trust is a separate taxpaying entity. Trusts may be created by transferring property to the trust. The property is administered by a trustee for the benefit of the beneficiary. The trustee may be either an individual or an institution, such as a bank. The tax is calculated on Form 1041. Tax rate schedules for estates and trusts for 1990 are shown here:

If taxable income is:		The tax is:			
Over	But Not Over				Of the Amount Over
$ 0	$ 5,450			15%	$0
5,450	14,150	$ 817.50	+	28%	5,450
14,150	28,320	3,253.50	+	33%	14,150
28,320	—			28%	-0-

Estate taxes apply to the disposition of property that occurs as a result of the transferor's death. The estate tax is a wealth transfer tax, not an income tax. The tax base for the federal estate tax is the total of the decedent's (1) taxable estate and (2) adjusted taxable gifts (post-1976 taxable gifts). After the gross tax liability on the tax base is determined, various credits, including the unified credit, are deducted to arrive at the net estate tax payable. Form 706 is used for the U.S. estate tax return if the gross estate exceeds a $600,000 exemption. The unified federal estate and gift tax rates are applicable to estates of decedents dying, or to gifts made, after 1983 but before 1993.

CONSOLIDATED TAX RETURNS

An affiliated corporation consists of a parent corporation and at least one subsidiary corporation. Affiliated corporations have two options for filing their federal income tax returns:

1. Each member of the group can file separate tax returns. The group can elect to claim a 100 percent dividends-received deduction for intragroup dividends.

2. The affiliated group can file a single tax return (a consolidated return) that reports the results for all group members.

When a consolidated return is filed, special treatment is given to transactions between group members for such transactions as gains and losses on intercompany transactions and intragroup dividends. Code Sections 1501 through 1504 contain the primary statutory provisions governing the filing of a consolidated tax return.

To file a consolidate return, certain stock ownership requirements must be satisfied:

1. A parent corporation must directly own stock having at least 80 percent of the total voting power of all classes of stock entitled to vote and at least 80 percent of the total value of all outstanding stock in at least one includable corporation.

2. For each other corporation eligible to be included in the affiliated group, stock having at least 80 percent of the total voting power of all classes of stock entitled to vote and at least 80 percent of the total value of all outstanding stock must be owned directly by the parent corporation and the other group members.

BANK SPECIFIC TAX RULES

Commercial banks and thrift institutions generally have the same income and deductions as other corporations and are subject to the same income taxes as such corporations. However, there are certain rules that apply specifically to commercial banks and thrift institutions.

For purposes of the Internal Revenue Code, the term "bank" includes those institutions subject to federal or state bank supervisory authorities and a substantial part of whose business involves receiving deposits and making loans and discounts or of exercising fiduciary powers similar to those allowed national banks. Thrift institutions are domestic building and loan associations, savings and loan associations, mutual savings banks, or cooperative nonprofit mutual banks. At least 60 percent of these institutions' assets must consist of certain "qualifying assets."

The Tax Reform Act of 1986 made significant changes in the tax law. It has a major impact on banks and banking activities. Several of these will be noted.

A bank can deduct bad debts using the reserve method (experience method). The Act did away with any deduction under the reserve method for large banks (banks with more than $500 million in assets). The effect was to require large banks to use the direct charge-off method (deduct band debts in the year that specific loans are identified as worthless).

Net operating loss deductions can be carried back 3 years, but forward 15 years. A commercial bank is allowed that portion of the net operating loss which is attributed to the bad debt deduction to be carried back 10 years and forward 5 years.

Interest expense incurred to acquire or carry tax-exempt obligations is disallowed to the extent of 100 percent disallowance beginning with the bank's first taxable year ending after 1986. Banks can continue to take a 20 percent disallowance for tax-exempt obligations acquired after January 1, 1983, and on or before August 7, 1986. An exception to the 100 percent disallowance rule is made for "qualified tax exempt obligations," which are subject to the 20 percent rule.

The cash method of accounting cannot be used for any corporation (except S corporations) having average annual gross receipts of more than $5 million for the three preceding taxable years. Adjustments to taxable income resulting from the change to the accrual method will be absorbed over a period of not more than 4 years.

The investment tax credit of 6 percent to 10 percent has been repealed for any property placed in service after December 31, 1985, unless acquired under a binding contract that was binding on the taxpayer prior to December 31, 1985.

Deductions for certain travel and entertainment expenses have been reduced to 80 percent of the expenses incurred. Meal expense is deductible only if directly related to business and the meal followed or preceded a substantial business discussion. Detailed records must be kept by the taxpayer.

The tax law allows qualified individuals to elect to deduct losses on deposits arising from the insolvency or bankruptcy of a qualified financial institution as a casualty loss in the year in which the amount of the loss is reasonably estimated. A commercial bank (as defined in Sec. 581) is a qualified financial institution. Qualified individuals can claim the loss in a later year either as a casualty loss deduction or as a bad debt deduction. The amount of the loss recognized is the difference between the taxpayer's basis in the deposit and the amount which is a reasonable estimate of the deposit amount that will eventually be received. If a loss has been deducted but is later recovered, then the lesser of the recovery amount or the tax benefit received from the election is included in income in the year of the recovery.

TAX PLANNING

Tax law offers many opportunities for tax planning. Staff accountants and lawyers as well as outside tax advisors should be able to provide adequate tax advice to bank officers. Reducing tax liabilities can obviously have a significant impact on a bank's earnings and cash flows.

Tax planning includes (1) avoiding detrimental results and (2) achieving favorable results. Some tax plans involve one isolated transaction. Others reflect an ongoing program that requires periodic review.

Some tax planning opportunities are mentioned in this section to indicate some areas where planning can be productive.

Deferring Taxes As a general rule, taxable income should be deferred as long as possible and tax deduction should be taken as soon as available. This works well when tax rates between years either stay the same or decrease in the succeeding year. However, if tax rates are expected to be higher in succeeding years, it may be wise to accelerate income and defer deductions. Deferring taxes generally has the same impact as interest-free time deposits.

Investment Income It may be possible for a bank to arrange its investments activities to defer income to next year or to accelerate income into the current year. For example, a bank could purchase Treasury bills that do not pay interest until next year. Or, a bank could purchase notes that pay interest before year-end.

Reduced Tax Rate Benefit An affiliated group may elect to apportion the tax benefits of the 15 percent and 25 percent tax rates to the member corporations in any manner that they elect. Otherwise, the $50,000 and $25,000 amounts for the two reduced tax rate brackets are divided equally among all the corporations in the group.

Net Operating Loss Carryovers/Carrybacks The tax law allows a corporation that incurs a net operating loss (NOL) for the year two choices:

1. Carry the NOL back to the third, second, and first preceding years in that order, and then forward to the succeeding 15 years in order until it is used up. Banks usually make this election. (The Tax Reform Act of 1986 allows banks to carry back a loss attributable to bad loans 10 years until 1994.)

2. Carry the NOL forward to the 15 successive years.

A company might elect to carry the NOL forward to the 15 successive years if it anticipates that future income will be taxed at higher income tax rates than in the past. Income taxes in the future may be greater than in the past because (1) enacted income tax rates may increase or (2) a higher level of future income may place the company in a higher income tax bracket. If the loss is carried back, the company can expect to receive the tax refund in the near future. If the company required immediate cash, the carryback option can be attractive.

Alternative Minimum Tax Elections (AMT) The Tax Reform Act of 1986 requires that banks and other corporations, individuals, estates and trusts pay the higher of their regular income taxes or an alternative minimum tax. This tax equals the amount by which the tentative minimum tax exceeds the regular tax. This usually requires the bank to calculate its taxes twice. Currently banks are subject to a 20 percent AMT computed on regular taxable income plus tax preferences and adjusted for income, gain, deduction, and loss items that must be recomputed under the alternative minimum tax system. If the AMT is larger than the regular tax, the bank must pay the AMT.

The tax law makes available under AMT rules the opportunity to defer the claiming of certain deductions for income tax purposes. By deferring these deductions, the taxpayer will increase regular tax liability but can obtain an overall savings by reducing the taxpayer's AMT liability. First, Code Section 59(e) allows an extended write-off period to apply to certain expenditures that otherwise would be a tax preference item. If the extended write-off period is elected, the Code exempts each expenditure from being a tax preference item.

Another election allows a taxpayer to elect to use the depreciation method generally required for AMT purposes (the 150 percent declining balance method over the property's class life) in computing the regular tax liability. This election allows the taxpayer to change the depreciation method from the 200 percent declining balance method to the 150 percent declining balance method, and the depreciation period from the property's recovery period specified in Accelerated Cost Recovery System (ACRS) rules to its class life.

Filing a Consolidated Tax Return An affiliate group is a chain of corporations connected through stock ownership with a common parent corporation. An election to file a consolidated return is binding on all subsequent tax years unless the IRS allows the group permission to discontinue filing a consolidated return or until the affiliated group is terminated. Some states do not allow the filing of a consolidated tax return for state income tax purposes.

By filing a consolidated tax return, an affiliated group has the opportunity to offset one member's current NOL against the taxable income of other group members. The separate return losses of one affiliated group member may be offset against the taxable income of other group members in the current tax years, providing an immediate tax benefit. Capital losses of one group member may also be offset against the capital gains of other group members in the current tax year. This allows the taxpayer to avoid carrying losses to subsequent tax years. On the other hand, operating losses and capital losses of group members may reduce or eliminate the opportunity for profitable group members to take advantage of credits or deductions by lowering certain credit or deduction limitations.

Dividends paid from one group member to a second group member are eliminated in the consolidated tax return. The 100 percent dividends-received deduction election could be used by the affiliated group to exempt from taxation dividends received from corporations that are not eligible to be included in the consolidated return.

Gains on intercompany transactions are deferred until a subsequent year. Loses on inter-company transactions are deferred until a subsequent year, which could be a disadvantage.

Calculation of the alternative minimum tax liability is computed on a consolidated basis and might reduce the negative impact of the tax preference items and certain other adjustments, thereby allowing the affiliated group to avoid paying an alternative minimum tax liability.

Accumulated Earnings Tax Corporations that do not distribute their earnings for a taxable year may be subject either to a tax on improper accumulation of earnings or to a tax on undistributed personal holding company income. Controllers should take the necessary measures to avoid such taxes.

Bank Acquisitions If a bank acquires a corporation and pays in excess of fair market value, the excess is assigned to goodwill. Deductions for goodwill are not tax deductible. Every effort should be taken to allocate the excess to assets which can be depreciated or amortized to obtain the maximum deductions.

Loan Points It may be possible to defer loan points and loan fees by carefully structuring the transaction. If a borrower pays the points, the bank has taxable income. If the bank arranged to finance the points, the income can be deferred over the life of the loan.

Reimbursing Business Travel Expenses Currently the deduction allowed for business meals is limited to 80 percent of cost. When a bank reimburses employees for travel away from home at a fixed per diem rate, the bank can deduct 100 percent of the reimbursement if adequate records are kept.

Executive Compensation Corporate executives may be provided with various "perks" that can be either taxable or nontaxable to them personally. A list of perks that can, under certain circumstances, exempt that item from taxation either partially or wholly include

Health and accident insurance (Sec. 106)

Group term life insurance (Sec. 79(a))

Meals and lodging (Sec. 119)

Certain death benefits (Sec. 101)

Employee discounts (Sec. 132(a)(2))

Qualified pension, profit-sharing, stock-bonus and stock-option plans, and deferred compensation arrangements

Working condition fringes (Sec. 132(A)(3))

The form in which a business acquisition or disposition is structured

Some tax plans do not succeed because of statutory provisions that were enacted specifically to counteract what Congress considered to be unduly generous tax results. Others fail because of judicial doctrines that courts apply to offset what they consider to be unduly onerous tax positions.

OFFICIAL PUBLICATIONS

There exists a presumption that final IRS regulations have the same authoritative weight as the statute. The IRS publishes *Administrative Interpretations* as a method of interpreting the statute. *Revenue Rulings* reflect the IRS position on the tax consequences of a particular transaction in which taxpayers might be interested. Such rulings appear in the weekly *Internal Revenue Bulletin* published by the Government Printing Office. *Revenue Procedures* are pronouncements by the IRS that usually deal with the procedural features of tax practice. *Letter Rulings* are responses by the IRS to taxpayers' inquiries. *Information Releases* are also used by the IRS to communicate a particular interpretation that the IRS thinks would be of interest to the general public.

Judicial decisions also reflect important sources of tax law. Courts often apply the legislative reenactment doctrine. This doctrine implies that a regulation is considered to have Congressional approval if such regulation was finalized years earlier and during the interim period Congress did not amend the statutory language involved.

General guidelines for evaluating the relative authority of tax sources is as follows:

1. The Code is the primary authority.

2. Treasury Regulations are considered a strong authority. Legislative Regulations generally tend to have greater weight than Interpretive Regulations.

3. Court decisions are considered a strong authority. The higher the court, the greater
   the precedent.

4. Published IRS rulings bind the IRS but not the courts.

5. Letter rulings bind the IRS as to the particular taxpayer requesting the ruling. They
   cannot serve as legal precedents by either the IRS or taxpayer.

6. Text material taken from tax services is given little weight by the IRS or the courts.
   However, Mertens' *Law of Federal Income Taxation* is often quoted in judicial
   decisions.

TAX RESEARCH

Tax research is a part of the process of resolving tax-related questions on the basis of tax law
sources and the circumstances associated with the particular situation. Tax research is also
undertaken to determine the tax consequences of a particular business transaction in specified
circumstances. The research process generally consists of the following procedures:

1. Determine the facts in the case.

2. Determine the tax issue(s).

3. Determine which tax authorities are applicable to the case.

4. Evaluate the authorities and select which authority to follow where conflicts exist.

5. Communicate the conclusions and recommendations of the research to the interested parties.

A broad array of tax books, services, journals, and citators are from authoritative sources.
A sampling of these are presented here.

Books

Federal Income Taxation of Corporations and Shareholders, Bittker and Eustice, Warren,
Gorham & Lamont

Federal Taxes, Prentice-Hall

Federal Tax Handbook, Commerce Clearing House

Master Federal Tax Manual, Research Institute of America

Standard Federal Tax Reporter, Commerce Clearing House

Tax Concepts for Decision Making, Raabe and Parker, West Publishing

Tax Guide, Research Institute of America

Tax Management Portfolios, Bureau of National Affairs

Tax Periodicals

Estate Planning

The Journal of American Taxation Association

The Journal of Corporate Taxation

The Journal of Partnership Taxation

The Journal of Real Estate Taxation

The Journal of Taxation

The Review of Taxation of Individuals

The Tax Advisor

Taxation for Accountants

Taxes—the Tax magazine

Tax Law Review

Tax Management

Tax Notes

Tax Services

Federal Taxes, Prentice Hall

Federal Tax Guide, Commerce Clearing House

Standard Federal Tax Reporter, Commerce Clearing House

The Tax Coordinator, Research Institute of America

Tax Guide, Research Institute of America

The Law of Federal Income Taxation, Callaghan & Company

Tax Management Portfolios, Bureau of National Affairs

Tax Newsletters

Daily Tax Report, Bureau of National Affairs

U.S. Tax Week, Matthew Bender & Company

Citators can be used to assess tax authorities. Citators give a history of tax cases and list authorities that have cited the case in question. Prentice Hall and Commerce Clearing House provide authoritative citators.

Tax research currently relies heavily on computers. Computer data bases cover federal and state income tax subjects. Data bases include full texts of cases, revenue rulings, and other sources of tax law. The name of the data base and the provider are listed here:

Data Base	Provider
ACCESS	Commerce Clearing House
LEXIS	Mead Data Central

Data Base	Provider
PHINet	Prentice Hall
WESTLAW	West Publishing

THE TAX AUDIT

The tax system relies heavily on voluntary compliance and self-assessment to collect tax revenues. To maintain the integrity of the system, Congress has imposed on the Secretary of the Treasury the responsibility of administering and enforcing the Internal Revenue Code. The Secretary has delegated this authority to the Commissioner of the Internal Revenue Service.

When the IRS receives a tax return, it performs various clerical checks to be assured that the numbers are correct, to verify signatures, to deposit checks, to process refunds, to scan for math and clerical errors, and additional activities. This is merely a preliminary examination. These situations can usually be resolved by telephone or written correspondence with the IRS.

An audit is an examination of a tax return to determine its accuracy. Returns are selected for a formal audit by a variety of methods: (1) randomly, in a Taxpayer Compliance and Measurement Program, (2) because of their high discriminant function score (a score given to each taxpayer's return by a classified computer program to assesses the return's potential for audit), (3) because of the large income reported, unusually large deduction, or some other characteristic considered important to the IRS.

The probability of an audit is substantially larger for high-income taxpayers. In recent years the IRS has audited approximately 1 1/2 percent of returns filed.

Audits are performed by an examination division of an IRS district office. The audit may take place at the IRS office (an office audit) or at the taxpayer's office (a field audit). An office audit is conduced by an office auditor. A field audit is conducted by revenue agents. If the IRS does not agree with the return as filed, it may propose adjustments to the tax liability. The IRS findings are set down in a report called "Income Tax Examination Changes" when the audit is finished. The taxpayer might agree with the proposed adjustments and sign certain documents or not agree with the proposed adjustments. By signing, the taxpayer waives the right to pursue an appeal within the IRS or the Tax Court. The taxpayer could sign the form, pay the deficiency, and sue for a refund in the U.S. District Court or U.S. claims court. By not signing, the taxpayer will receive a letter explaining the appeal process. A taxpayer who does not agree with the outcome of an audit can appeal the case to a higher level of the IRS. The IRS does not allow the taxpayer an appellate conference as a right but as a privilege. The appeals division has the authority to settle all cases.

To audit a return and assess a deficiency, the IRS typically has three years from the later of (1) the initial due date or (2) the date a return is filed. The statute of limitations will ordinarily be extended if (1) a taxpayer understates gross income by more than 25 percent in any year (which extends the limits from three to six years); any part of a tax deficiency is due to fraud (an indefinite limitation).

A taxpayer generally has the burden of proof in contesting a tax deficiency. Cases involving fraud are an exception to this general rule.

Many administrative procedures are available to a taxpayer and the IRS to resolve disputes before resorting to a court. The following two such procedures: (1) an appeals division conference can be arranged or (2) a request for technical advice can be sought from the national IRS Office in unusual or complex cases or where courts have differed on an interpretation of the law.

A statutory notice of deficiency, or ninety-day letter, is filed before a tax deficiency can be assessed and collected. The taxpayer is given 90 days to decide how to proceed, using one of the following options:

1. File a petition with the Tax Court.

2. Pay the deficiency and file a claim for refund, suing either in either a federal court or the Claims Court.

The IRS may assess both interest and penalties for the underpayment of any tax. Criminal penalties may also be imposed.

PART II INCOME TAX ALLOCATION

Federal, state, and local governments impose taxes against individuals, businesses, and other entities. Taxable income is determined by applying the tax rules and regulations. Because tax rules and regulations are used to compute taxable income and because accounting principles are used to compute income reported on financial statements, taxes payable can differ from the provision for income taxes (income tax expense) reported on the income statement. This difference can result in a special liability or deferred charge item being reported on the balance sheet. Accounting for these differences is generally accomplished by a process referred to as income tax allocation (Sources: SFAS No. 96, "Accounting for Income Taxes." SFAS No. 109, "Accounting for Income Taxes," which supersedes Statement No. 96).

OBJECTIVE OF ACCOUNTING FOR INCOME TAXES

The objective in accounting for income taxes on an accrual basis is to recognize the amount of current and deferred taxes payable or refundable at the date of the financial statements (1) as a result of all events that have been recognized in the financial statements and (2) as measured by the provisions of enacted tax law. A second objective is to recognize deferred tax liabilities and assets for the future tax consequences of events that have been recognized in an enterprise's financial statements or tax returns.

The basic principles of accounting for income taxes at the date of the financial statements include the following:

1. A current tax liability or asset is recognized for the estimated taxes payable or refundable on the tax returns for the current year.

2. A deferred tax liability or asset is recognized for the estimated future tax effects attributable to temporary differences and carryforwards.

3. The measurement of current and deferred tax liabilities and assets is based on provisions of the enacted tax laws; the effects of future changes in tax laws or rates are not anticipated.

4. The measurement of deferred tax assets is reduced, if necessary, by the amount of any tax benefits that, based on available evidence, are not expected to be realized.

Income Tax Allocation

It is possible for some revenue and expense items to be included in accounting and taxable income in different accounting periods. Some items may be recognized earlier or later for accounting purposes than for tax purposes. These differences are called *temporary differences*, and result in establishing deferred credits or deferred charges in the financial statements. When the item reverses in subsequent periods, the deferred balance is eliminated. For example, a company may use straight-line depreciation for accounting purposes and accelerated deprecia-tion when preparing its income tax return. Other temporary differences include a reduction to the tax basis of depreciable assets because of tax credits, an investment tax credit accounted for by the deferral method, and an increase in the tax basis of assets because of indexing for inflation. The accounting procedure developed to deal with these temporary differences is called *interperiod tax allocation*. Comprehensive income tax allocation requires allocation for all timing differences, including those not expected to recur in the future.

The accounting for income taxes requires that reported income taxes should recognize the current and deferred income taxes payable or refundable at the date of the financial statements that result from transactions and events already recognized in the financial statements. The income tax expense for the period is calculated by netting the current period change in the deferred income tax accent from the last period with the current income tax payable. The income tax expense is not determined directly from the effect of temporary differences but is a residual calculation. For example, an increase in the deferred income tax payable during the period causes the income tax expense to be larger than the amount of the taxes currently payable. This method reflects the asset/liability (a balance sheet) approach to interperiod income tax allocation that is currently required by generally accepted accounting principles.

When using the liability method (or asset/liability method; or balance sheet method), the deferred tax amount reported on the balance sheet is the effect of temporary differences that will reverse in the future and that are measured using the currently enacted income tax rates and laws that will be in existence when the temporary differences reverse. Income tax expense is the sum of (or differences between) the change in deferred taxes for the period and the income taxes currently payable. Recognition of deferred income taxes reflects accrual account-ing. Under the liability method, the deferred tax consequences of temporary differences are recognized as liabilities and assets on the balance sheet.

A deferred tax liability is recognized for temporary differences that will result in taxable amounts in future years.

A deferred tax asset is recognized for temporary differences that will result in deductible amounts in future years and for carryforwards. A valuation allowance is recognized if, based on the weight of available evidence, it is more likely than not that some portion or all of the deferred tax asset will not be realized.

Computing the Deferred Tax Liability

The following are the basic steps required to compute the amount of the year-end deferred tax liability (assuming no operating loss carryforward for tax purposes):

1. Identify the temporary differences.
2. Estimate the particular future years in which the temporary differences will result in taxable or deductible amounts (only completed transaction can be considered).
3. Determine the net taxable or deductible amount in each future year.
4. For net deductible amounts in a particular future year, carry back or carry forward that amount to offset net taxable amounts that are scheduled to occur in prior or subsequent years (according to the tax law).
5. Compute the amount of tax for the remaining net taxable amounts that are scheduled to occur in each future year by applying presently enacted tax rates for those years to the net taxable amounts.
6. Sum the amounts of tax in each future year to determine the amount of deferred tax liability at the end of the current year.
7. Prepare the required journal entry to record the income tax expense for the period, income taxes payable, and any deferred income tax liability or asset.

Illustration of Income Tax Allocation

To illustrate income tax allocation, assume the following information:

1. Pretax financial income was $30,000.
2. The company has excess deductions of plant assets for income tax purposes over depreciation taken for financial reporting purposes of $10,000 in 1990. This is expected to reverse over the next five years at the amount of $2,000 per year. The company recognized an expense in its current financial statements of $5,500 related to litigation. This amount will be deductible for tax purposes in 1994 when the case is expected to be resolved.
3. Future tax rates provided in enacted tax laws are as follows: 1990–1991 35%; 1992–1993 33%; after 1993 32%.

Schedule to Compute Income Tax Liability

	1990	1991	1992	1993	1994	1995
Pretax book income	$30,000					
Temporary differences						
Depreciation	(10,000)	$2,000	$2,000	$2,000	$2,000	$2,000
Litigation	5,500				(5,500)	

	1990	1991	1992	1993	1994	1995
Taxable income						
before carryback	25,500	2,000	2,000	2,000	(3,500)	2,000
Carryback (3 years)		(2,000)	(1,500)		3,500	
Taxable income	25,500	—	500	2,000	—	2,000
Tax rates	35%		33%	33%		32%
Tax liability	$ 8,925		$ 165	$ 660		$ 640

Based on the information in this schedule, the following journal entry can be made to accrue income taxes and record the tax liabilities:

12/31/1990	Current Federal Income		
	Tax Expense (to balance entry)	10,390	
	Federal Income Tax Payable—Current		8,925
	Federal Income Tax Payable—Deferred		1,465*
	*165 + 660 +640.		

Note that the $3,500 1994 reversal litigation item resulting in a deductible amount in that year offsets the 1994 $2,000 depreciation item, which is a taxable amount. The $3,500 excess deductible amount can be carried back three years and offset against the taxable $2,000 in 1991 and $1,500 in 1992 that otherwise would be payable, similar to what is allowed for net operating loss carrybacks for tax purposes (carried back three years and carried forward for fifteen years).

The 1989 $10,000 difference for depreciation is referred to as an originating difference; the series of $2,000 offsetting amounts are referred to as reversing differences. The 1990 $5,500 difference for the litigation loss is referred to as an originating difference; the 1994 $5,500 is referred to as a reversing difference.

Deferred tax assets and liabilities are subject to current and noncurrent classification. On a balance sheet where current and noncurrent liability sections are used, the Federal Income Tax Payable—Deferred is classified as a long-term liability because it originates in 1992. Federal Income Tax Payable—Current is classified as a current liability. Current Federal Income Tax Expense is reported on the Income Statement.

The financial reporting of income taxes is complicated by the alternative minimum tax (AMT) provision of the income tax law.

INTRAPERIOD TAX ALLOCATION

The amount of income tax expense (or benefit) should be allocated to continuing operations, discontinued operations, extraordinary items, the cumulative effect of accounting changes and prior period adjustments during that same period. This process is referred to as *intraperiod tax allocation.*

The amount of income tax expense or benefit allocated to continuing operations is the amount of income tax expense that would result if the only item occurring during the year was the income or loss from continuing operations. The difference between that amount and total income tax expense is then allocated to the remaining items.

KEY DEFINITIONS

Income Taxes

AMT Alternative minimum tax. A tax imposed to ensure that every individual and corporation with substantial economic income pays a significant amount of tax in spite of exclusions, deductions, and credits.

Appellate Court A court to which other court decisions are appealed. The appellate courts for federal tax purposes include the Court of Appeals and the Supreme Court.

Assessment of tax The imposition of an additional tax liability as the result of an audit.

Audit The examination of a taxpayer's tax return or other transactions by the IRS to determine the correct tax liability.

Basis The value allowed by the tax laws representing the tax value of an asset.

Burden of proof The weight of evidence in a legal case or proceeding.

Business purpose A judicial doctrine that is cited as authority to tax a transaction in a manner that is inconsistent with the literal terms of the Code because the transaction has no apparent business purpose other than saving taxes; the business reason for adopting a particular course of action.

Capital asset Any property other than those specifically identified in Section 122(1)–(5). (114), such as a taxpayer's house, car, clothing, investments, inventory, and depreciable and real property used in a trade or business, except those specifically excluded from the definition.

Capital gain The gain realized on the sale or exchange of a capital asset.

Capital loss The loss realized on the sale or exchange of a capital asset.

Circuit courts of appeal Twelve geographically bounded federal courts of appellate jurisdiction. These courts hear appeals from the tax court and federal district courts.

Citation A reference to a tax authority made in standard format.

Claims court One of three courts of original jurisdiction in federal income tax litigation.

Code An integrated compilation of the numerous federal income tax laws during various time periods. The current Code is The Internal Revenue Code of 1986, as amended.

Conduit principle A provision in the tax law that allows specific tax characteristics to be passed through to the owners of the entity without losing their identity.

Consolidated tax return A single tax return filed on behalf of two or more legally separate corporations that are members of an affiliated group.

Court of Appeals for the Federal Circuit A federal court of appeals jurisdiction that hears cases on appeal from the claims court.

District court One of three courts of original jurisdiction in federal income tax litigation.

District office One of 63 IRS offices located throughout the United States that conducts audits of tax returns, assists taxpayers in their compliance efforts, and collects overdue tax liabilities.

Enrolled agent An individual who is not an attorney or a CPA but who is authorized to practice before the IRS.

Estate A fiduciary entity that exists from the moment of death of an individual taxpayer until the final distribution of the estate assets.

Exclusions Items of income that are not required by law to be reported as gross income.

Gift tax A tax on the right to transfer property, paid by a donor.

Global tax An income tax system that taxes a taxpayer's income without consideration of where it is earned.

Income All income from whatever source derived.

Income taxes Domestic and foreign federal, state, and local taxes based on income.

Intent of Congress The reason underlying Congress's enactment of any particular provision in the Code.

Investment tax credit A credit against the tax allowed for investing in depreciable tangible property before 1986, equal to 10 percent of the qualified investment.

Judicial doctrine General rules of law that come from the decisions rendered by various courts.

Judicial tax law Interpretations of the Code rendered by courts in the United States.

Marginal tax rate The tax rate that applies to any incremental amount of taxable income.

Net operating loss (NOL) The excess of a taxpayer's deductions (after certain adjustments) over gross income for a year.

Net operating loss deduction The amount that a taxpayer can deduct in a carryback or carryforward year because of an NOL.

Net tax liability Gross tax liability less prepayments and tax credits.

Net worth method A method of determining a taxpayer's income used by the IRS when the necessary records are absent.

Ninety-day letter A statutory notice of deficiency.

Passive activity Any activity which involves the conduct of a trade or business in which the taxpayer does not materially participate.

Phantom income A term for income that is attributable to the fact that any reduction in the taxpayer's debt must be included as part of the amount realized on a disposition of property.

Primary authority Statutory law (Code) and interpretations made by various administrative and judicial officials.

Private letter ruling The IRS's response to a taxpayer's inquiry concerning the interpretation of a tax law to a specific situation.

Progressive tax rate Any tax rate schedule that imposes a higher tax rate for incrementally larger amounts of a tax base.

Qualified pension plan A pension plan that has preferential tax treatment as a result of satisfying certain legal requirements.

Secondary authority Any unofficial interpretation of federal or state tax law.

Sham transaction A transaction without tax substance.

Statute of limitations A provision in the law which limits the period of time in which an action can be taken.

Substance over form A judicial doctrine that is cited as authority to tax a transaction based on the economic consequences of what has happened rather than on the technical legal form in which it was achieved.

Supreme Court The final appellate authority in federal litigation.

Surtax An additional tax imposed above a normal tax.

Taxable entity A unit designated by law as the one responsible for the reporting of income and the payment of the tax.

Taxable income The legally defined amount that is the tax base for the U.S. income tax.

Tax avoidance The act of using a legitimate part of the law to avoid paying taxes or to reduce a tax liability.

Tax conduit A business or legal entity that is not subject to taxes but whose items of gross income and deductions are attributed to its owners without regard for any actual distribution of assets.

Tax Court One of three trial courts that share cases dealing with federal income tax affairs.

Tax credit A direct deduction in a taxpayer's tax liability authorized by Congress. Credits are subtracted from the income tax; examples include child care credit, earned income credits, credit for the elderly and permanently disabled, and others.

Tax deficiency The difference between the correct tax liability and the tax liability as determined by a taxpayer, plus related interest and penalties.

Tax evasion A scheme used by a taxpayer to reduce taxes or defer the payment of taxes illegally.

Tax liability Taxable income multiplied by the tax rate equals the gross tax liability; the gross tax liability minus tax credits and prepayments equals net tax liability.

Taxpayer identification number A number used to identify, file, and retrieve tax returns. For most individuals, the TIN is their Social Security Number; for others it is a number assigned by the IRS.

Tax penalty An increase in a tax assessment, in addition to interest.

Tax planning Efforts to reduce a tax liability consistent with the taxpayer's business objectives.

Tax service A privately published compilation of primary and secondary authorities used by professionals in dealing with tax questions.

Tax-sheltered investments Investments that usually decrease an investor's income tax liability.

Trial court The first court that considers a case (not an appellate court).

Unified Transfer Tax A federal tax that applies to estate and gifts after 1976.

Financial Accounting

Current tax expense The amount of income taxes paid or payable (or refundable) for a year as determined by applying the provisions of the tax law to taxable income or excess of deductions over revenues for that year.

Deferred tax asset The amount of deferred tax consequences attributable to temporary differences that will result in net tax deductions in future years that could be recovered (based on operating loss carryback provisions in the tax law) by refund of taxes paid in the current or a prior year.

Deferred tax expense (benefit) The net change during the year in a company's deferred tax liability or asset.

Deferred tax liability The amount of deferred tax consequences attributable to temporary differences that will result in net taxable amounts in future years. The liability is the amount of taxes that would be payable on those net taxable amounts in future years based on the provisions of the currently enacted tax law.

Income tax expense (or benefit) The sum of income taxes payable (or refundable) and deferred tax expense (or benefit).

Income taxes payable (or refundable) The amounts of income tax paid or payable (or refundable) for a year as determined by applying the provisions of the tax law to the taxable income or operating loss for that year. Sometimes called *current tax expense (or benefit)*.

Interperiod income tax allocation The allocation of income tax expense among periods to compensate for a temporary difference between reported book income and taxable income.

Liability method Under the tax liability method of income tax allocation, the deferred tax amount reported on the balance sheet is the effect of temporary differences that will reverse in the future and that are measured using the currently enacted income tax rates and laws that will be in existence when the temporary differences reverse. The liability method is balance-sheet focused. Under the liability method the deferred tax consequences of temporary differences are generally recognizable liabilities and assets.

Operating loss carryforward For financial reporting purposes, the amount of an operating loss carryforward for tax purposes (a) reduced by the amount that offsets temporary differences that will result in net taxable amounts during the carryforward period and (b) increased by the amount of temporary differences that will result in net tax deductions for which a tax benefit has not been recognized in the financial statements.

Originating difference A temporary difference which first arises. Refer to reversing differences.

Permanent differences The difference between pretax financial income and taxable income in an accounting period that will never reverse in a later accounting period. Differences that affect either reported pretax financial income or taxable income, but not both. Permanent differences do not require interperiod income tax allocation. Examples of permanent differences include interest on municipal bonds, life insurance proceeds payable to a corporation upon the death of an insured employee, life insurance premiums on officers, amortization of goodwill, and percentage depletion in excess of cost depletion.

Reversing difference The offsetting amount to an originating temporary difference which occurs in a future period. See originating difference.

Taxable income The excess of taxable revenues over tax deductible expense and exemptions for the year as defined by the governmental taxing authority.

Tax planning strategies A transaction or series of transactions that meet certain criteria and that, if implemented, would affect the particular future years in which temporary differences result in taxable or deductible amounts. A tax planning strategy either reduces the amount of a deferred tax liability or increases the amount of deferred tax asset that would otherwise be recognized.

Temporary differences A difference between the tax basis of an asset or liability and its reported amount in the financial statements that will result in taxable or deductible amounts in future years when the reported amount of the asset or liability is recovered or settled, respectively. A temporary difference will result in either a tax liability that will be paid in the future or a prepaid tax that will result in a decrease in future tax payments at the then current tax rate.

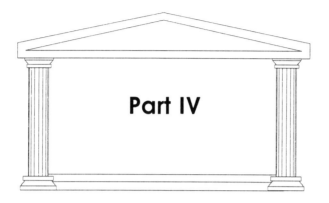

Part IV

Foreign Transactions and Operations and Business Combinations

Chapter 10

International Transactions and Operations

I nternational transactions and operations have become increasingly important because capital and credit markets have become integrated internationally, competition has intensified between global businesses, joint ventures between international entities have increased in number and size, and bank and money managers maintain portfolios of international securities. When accounting and reporting standards among countries differ, attempts to analyze and evaluate the performance of international companies becomes increasingly difficult.

THE INTERNATIONAL ENVIRONMENT

The emergence of multinational corporations, including banks, the internationalization of world commerce and financial markets, and the development of global economic interdependence set the stage for the evolution of international accounting. Accounting reacts to its environment. It is important for users of foreign financial statements to understand the business environment of a company's country in order to interpret accurately its financial reporting.

An international bank has problems that a domestic bank has measuring the financial position and performance of divisions or subsidiaries. Centralization versus decentralization issues are common to both domestic and international operations as are transfer pricing, cost allocations, and investment centers. Issues that are associated specifically with international operations include

1. Controlling widely separate geographical operations

2. Accounting records kept in units of different currencies

3. Different accounting principles and reporting standards

4. Interest rates, growth rates, country risks, and inflation rates that vary from country to country

5. Political, economic, and cultural differences that differ among nations

6. Language differences

International associations have made efforts to standardize accounting principles and practices across international boundaries. The International Accounting Standards Committee (IASC), European Community (EC), Organization for Economic Cooperation and Development (OECD), United Nations (UN), International Federation of Accountants (IFAC), and international accounting firms have made studies and recommendations leading to the development of international accounting principles and practices.

The International Accounting Standards Committee was formed in 1973 to promote harmonization of accounting standards among countries. IASC pronouncements have not had much of an impact on U.S. accounting standards to date. This may change as accounting evolves to meet the needs of a global economy. Many differences exist between accounting principles throughout the world. These differences exist for a variety of reasons including historical, philosophical, legal, institutional, and economic.

The American-British accounting model has been adopted by many countries and is directed toward the decision needs of creditors and creditors. The continental European model, which includes Japan, is designed primarily for companies with strong ties to their banks that supply capital to commercial enterprises. As a result, accounting is oriented toward the needs of the capital providers and to satisfy the needs of governmental requirements. The South American model, which is used by most countries in South America except for Brazil, makes provision for inflation, which has been pervasive throughout the South American countries. Uniformity of accounting is rather common. Accounting focus is generally towards the needs of government planners.

Many countries have attempted to deal with the problem of inflation through indexing. Prices adjusted for inflation have often been provided as supplemental. The trend appears to be toward current cost accounting or fair value accounting as contrasted with a general price level approach.

The majority of banks throughout the industrial world are shareholder owned. In certain European countries larger banks have come under varying degrees of government control. The amount to be reserved by banks to provide for potential loan losses differs among countries. In a majority of countries the amount is fixed by law. A majority of banks value marketable securities at the lower of cost or market. Over 50 percent of the banks value investment assets at original cost.

The majority of banks segregate assets and liabilities on the balance sheet by type of asset or liability. Loans are often segregated by maturity date and by type of borrower. Non-performing loan data is not usually provided although banks in the United States, the United Kingdom, and Canada do disclose such information. Investment assets are usually reported by type of security. Deposits are typically reported by type of deposit. Interest income and interest expense is usually reported in gross amounts on the income statement.

A sampling of international commercial banks indicates that the following information is customarily provided in annual reports:

1. General Information:

    Financial summary

    Organization by groups

    Key executives and Board of Directors

    Management report

2. Financial Information:

    Auditor's report

    Financial statements and supporting schedules

    Significant accounting policies

    Notes to financial statements

3. Supplementary information:

    Segment and geographic area information

    Key financial ratios

    Analysis of loans

    Analysis of earning assets

    Analysis of interest-bearing liabilities

    Capital requirements

    Selected financial data for subsidiaries, branches, and offices

    Shareholders' information including capital changes

International entities are listing securities on major stock exchanges outside of their own countries, resulting in an significant increase in international shareholders. Preparers of financial statements will need to provide additional information to meet the expanding needs of such shareholders (such as restated financial data). The development of international accounting standards will attract the attention of standard setters, resulting in a standardization of accounting standards and practices. The needs for increased cooperation between stock exchanges and accounting regulators will be recognized.

The harmonization of financial reporting is essentially a process of increasing the compatibility of accounting theory and practice by establishing boundaries. Standardization implies the setting of rigid and narrow rules and procedures. The trend worldwide appears to be one of standardization on a worldwide or regional basis. However, a strong move towards harmonization can be observed, especially in Common Market countries.

FOREIGN CURRENCY EXCHANGE RATES

An exchange rate is the ratio between a unit of one currency and the amount of another currency for which the unit can be exchanged (converted) at a particular time. A foreign currency (English pound) is a currency other than the entity's functional currency (U.S. dollar). Foreign exchange rates between currencies are established daily by foreign exchange brokers who act as agents for individuals, companies, or countries desiring to deal in foreign currencies. Some countries maintain an official fixed rate of currency exchange.

A currency is like most other commodities. Exchange rates are affected by the supply of and demand for a nation's currency. If a nation is experiencing high levels of inflation, the purchasing power of its currency will decrease and is reflected by a decrease in the positioning of its currency relative to other nations' currencies. Also, if a country has a higher average interest rate than another, the international investment community would normally seek to invest in the country with the higher average interest rate, thus increasing the demand for the country with the higher interest rate.

The relative value of one currency to another can be expressed either directly or indirectly. The direct exchange rate is the number of local currency units (LCU) required to acquire one foreign currency unit (FCU), i.e., \$.60 = 1 German Mark. The indirect exchange rate is the reciprocal of the direct exchange rate, i.e., \$1 = 1.6667 German Marks (1DM/\$.60 = 1.6667 DM). A change in an exchange rate is referred to as a strengthening or weakening of one currency against another. A strengthening for the U.S. dollar occurs when the dollar has risen relative to the mark.

INTERNATIONAL OPERATIONS

International operations expose banks and other companies to special risks not usually associated with domestic transactions. Assets held in foreign countries have additional risks:

1. Expropriation or the seizure of assets
2. Adverse changes in the exchange rate
3. Restrictions on currency transfer
4. Wars and civil disorders

Foreign exchange risks exposes an asset, liability, or income stream to exchange risk when a currency movement can adversely change its home currency value. Exposure indicates that a company has assets, liabilities, or income streams denominated in currencies other than its own. For banks this exposure can consist of trading items (receivables and payables) and capital items (foreign currency dividends and loan payments) as well as exposure related to the ownership of foreign currency denominated assets and liabilities.

Banks and other companies attempt to find ways to manage the foreign exchange risk. One method is to cover all exposed transactions on the foreign currency markets. In other cases, economic exposure to exchange risk can be obtained by structuring cash flows so that a change in cash inflows or outflows produced by a currency movement is offset by a counter change in cash outflows or inflows.

When business transactions are undertaken abroad, accounting for these transactions by a U.S. company is done in U.S. dollars—the unit of measurement in the United States. The accountant normally becomes involved in foreign transactions and operations in one of two ways:

1. Foreign currency transactions—transactions that require settlement in a foreign currency, including buying and selling, borrowing or lending, and investing.

2. Translation of financial statements of a foreign subsidiary or branch office whose statements are denominated in foreign currency.

The current accounting standard for foreign currency transactions and financial statements is SFAS No. 52, "Foreign Currency Translation," which was issued in December 1981.

FOREIGN CURRENCY TRANSACTIONS

Foreign currency transactions are accounted for as follows according SFAS No. 52:

1. Receivables, payable, revenues, and expenses are translated and recorded in dollars at the spot rate existing on the transaction date. An exchange rate that indicates the price of foreign currencies on a particular date for immediate delivery is called a spot rate.

2. At the balance-sheet date, receivables and payables are adjusted to the spot rate.

3. Exchange gains and losses resulting from changes in the spot rate from one point in time to another are usually recognized in the current period's income statement.

Banks frequently engage in foreign lending and borrowing activities. Such activities include

- Investment in securities of foreign companies, banks, and governments
- Borrowing from foreign lenders
- Direct investment in branches and subsidiaries abroad

Investments and loans in securities of foreign entities require the U.S. bank to convert dollars into foreign currency to acquire the security and then to convert the foreign currency into dollars when the security matures or is sold. Borrowing from abroad usually requires the U.S. bank to borrow a quantity of foreign currency, convert it into dollars, and later purchase foreign currency to repay the borrowed funds.

To illustrate a foreign currency transaction involving investments, assume that a U.S. bank purchased marketable securities in a foreign company for FC 1,500,00, on November 15, 199A. The U.S. company intends to convert the marketable securities, measured in the functional currency of the foreign entity, into cash within the normal operating cycle of the bank. Exchange rates for selected dates are shown here:

November 15, 199A, FC 1 = $.90 $1,350,000 (FC 1,500,000 × $.90)
December 31, 199A, FC 1 = $.95 $1,425,000 (FC 1,500,000 × $.95)
Exchange gain on December 31 , $ 75,000

The journal entry to record the purchase of the securities is:

Nov. 15, 199A   Marketable Securities   1,350,000
                       Cash   1,350,000

The journal entry on December 31 to record the exchange gain is:

Dec. 31, 199A   Marketable Securities   75,000
                       Exchange Gain   75,000

    The marketable securities would be classified as a current asset. The exchange gain would be included in the nonoperating section of the income statement. When the marketable securities were subsequently sold, the difference between the year-end exchange rate ($.95) and the rate on the date of the exchange would be recorded as an exchange gain or loss.

    To illustrate a foreign lending transaction, assume that a U.S. bank invests in a foreign bank certificate. On August 15, 19X1, a U.S. bank purchases a 90-day certificate of deposit from a Swiss bank, the face amount of which is one million Swiss francs at a cost of $600,000 (the spot rate is $.60SF). The CD carries an annual interest rate of 10 percent. The U.S. bank records the purchase of the CD as

August 15, 19X1

Temporary Investments   600,000
    Cash   600,000
To record purchase of a Swiss CD with a face value of
SF1,000,000 when the spot rate was $.60SF.

    When the CD matures on November 13, the U.S. bank receives principal and interest of SF1,025,000 [= SF1,000,000 + (SF1,000,000 × .10)/4]. The spot rate of exchange is $.59SF. To adjust the investment to $.59SF:

Exchange Loss   10,000
    Temporary Investments   10,000
Loss of $10,000 = ($.60 − $.59)1,000,000.

To record receipt of foreign currency and interest earned:

Foreign Currency ($.59 × 1,025,000)   604,750
    Temporary Investment   590,000
    Interest Income ($.59 × 25,000)   14,750

To record the exchange of the foreign currency for dollars:

Cash   604,750
    Foreign Currency   604,750

FORWARD EXCHANGE TRANSACTIONS: HEDGES AND SPECULATION

Companies often can avoid gains/losses on foreign exchange transactions by hedging operations. Forward contracts are often used for this purpose. A forward exchange contract is an agreement to exchange different currencies at a specified future date and at a specified rate (the forward rate). Currency swaps are essentially the same as forward contracts and are considered forward contracts for accounting purposes.

Accounting required for forward exchange contracts depend upon management's intent when entering into the contract. A summary of accounting for forward exchange contracts is shown here.

Type of forward contract	Accounting for exchange gain or loss	Accounting for forward contract premium or discount
1. Hedge of an exposed position	Generally no net exchange gain or loss	Amortized against operating income over term of contract
2. Hedge of an identifiable foreign currency commitment	Deferred to transaction date; then adjustment of dollar basis of the transaction price	May be deferred to transaction date as with exchange gain or loss
3. Speculation	Included currently in income statement	No separate accounting recognition

A premium or discount on a forward purchase contract (debit or credit) is the difference between the current and future values of the foreign currency to be purchased. A premium exists when the forward rate exceeds the spot rate; a discount exists when the forward rate is less than the spot rate. Premiums or discounts are usually the result of interest rate differentials or expected changes in the exchange rate. Premiums or discounts are considered a financing revenue or expense. Amortization of a premium or discount is accounted for independently of any transaction gain or loss on the contract.

To illustrate the hedging of an exposed asset position, assume that a bank has an exposed liability position of 100,000 pounds. Relevant exchange rates are provided here:

		Spot Rate	Forward Rate
Dec. 11, 19X1	Date the forward exchange contract was made	$1.50	$1.54
Dec. 31, 19X1	Balance sheet date	1.55	

		Spot Rate	Forward Rate
Jan. 10, 19X2	Settlement date	1.57	
Dec. 11	Foreign Currency Receivable (spot rate)	150,000	
	Premium on Contract	4,000	
	Liability to Currency Dealer (forward rate)		154,000
	To record the contract		
Dec. 31	Foreign Currency Receivable	5,000	
	Exchange Gain		5,000
	To adjust receivable to current spot rate and recognize gain ($1.55 − $1.50) × 100,000 pounds		
Dec. 31	Amortization Expense	2,667	
	Premium on Contract		2,667
	To amortize premium (2/3 × $4,000)		
Jan. 10	Foreign Currency Receivable	2,000	
	Exchange Gain		2,000
	To adjust receivable to current spot rate ($1.57 − $1.55) × 100,000		
Jan. 10	Amortization Expense	1,333	
	Premium on Contract		1,333
	To amortize premium (1/3 × $4,000)		
Jan. 10	Liability to Currency Dealer	154,000	
	Cash		154,000
	To pay currency dealer on contract		
Jan 10	Foreign Currency (spot rate)	157,000	
	Foreign Currency Receivable		157,000
	To record the receipt of the foreign currency in exchange for the receivable		

To illustrate accounting for a forward exchange contract involving a speculation. Contracts entered into for speculative purposes are for the purpose of obtaining a gain from anticipated changes in the exchange rate. In speculative forward contracts, neither discount nor premium is separately measured and accounted for. The amount due to or from an exchange broker and the forward exchange contracts are recorded at the forward rate. Transaction gains and losses are based on the difference between the forward rate specified in the contract and the forward rate for the period remaining until the contract is settled. Transaction gains and losses are recognized currently in income. To illustrate, assume that on December 1, 19XA, a U.S. bank purchases a ninety-day future contract for 10,000 German Marks at a time that the current quotation for ninety-day futures in Marks is $.550. The spot rate for the Mark on December 1 is $5.190. Selected foreign exchange rates at December 31, 19XB, and January 30, 19XB, are as follows:

	12/31/19X4	1/30/19XB
30-day futures	$.5200	$.5230
Spot rate	.5250	.5280

Journal entries to account for the speculation are as follows:

Dec. 1	Contracts receivable	5,150	
	Contract payable		5,150
	To record the purchase of the contract		
Dec. 31	Contracts receivable	50	
	Exchange gain		50
	To adjust the contract for the difference between the spot rate (.5250) and the 30-day futures ($.5200) on December 31, 19XA and to recognize the transaction gain.		
Jan. 30	Cash (.5280 spot rate)	5,280	
	Exchange gain		80
	Contract receivable		5,200
	To record receipt of the foreign currency from the broker and its sale on the spot market		
Jan. 30	Contract payable	5,150	
	Cash		5,150
	To record payment to the broker		

FOREIGN CURRENCY FINANCIAL STATEMENTS

Accounting principles for purposes of consolidation, combination, or reporting on the equity method for foreign operations (branches, subsidiaries) can be summarized in broad terms as follows:

1. Foreign currency financial statements must be in conformity with generally accepted accounting principles before they are translated.

2. The *functional currency* of an entity is the currency of the primary economic environment in which the foreign entity operates. The functional currency may be the currency of the country in which the foreign entity is located, the U.S. dollar, or the currency of another foreign country. If the foreign entity's operations are self-contained and integrated in a particular country and are not dependent on the economic environment of the parent company, the functional currency is the foreign currency. The functional currency of a foreign company would be the U.S. dollar if the foreign operation is an integral component or extension of the parent company's operations. The daily operations and cash flows of the foreign operation of the foreign entity are dependent on the economic environment of the parent company.

3. If the functional currency is the local currency of the foreign entity, the current rate method is used to translate foreign currency financial statements into U.S. dollars. All

assets and liabilities are translated by using the current exchange rate at the balance sheet dates. This method provides that all financial relationships remain the same in both local currency and U.S. dollars. Owners' equity is translated by using historical rates; revenues and gains and expenses and losses are translated at the rates in existence during the period when the transactions occurred. The translation adjustment which result from the application of these rules are reported as a separate component in owners' equity of the U.S. company's consolidated balance sheet (or parent-only balance sheet if consolidation was not deemed appropriate). See Figure 10-1.

4. If the functional currency is the reporting currency (the U.S. dollar), the foreign currency financial statements are remeasured into U.S. dollars using the temporal method. All foreign currency balances are restated to U.S. dollars using both historical and current exchange rates. Foreign currency balances which show prices from past transactions are translated by using historical rates; foreign currency balances which show prices from current transactions are translated by using the current exchange rate. Translation gains or losses that result from the remeasurement process are reported on the U.S. company's consolidated income statement. See Figure 10-2.

Current Rate Method

Proponents of the current rate method maintain that the use of this method will reflect most clearly the true economic facts since presenting all revenue and expense items at current rates reflects the actual earnings (those that can be remitted to the home country) of a foreign operation at that time. Also, stating all items at the current rate retains the operating relationships after the translating intact with those that existed before the translation. Critics of the current rate method claim that since fixed assets are translated at the current rate and not at the rate that existed when they were acquired, the translated amounts do not represent historical costs and are not consistent with generally accepted accounting principles.

Temporal Method

Since the temporal method states monetary assets at the current rate, proponents of the temporal method claim that this reflects the foreign currency's ability to obtain U.S. dollars. Since historical rates are used for long-term assets and liabilities, the historical cost principle is maintained. However, the use of the temporal method distorts financial statement relationships that exist before and after remeasurement.

Illustrations of the Temporal and Current Rate Methods

The appended exhibits illustrate the temporal method and the current rate method. The temporal method illustration assumes that the functional currency of a Canadian subsidiary is the U.S. dollar. The current rate method assumes that the functional currency of the Canadian subsidiary is the Canadian dollar. The Canadian subsidiary was established at the beginning of the year. The current rate of exchange is $.80; the historical rate used for the building and common stock is $.90; the average rate for the year is $.85. The computation of the exchange loss for the year is shown in an accompanying schedule. The temporal method's $10,406

Figure 10-1
Translation of Foreign Financial Statements—All Current Methodology

	Canadian Dollars	Exchange Rate	U.S. Dollars
Balance Sheet:			
Assets			
Cash	C$ 77,555	.80	US$ 62,044
Rent Receivable	25,000	.80	20,000
Building (net)	475,000	.80	462,044
	C$ 577,555		US$ 509,544
Liabilities and Equity			
Accounts Payable	6,000	.80	4,800
Salaries Payable	4,000	.80	3,200
Common Stock	555,555	.90	500,000
Translation Adjustment			(59,156)
Retained Earnings	12,000	See below.	13,200
	C$ 577,555		US$ 462,044
Income Statement:			
Rent Revenue	C$ 125,000	.85	US$ 106,250
Operating Expenses	(28,000)	.85	(23,800)
Depreciation Expense	(25,000)	.90	(21,500)
Net Income	C$ 72,000		US$ 61,200
Retained Earnings Statement:			
Balance, January 1, Year 1	C$ —		US$ —
Net Income	72,000	See above.	61,200
Dividends	(60,000)	.80	(48,000)
Balance, December 31, Year 1	C$ 12,000		US$ 13,200
Computation of Translation Adjustment for S for Year 1			
Net Asset Position			
January 1, Year 1	C$ —		US$ —
Plus:			
Cash Invested by P	555,555	.90	500,000
Net Income	72,000	.85	61,200
Less:			
Dividends	(60,000)	.80	(48,000)
Subtotal:			513,200
Net Asset Position, December 31, Year 1	C$ 567,555	.80	454,044
Translation Adjustment			US$ 59,156

Source: Belcher, Finley E., and Stickney, Clyde P., *Business Combinations and Consolidated Financial Statements* (Richard D. Irwin, Homewood, IL).

Figure 10-2
Temporal Method—Remeasurement under FASB Statement No. 52

	Canadian Dollars	Exchange Rate	U.S. Dollars
Balance Sheet:			
Assets			
Cash	C$ 77,555	.80	US$ 62,044
Rent Receivable	25,000	.80	20,000
Building (net)	475,000	.90	427,500
	C$ 577,555		US$ 509,544
Liabilities and Equity			
Accounts Payable	6,000	.80	4,800
Salaries Payable	4,000	.80	3,200
Common Stock	555,555	.90	500,000
Retained Earnings	12,000	See below.	1,544
	C$ 577,555		US$ 509,544
Income Statement:			
Rent Revenue	C$ 125,000	.85	US$ 106,250
Operating Expenses	(28,000)	.85	(23,800)
Depreciation Expense	(25,000)	.90	(22,500)
Translation Exchange Loss	—		(10,406)
Net Income	C$ 72,000		US$ 49,544
Retained Earnings Statement:			
Balance, January 1, Year 1	C$ —		US$ —
Net Income	72,000	See above.	49,544
Dividends	(60,000)	.80	(48,000)
Balance, December 31, Year 1	C$ 12,000		US$ 1,544

Computation of Translation Exchange Loss for S for Year 1

Net Monetary Position			
January 1, Year 1	C$ —		US$ —
Plus:			
Cash Invested by P	555,555	.90	500,000
Cash and Receivable from rents	125,000	.85	106,250
Less:			
Cash Disbursed for Building	(500,000)	.90	(450,000)
Cash Disbursed and Liabilities	(28,000)	.85	(23,800)
Incurred for Operating Expenses			
Cash Disbursed for Dividends	(60,000)	.80	(48,000)
Subtotal:			84,450
Net Monetary Position, December 31, Year 1	C$ 92,555	.80	74,044
Translation Exchange Loss			US$ 10,406

Source: Belcher, Finley E., and Stickney, Clyde P., *Business Combinations and Consolidated Financial Statements* (Richard D. Irwin, Homewood, IL).

exchange loss occurred because the subsidiary held net monetary assets denominated in Canadian dollars when the Canadian dollar decreased in value relative to the U.S. dollar. The current rate method's translation adjustment for the year which results from the impact of rate changes on the net monetary position during the year is also shown in a separate schedule.

Translation Losses and Economic Exposure

The exposure to exchange translation gains and losses is not usually the same as the economic exposure to exchange gains and losses. Economic exposure is due to many factors including rates of inflation, regulation, interest rate changes, and other factors. Translation exposure is related to what accounts have to be translated at current exchange rates. A company's exposed position represents the net balance of all accounts translated at current exchange rates. Accounts translated at historical rates are not exposed to translation adjustments because the same conversion rate is used each year. The net translation exposure position of a firm can be explained as follows:

Items contributing to exposure:

a.   Current assets (not including prepaid expenses)

b.   Investments denominated in fixed amounts of local currency (German marks; English pounds)

c.   Long-term receivables (net of allowances)

Items lessening exposure:

a.   Inventories

b.   U.S. dollar assets included in a, b, and c above

c.   Local currency liabilities

The algebraic sum of the items listed represents the company's net exposure to risk of loss (or exposure to gain) through exchange fluctuations. An exposed position can usually be managed by controlling the company's position in listed securities and by the use of forward exchange contracts.

KEY DEFINITIONS

Absolute advantage The greater efficiency that one nation may have over another in the production of a commodity.

Basis for trade The forces that give rise to trade between two nations. See comparative advantage.

Comparative advantage The law of comparative advantage explains how mutually beneficial trade can occur even when one nation is less efficient than another nation in the production of all commodities. The less efficient nation should specialize in and export the commodity in which its absolute disadvantage is smallest (the commodity of its comparative advantage), and should import the other commodity.

Conversion The exchange of one currency for another.

Current exchange rate The rate at which one unit of currency can be exchanged for (converted into) another currency.

Current rate method A translation method under which all assets and liabilities are translated at the current rate of exchange and stockholders' equity accounts are translated at historical rates of exchange and income statement accounts are translated at weighted-average rates of exchange.

Denominated Assets or liabilities expressed in one currency in an amount that is fixed in terms of that currency.

Direct exchange rate An exchange rate that reflects the number of local currency units required to acquire one foreign currency unit.

Discount (premium) on a forward contract The foreign currency amount of the contract multiplied by the difference between the contracted forward rate and the spot rate at the date of inception of the contract.

Exposed net asset position The net amount of outstanding receivables in excess of outstanding payable with both denominated in a foreign currency.

Exposed net liability position The net amount of outstanding liabilities in excess of outstanding receivables with both denominated in a foreign currency.

Foreign currency A currency other than the functional currency of the entity being referred to.

Foreign currency transactions Transactions whose terms are denominated in a currency other than the entity's functional currency.

Foreign exchange markets The market framework for the exchange of one national currency for another.

Foreign exchange rate The price of one currency in terms of another.

Forward exchange contract An agreement to exchange at a specified future date currencies of different countries as a specific rate (forward rate).

Forward exchange rate A rate at a specified time in the future.

Functional currency The currency of the primary economic environment in which the entity operates.

Functional currency translation The primary currency of the economic environment in which the entity operates; the process of expressing in the reporting currency of the enterprise those amounts that are determined or measured in a different currency.

Hedging Purchasing a currency for future delivery when that currency comes due or selling a currency at a future date when revenues in that currency are anticipated.

Highly inflationary environment A cumulative inflation rate that reaches 100 percent or more over a three-year period.

Historical rate of exchange The rate of exchange on the date a transaction occurred.

Indirect exchange rate An exchange rate that is the reciprocal of the direct exchange rate and is the number of foreign currency units that may be obtained for one local currency unit.

International finance The study of foreign exchange markets, the balance of payments, and adjustment to balance-of-payments disequities.

Measurement The recording of a foreign currency transaction by an entity using the local currency to value the transaction.

Monetary Assets and liabilities that are expressed in terms of a fixed number of foreign currency units.

Monetary-nonmonetary method Monetary assets and liabilities are translated at the current rate of exchange, while nonmonetary assets and liabilities are translated at historical rates of exchange.

Nonmonetary Assets and liabilities that are not monetary (not expressed in terms of a fixed number of foreign currency units).

Remeasurement The process of translating one foreign currency into another foreign currency at a rate prevailing on the date of remeasurement when a subsidiary keeps its books and records in a currency other than its functional currency.

Reporting currency The currency in which an enterprise prepares its financial statements.

Spot rate The exchange rate for immediate delivery of currencies exchanged.

Temporal method The process of expressing financial statements measured in one unit of currency in terms of another unit of currency.

Transaction gain or loss Gains or losses that result from a change in exchange rates between the functional currency and the currency in which a foreign currency transaction is denominated.

Translation The conversion of the assets, liabilities, and operating accounts of a foreign branch or subsidiary from stated amounts of foreign currency into U.S dollars.

Translation adjustments The result of the process of translating financial statements from the entity's functional currency into the reporting currency.

Weighted-average rate of exchange A rate that approximates the simple average rate of transaction occurring evenly during the accounting period.

Chapter 11

Business Combinations

Expansion has always been a major activity for most business organizations, including banks. Companies may expand internally or externally. When external expansion is the method, businesses attempt to expand by acquiring one or more firms. External expansion allows for rapid growth without increasing competition. Significant cost savings may also be a consequence of external expansion. Expansion by banks is becoming an increasing factor in banking activities.

AN OVERVIEW

A business combination occurs when a corporation and one or more incorporated or unincorporated businesses are brought together into one accounting entity. The single entity carries on the activities of the previously separate, independent entities. The basic objectives of business combinations are profitability and the maximization of shareholders' wealth. A concern of many combinations is with operating efficiencies through the integration of operations, or diversification of business risks through conglomerate operations.

Business combinations can be classified structurally into three types: horizontal, vertical, and conglomerate. A horizontal combination is one that involves companies within the same industry that have previously been competitors; a vertical combination involves a company and its suppliers or customers; and a combination resulting in a conglomerate is one involving companies in unrelated industries having few, if any, production or market similarities.

Method of Combination

Business combinations can also be classified by method of combination as statutory mergers, statutory consolidations, and stock acquisitions. A statutory merger occurs when one company acquires all of the net assets of one or more other companies. The acquiring company survives; the acquired company or companies cease to exist as a separate legal entity. For example, a merger occurs between corporations A and B if A remains the same legal entity (essentially with the combined assets and liabilities of A and B) and B goes out of existence.

A statutory consolidation requires the formation of a new corporation that acquires two or more other corporations; the acquired corporations then cease to exist as separate legal entities. For example, corporations A and B agree to transfer their assets and liabilities to a new corporation C and then go out of existence, leaving C as the corporation to carry on the activities of A and B.

A stock acquisition occurs when one corporation pays cash or issues stock or debt for more than 50 percent of the voting stock of another company and the acquired company remains intact as a separate legal entity. The relationship of the acquiring company to the acquired company in a stock acquisition is described as a parent-subsidiary relationship. The acquiring company is referred to as the parent (investor) and the acquired company as a subsidiary. The related companies are called affiliated companies. Each of the affiliated companies continues as a separate legal entity. The parent company carries its interest in a subsidiary as an investment in its accounts. Consolidated financial statements are prepared only when the business combination was carried out as a stock acquisition.

The relationship between mergers, consolidations, and stock acquisitions can be summarized as follows:

	Prior to Combination	Survivor(s)
Statutory merger	A and B	A or B
Statutory consolidation	A and B	C
Acquisition	A and B	A and B

Antitrust Restrictions

Certain business combinations are prohibited by law. Federal laws prohibit combinations that would be in restraint of trade or would impair competition. Section 7 of the Clayton Act (1914) prohibits any business combination in which "the effect of such acquisition may be substantially to lessen competition or tend to create a monopoly."

Federal *antitrust laws* are enforced by the Justice Department, the Federal Trade Commission, the Federal Reserve Board, and the Securities and Exchange Commission. These agencies have developed over the years certain precombination notification regulations: A company with assets or sales of at least $10 million that plans to acquire a manufacturing company with assets or sales of at least $10 million must file a detailed 21-page form 30 days before the planned date of consummation. If the target company is not a manufacturing company, notification is required if one company has at least $100 million in sales or assets and the other company has sales or assets of at least $10 million. These regulations enable the enforcing agents to review proposed business combinations before they occur. The agents are empowered to obtain a preliminary court injunction against the proposed sale and have used this authority.

Cost-Benefit Analysis for Bank Mergers and Acquisitions

Basic techniques of cost benefit analysis can be used to broadly conceptualize whether the benefits of a bank merger or acquisition exceed its costs. The benefit of a bank merger or acquisition is the difference between (1) the present value of the merged or acquired banks and (2) the sum of their present values if they do not merge or are not acquired. The cost of merger or acquisition is the difference between the amount paid for the acquiree and its value as a separate bank. Obviously care should be taken in applying this conceptualized cost-benefit analysis because there are many costs or benefits that cannot be quantified.

Alternate methods can be used to place a valuation on an acquiree. Such methods use book values, earnings per share, price-earnings ratios, and market values to evaluate the merger or acquisition.

PURCHASE AND POOLING ACCOUNTING

There are two methods of accounting for business combinations—the pooling of interests method and the purchase method. A business combination that meets the criteria of APB Opinion No. 11 must be accounted for under the pooling method. The criteria for a pooling of interests can be summarized as follows:

Attributes of the combining companies:

1. Autonomous (two-year rule)

2. Independent

Manner of Combining interests:

3. Single transaction (or completed in one year after initiation)

4. Exchange of common stock (90 percent "substantially all" rule)

5. No equity changes in contemplation of combination

6. Shares reacquired only for purposes other than combination

7. Voting rights immediately exercisable

8. Combination resolved at consummation (no pending provisions)

Absence of planned transactions:

9. Issuing company does not agree to reacquire shares

10. Issuing company does not make deals to benefit former stockholders

11. Issuing company does not plan to dispose of assets within two years

The pooling of interest method accounts for a business combination as the uniting of the ownership interests of two or more companies by exchange of equity securities. The purchase method accounts for a business combination as the acquisition of one enterprise by another. A comparison of the pooling and purchase method follows:

Purchase	*Pooling of interests*
Assets and liabilities acquired at fair values. Any excess of cost over fair value of net assets acquired is goodwill.	Assets and liabilities acquired are recorded at their book value.
The acquired company's retained earnings do not become a part of the acquiring company's retained earnings.	The acquired company's retained earnings becomes a part of the acquiring company's retained earnings. Some adjustment may be required to maintain legal capital.
The excess of cost over book value becomes an amortizable intangible asset that reduces the reported income of the acquiring company.	No excess of cost over book exists.
The acquired company's earnings are included with the acquiring company's earnings from the date of combination.	The acquired company's earnings are included with the acquiring company's earnings from the beginning of the combination year.
Direct costs incurred in the combination are included as part of the cost of the acquired company.	Direct costs incurred in the combination are expensed in the year incurred.
Indirect costs related to the acquisition are expensed in the year incurred.	Same as for purchase method.
Comparative statements for prior years are not restated.	Comparative statements for prior years are restated on a combined basis.

In purchase accounting the assets and liabilities of the acquired business must be recorded on the books of the combined bank at their fair value. To the extent possible, the cost of the acquisition is allocated to each identifiable asset or liability being acquired. Identifiable assets may be tangible or intangible. Any excess of the cost of the acquisition over the net fair value of the identifiable assets and liabilities acquired or assumed is purchased goodwill. Identifiable and unidentifiable intangible assets (i.e., goodwill) are reportable in Schedule RC, Item 10, "Intangible Asset." In accordance with regulatory instructions intangible assets should be amortized over their estimated useful lives, not to exceed 15 years, except in those cases where a shorter amortization period has been prescribed by the bank's primary federal bank supervisory authority. If the net fair value of the identifiable assets and liabilities acquired or assumed exceeds the cost of the acquisition, the values otherwise assignable to the acquired fixed assets, intangible assets, and other assets of a noncurrent nature shall be reduced proportionately for the amount of such excess. Negative goodwill shall not be recorded unless these categories of assets acquired are reduced to a zero value. Negative goodwill should be reported as "Other

Liabilities," and should be amortized systematically to income over the period estimated to be benefitted.

CONSOLIDATED FINANCIAL STATEMENTS

A stock acquisition is one form of business combination. In a stock acquisition one corporation acquires all or part of the voting stock of another company, and the acquired company remains intact as a separate legal entity. The relationship of the acquiring company to the acquired firm is described as a parent-subsidiary relationship. The acquiring company is referred to as the parent (investor) and the acquired company as a subsidiary. The related companies are called affiliated companies. Consolidated financial statements are generally prepared for affiliated companies.

The purpose of consolidated statements is to present the financial position, results of operations, and cash flows of a company and its subsidiaries essentially as if the group were a single company with one or more branches or divisions. Consolidated financial statements provide considerable information that is not found in the separate statements of the parent corporation and are often required for fair presentation of the financial position and results of operations for a group of affiliated companies.

When preparing consolidated financial statements, consideration should be given to the following:

- The objective should be to issue the most meaningful financial presentation in the circumstances.

- The usual condition for controlling financial interest is ownership of a majority voting interest in common stock. As a general rule, ownership by one company, directly or indirectly, of over 50 percent of the outstanding voting shares of another company is required for consolidation.

- A majority-owned subsidiary should not be consolidated if control is likely to be temporary or if control does not rest with a majority owner (e.g., the subsidiary is in legal reorganization or bankruptcy)

- A difference in the fiscal periods of a parent and a subsidiary does not, of itself, justify the exclusion of the subsidiary from consolidation; the differences of not more than 93 days between the date of the subsidiary's financial statements and the parent company's financial statements are acceptable, although lesser differences are more desirable (see Rule 3-A-02 of SEC Regulation S-X).

Consolidated financial statements include a complete set of statements prepared for the consolidated entity and include the sum of the assets, liabilities, revenue and expenses of the affiliated companies after eliminating the effect of any transactions among the affiliated companies. The consolidated statements present the financial position and results of operations of the economic unit controlled by the parent company as a single accounting entity. Emphasis is placed on the economic unit under control of one management rather than upon the legal form of the separate entities. The consolidated financial statements are prepared primarily for the benefit of the shareholders and creditors of the parent company. There is a presumption that consolidated statements are more meaningful than the separate statements of members of the affiliation. However, subsidiary creditors, minority shareholders, and regulatory agencies must rely on the statements of the subsidiary to assess their claims.

Consolidated statements eliminate intercompany items, such as amounts one affiliated company owes another, securities one affiliated company holds in another, as well as intercompany income account items (intercompany sales and purchases). Any minority interest (stockholders of a subsidiary who are outside the affiliation structure) represents the investment in the consolidated net assets by stockholders outside the affiliation structure, and is reported on the consolidated statement as a separate ownership interest, a liability, or separately between liabilities and stockholders' equity.

A description of significant consolidation policies is required to be included in corporate financial reports as an integral part of the financial statements. For example, principles of consolidation could be reported in the annual report of a publicly owned corporation as follows: The consolidated financial statements include the accounts of the company and its subsidiaries, all of which are wholly owned. All significant intercompany amounts are eliminated in consolidation. The excess of net assets of acquired subsidiaries over cost is being amortized over a twenty-year period from their respective dates of acquisition.

Earnings Per Share

Consolidated earnings-per-share computations are identical to those of the parent company. Procedures used in computing parent company's earnings per share apply to investor accounting under the equity method. Parent company's relationships do not affect EPS computations unless the subsidiary has outstanding common stock equivalents or other potentially dilutive securities. In such cases a subsidiary's EPS computation differs according to whether the subsidiary's potentially dilutive securities are convertible into subsidiary's common stock or parent company's common stock.

Income Tax Considerations

Some consolidated entities prepare consolidated income tax returns and pay taxes on consolidated taxable income. Others prepare separate income tax returns for each affiliated company and pay taxes on the taxable income included in the separate returns.

The major advantages of filing a consolidated return include:

1. Losses of one affiliate are offset against income of other members of the group.
2. Intercorporate dividends are excluded from taxable income.
3. Intercompany profits are deferred from income until realized.

The right to file a consolidated income tax return is based upon classification as an affiliated group under sections 1501 through 1505 of the Internal Revenue Code. According to these sections of the Code, an affiliated group exists when a common parent corporation owns at least 80 percent of the voting power of all classes of stock and 80 percent or more of the total value of all outstanding stock of each of the includable corporations. The common parent company must meet the 80 percent requirements directly for at least one includable corporation.

When separate tax returns are filed, separate affiliates pay a tax on unrealized profits. As a result, income tax allocation is required to defer any taxes paid on unrealized profits or losses.

PUSH-DOWN ACCOUNTING

Push-down accounting is the establishment of a new accounting basis for a bank in its separate financial statements as a result of a substantive change in control. Push-down accounting is an approach to accounting for an acquisition that involves establishing a new basis of accounting and reporting for a subsidiary in its separate financial statements. According to this method, the parent company's cost of acquiring a subsidiary is "pushed down" and used to establish a new accounting basis for the assets and liabilities of the subsidiary. The assets and liabilities of the subsidiary would be updated to report the amounts at which they are shown on the parent's consolidated statements. The SEC has required push-down accounting under special circumstances since 1983.

Push-down accounting is required for banking purposes if a direct or indirect change in control of at least 85 percent of the voting stock of the bank has occurred, and the bank does not have an outstanding issue of publicly traded debt or preferred stock. Push-down accounting will also be required if the bank's separate financial statements are presented on a push-down basis in reports filed with the SEC. Push-down accounting may also be used when a direct or indirect change in control of at least 80 percent, but less than 85 percent, of the voting stock of the bank has occurred. The bank's primary federal supervisory authority reserves the right to determine whether or not a bank can use push-down accounting for purposes of the Reports of Condition and Income.

When push-down accounting is used, all of the following conditions should be met: (1) an arm's length purchase acquisition resulting in a substantive change in control of at least 80 percent must have occurred, (2) the bank's independent accountant has concurred that the use of such accounting is appropriate and that the necessary adjustments have been made and are appropriate, and (3) the adjusting entries eliminated the undivided profits account.

PROPORTIONATE CONSOLIDATION

When an enterprise owns a substantial but not controlling interest in another company, some accountants prefer to use "proportionate consolidation" for the arrangement. For example, if a company has a one-third interest in a noncorporate joint venture, the investor company would include in the consolidated financial statements one-third of each of the assets, liabilities, revenues, and expenses of the venture. Proportionate consolidation of joint ventures is used primarily in the real estate and construction, oil and gas, and utilities industries.

ONE-LINE CONSOLIDATION

One-line consolidation occurs when an investment in another company is accounted for by the equity method of accounting. The effect of using the equity method on reported income and the total balance sheet assets of the investee are identical to those that would be reported if the investee were consolidated. The difference would be that income and total assets of the investee would be reported on a single line in the income statement and balance sheet of the investor.

REORGANIZATION

A combination of two or more entities involving related parties is considered a reorganization, not a business combination. For example, two subsidiary banks of a bank holding company may combine into one bank, which is a change in organization but not a change in the entity. The assets and liabilities transferred in the combination are accounted for at historical cost in a manner similar to that in pooling of interests accounting.

COMBINED STATEMENTS

In some situations enterprises are affiliated as a result of common management or common control instead of as a result of a majority voting interest held by a parent in its subsidiaries. Combined statements are sometimes prepared for some arrangements. Combined financial statements could also be used in these cases:

- Where an individual owns a controlling interest in several corporations that are related in their operations, and
- To present the financial position and the results of operations of a group of unconsolidated subsidiaries

The procedures used to prepare combined statements are similar to those used when preparing consolidated statements. Any intercompany investment is eliminated against the related equity of the other enterprise. Where there is no intercompany investment but merely common management, the individual company equities are combined.

BANK SPECIFIC

For uniform bank call reports, the consolidation process eliminates the results of all transactions and all outstanding asset/debt relationships between offices included in the consolidated bank's consolidated Reports of Condition and Income. Each subsidiary shall consolidate its majority-owned subsidiaries in accordance with the general consolidation rules. Each subsidiary or consolidated subsidiary shall be carried upward to the next succeeding level to determine whether consolidation is required.

Minority interest consists of the shares of stock now owned by the reporting bank. Minority interest in the reporting bank's consolidated subsidiaries is shown along with "Other

Liabilities." Income associated with a minority interest is shown in the Report of Income as "Other Noninterest Expense."

The recognition of goodwill under the purchase method applies to banks and thrift institutions with certain exceptions. One exception relates to accounting for identifiable existing deposits and loan accounts. Existing deposits and loan accounts may have the ability to generate new banking business reflecting an intangible asset. The fair value of such assets should be determined using the expected benefit existing on the date the entity is acquired. Consideration should not be given to additional loans issued or deposits received after consummation of the combination.

Banks and thrift institutions may be acquired in periods with high interest rates. Discounting low-yield assets using high current interest rates can result in low fair values for the assets. In such cases the fair value of the liabilities assumed over the fair value of tangible and identifiable intangible assets acquired should be accounted for as an unidentifiable intangible asset. This asset would be charged to expense over a period of time not to exceed the remaining life of the noncurrent interest-bearing assets acquired in the combination using a modified interest method. This method applies a constant rate of interest to the carrying amount of the interest-bearing assets that are expected to exist at the beginning of the subsequent year.

Furthermore, an entity might sell a large segment of the operating assets or the bank or thrift institution acquired. If operating assets are disposed of, a pro rata amount of unidentifiable intangible assets must be removed and accounted for as part of the cost of the asset disposition. If the assets sold are interest-bearing, a proportion of the unidentifiable intangible asset should be written off against income if the benefit of the asset has diminished significantly.

On occasion, regulatory agencies have encouraged banking mergers by providing financial assistance to entities willing to assume the assets and liabilities of banking institutions in financial distress. Where a regulatory agency agrees to pay amounts by which future interest received or receivable on the interest-bearing assets acquired is less than the interest cost of carrying those assets for a period by a stated margin, the financial assistance is accounted for as additional interest in computing the fair value of the asset acquired in the combination. The interest rate margin in effect on the acquisition date is used in computing the fair value of the asset. As the actual financial assistance accrues, it should be included in income.

In certain circumstances it will be necessary for the combined companies to repay the regulatory authority. This can result in a loss contingency. An expense and liability should be recognized for the contingency when it is probable that a repayment will be made and the amount of the payment can reasonably be estimated.

EQUITY METHOD OF ACCOUNTING

The equity method of accounting is used for investments in common stock where the investor owns over 20 percent of the outstanding voting stock of another company and can exercise significant influence. When an investor corporation can exercise significant influence over the operations and financial policies of an investee corporation, generally accepted accounting principles require that the investment in the investee be reported using the equity method.

Significant influence can be determined by such factors as representation on the board of directors, participation in policy-making processes, material intercompany transactions, interchange of managerial personnel, and technological dependency. It is presumed that an investor can exercise significant influence if he or she owns 20–25 percent of the outstanding common stock of the investee, unless evidence to the contrary is available.

The equity method of accounting for common stock investments reflects the economic substance rather than the legal form that underlies the investment in common stock of another company. When the equity method of accounting is used, the investor initially records the investment in the stock of an investee at cost. The investment account is then adjusted to recognize the investor's share of the income or losses of the investee after the date of acquisition when it is earned by the investee. Such amounts are included when determining the net income of the investor in the period they are reported by the investee. This procedure reflects accrual-basis accounting in that revenue is recognized when earned and losses when incurred. Dividends received from an investee reduce the carrying amount of the investment and are not reported as dividend income. As a result of applying the equity method, the investment account reflects the investor's equity in the underlying net assets of the investee. As an exception to the general rule of revenue recognition, revenue is recognized without a change in working capital.

In the investor's income statement the proportionate share of the investee's net income is reported as a single-line item, except where the investee has extraordinary items that would be material in the investor's income statement. In such a case the extraordinary item would be reported in the investor's income statement as extraordinary. Intercompany profits and losses are eliminated. Any excess of price paid for the shares over the underlying book value of the net assets of the subsidiary purchased must be identified (for example, purchased goodwill) and, where appropriate, amortized or depreciated.

When an investor owns over 50 percent of the outstanding common stock of an investee and so can exercise control over the investee's operations, consolidated financial statements for the affiliated group are normally presented.

Investments in unconsolidated subsidiaries are reported in consolidated financial statements by the cost method. In unconsolidated financial statements of the parent company, investments in subsidiaries are reported by the cost method.

ACQUISITION OF A TROUBLED BANK

SFAS No. 72, "Accounting for Certain Acquisitions of Banking or Thrift Institutions," and FASB Interpretation No. 9, "Applying APB Opinion Nos. 16 and 17, "When a Savings and Loan Association or a Similar Institution is Acquired in a Business Combination Accounted for by the Purchase Method," should be consulted when a bank or thrift institution is acquired.

SFAS No. 72 is applicable to the acquisition of a troubled bank or thrift, specifically to that portion of goodwill that arises from the excess of the fair value of assumed liabilities over the fair value of acquired identifiable assets. This document also governs accounting and reporting for financial assistance that may be granted by a regulatory authority in connection with an enterprise's acquisition of a troubled banking or thrift institution. SFAF No. 72 is applicable to acquisitions of commercial banks, savings and loan associations, mutual savings banks, credit unions, and other depository institutions.

FASB Interpretation No. 9 requires that the net-spread method should not be used in determining the amount of goodwill or other intangible assets that are acquired in a business combination accounted for by the purchase method. Rather, the separate-valuation method should be used. The Interpretation discusses the circumstances in which goodwill recorded in an acquisition can be amortized by accelerated methods.

The separate-valuation method is based on recording the acquired identifiable assets at fair value at the date of purchase. Any difference between the fair value of separate tangible and intangible assets acquired less liabilities assumed is recorded as purchased goodwill. Independent appraisals and/or subsequent sales of acquired assets can provide evidence of fair value. The fair value of long-term interest-bearing assets is the present value of the amount that will be received, less an allowance for uncollectible accounts. The present value of assumed liabilities is its present value at the prevailing interest rates at acquisition. A portion of the acquisition cost must be allocated to contingent assets, liabilities, and impairments, if any.

Goodwill recorded in an acquisition of a savings and loan association can be amortized by accelerated methods if both of the following circumstances are present:

1. Goodwill includes an indeterminable amount for the acquired assets to generate future income or new business, but these factors cannot be separately valued.

2. The expected benefits from such factors are expected to decline over their useful life.

Preacquisition contingency for goodwill would be required for that portion of the total acquisition cost under the purchase method allocated to contingent assets, liabilities, and impairments, if it is probable that the contingent item existed at the consummation date of the combination and the amount of the contingent item can be reasonably estimated.

When a regulatory agency provides periodic financial assistance approximately equal to the difference between the average yield on the long-term interest-bearing assets acquired in an acquisition and the current interest cost of carrying such assets, SFAS No. 72 requires that the computation of this type of financial assistance be made at the acquisition date and be based on the difference between the average yield on the long-term interest-bearing assets and the current interest cost of carrying such assets. This amount is considered as an additional interest on the long-term interest-bearing assets. The additional interest is reported as income of the period in which it is accrued.

If assets and/or liabilities are transferred to a regulatory agency as part of the plan of financial assistance, the fair value of the items transferred to the regulatory agency are excluded from the fair market value of the assets and liabilities acquired in the transaction.

Financial assistance received after the date of acquisition of a thrift is recognized in the financial statements of the period(s) in which it becomes probable and the amount can be reasonably estimated. In such cases the assistance is reported as a reduction of the balance of the unamortized goodwill. The nature and amount of financial assistance received from a regulatory agency in connection with the acquisition of a bank or thrift must be disclosed in the financial statements.

If the financial assistance is repaid to the regulatory agency, the repayment is recognized as a liability and a charge to income of the period in which the repayment is probable and the amounts can be reasonably estimated.

A 1990 study by the FMCG Capital Strategies in conjunction with the Bank Administration Institute (*Analyzing Success and Failure in Banking Consolidations*) concluded that there are four preconditions for successful acquisitions:

- *Expense control* A strong, well-established expense control ethic, a track record of actually cutting expenses, and negotiated before-the-fact understandings with the acquiree or merger partner to facilitate the structural changes required after the deal is done.

- *The right price* Pricing discipline is a prerequisite for successful merger and acquisition transactions.

- *Business mix* Increasing shareholder value by consciously seeking to balance the bank/nonbank mix, industry/customer/product concentrations, and geographic coverage. Mergers and acquisitions are probably the easiest way to achieve or destroy this balance.

- *Geographic proximity* Limiting a bank's focus to a limited geographic area because there are real benefits of not being too far away—easier management coverage, greater potential for operations, systems and branch consolidations, and advertising synergies.

Success in this context is considered by some as growth in absolute assets, absolute earnings, or total number of employees. Other banks have tended to measure success in acquisitions by the impact on growth in earnings per share or the lack of dilution to earnings, and the impact on a bank's stock price over the long term. No single measure can adequately measure or define success.

The study identified two major factors that will determine if the acquisition is ultimately value-creating: whether the merged bank will be able to cut costs, and whether the premium paid over discounted cash flow value is low enough. This is a matter for the negotiating process. Implementing a transaction involves having a standing team ready to work full time on the consolidation. It also involves creating a process where management can agree on what exactly should be done. Part of this process is setting performance standards that are recognized by all parties involved. Benefits are related to good communications through the entire process. The acquisition will not be successful until the joined institutions possess a set of shared values and ways of doing things that ensure that synergy is a reality.

KEY DEFINITIONS

Conglomerate A business combination that occurs between companies in unrelated industries.

Consolidated financial statements Financial statement prepared for a parent company and its subsidiaries. They include a complete set of statements normally prepared for a separate entity.

Consolidated tax return An election to file a separate or consolidated tax return is available to member corporations of an affiliated group. To qualify as an affiliated group, a parent company must own at least 80 percent of the common shares of its subsidiary. If a consolidated tax return is filed, intercompany dividends avoid taxation. Losses of one affiliate may be used to offset current income of another. Profit on intercompany sales are not taxed until the purchasing affiliate sells the assets to a nonaffiliate.

Consolidation The process of combining the financial statements of a parent and one or more subsidiaries, resulting in statements reflecting a single company.

Cost method A method of accounting for an investment in common stock used by a parent company for its investment in which income is recorded when dividends are declared or received and the amortization of the excess of cost over book value is not recorded on the books of the parent company. The method is considered a cash basis method.

Eliminating entries Entries which remove the intercompany financial relationships.

Entity theory of consolidated statements A theory that reports all identifiable assets and liabilities acquired, including the minority's share, at fair value and would impute goodwill to the minority interest.

Equity method A method of accounting for an investment in common stock that is a full accrual method used by a parent company to account for its investment. The parent company records its share of a subsidiary's net income by debiting the Investment in Subsidiary account and crediting Equity in Earnings of Subsidiary. Dividends received by a parent reduce the Investment in Subsidiary account. The parent amortizes any excess of cost on its book.

Goodwill The amount by which the total cost of the investment is above the current value of an acquired business's net assets.

Horizontal method A business combination that occurs between companies involved as competitors at the same level in a given industry.

Indirect holdings Holdings when the parent company's controlling interest in a subsidiary enables it to control a second subsidiary even though the parent owns few or none of the second subsidiary's shares directly.

Minority interest The shares of stock of a subsidiary held by stockholders other than the parent company.

Modified entity theory of consolidated statements A theory that states at fair value all assets and liabilities acquired, including the minority interest, but does not impute goodwill to the minority interest.

Mutual holdings Holdings when one or more subsidiaries own stock in the parent or in each other.

Parent A company that owns more than 50 percent of the outstanding common stock of another company.

Parent theory of consolidated statements A theory which requires the valuation of the minority interest and the minority's related portion of the subsidiary's assets and liabilities at book value.

Pooling of interest A method of recording a business combination that assumes that the stockholders of the two constituent companies have merely exchanged common stock and that the separate businesses have been combined into one.

Purchase accounting A method of recording a business combination that assumes that one company purchased another company and that a new basis of accountability exists.

Push-down accounting An accounting method that adjusts the subsidiary's assets and liabilities to their current values in the general ledger based on the parent's cost.

Statutory consolidation A legal term referring to a type of business combination in which a new corporation is formed to carry on the businesses of two predecessor companies that are liquidated.

Statutory merger A legal term referring to a type of business combination in which a newly acquired company is liquidated into a division at the time of the business combination.

Subsidiary A company whose outstanding common stock is more than 50 percent owned by another company.

Vertical combination A combination that takes place between companies involved at different levels in a given industry.

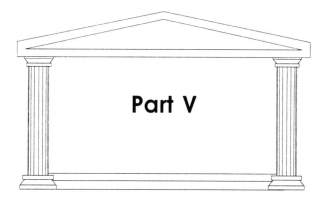

Part V

Overview of Financial Statement Analysis

Chapter 12

Financial Statement Analysis

T he purpose of financial statement analysis is to examine past and current financial data so that a company's performance and financial position can be evaluated and future risks and potential estimated. Financial statement analysis can yield valuable information about trends and relationships, the quality of a company's earnings, and the strengths and weaknesses of its financial position.

OVERVIEW OF ANALYSIS OF BANK FINANCIAL STATEMENTS

A bank's financial soundness is related primarily to four variables (LACE): liquidity, asset quality, capital adequacy, and earnings. Liquidity is determined on a net basis where short-term volatile liabilities are subtracted from temporary investments. The quality of a bank's assets impacts the income stream and the capital base. A bank's capital serves as a cushion to absorb losses. Earnings and the quality of the earnings are considered by most analysts to be the most important measures of a bank's soundness.

A bank's operating objectives are to maximize revenues, minimize costs, and avoid taxes (shelter income) while maintaining a sound asset base. A bank attempts to increase profitability by various techniques including the following:

1. Managing spread
2. Controlling loan quality
3. Controlling interest expense and overhead

4.   Generating fee and service-charge income

5.   Avoiding taxes

Bank rating services typically rate banks according to the following procedures:

1.   Use of identical criteria for each bank, often the Federal Reserve Board's reports of condition and income

2.   Analytical review of individual banks by bank analysts

BASICS OF FINANCIAL STATEMENT ANALYSIS

Financial statement analysis begins with establishing the objective(s) of the analysis. For example, is the analysis undertaken to provide a basis for granting credit or making an investment? After the objective of the analysis is established, the data is accumulated from the financial statements and from other sources. The results of the analysis are summarized and interpreted. Conclusions are reached and a report is made to the person(s) for whom the analysis was undertaken.

To evaluate financial statements, a person must:

1.   Be acquainted with business practices

2.   Understand the purpose, nature, and limitations of accounting

3.   Be familiar with the terminology of business and accounting

4.   Be acquainted with the tools of financial statement analysis

Financial statement analysis includes comparing some or all of the following:

1.   Financial information for comparable prior period(s)

2.   Budgets or forecasts

3.   The industry in which the entity operates

4.   Peer businesses

5.   Relevant nonfinancial data

Financial service organizations (e.g., Moody and Standard & Poor), credit collection agencies (e.g., Dun and Bradstreet), industry trade associations, investment and brokerage companies, federal government departments, commissions, and regulatory agencies publish key business and banking ratios. Computerized financial data is becoming widely available from information service companies.

The analysis should identify major changes or turning points in trends, amounts and relationships. Major tools used in financial statement analysis include ratios, vertical and horizontal analysis, time-series analysis, regression analysis and correlation analysis.

A starting point for analyzing a bank's financial statement is the auditor's opinion (see Chapter 16). A bank auditor typically verifies the fairness of the bank's financial statement to determine if the financial statements fairly present the bank's financial activities in accordance with generally accepted accounting principles. Reading the opinion introduces the analysts to the bank's annual report. The analysts would usually review the annual report's footnotes, which are an integral part of the financial statements and supplementary data. The footnotes can provide information concerning significant accounting policies and more detailed related to activities affecting the annual report.

Comparative financial statements provide analysts with significant information about trends and relationships over two or more years. Comparative statements are more significant for evaluating a company than are single-year statements.

RATIO ANALYSIS

Financial statement ratios are additional tools for analyzing financial statements. A ratio is an expression of a mathematical relationship between one quantity and another. The ratio of 400 to 200 is 2:1 or 2. If a ratio is to have any utility, the elements which constitute the ratio must express a meaningful relationship. Financial ratios establish relationships between various items appearing on financial statements. Ratios can be classified as follows:

1. *Liquidity ratios* Measure the ability of the enterprise to pay its debts as they mature.

2. *Activity (or turnover) ratios* Measure how effectively the enterprise is using its assets.

3. *Profitability ratios* Measure management's success in generating returns for those who provide capital to the enterprise.

4. *Coverage ratios* Measure the protection for long-term creditors and investors.

Figure 12-1 presents financial statement ratios which have major applications to businesses in general. Ratios which are specifically related to the statement of cash flows are included in Chapter 7.

BANK SPECIFIC RATIOS

Banks often measure performance under three basic categories: financial, operating, and marketing performance. Figure 12-2 presents ratios which are of special significance to banks. When these categories are used, financial information is divided into basic subunits: profitability, earnings, capital adequacy, credit risk management, and asset/liability management. Operating performance is evaluated using standard ratios.

The best measurement of a bank's earnings is its pretax operating income. Analysts also compute a bank's performance ratios with income before securities transactions instead of net income to avoid distortions that can result from including such data.

Additional ratios or amounts not shown on Figures 12–1 or 12–2 that are often computed by bank analysts include the number of full-time equivalent employees (FTE), salary and benefits per employee (total employee expenses/total number of employees), total assets per employee (dollar total assets/FTE), percentage change in salary and benefits, and many others. Figure 12-3 shows the relationship of ROA to banking.

Marketing effectiveness is evaluated in terms of target objectives such as new loans, new deposits, share of market or as related to the specific objective of the marketing effort.

Figure 12-1
Financial Statement Ratios

Ratio	Formula	Interpretation
Liquidity ratios		
a. Current (or working capital) ratio	$\dfrac{\text{Current assets}}{\text{Current liabilities}}$	Short-term debt-paying ability (i.e., dollar amount of current assets from which to obtain funds necessary to liquidate each dollar of current liabilities).
b. Acid-test (or quick) ratio	$\dfrac{\text{Quick assets, i.e., cash marketable Securities, receivables}}{\text{Current liabilities}}$	A more severe test of the short-term debt-paying ability than the current ratio since it excludes inventory (which awaits sale) and prepaid expenses.
c. Cash ratio	$\dfrac{\text{Cash}}{\text{Current liabilities}}$	The severest test of short-term debt-paying ability.
Measures of the movement or turnover of current assets and liabilities		
a. Receivables turnover	$\dfrac{\text{Sales (net)}}{\text{Average receivables (net)}}$	The efficiency in collecting receivables and in managing credit.
b. Age of Receivables	$\dfrac{365}{\text{Receivables turnover}}$	The number of days it takes on the average to collect accounts receivable; the extent of control over credit and collection.
c. Inventory turnover	$\dfrac{\text{Cost of goods sold}}{\text{Average inventory}}$	Marketability of inventory, efficiency in the management of inventory, and the resonableness of the quantity of inventory on hand.
d. Days in inventory	$\dfrac{365}{\text{Inventory turnover}}$	The average number of days required to use or sell inventory (e.g., the average period that an item is held in inventory). For a manufacturing company, the number of days should correspond closely with production time.
e. Working capital turnover	$\dfrac{\text{Net sales}}{\text{Average working capital}}$	The extent to which a company is using working capital to generate sales.
f. Number of days' purchases in ending accounts payable	$\dfrac{\text{Accounts payable}}{\text{Average daily purchases}}$	The extent to which the company its paying bills promptly.

Ratio	Formula	Interpretation
Solvency ratios		
1. Measures of capital structure:		
a. Owners' equity to total sales	$\dfrac{\text{Total owners' equity}}{\text{Total assets (net)}}$	Proportion of firm's assets provided by owner.
b. Owners' equity to total liabi8lities	$\dfrac{\text{Total owner's equity}}{\text{Total liabilities}}$	Relative claims of owners and creditors to rest of firm.
c. Fixed assets to total equity	$\dfrac{\text{Total owners' equity}}{\text{Fixed assets (net)}}$	Relationship of owners' investment to the company investment in fixed assets (i.e., the higher the ratio, the less owners' capital is available for working capital).
d. Book value per share of common stock	$\dfrac{\text{Common stock equity}}{\text{Number of common shares outstanding}}$	Net assets reported on financial statement per share of common stock.
2. Measures of debt structure (debt management)		
a. Total liabilities to total assets	$\dfrac{\text{Total liabilities}}{\text{Total assets (net)}}$	Protection available to creditors and the extent to which the company is trading on equity.
b. Total liabilities to owners' equity	$\dfrac{\text{Total liabilities}}{\text{Owners' equity}}$	Relationship between total debt and equity financing. "What is owed to what is owned."
Profitability (earnings) ratios		
1. Net income to sales	$\dfrac{\text{Net income}}{\text{Net sales}}$	Profit margtin per dollar of sales.
2. Operating ratio	$\dfrac{\text{Cost of goods sold} + \text{operating expenses}}{\text{Net sales}}$	Profit margin per dollar of sales.
3. Sales to total assets (or asset turnover)	$\dfrac{\text{Net sales}}{\text{Average total assets}}$	Productivity of all assets in generating sales.
4. Earnings per share of common stock	$\dfrac{\text{Net income} - \text{preferred dividend measurements}}{\text{Average number of common stock}}$	Return on common shareholders' investment per share of common stock.

Figure 12-2
Financial Statement Ratios for Banks

Area Measured	Ratio	Formula	Description
LIQUIDITY	Liquid Assets to Borrowings	$\dfrac{LIQA}{BORR}$	Liquid Assets (Due from Banks plus Fed Funds Sold plus Trading Securities plus Securities with less than 1 year to maturity) divided by Federal Funds purchased plus Other Borrowings
	Liquid Assets to Borrowings & Large CDs	$\dfrac{LIQA}{BORR \& CD}$	Liquid Assets (see preceding description) divided by Federal Funds Purchased plus Other Borrowings plus Large Denomination CDs with less than 1 year maturity.
	Loans to Deposits	$\dfrac{TLOANS}{TDEP}$	Total Loans divided by Total Deposits. Measures amount of deposits committed to loans by the bank.
RISK	Earnings Volatility Index	$\dfrac{SD}{Mean}$	Standard Deviation of annual year-to-year earnings growth divided by the Mean of the year-to-year earnings growth (5 years if available). Measures earning volatility.
	Rate Sensitivity Mismatch	$\dfrac{VRA-VRL}{TA}$	Variable Rate Assets minus Variable Rate Liabilities divided by Total Average Assets.
	Loss Coverage Rate	$\dfrac{NI + TAX + LP}{NCO}$	Net Income plus Taxes plus Loss Provision divided by Net Charge-offs.
	Loan Loss Reserve to Loans	$\dfrac{LLR}{TLOAN}$	Loan Loss Reserve divided by Total Average Loans. Measures loan quality.
	Equity to Assets or Capital Ratio	$\dfrac{EQ}{TA}$	Total Shareholders' Equity divided by Total Assets.
	Equity + LLR to Loans	$\dfrac{EQ + LLR}{TLOANS}$	Total Shareholders' Equity plus Loan Loss Reserve to Total Loans.
	Capital to Risk Assets	$\dfrac{EQ + DST + LLR}{TA-CASH-LIQA}$	Total Shareholders' Equity plus Long-Term Subordinated Debt plus Loan Loss Reserve divided by Total Assets less Cash and Liquid Assets.
	Net Charge-Offs to Loans	$\dfrac{NCO}{TLoans}$	Net Charge-offs to Total Average Loans. Measures loan quality.
GROWTH	Earnings per Share	$\dfrac{CYE/S}{PYE/S} - 1$	Current Year Earnings per Share divided by Prior Year Earnings per Share minus 1.

Figure continues

Figure 12-2
Continued

Area Measured	Ratio	Formula	Description
GROWTH	Dividends per Share	$\dfrac{CYD/S}{PYE/S} - 1$	Current Year Dividends per Share divided by Prior Year Dividends per Share minus 1
	Total Assets	$\dfrac{CYTA}{PYTA} - 1$	Current Year Total Average Assets divided by Prior Year Total Average Assets minus 1.
	Total Loans	$\dfrac{CYTL}{PYTL} - 1$	Current Year Total Loans divided by Prior Year Total Loans minus 1.
	Total DDA & Savings	$\dfrac{CYDDA + S}{PYDDA + S} - 1$	Current Year Total DDA & Savings divided by Prior Year Total DDA & Savings minus 1.
	Total Deposits	$\dfrac{CYTD}{PYTD} - 1$	Current Year Total Deposits divided by Prior Year Total Deposits minus 1.
	Equity	$\dfrac{CYEQ}{PYEQ} - 1$	Current Year Total Shareholder Equity divided by Prior Year Total Shareholder Equity minus 1.
	Growth in assets	$\dfrac{\text{Current year's assets}}{\text{Previous year's assets}} - 1$	
	Growth in loans	$\dfrac{\text{Current year's loans}}{\text{Previous year's loans}} - 1$	
	Growth in deposits	$\dfrac{\text{Current year's deposits}}{\text{Previous year's deposits}} - 1$	
	Growth in income	$\dfrac{\text{Current year's income}}{\text{Previous year's income}} - 1$	
	Growth in equity	$\dfrac{\text{Current year's equity}}{\text{Previous year's equity}} - 1$	
	Growth in dividends	$\dfrac{\text{Current year's dividends}}{\text{Previous year's dividends}} - 1$	
	Dividend payout ratio	$\dfrac{\text{Current year's dividend}}{\text{Net income}}$	
PROFITABILITY	Return on Assets (ROA)	$\dfrac{NOI}{TA}$	Net Operating Income (after tax) divided by Total Average Assets.
	Net Interest Margin	$\dfrac{NII}{TA}$	Net Interest Income divided by Total Average Assets. Measures ability of management to generate net income.
	Other Income Contribution	$\dfrac{TOI}{TA}$	Total Other Income divided by Total Average Assets.
	Loss Provision	$\dfrac{LP}{TA}$	Provision for Loan Loss divided by Total Average Assets.

Figure continues

Figure 12-2
Continued

Area Measured	Ratio	Formula	Description
PROFITABILITY	Shareholder Return	$\dfrac{\text{DIV.} + \text{APPREC.}}{\text{BEG. MV}}$	Cash Dividends per share plus share price appreciation (Ending share price minus Beginning share price) divided by Beginning Market Value (i.e., share price)
	Return on Equity (ROE)	$\dfrac{\text{NOI}}{\text{EQ}}$	Net Operating Income (after tax) divided by Average Shareholder's Equity.
	Dividend Payout	$\dfrac{\text{DIV}}{\text{NI}}$	Cash Dividends declared divided by Net Income.
	Security Gains & Losses	$\dfrac{\text{SB/L}}{\text{TA}}$	Security Gains and Losses (net of Taxes) divided by Total Average Assets.
Yield on Average Earning Assets		$\dfrac{\text{Interest Income}}{\text{Average Earning Assets}}$	Earning assets include balance of loans securities, and other interest-bearing assets. Measures the yield on earning assets.
Rate Paid on Funds		$\dfrac{\text{Interest Expenses}}{\text{Average Interest–Bearing Liabilities}}$	Measures the cost of funds employed by the bank.
Net Interest Margin		$\dfrac{\text{Interest Income} - \text{Interest Expense}}{\text{Average Earning Assets}}$	Measures the spread and relationship of interest-bearing assets to interest-bearing liabilities.
CAPITAL STRUCTURE			
Capital Ratio		$\dfrac{\text{Shareholders' Equity}}{\text{Total Assets}}$	Relationship of stockholders' equity to total assets. Measures the adequacy of capital.
Capital to Debt		$\dfrac{\text{Shareholders' Equity}}{\text{Total Liabilities}}$	Relationship of stockholders' equity to total debt.

Figure 12-3
ROA Bank Relationships

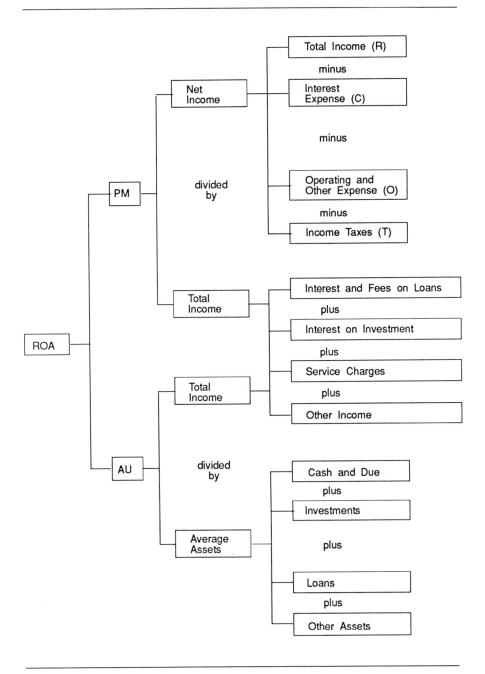

INDUSTRY GUIDE 3—SELECTIVE REPORTING

The SEC's Industry Guide 3, *Statistical Disclosure by Bank Holding Companies*, provides a description of business portions of those bank holding company registration statements for which financial statements are required. This guide for banks provides specific reporting on the following financial ratios:

1. Return on assets (net income/average total assets)

2. Return on equity (net income/average equity)

3. Dividend payout ratio (dividends, declared per share divided by net income per share)

4. Equity to assets ratio (average equity divided by average total assets)

The Industry Guide also requires the presentation of detailed account analyses. The Guide prescribes a format for balance sheets that requires the reporting of significant categories of assets and liabilities, including all major categories of interest-earning assets and interest-bearing liabilities reported. For each reporting period, an analysis of net interest earnings must be presented:

1. For each major category of interest-earning asset and each major category of interest-bearing liability, and the average amount outstanding during the period and the interest earned or paid on such amount

2. The average yield for each major category of interest-bearing assets

3. The average rate paid for each major category of interest-bearing liability

4. The average yield on all interest-earning assets and the average effective rate paid on all interest-bearing liabilities

5. The net yield on interest-earning assets (net interest-earnings divided by total interest-earning assets, with net interest earnings equaling the difference between total interest earned and total interest paid).

For the last two fiscal years, a bank must present (1) the dollar amount of change in interest income and (2) the dollar amount of change in interest expense. The changes should be segregated for each major category of interest-earning asset and interest-bearing liability into amounts attributable to (a) changes in volume (change in volume times old rate), (b) changes in rates (change in rate times old volume), and (c) changes in rate/volume (change in rate times the change in volume.

Investment Portfolio

The Guide requires that as of the end of each reported period, the bank must present the book value of investments in obligations of (1) the U.S. Treasury and other U.S. government agencies and corporations; (2) States of the U.S. and political subdivisions; and (3) other securities including bonds, notes, debentures and stock of business corporations, foreign governments and political subdivisions, intergovernmental agencies and the Federal Reserve bank. These categories must present the amount which is due (1) in one year or less, (2) after one year through five years, (3) after five years through ten years, and (4) after ten years. In addition, the weighted average yield for each range of maturities must be stated.

As of the end of the latest reported period, the Guide requires that the name of any issuer, and the aggregate book value and aggregated market value of the securities of such issues, when the aggregate book value of such securities exceeds 10 percent of stockholders' equity, be stated.

Loan Portfolio

At the end of each reported period, the amount of loans in various categories must be presented:
Domestic:

1. Commercial, financial, and agricultural

2. Real estate—construction

3. Real estate—mortgage

4. Installment loans to individuals

5. Lease financing

Foreign:

6. Governments and official institutions

7. Banks and other financial institutions

8. Commercial and industrial

9. Other loans

Maturities and Sensitivities of Loans to Changes in Interest Rates

As of the end of the latest fiscal year reported, the bank must present separately the amount of loans in each category that are due in one year or less, due after one year through five years, and due after five years.

Risk Elements

Regarding risk elements in loans, a bank must report as of the end of each reported period: (a) loans accounted for on a nonaccrual basis; (b) accruing loans which are contractually past due 90 days or more as to principal or interest payments; and (c) loans not included above that are "troubled debt restructurings" as defined in SFAS No. 15.

A discussion of the bank's policy for placing loans on nonaccrual status must be provided. As of the end of the most recent reported period, the bank must describe the nature and extent of any loans that are not disclosed above, but where known information about possible credit problems of borrowers causes management to have serious doubts as to the ability of such borrowers to comply with the present loan repayment terms and that could result in disclosure of such loans at a later date.

Loan Loss Experience

Banks must also provide a summary of loan loss experience. The analysis involves an analysis of the Allowance for Loan Losses. The report should show

- The balance at the beginning of the period
- Charge-offs during the period (domestic, foreign)
- Recoveries (domestic, foreign)
- Net charge-offs; additions charged to operations
- Balance at end of period
- Ratio of net charge-offs during the period to average loans outstanding during the period

The analysis should also show an allocation of the Allowance for Loan Losses account balance at the end of the period in dollar amounts and as a percent of loans in each category to total loans.

Deposits

The Guide also requires for each reported period the average amount of and the average rate paid on each of the following deposit categories that are in excess of 10 percent of average total deposits:

Deposits in domestic bank offices:

1. Noninterest bearing demand deposits
2. Interest bearing demand deposits
3. Savings deposits
4. Time deposits

Deposits in foreign banking offices:

5. Banks located in foreign countries
6. Foreign governments and official institutions
7. Other foreign demand deposits
8. Other foreign time and savings deposits

If amounts are material, the registrant should disclose separately the aggregate amount of deposits by foreign depositors in domestic offices. Identification of the nationality of the depositors is not required. As of the end of the latest reported period, the bank must state the amount outstanding of time certificates of deposits and other time deposits in amounts of $100,000 or more issued by foreign offices.

Short-Term Borrowings

For short-term borrowings the bank must provide the following information:

1. The amount outstanding at the end of the reported period, the weighted average interest rate thereon, and the general terms thereof

2. The maximum amount of borrowings in each category outstanding at any month-end during each reported period

3. The approximate average amounts outstanding during each reported period and the appropriate weighted average interest rate thereon

REPORT FORMAT

Financial statement analysis data can be compiled in various formats. Several formats are illustrated here.

1. Ratio comparisons of banks—reporting period:

| | | Competitor Banks | | |
Ratios	Our Bank	Bank A	Bank B	Bank C

2. Statement of Financial Position:

Same Month Last Year	YTD	Balance Sheet Accounts	Average of Last Month	Budget for Last Month	Budget Variance

3. Income Statement—reporting period:

Same Month Last Yr	Income Statement Accounts	Last Month	Last Month YTD	Budget Variance

4. Key Ratios—Quarters

Same Qt. Last Yr	YTD	Variance Ratios	Quarter	Year to Date	Budget YTD	YTD from Budget

SEGMENT REPORTING

Financial analysis is improved through the presentation of disaggregated segment financial information. SFAS No. 14, "Financial Reporting for Segments of a Business Enterprise," requires that a company's financial statements include information about its operations in different industries, its foreign operations and export sales, and its major customers. An industry segment is a component of an enterprise that provides a product or service or group of related products and services, primarily to unaffiliated customers, for a profit.

Different industry segments and/or geographic areas may possess different levels of profitability, risk, and growth. Assessing profitability, risk, and growth can be assisted by having segmental data available.

Reportable Industry Segments

An industry segment is considered a reportable segment if it satisfied one of the three 10 percent tests:

1.   *Revenue test* Segment revenue is at least 10 percent of the combined revenue of all industry segments.

2.   *Operating profit and loss test* The absolute amount of segment operating profit or loss is equal at least 10 percent of the greater, in absolute amounts, of

     a.   Combined operating profit of all segments reporting a profit

     b.   Combined operating losses of all segments reporting a loss

3.   The identifiable assets of the segment are 10 percent or more of the combined identifiable assets of all industry segments.

The combined unaffiliated revenue of all reportable segments must be at least 75 percent of the combined unaffiliated revenue of all segments. If the 75 percent is not satisfied, additional segments must be designated as reportable until the test is satisfied.

Also, the number of reportable segments should not be so large as to decrease the usefulness of segment reporting. The FASB suggests that if the number of reportable segments exceeds ten, segment information may become too detailed. The most closely related industry segments should be combined into broader reportable segments.

Another possibility is the presence of a dominant segment. A dominant segment is one whose revenue, operating profit or loss, and identifiable assets all exceed 90 percent of the combined totals when no other segment meets any of the 10 percent tests. The dominant segment must be identified, but detailed segment reporting is not required.

Certain disclosures are required for each reportable segment and in the aggregate for the remainder of the industry segments. These disclosures include revenue information, profitability information, identifiable assets information, and other disclosures (aggregate amount of depreciation, depletion, and amortization, the amount of capital expenditures; equity in unconsolidated but vertically integrated subsidiaries and their geographic location; and the effect of a change in accounting principles on segment income). These disclosures can be presented within the body of the financial statements, in the footnotes to the statements, or in a separate schedule that is an integral part of the financial statements.

Foreign Operations, Geographic Areas, and Export Sales

An enterprise's foreign operations are considered reportable if one of two 10 percent tests are satisfied:

1.   Unaffiliated revenue is at least 10 percent of consolidated revenue

2.   Identifiable assets test. Identifiable assets are at least 10 percent of consolidated total assets

If an enterprise operates in two or more foreign geographic areas, the above tests are also applied to each area to determine if any individual areas are reportable. A geographic area is an individual country or group of countries. Information to be disclosed about the foreign operations in aggregate or foreign geographic areas individually include

1.   Unaffiliated and intraenterprise revenues

2.   Operating profit or loss or net income or some measure of profitability

3.   Identifiable assets

Information About Major Customers

If an enterprise earns 10 percent or more of its revenue on sales to a single customer, that fact and the amount of revenue from each such customer must be disclosed.

CAPITAL ADEQUACY

In 1989 federal banking regulators composed of the Federal Reserve, the Comptroller of the Currency, and the Federal Deposit Insurance Commission issued new capital guidelines for commercial banks. The basic purpose of the guidelines is to increase capital levels of commercial banks as their financial structures increase since capital adequacy is basic to bank safety and soundness regulation. Recent emphasis has focused on standardizing banks' capital requirements.

Risk-based capital requirements assess the riskiness of a financial institution's balance sheet assets and off-balance sheet commitments, (letters of credit and swap exposures) in relation to its capital structure. Hopefully, the general regulations should

1.   Make regulatory capital evaluation and requirements more sensitive to differing risk profiles

2.   Include off-balance sheet items in that evaluation

3.   Reduce disincentives to holding liquid low-risk assets

4.   Foster coordination of supervisory authorities from major industrial countries

The Board of Governors of the Federal Reserve System monitors the implementation of the risk-based capital regulations.

Risk-based capital requirements redefine capital. Under the 1989 guidelines risk-weighted capital ratios must equal 7.25 percent by the end of 1990 and 8 percent, with half the capital composed of core capital instruments or contributions, by the end of 1992. Transitional rules are in effect during the transitional period beginning January 1, 1990. The regulations are considered a *minimum*. Most banks will have no problem meeting the new guidelines. Currently regulators are pressing for institutions to exceed the 8 percent minimum.

Under the guidelines capital consists of "Tier One" (core capital) and "Tier Two" (supplementary capital). The sum of Tiers One and Two must equal or exceed 8 percent of the sum of risk-weighted assets and credit equivalents. Tier One capital consists of equity capital (common, cumulative/noncumulative, perpetual preferred stock—excluding auction rate issues) and minority interests that are held by others in consolidated subsidiaries, plus disclosed reserves, with two adjustments. Goodwill is deducted from the sum of equity capital and disclosed reserves. Bank holding companies may count both cumulative and noncumulative perpetual preferred stock. Tier Two capital (supplementary capital) consists of five elements that can serve the loss-absorption function: undisclosed reserves, revaluation reserves, general loan loss provisions, hybrid instruments, and subordinated term debt. Tier Two is limited to the amount of Tier One and cannot include loan reserves in excess of 1.25 percent of risk-weighted assets. Regulators are required to monitor compliance with the guidelines and can make exceptions or require higher capital levels.

According to the guidelines, assets are classified into one of four categories from the least risky to the most risky: (1) cash and direct debt of the U.S. government and its agencies (0 percent weighing), (2) claims on domestic depository institutions, debt conditionally guaranteed by the U.S. government and debt of government-sponsored agencies (20 percent weighing), (3) accruing loans secured by first liens on one- to four-family houses, mortgage-backed securities backed by conventional mortgages and certain state or local revenue bonds or revenue-backed obligations (50 percent weighing) and (4) all other assets (100 percent weighing).

Off-balance-sheet risks such as letters of credit, assets sold with recourse and formal loan commitments are included in assets through conversion to "credit equivalents." To determine a credit equivalent amount, each off-balance-sheet risk is weighted (0 percent, 20 percent, 50 percent, or 100 percent) and assigned to the appropriate risk category based on the obligor, guarantor, or type of collateral.

The capital ratio is computed as the sum of Tiers One and Two capital divided by the sum of risk-weighted assets and credit equivalent (qualifying assets/weighted risk assets).

The capital guidelines are comprehensive and detailed. It is anticipated that bank auditors will give special attention to the classification of home loans and securities, how off-balance-sheet risks are reported, procedures used to compute loan loss reserves that could be used to minimize specified losses, accounting used to avoid consolidating subsidiaries, underwriting standards for home loans, analyzing competitor banks to determine their risk-based capital positions, pricing off-balance-sheet risks and loan products, computing and applying risk-based capital ratios, and analyzing bond portfolio records to ensure proper classification.

The 1989 guidelines have significant impacts on commercial banks and their customers. Many banks will undoubtedly attempt to improve their capital leverage. Banks with capital in excess of the requirements may opt for aggressive growth to improve bank leverage. Also, because of the requirements of the guidelines, it is possible that home mortgages will become more attractive (qualifying home loans require only half the capital of other loans); as a result, rates for first mortgage home loans may decrease while rates for personal and commercial loans may increase, other things remaining the same.

An example of applying risk-based capital guidelines is presented in Figure 12-4 adapted from an example provided in the January 1990 issue of the *Journal of Accountancy*, "Risk-based Capital Guidelines for Banks," by J. Robert Kelly.

Capital adequacy regulations approved by the Board of Governors of the Federal Reserve System were issued in the January 27, 1989, issue of the *Federal Register*. They took effect on March 15, 1989 (54 Fed. Rg. 4186). The Office of the Comptroller of the Currency also issued

Figure 12-4
Example of Applying Risk-based Capital Guidelines (000's omitted)

	Balance Sheet Amount	Credit Conversion Factor	Amount	Risk-weighted category				
				0%	20%	50%	100%
Qualifying real estate loans	$1,500	N/A	$1,500			$1,500	
Other loans, net of $50 reserve	1,000	N/A	1,000				$1,000
U.S. Treasury bonds	500	N/A	500	$500			
Nonguaranteed agency bonds	500	N/A	500		$500		
Other bonds	500	N/A	500				500
Other Assets	330	N/A	330				330
Total Assets	$4,330						
Off-balance-sheet items	$400	50%[1]	200				200
Category totals				$500	$500	$1,500	$2,030
Risk-weighted totals				$ 0	$100	$ 750	$2,030 $2,880

Table continues

Figure 12-4
Continued

Capital		Amount	Tier 1	Tier 2	Total
Shareholder's equity—common		$216	$216		$216
Capital notes		20		$20	20
Loan Reserve		50		36	36[2]
			$216	$56	$272
Capital ratios:					
Old guidelines	—Primary	6.07%[3]			
	—Total	6.53%[4]			
New guidelines	—Tier 1	7.50%[5]			
	—Tier 2	1.04%[5]			
	—Total	9.44%[5]			

1. Assumed that the off-balance-sheet item involved qualified for the 50% credit conversion factor and the 100% risk weight category.
2. Limited to 1.25% of total risk-weighted assets ($2,880).
3. Computed as the sum of common equity ($216) plus the loan reserve ($50) divided by the sum of total assets ($4,330) plus loan reserves ($50).
4. Primary capital ($266) plus capital notes ($20) divided by the primary capital ratio denominator ($4,380).
5. Tier 1 ($216), tier 2 ($56) and total capital ($272) divided by risk-weighted assets ($2,880).

Source: Kelley, J.R. "Risk-Based Capital Guidelines for Banks," *Journal of Accounting*, January, 1990. Adapted with permission.

regulations that were published in *Federal Register* (January 27, 1989). These regulations apply to all nationally chartered banks and are almost identical to the Board's regulations. The Federal Deposit Insurance Corporation also issued risk-based capital regulations that were published in the *Federal Register* (March 21, 1989). These regulations apply to state-chartered banks that are not members of the Federal Reserve System and are similar to the Board's final regulations.

Regulator-determined capital is designed to absorb losses, particularly unexpected losses, arising from a bank's asset portfolio or its off-balance-sheet activities. It is also maintained that regulatory-determined capital is required to instill public confidence in the banking system.

The Federal Financial Institutions Examination Council Final Regulation approved changes in bank Call Reports designed to give regulators data on risk-based capital levels and off-balance sheet activities. The revision includes a simplified test for banks to determine if they meet minimum risk-based capital ratios. Banks with assets under $1 billion meeting this test will not have to answer a number of detailed questions. After December 1990, the reported data will be publicly available.

Risk-based capital planning can assist a bank in evaluating the impact of varying interest rates, profitability, and growth assumptions on it future operations. For example, in attaining the capital ratio, several choices can be made:

Control the rate of growth

Control the level of retained earnings

Restructure the assets to provide a lower applicable risk weight category

Sell assets

Issue new debt or equity securities

Merge with or acquire better capitalized institutions

Source: *Overview of Risk-Based Capital Requirement: A management guide to compliance,* Regulatory Compliance Associates, Inc., Bank Administration Institute.

GOING CONCERN CONSIDERATIONS

External financial reports are prepared on the assumption that the business entity will continue to operate indefinitely and will not be liquidated in the foreseeable future. When this is not the case, the going-concern assumption is no longer valid.

While there are many causes of financial distress, the following factors have been identified as usually directly or indirectly involved:

1. Financial problems—difficulties in meeting obligations:
    (a) Liquidity deficiency
    (b) Equity deficiency
    (c) Debt default
    (d) Funds shortage
2. Operating problems—apparent lack of operating success:

(a)   Continued operating losses

(b)   Prospective revenues doubtful

(c)   Ability to operate is jeopardized

(d)   Incapable management

(e)   Poor control over operations

Specific signs of financial distress include the following: liquidation process begun; declining share of major product markets, deferment of payment to short-term creditors, omission of preferred stock dividends, the filing of Chapter 7 or Chapter 11 bankruptcy, efforts to dispose of a segment of a business, bond defaults; overdrawn bank account, debt restructuring; externally forced revisions of operation, insolvency and illiquidity. The financially healthy firm usually has an adequate return on investment and a sound balance sheet.

The auditor's responsibility is to evaluate whether there is substantial doubt for a reasonable period of time about the going-concern condition of the firm. If substantial doubt exists, the auditors obtain management's plans and assess the likelihood of the plans being implemented. If substantial doubt remains, the auditor considers the adequacy of disclosures on the firm's inability to continue and whether to include an explanatory paragraph following the opinion paragraph in the audit report. Auditors are not responsible for predicting future conditions and events.

HORIZONTAL AND VERTICAL ANALYSIS

Horizontal analysis and vertical analysis of financial statements are additional techniques that can be used effectively when evaluating a company. Horizontal analysis spotlights trends and establishes relationships between items that appear on the same row of a comparative statement thereby disclosing changes on items in financial statements over time. Each line item (such as sales) on a row for one fiscal period is compared with the same item in a different period. Horizontal analysis can be performed in terms of changes in dollar amounts, in percentage of change, or in a ratio format (year to year).

Vertical analysis involves the conversion of items appearing in statement columns into terms of percentages of a base figure to show the relative significance of the items and to facilitate comparisons. For example, individual items appearing on the income statement can be expressed as percentages of sales. On the balance sheet individual assets can be expressed as a percentage of total assets. Liabilities and owners' equity accounts can be expressed in terms of their relationship to total liabilities and owners' equity.

When horizontal analysis is used, care should be taken in computing percentage changes. If a base figure is zero or negative, although an amount of the change may be shown, no percentage change may be validly expressed mathematically. In cases where changes are expressed as percentages, no vertical addition or subtraction of the percentages can be made because the percentage changes result from the use of different bases. For items having a small base amount, a relatively small dollar change can result in a very high percentage change.

TIME-SERIES ANALYSIS

Time-series analysis is used where data classified on the basis of intervals of time represent vital information in the control and operation of a business or bank. The changes that can be isolated in time-series analysis are of the following major types:

1. *Secular trend* reflects the effect of forces making for gradual growth or decline over a long period of time.

2. *Seasonal variations* regular recurring variations with the seasons of the year.

3. *Cyclical fluctuations* A recurring type of change not having a fixed period.

4. *Random or erratic fluctuations* innumerable small variations that are essentially random in nature, resulting from a number of factors, most of which are relatively unimportant.

REGRESSION AND CORRELATION ANALYSIS

Regression analysis uses the relationship between a known variable and an unknown variable to estimate the unknown variable. Correlation analysis measures the degree of relationship between two or more variables.

THE AUDITOR'S REPORT

Financial analysis of a company should include an examination of the financial statements of the company by an external auditor, including notes to the financial statements, and the auditor's report. The auditor's report will state whether the financial statements have been audited in accordance with generally accepted auditing standards. The report also indicates whether the statements fairly present the company's financial position, results of operations, and statement of cash flows in accordance with generally accepted accounting principles. Notes to the financial statements are considered an integral part of the statements. Notes are often more meaningful than the data found within the body of the statements. The notes explain the accounting policies of the company and usually provide detailed explanations of how those policies were applied, along with supporting details.

In a typical report management includes an analysis of the current and previous years, which is referred to as the "Management's Discussion and Analysis." In this section of the report, management discusses the company's operations, financial position, and other important matters. This section should be read with caution. Refer to Chapter 15, "Bank Examinations and Audits" for additional information.

LIMITATIONS OF FINANCIAL STATEMENT ANALYSIS

Financial statement analysis has its limitations. Statements represent the past and do not necessarily predict the future. However, financial statement analysis can provide clues or suggest a need for further investigation.

What is found on financial statements is the product of accounting principles and methods (LIFO or FIFO inventory, straight-line or accelerated depreciation) that sometimes distort the economic reality or substance of the underlying situation. Furthermore, many of the numbers found on financial statements are estimates, which can introduce an element of subjectivity into the underlying data.

Financial statements are subject to manipulation by management. Cost and revenue estimates can be understated or overstated; expenses and revenues can be shifted from one period to another. Ratios are no more relevant and reliable than the data that goes into the computations. Professional judgment is always subject to question.

Financial statements say little directly about changes in markets, the business cycle, technological developments, laws and regulations, management personnel, price-level changes (inflation and deflation), the quality of earnings, and other critical analytical concerns. Financial ratios reflect symptoms of good or bad performance, not causes. An attempt should be made to determine the causes of good or bad performance.

ELEMENTS OF A GOOD FINANCIAL ANALYSIS REPORT

A committee of the Financial Analysts Federation outlined the elements of good financial reporting:

1. Clear presentation of information that goes beyond the minimum reporting requirements and puts company operations in perspective.

2. Written commentary that explains why important developments occurred.

3. A timely, consistent, and responsible investor relations program that informs the financial analyst in an unbiased manner.

4. An ability to articulate and communicate the business philosophy and principal strategies of management and the way in which management is organized to carry them out.

Many analytical tools and techniques of financial statement analysis are available and their use should be selective. In determining which ones to use, consider its relevance, controllability, consistency, comparability, and simplicity.

KEY DEFINITIONS

Capital adequacy See the Glossary at the end of this chapter.

Capital structure The debt and equity of an organization.

Common-size statements Statements in which each element is shown as a percentage of some major total.

Comparative financial statements Current and past financial statements of a company.

Equities Interests in assets of owners and creditors.

Financial statement analysis The analysis of financial statements to evaluate the strengths and weaknesses and future operating prospects of a company. Financial analysis often involves liquidity, profitability, activity, financial structure, and solvency analysis.

Going concern A business entity that is assumed to remain in operations long enough for all of its current plans to be carried out.

Horizontal analysis Current and past financial statement accounts of a company presented side by side with the dollar amount of increase or decrease together with the percentage of proportionate increase or decrease.

Leverage The use of long-term debt in securing funds for the entity. Operating leverage refers to the tendency of net income to rise at a faster rate than sales when there are fixed costs. Financial leverage refers to the increased rate of return on owners' equity when an investment earns a return larger than the pre-tax interest rate paid for debt financing.

Liquidity The ability to pay currently maturing debts.

Ratio The relationship of one amount to another.

Ratio analysis The analysis of the proportion of financial items from period to period by converting the dollar amounts to a percentage, a decimal, or a fraction.

Segment A component of an entity whose activities represent a separate major line of business or class of customers. It can be a subsidiary, a division, or a department provided its assets, results of operations, and assets can be clearly distinguished.

Segment reporting Line of business reporting.

Solvency The excess of the fair market value of total assets over total liabilities.

Vertical analysis Current and past financial statements of a company presented side by side with comparisons made of each component as a percentage of a base total within those statements.

Working capital The excess of current assets over current liabilities.

Capital Adequacy

Capital Most generally, the difference between total assets and total liabilities. In the context of banking regulation, those items included in the numerator when the capital/asset ratio is calculated.

Capital/asset ratio The amount of capital maintained, divided by the total assets owned. Also known as a leverage ratio or gearing ratio.

Capital/risk-weighted assets ratio The amount of capital maintained, divided by the sum of (1) the total assets owned, where the value of each asset is assigned a risk weight and (2) the credit equivalent amount of all off-balance sheet activities, where each credit equivalent amount is assigned a risk weight.

Common stock Shares of ownership in a corporation that entitle the holder to dividend distributions made by the issuer. Common stock counts as Tier One capital.

Core capital Tier One capital.

Counterparty The other or opposite party to a contract.

Credit conversion factor A percentage amount applied to the full face value of off-balance-sheet activities other than interest or foreign exchange rate contracts to determine a credit equivalent amount.

Credit equivalent amount The deemed actual credit exposure arising from an off-balance-sheet activity. A credit conversion factor is applied to the full face value of the activity. A risk weight is then applied to the credit equivalent amount to calculate the risk-weighted value for the activity.

Credit risk The risk of financial loss from a default on an obligation.

Currency risk The risk of financial loss from an adverse foreign exchange rate movement.

Current credit exposure The mark-to-market value of a foreign exchange rate contract or interest rate contract.

Current exposure method The method prescribed in the Basle Agreement to calculate the credit equivalent amount on foreign exchange and interest rate contracts. It involves calculation of the current credit exposure and the potential future credit exposure. The sum of these is the replacement cost, which is taken to be the credit equivalent amount. A risk weight is then applied to this amount.

Disclosed reserves Reserves that are created or increased by appropriations of retained earnings or other surplus disclosed on the balance sheet. Essentially, disclosed reserves consist of retained earnings and paid-in capital in excess of par value (or capital surplus if no-par stock is issued).

Equity capital Under the Basle Agreement, equity capital consists of common stock, noncumulative preferred stock, and (for bank holding companies) perpetual cumulative preferred stocks.

Floating-rate preferred stock Preferred stock whose yield varies with a certain index. The index may be a market interest rate, the issuer's credit standing, or the issuer's financial condition. Also called adjustable-rate preferred stock.

General provisions and general loan loss reserves Provisions and reserves that are held against future unidentified losses and are freely available to meet any subsequent losses.

Goodwill An intangible asset reflecting the excess of the purchase price over the fair market value of net assets in an acquisition in which the purchase method of accounting is used.

Hidden reserves See Undisclosed reserves.

Hybrid instruments Financial instruments that combine features of debt and equity. An example is mandatory convertible debt. Hybrid instruments may be included in Tier Two capital.

Interest rate risk The risk of financial loss from an adverse interest rate movement.

Leverage ratio See Capital/asset ratio.

Limited life preferred stock Preferred stock with a stated maturity.

Loan loss provisions See General provisions and general loan loss reserves.

Loss absorption The reduction in a capital account that corresponds with the reduction in an asset account.

Mark-to-market value The current market value of an item.

Netting Treating several transactions between the same counterparties not individually but as a whole. That is, considering the net claim arising from all transactions between the same counterparties, rather than the gross claims.

Obligor The party obligated to perform on a contract.

Perpetual preferred stock Preferred stock that has no fixed maturity and cannot be redeemed at the holder's options. Perpetual preferred stock may be noncumulative, which means that dividends do not accrue (if they are not paid, they do not accumulate as arrearages). By contrast, unpaid dividends on cumulative perpetual preferred stock do accrue and must be paid off before any dividends on common stock are paid.

Preferred stock Stock that entitles the holder to a preference in dividend distributions and/or a liquidation distribution over common stockholders.

Replacement cost The cost to the nondefaulting party of replacing the cash flows that it was entitled to under a foreign exchange or interest rate contract but that were lost because of counterparty default.

Revaluation reserves Reserve accounts on the right-hand side of the balance sheet that are increased whenever an asset on the left-hand side is revalued to reflect its market value. A revaluation reserve thus reflects the unrealized appreciation in an asset. The full amount of unrealized appreciation of fixed asset may be included in Tier Two capital, as may 45 percent of the unrealized appreciation of common stock. U.S. banks and bank holding companies are not permitted to revalue assets, but banking organizations in some other countries, such as Japan, are permitted to do so.

Risk weight A percentage amount applied to the full value of each on-balance-sheet asset and the credit equivalent amount of each off-balance-sheet activity.

Risk-weighted assets The denominator of the capital/risk-weighted assets ratio. This denominator consists of the sum of (1) the risk-weighted amounts of all on-balance-sheet assets and (2) the risk-weighted credit equivalent amounts of all off-balance sheet activities.

Subordinated term debt Fixed-term debt obligations that are subordinated in some way to other securities of the issuer. The amount of subordinated term debt that can be included in Tier Two is limited to 50 percent of the value of Tier one. Further, the amount of any particular subordinated term debt instrument that can be included diminishes as the instrument nears maturity. Specifically, during the final five years of any subordinated term debt instrument's life, a 20 percent discount is applied.

Supplement capital Tier Two capital.

Tier One capital The sum of equity capital and disclosed reserves, as adjusted. Bank holding companies may include cumulative perpetual preferred stock in Tier One. Also known as core capital.

Tier Two capital The sum of general provisions and general loan loss reserves, hybrid debt/equity instruments, revaluation reserves, subordinated term debt, and undisclosed reserves. Also known as supplementary capital.

Total capital The numerator of the capital/risk-weighted assets ratio. This numerator consists of the sum of Tier One capital, as adjusted, the Tier Two capital, minus investments in certain unconsolidated subsidiaries.

Undisclosed reserves Accumulated after-tax retained profits that are not disclosed on a balance sheet. The Federal Reserve Board does not permit U.S. banks or bank holding companies to maintain undisclosed reserves. Regulators in other countries, such as Japan, do permit all their banking organizations to maintain Undisclosed Reserves. These may be included in Tier Two. Also known as hidden reserves.

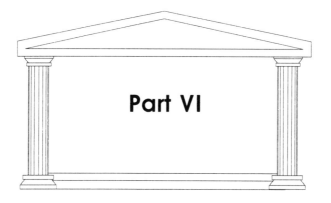

Part VI

Managerial Accounting: Concept, Methods, and Uses

Chapter 13

Managerial Accounting

The primary objective of managerial accounting for banks is to explain how accounting data can be applied and interpreted by bank management in planning, evaluating, and controlling banking activities. In managerial accounting the objective is to organize financial and other information so that it can be used more efficiently and effectively by the internal management of the bank. In Chapter 3 the basics of institutional planning and controlling were discussed in some detail. In this and the following chapter specific procedures for carrying out major bank functions as related to managerial accounting will be explained.

RESPONSIBILITY ACCOUNTING

Responsibility accounting can serve as the basis for a bank's accounting and financial reporting systems. Responsibility accounting focuses on the collection of data to place responsibility for profit, revenue, expenses, or investments to achieve control over one or more of these four centers. The emphasis is on people—who are responsible for profit, revenue, expenses, or investments. Responsibility accounting is also referred to as profit-centered accounting and performance reporting.

In a responsibility accounting system the accountant reports to each manager only information that is relevant to that manager's responsibility. Higher-level managers or administrators assign responsibilities to their subordinates. There are three major patterns of banking activity by which managerial authority can be delegated: (a) function, (b) product or service line, and (c) geographic region. A combination of patterns is sometimes desirable. Banking functions typically consist of operations, marketing, finance, and human resources.

Responsibility accounting is based on these assumptions:

1. All profit, revenues, expenses, and investments can be controlled.

2. Responsibility for profit, revenues, expenses, and investments must be assigned—and assigned fairly.

Assigning responsibility in an organization requires that authority to act be clearly assigned, and that when responsibilities are assigned, commensurate authority to carry out those responsibilities is also assigned. These relationships are usually presented in the bank's organizational chart and its chart of accounts. The organizational chart should reflect a plan of organization that provides an appropriate segregation of functional responsibilities. Accounting reports should be prepared to summarize the performance of each responsibility center. Such reports should include only those items over which the center has control. Controllability varies with a manager's level of authority and the time period in which a decision must be made.

Not all managers have the same type of financial responsibility. Management practice has accepted four major types of responsibility centers:

1. Expense (or cost) center: an organizational unit that is held accountable for the incurring of expense.

2. Revenue center: an organizational unit that is held accountable only for revenue.

3. Profit center: an organizational unit that is held accountable for revenue and expense.

4. Investment center: an organizational unit whose management is held accountable for attaining a satisfactory rate of return on capital.

A bank could establish profit centers to measure, control, and evaluate products, classes of products, customers, departments, geographic areas and similar profit producing centers. An expense center could be organized for any subunit or function to which the bank can trace direct costs. Branch offices or the loan function could be organized as revenue or investment centers. An analysis of major activities groupings can assist in identifying activities associated with a responsibility center:

■ Support activities

■ Administrative activities

■ Customer-related activities

■ Revenue generating activities

A typical report for a bank's profit center is illustrated below. This report could be modified to accommodate other types of centers.

Responsibility Center Report
for Personal Loan Department

	Budget This Month	Actual This Month	Variance	Budget This Year	Actual This Year	Variance
Revenues						
Interest costs						
Net interest income						
Other income		(Data omitted)				
Direct costs						
Common costs						
Net income before taxes						

Assigning costs to responsibility centers often involves cost allocations. Cost allocation refers to the assignment of various costs to functions, departments, products, or services. To allocate costs, a bank must first set an allocation base, which is a reasonable common denominator for assigning a given cost to two or more functions, departments, products, or services. There are two criteria for resolving cost allocation issues:

1. What costs can the manager control (controllability)?

2. What type of allocation will motivate a manager to make decisions in the best interest of the bank (motivation)?

When transactions are recorded in the journals and ledgers of a bank, revenues and costs should be classified by responsibility center along with of other classification procedures. This will facilitate the implementation of responsibility accounting.

Responsibility accounting requires that an effective and efficient internal reporting system be established. An effective internal reporting system should be goal oriented, useful, timely, accurate, responsibility centered, integrated with the accounting system and financial statements, capable of flagging exceptions, and provided in a standardized format. Management reports would ordinarily be related to planning, controlling, and evaluating functions. The reports would typically include statistical data, narrative, and graphics.

BUDGETS

A bank's budget is an orderly and coordinated plan of financial planning and management. It is a major tool for effective planning, motivating, and controlling bank operations. The budgeting process forces management to determine its goals and objectives and to develop a coordinated plan for achieving these ends. All levels of management must be committed to budgeting planning. The budget plan that is the result of the budgeting process must be achievable, realistic, and understandable.

The budget is a relatively complete "blueprint" of the future operations of the bank. The budget period is usually short enough to permit reasonably accurate predictions and long enough to allow time for implementation. The budget period usually coincides with the fiscal period of the business so that actual results of operations can be compared with budgetary estimates. An operating budget is usually prepared for a year, with supporting schedules in monthly or quarterly terms. A capital expenditure or project budget is usually developed for a longer time period.

The Budgetng Process—An Overview

The budgeting process involves the determination by a budget committee of basic assumptions (such as the economy, regulatory issues, demographics and marketing) under which the details of the budget are to be prepared. For example, a bank would stipulate budgeting assumptions about such items as interest rates for the coming year, growth in personal income, and housing starts and sales in the bank's market area. These assumptions should be consistent with those being used by the asset/liability management staff when analyzing the bank's ALM risk profiles. The board of directors (or another high-level, decision-making group) approves the assumptions set forth by the budget committee.

Detailed budgeting usually begins with a forecast of revenue from products or services. Three basic sources of revenue exist in a revenue plan:

1. Fee revenue (volume, pricing, new products, products to be discontinued)

2. Net interest income: net interest income = gross interest income − cost of funds

3. Other income

Estimates are then made of expenses, costs, collections, and payments. Budgeted financial statements are then compiled and analyzed to determine how the budgeted activities will affect the bank, stockholders, creditors, and other parties. The budget would then be implemented and monitored.

The Comprehensive Budget—Preparation

The comprehensive budget, sometimes referred to as the master budget, is a complete expression of the planned operations of the bank for a period of time. The comprehensive budget typically has two elements: an operating budget and a financial budget.

The operating budget describes the relationship of the input (efforts) of the bank to final output and revenue (accomplishments). The financial budget describes the impact of budgeting on the balance sheet, especially as it relates to economic resources and obligations.

At the beginning of the budget process, budget instructions should provide a brief statement of the bank's budgeting objectives. The instructions should also give general guidelines to control the budgeting process including financial objectives, targets, variances, documentation, forms, support materials, and schedules.

The preparation of a comprehensive budget usually begins with the anticipated volume of a bank's revenue from product sales and services, which is the crucial factor that determines the level of activity for a period. In other cases capacity or the availability of resources could be the starting point.

A top-down or a bottom-up approach can be used to forecast revenue from product sales and services. The top-down approach would first forecast bank revenue based on an examination of the economy, then the bank's share of the market and the bank's revenue sources, and would proceed to a forecast of revenue by products, services, or other category. The bottom-up approach would forecast revenue by product, services, or other category, then the bank's revenue sources, and then market share. Bottom-up budgeting compiles data received from different subunits. Both methods should result in sales forecasts of materially the same amount. Quantitative methods of forecasting include historical projections; time series analysis relating to secular trend, cycles, seasonal fluctuations, and random fluctuations using methods such as moving average, exponential smoothing, and time series analysis; and regression analysis.

Unit managers are usually required to budget and are held accountable for revenues and expenses that they directly manage and control. This reflects responsibility accounting as described earlier. For example, line managers can be held accountable for the number of new accounts obtained and, to some extent, the number of deposit accounts closed. They would not ordinarily be expected to forecast portfolio volumes. Managers would have normal budget authority for fees and service charges but only limited control over rates and yields.

Budget—Testing and Appraisal

The annual budget should ordinarily be tested and appraised (analyzed) after it has been prepared. The budget officer or controller would ordinarily be responsible for summarizing the appraisals. Tests used to evaluate budget performance should ordinarily include some or all of the following (the list is not inclusive):

1. Budget against management goals, objectives, or targets:

    (a) Revenues (total, units, dollars, segments, percentage of market; growth rate)

    (b) Net income (total, segment, percent of sales, compared to industry, growth rate)

    (c) Return on assets (total, organization segment, peer banks, industry norms)

    (d) Return on shareholders' equity (total, industry norms, major competitors)

    (e) Gross margin (to total revenue, segment, trends, industry norms, major competitors)

    (f) Employment levels (total, classification)

    (g) Profit structure

    (h) Asset turnover (loans, investments)

    (i) Other significant ratios (current ratio, quick ratio, cash flows ratios, working capital ratio, total liabilities to shareholders' equity ratio, long-term debt to shareholders' equity ratio, times interest charges earned, dividend payout ratio, price/earnings ratio, and other banking related ratios)

2. Budget against prior year (interim period) actual performance: revenues, gross margin (amount and percentage), net income (amount and percentage of revenue, per share), return on assets, return on shareholders' equity.

The budget appraisal would be presented to management for its consideration and comment. The report would ordinarily include a summary of assumptions used in budgeting (inflation rate, status of economy, interest rates, tax rates, and others), budgetary and actual operating and financial highlights, budgeted and actual cash flows, impact on profit structure (contribution margin, return on assets, return on shareholders' equity and other significant ratios) and interpretative commentary.

Monitoring the Budget

After the budget is prepared and appraised (tested), the budget is implemented. The second phase of the budgetary control process involves monitoring operations so that operating plans and targets can be attained. The monitoring process should be viewed as a continuous process with emphasis on interim periods and the year's end.

Budgetary control relies primarily on analyses of differences between actual costs/revenues and budgeted costs/revenues and between actual costs and standard costs. Aspects of the control process involve establishing lines of responsibility for performance, communicating plans to those assigned performance responsibilities, evaluating variances between actual results and budgeted estimates, and taking appropriate action thereon.

A budget should provide the basis for determining cost control responsibilities. Actual results of operations during the budget period should be compared to predetermined (budgets) data, and identifying variations from budgets in a timely and relevant manner. Standard costing is widely used as measure of what a product or service should cost as compared with the actual reported costs. When standards are based on current operating levels during the budget process, the budget reflects standard costs.

Standard costs are composed of a standard measurement unit and a unit cost. The components of standard costs are outlined here:

Component	Source document	Source
Quantity of material	Bill of material	Supervisor's report
Material unit cost	Purchasing records	Vendor
Operating times	Routing slips	Supervisor's report
Wage rate	Payroll records	Labor agreements
Overhead rate	Overhead rate determination process	Budget system

Because predetermined standards usually differ from actual costs incurred, a variance typically exists. An unfavorable variance results when actual cost exceeds standard cost; a favorable variance results when standard cost exceeds actual cost. The usual approach followed in standard cost analysis is to separate price factors from efficiency factors. When the actual amount paid differs from the standard amount, the variance is referred to a price, rate, or spending variance. When the actual input quantity (e.g., labor hours) differs from the standard input quantity, the variance is referred to as a quantity, volume or yield variance. The relationship between actual and standard price/quantity is illustrated below. The diagram shows two types of price and quantities: actual and standard. A price variance is conceptualized as the difference between quadrants 1 and 2. A quantity variance is reflected in the difference between quadrants 2 and 4.

		Actual Price		Standard Price
Actual Quantity	1	Actual quantity at actual price	2	Actual quantity at standard price
Standard Quantity	3	Standard quantity at actual price	4	Standard quantity at standard price

The use of standards employs the principle of management referred to as management by exception. Actual results that correspond with the standards require little or no attention. The exceptions must be examined and explained. Management by exception calls attention to areas that require control.

Responsibility accounting requires the breakdown of costs by management responsibility. Costs are assigned to managers on the basis of their ability to control specific costs. Typically only controllable costs are assigned to individual managers.

Accountants have taken a special interest in dealing with overhead by using what has come to be referred to as activity based overhead rate. An activity based overhead rate is found by separating overhead costs by activity and developing a predetermined overhead rate for each activity. Accountants trace overhead costs to the activities in which those costs were incurred. A cost driver (or activity base or measure) is an activity measure common to a product or service. The cost driver should be the one that best relates overhead costs to production volume (the thing that causes an activity's total overhead to change). Costs traceable to an activity can now be measured rather than allocated. Measurement is more precise than allocation.

Activity-based overhead rates have two advantages over bank-wide overhead rates. With activity-based rates, only products or services are charged for overhead use. Each activity uses the cost driver that best relates its costs to its activity.

Fixed and Variable Budgets

The budget is primarily a planning tool. It is often developed as a static or inflexible budget in which case it is prepared for one level of activity or volume level—the anticipated or normal, level of output. In many instances a flexible, or variable, budget can be used more appropriately as the tool for controlling costs and evaluating performance.

A flexible budget is prepared for a range of activities or volume because certain costs are affected by changes in the level of activity or volume. Flexible budgets are often expressed in terms of units of output or in standard units allowed for that output. Noncontrollable costs are sometimes excluded from the budget of a unit or department. Costs incurred in a separate service department would ordinarily be allocated to an operating department based on the amount of service used. Bank management should develop a rational cost allocation strategy.

Flexible budgeting has many applications for banks. A simplified flexible budget prepared in terms of a bank product output for three activity levels is:

	Levels of Service Output		
	10,000	15,000	20,000
Direct materials	$100,000	$150,000	$200,000
Direct labor	50,000	75,000	100,000
Variable overhead	20,000	30,000	40,000
Fixed overhead	30,000	30,000	30,000
Total costs	$200,000	$285,000	$370,000

If the actual level of output for the period is 15,000 units, actual costs would be compared with the flexible budget prepared at the 15,000 unit level. Any cost variances—favorable and unfavorable—between actual and budgeted should be explained and corrected, if necessary. A performance report could be prepared using the following format:

Item	Actual Cost	Budgeted Cost	Variance	Explanation

(Detailed data)

Types of Budgets

Bank administrators should be familiar with the various types of budgeting used in business (including banking), government, and not-for-profit institutions:

1. Incremental budget (used with object-of-expenditure, or line item, budgets); also baseline budget
2. Formula budget
3. Planning, programming, and budgeting systems (PPBS)
4. Zero-base budgeting
5. Performance budgeting

Incremental budgeting incorporates an object-of-expenditure approach to budgeting. Incremental budgets show line-item categories of expenditures to be made during the year. Line item refers to objects of expenditures, such as salaries and supplies. In incremental budgeting either each line item is considered for an increment or it remains unadjusted in the base. Frequently, increments are calculated as uniform percentage adjustments for every line item or group of line items. The basic philosophy is that the current budget is distributed properly among both the functions and objects of expenditures and that little programmatic change needs to occur. Changes in institutional priorities often result through ad hoc determination concerning what increase is needed to effect a programmatic change. When resources become scarce, incremental budgeting tends to perpetuate the existing programs regardless of how ineffective or inefficient they may be. High-cost programs continue to receive high levels of support. The status quo is reinforced and extended. Incremental budgeting emphasizes the short-run and continuity at the possible expense of the long-run goals of the organization. It also encourages spending at the risk of jeopardizing cost control efforts.

Formula budgeting is a technique by which the financial needs or operating requirements of an institution may be determined through the application of a formula. Formula budgeting is an objective procedure for estimating the future budgetary requirements of an institution by manipulating data about future programs and by utilizing relationships between program and cost. Formula budgeting is frequently used in not-for-profit institutions, such as colleges and universities.

Planning, programming, and budgeting systems (PPBS) is a managerial technique designed to merge the planning process with the allocation of funds by making it difficult to allocate funds without planning. PPBS emphasize performance (that is, output and efficiency). The focus of PPBS is essentially a planning device that ultimately leads to a conventional department budget for operation and control. PPBS is also described as a macroeconomic, centralized, top-down policy and long-range planning tool. In PPBS planning involves the selection and identification of long-range objectives of the organization and benefit-cost analysis of various courses of action.

Zero-base budgeting demands a total rejustification of every activity from base zero, instead of incrementing the new on the old. The objective of zero-base budgeting is to examine each activity in a manner similar to a proposed new activity to determine whether the activity is necessary. The major focus of zero-base budgeting is on ensuring that managers evaluate their areas of responsibility more completely and more objectively than under other budgeting procedures.

Performance budgeting is a budgeting structure that either focuses on activities or functions that produce results and from which resources are used, or promotes a budgetary process that attempts to link organizational objectives to resource utilization. Its primary focus is to improve efficiency by means of activity classifications and cost measurements. The common components of most performance budgeting systems are activity classifications, performance measurements, and performance reports. A major problem in implementing performance budgeting has been the difficulty in determining appropriate performance criteria.

Banks have used all of these budget types or variations thereof. Incremental budgets and planning, program, and performance evaluation budgets are common in current banking practice.

Bank Specific

Bank budgeting officers ordinarily begin with a balance sheet approach to budgeting. Balance sheet planning starts with relating the balance sheet to sources and uses of funds:

Source of funds	Uses of funds
Consumer-based funds	Loans
Market-based funds	Leases
Long-term debt	Time deposits

Source of funds	Uses of funds
Capital leases	Other earning assets
Equity	Other assets

A cost of funds would be calculated for each source of funds (liabilities and capital). For the using side (assets), an anticipated income is computed for each asset category. The current net interest income is determined by subtracting the derived sources from uses. The amount of loan-loss provisions could be computed at this point.

In planning for asset balances, the bank would consider such factors as funding and capital constraints, credit and interest-rate risk, loan amortization, prepayments, and liquidity requirements. In planning liabilities and equity balances, the bank would consider such factors as funding requirements, liquidity risk, interest rates; capital requirements, and maturity gaps.

Expense planning involves all non-interest expenses: staffing; compensation expense, and other operating expenses, such as marketing, travel, contributions, postage, telephone, and many others. Each responsibility center would prepare an expense plan.

Significant ratios of special interest to a bank in evaluating its operations can be broadly grouped as follows (not intended to be all-inclusive):

1. Profitability ratios:
    Return on assets
    Return on earning assets
    Return on equity
    Earnings per share
    Fully diluted earnings per share
    Price/earnings ratio
    Cash flow per share
    Operating activities cash flow per share

2. Interest margin ratios:
    Yield on earning assets
    Cost to fund earning assets
    Net interest margin

3. Earning assets ratios
    Loans to deposits
    Loans to assets

4. Noninterest expense ratios:
    Number of FTE employees
    Salary and benefits per employee
    Expense components as a percentage of operating income

5. Noninterest income ratios:
    Percentage of operating income
    Percentage of noninterest expense

6. Capital ratios:
   Capital to debt
   Capital to total assets
   Capital to risk-based assets
   Book value per share

7. Dividends ratios:
   Dividend payout ratio
   Dividend yield ratio

8. Productivity ratios:
   Total assets, operating income, deposits, personnel expense, overhead expense, and many additional factors as a numerator/per employee as a denominator.

9. Risk ratios and measurement:
   Interest rate risk spread Average earnings asset yield minus average rate on interest-bearing liabilities
   Liquidity Average loans to total deposits
   Capital adequacy Equity capital to assets. Tier One capital to total risk-based capital; Tier Two capital to total risk-based capital; Risk-based capital to total assets
   Credit risk Net losses to average loans; loss reserves to average loans
   Operating service level indicators; Timeliness, efficiency error rates

Bank management is ultimately interested in knowing how the bank is doing compared to previous performance, to its budget and other plans, and to peer banks. Responsibility accounting and responsive budgeting, accounting, and information systems should provide the answers.

Budgeting for capital expenditures would be assigned to each responsibility center and/or to the chief financial officer of the bank. Capital budgets are discussed in the following section.

CAPITAL BUDGETS

Budgets can also be classified under the headings operating budgets and capital budgets. Operating budgets are general-purpose budgets used to formalize activities in relation to financial considerations for a stated period, usually a fiscal year. They represent short-term planning and control techniques. Capital budgets represent the expenditures, and the means of financing these expenditures, to be expended for long-lived, or capital, assets, including land, buildings, and equipment. Banks typically acquire significant capital assets and use capital budgeting procedures to evaluate capital acquisitions.

A capital budget is a plan for acquiring and maintaining long-term assets and providing the means of financing these activities. Financial theory strongly supports the separation of the investment decision from the financing decision. A capital budget typically includes one or more of the following items:

1. New facilities and major additions

2. Major renovations and repairs to existing facilities

Several methods are used for making capital budgeting investment decisions. The net present value method or some modification thereof, is preferred. The application of the net present value method of capital budgeting involves the following processes:

1. Estimate the future cash inflows and outflows for each alternative project under consideration.
2. Discount the future cash flows to the present, using the firm's cost of capital.
3. Accept or reject the proposed project according to a decision rule that will maximize the firm's wealth.

Capital budgeting is a formal process of long-term planning for relatively large, permanent acquisitions and commitments of a firm's economic resources. Long-term investment decisions relate to the following basic areas that have for their objective profit maximization:

1. Equipment acquisition and replacement required (for example, to deal with obsolescence, competition, or legal requirements)
2. Cost-saving investments to promote efficiency
3. Expansion opportunities (for example, diversification, product lines, and research and development investments)

In evaluating capital budgeting projects, management must consider two major factors:

1. The cost of the investment
2. The potential net increase in cash inflows (or reduction in cash outflows) resulting from the proposed investment

Four methods of capital budgeting are widely used in business:

1. The accounting method
2. The payback method
3. The net present value method
4. The discounted cash flow method

Accounting Method

The accounting method is based on the application of the following equation to evaluate capital projects:

$$\text{Accounting rate of return} = \frac{\text{Expected increase in income}}{\text{Expected increase in investment}}$$

To illustrate the accounting method, assume that a bank is considering the purchase of new equipment for $11,000. The equipment has an expected useful life of five years and a scrap value of $1,000 at the end of this useful life. For the next five years, the machine will create cost savings of $4,000 per year. The accounting rate of return can be calculated this way:

$$\text{Accounting rate of return} = \frac{\$4,000}{(\$11,000 - \$1,000)}$$
$$= 40\%.$$

The firm must now decide whether a rate of return of 40 percent is adequate for this project. The accounting rate of return's most serious shortcoming is that it ignores the time value of money. Expected future dollars are regarded as equal to present dollars.

Payback Method

The payback period is the time required for the cash inflow from an investment to accumulate to a total equal to the original cash outlay required for the investment. Using the above data, the payback period for the new machine can be calculated as:

$$\text{Payback period} = \text{Initial investment/Annual cash savings}$$
$$= \$11,000/\$4,000$$
$$= 2.75 \text{ years}$$

When using this method, management chooses the investment that provides the quickest payoff regardless of which investment gives the highest rate of return over the long run. Also, management often sets a maximum payback period for acceptable investments. Investments that exceed the maximum period are rejected. A reasonable payback period is usually considered to be between two and five years.

If the inflow of cash savings is not the same from year to year, the payback period may be calculated by adding the cash proceeds in successive years until the total equals the original outlay.

Net Present Value Method

The net present value method uses present values of streams of earnings or costs for evaluating investment decisions. When this method is employed, expected future cash inflows and outflows associated with the investment are discounted to the present using a minimum discounting rate acceptable to management. The net present value is the difference between the present cost of the investment and the present value of the cash inflow expected from the investment. If the net present value is positive, the investment is acceptable. If the net present value is negative, the investment does not promise to provide a return at a minimum level and should be rejected. Net present value can be conceptualized as

$$\text{Net present value} = \text{present value of net cash inflows}$$
$$- \text{cost of the investment}$$

To illustrate the net present value method, consider an $11,000 machine with a scrap value of $1,000 and a useful life of five years. If the company expects a 16 percent minimum rate of return for this type of investment, the machine should not be purchased. The rationale for this decision is given in the illustration shown in Figure 13-1.

1. Dollar amounts of cash inflows and outflows are recorded in the columns for the appropriate periods.

Figure 13-1
Discounted Cash Flows

	Cash flows at end of period						Discount factor	Total present value
	0	1	2	3	4	5		
Initial cost	$(11,000)						1.0000	$(11,000)
Cash operating savings		$4,000	$4,000	$4,000	$4,000	$4,000	3.2741	13,096
Disposal value						1,000	.4761	476
Net present value								$2,572

(a) Direction of each cash inflow is indicated. Cash outflows are negative amounts, and cash inflows or savings are shown as positive amounts.

(b) The timing of each flow is indicated by recording it in the appropriate period.

2. Present value discounting factors are determined from present value tables and entered in the appropriate column (note that the cash operating savings can be treated as an annuity since they are equal each period).

3. Present values of each item are computed and entered in the last column whose figures are then totaled to determine the net present value of the investment.

Because the net present value of the investment in the machine is positive, the investment in the new machine is considered desirable. The underlying concept for this method is the idea that the company can earn more by buying the machine than it could by putting the same amount of cash into some other investment that earns a 16 percent rate of return. The effect of this decision rule is to accept any proposed investment that offers more than a 16 percent rate of return.

If income taxes are considered, the payment of income taxes represents a cash outflow; a tax savings represents a cash inflow. For a 48 percent income tax rate each dollar of cash revenue equals only $0.52 after-tax cash inflow, while each dollar of cash expense equals only $0.52 after-tax cash outflow. Cash savings on depreciation equals depreciation expense multiplied by the income tax rate. If the problem involving the machine is reworked to take a 48 percent income tax into consideration, the problem would be solved as shown in Figure 13-2. In this case the net present value of the investment is negative, so the investment in the machine is rejected.

Discounted Cash Flow Method

The discounted cash flow method of capital budgeting finds the discounting rate that results in a net present value of zero for the cash flows. This rate is the expected rate of return on the investment project. The discounting rate can be determined through the use of tables or with

Figure 13-2
Net Present Value Method Including Income Tax Implications

	Cash flows at end of period						Discount factor	Total present value
	0	1	2	3	4	5		
Initial cost	$(11,000)						1.0000	$(11,000)
Cash operating savings		$2,080	$2,080	$2,080	$2,080	$2,080	3.2741	6,810
Disposal value						1,000	.4761	476
Depreciation impact on income taxes		960	960	960	960	960	3.2741	3,143
Net present value								$ (571)

a trial-and-error approach. With the discounted cash flow approach, the decision rule takes the following form: if the computed rate of return on the investment exceeds a minimum acceptable rate imposed by management, the investment is considered acceptable. Otherwise, it is rejected.

Using data for the machine purchase above, and taking income taxes into consideration, the following computations are made:

1. Determine the expected after-tax savings from the investment ($2,080 + $960 = $3,040) per year for five years.

2. Determine the cash outflow for the initial cost of the investment, $11,000.

3. Determine the present value of other cash inflows such as salvage value, $1,000 at the end of five years or $476 now ($1,000 × .476 = $476).

4. Find the discount factor that will equate the expected cash inflows to the present value of the cash outflows.

5. Find the discounting rate that gives a discount factor of 3.4618 for a five-year annuity at an unknown discount rate. This is the discounting rate for which an annuity of $3,040 for five years has a present value of $10,524. Refer to the present value of annuity table to find the discount rate that, for five periods, equals or approximates the computed "factor value." The factor is about 14 percent, which is less than the 16 percent minimum rate acceptable to management. The project is rejected. Capital budgeting projects are frequently complicated when

    (a) the amounts to be invested occur over a period of time,

    (b) the amounts differ, and

    (c) the timing is irregular.

These problems can usually be dealt with by converting all investments and returns to their discounted total values, at a particular point.

BUDGETNG: BEHAVIORAL IMPLICATIONS

Humans are adaptive, problem-solving, decision-making creatures motivated by an assortment of differing needs and drives. The activities of individuals and organizations are enhanced or restricted by their environment, the availability of resources, administrative and managerial ability and experience, reward-punishment expectations, ability to accept responsibility and respond to authority. The behavioral sciences can serve accounting by helping practitioners understand and respond to the human condition.

Behavioral concepts have many implications for accounting, and it is expected that their application will increase in the future. Several of the areas where the behavioral sciences can affect budgeting activities will be explored.

From a behavioral viewpoint, budgeting is a process in which groups compete for a share of available resources. The behavioral scientist would be interested in the budgeting process as a situation in which

1. groups select projects to be submitted to a decision-making committee for approval and funding;

2. a decision-making group evaluates proposed projects after having established priorities and determined restraints;

3. decisions are communicated to project proposers; and

4. approved projects are initiated, controlled, and reviewed.

In studies of capital budgeting behavior scientists have shown that, where conflicts arise over proposals for use of resources, each competing group sees its project as superior to those of competitors. In capital budgeting, goal achievement is a primary motivating factor. Research studies indicate that failure to achieve a goal creates conflicts and influences behavior and attitudes negatively. Goal attainment or failure to attain a goal in one budget period affects behavior, attitude, and motivation in a subsequent period. When a group or individual has experienced success, subsequent action tends to improve; failure tends to lower levels of aspiration and achievement.

Behavioral studies also provide insights in the area of budgetary control, especially with regard to procedures of setting standards. The results of several of these studies indicate the following:

1. Control systems that encourage responsibility by self discipline rather than through inflexible rules are often more effective within complex business environments.

2. Employees tend to develop their own standards and to manipulate norms established by management, especially when the norms are considered unreasonable or unfair.

3. Feedback on variances from standards tends to emphasize under-achievement, unfavorable variances and punishment rather than over-achievement, favorable variances and reward.

Research studies have shown that the behavioral and decision-making patterns of management are conditioned to some extent by generally accepted accounting principles. Accounting principles impact directly on accounting measurement and reporting procedures and influence behavior and decision making. While generally accepted accounting principles narrow variations (and therefore choices) in processing and reporting practices, they do not eliminate them entirely. Alternative accounting principles and procedures are available that require a knowledge of consequences, and eventually a decision. Financial statements resulting from accounting principles do affect the behavior of their users.

Some examples will be presented here to illustrate how accounting principles can influence behavior and therefore have consequences. An accounting principle requires that research and development costs should be written off in the period in which they were incurred rather than capitalizing the costs and amortizing them over a period of years. This accounting principle could discourage a firm from undertaking or expanding research and development programs because such expenditures would be reflected on the current period's income statement as expenses. Accounting principle allows the use of various depreciation methods (straight line, accelerated, and others) and inventory methods (LIFO, FIFO, and other). The choice of a depreciation or inventory method influences the amount of net income reported on an income statement and income taxes payable on a tax return. Accounting principles and methods do influence human behavior, and managers should be aware of their consequences.

BUDGETING: EFFECTIVE TECHNIQUES

Research studies have shown that budgeting practices in successful firms do differ from those in firms which are not successful. The studies also have shown that there is a systematic approach for attaining budgetary effectiveness. A summary of conclusions produced in these studies provide interesting insights into the budgeting process.

Research has shown that successful companies have a commitment to budgets; have established the firm's mission, goals, and objectives; establish a relationship between the firm's long-, medium-, and short-term plans; establish detailed and comprehensive procedures to prepare budgets; analyze budget variances and take corrective action; accept budgeting as a major managerial function; recognize the motivational and morale implications of budgeting (the behavioral side of budgeting); provide feedback to employees directly involved in management; establish realistic targets when developing the budget; provide for a bottom-up process for developing budgetary targets (financial and nonfinancial) and data; require that managerial responsibilities are related to budgetary reports; invest resources in the budgeting process; standardize routine aspects of budgeting, especially in a budget manual; discourage dysfunctional "budget games"; and use budgeting data in decision making.

The management of successful companies have consistently demonstrated a strong commitment to the budgeting process. This commitment is recognized from the top down. The stronger the level of commitment in the organization, the more productive the budgeting process is to the overall success of the firm. Firms in which the senior executives are strongly committed to budgeting found that the budgeting exercise results in an improvement in performance, productivity, and profitability.

Firms that link their strategic goals to their tactical objective and their short-, intermediate-, and long-term goals and objectives typically are found to be successful firms. Programs and projects find their way into operating and capital budgets. By quantifying mission, goals, and objectives through budgeting, a firm breathes life into its enterprise.

The carefully planned budgetary process is more likely to produce results than one that is not as detailed or comprehensive. Budget preparation is taken seriously by the successful firms. Successful firms sometimes use "scientific" techniques in budget preparation, including the following: charts, Critical Path Method (CPM), Program Evaluation and Review Techniques (PERT); flexible budgeting; contingency plans.

Successful budgeting requires an understanding and application of interpersonal and small-group processes and leadership techniques. The behavioral aspects of budgeting cannot be ignored. Many firms commit significant resources to developing these techniques in their managers. Budgets can be one of the most effective motivational techniques available to management.

COST-BENEFIT ANALYSIS

Cost-benefit analysis is a procedure or system for evaluating a course of action or program by comparing the costs to the expected benefits from the action or program. If benefits exceed costs, the action or program is considered desirable. The cost-benefit ratio is conceptualized as the present value of the benefits divided by the present value of the costs (or average annual benefits over average annual costs).

The analysis is quantified as much as possible; all costs and benefits—direct and indirect, financial, social, and political—are taken into consideration. Difficulties arise when efforts are made to measure intangible costs and benefits, e.g., customer goodwill.

Cost-benefit analysis has been widely used

1. to determine whether a particular program, project, or activity is justified;

2. to rank alternative programs, projects, or activities; and

3. to determine the best course of action to attain an objective.

Cost-benefit analysis attempts to maximize benefits for a prescribed level of costs, determine the minimum level of expenditures to achieve a pre-specified level of benefits, or maximize net benefits (benefits minus costs). The methodology involves a comparison, in present value, of benefits and costs. Often, if the ratio of benefits to costs is greater than unity, the project will be selected (unless competing projects have a lower cost-to-benefit ratio). Benefits and costs include those which will flow from the project that can be converted into monetary values.

A standard classification for cost-benefit evaluations is (1) summative evaluations and (2) formative evaluations. Summative evaluations typically seek an answer concerning whether the program works or doesn't work. Answers to such questions as the following are sought: Does the value of the benefits exceed the costs? Given alternative programs that accomplish a particular task, which is less costly? Such evaluations are sometimes referred to as "cost-effectiveness" evaluations. Formative evaluations typically inquire as to whether the program can be improved.

Cost-benefit analysis has occasionally been applied to the auditing and accounting processes. As applied to auditing, costs often include audit fees and other costs incurred by the entity being audited. Benefits often relate to the reliability of the financial statements being audited and to the discovery or prevention of fraud. It is important to note that many of the benefits associated with an audit are usually paid for by a particular entity.

BREAK-EVEN ANALYSIS

Break-even analysis is conducted by bank managers in an attempt to identify a level of output at which to operate in the short run so as to cover all of their fixed and variable costs associated with the operation. This output level corresponds to the level at which total revenue becomes greater than total costs. This output level is also a level of operations at which a bank neither makes a profit nor incurs a loss on a particular product or service or on the bank as an entity. Operating below this break-even volume results in a loss; operating above the break-even volume results in a profit.

In many situations managers have information about what their total revenue and total costs will be at various output levels and within a relevant range. A relevant range is a given volume in which a specific relationship between cost and volume is valid. Bank managers can often intuitively estimate a minimum level of revenues that is needed to make a profit. Break-even analysis can be helpful to bankers in evaluating prices, variable and fixed expenses, product mix, volume, and other variables affecting earnings.

The Break-even Formula

The formula used to compute the break-even point (b/e) is expressed as

Revenue at b/e point = Variable expenses + Fixed expenses.

Fixed expenses tend to remain constant in total within a given period of time and over a wide range of activity (the relevant range) regardless of sales volume. Variable expenses tend to remain uniform per unit but vary in total in direct proportion to changes in the level of activity. Mixed expenses (semivariable) represent a combination of fixed and variable expenses. Mixed expenses increase with volume but not in the same proportion.

To illustrate the computation of the break-even formula, assume the following data:

Revenues (60,000 units @ $20 per unit)	$1,200,000
Less: Variable expenses (60,000 @ $12 per unit)	720,000
Contribution margin	480,000
Less: Fixed expenses	400,000
Net income	$ 80,000

The computation of the break-even point follows where S equals revenue (sales of product or service at the break-even point); variable expenses are expressed as a percentage of revenue:

$S = (\$720,000/\$1,200,000)(S) + \$400,000$

S = (.60)(S) + $400,000
.40S = $400,000
S = $1,000,000

Figure 13-3 illustrates a break-even chart prepared for this problem.

The basic relationship contained in the break-even model can be used to make additional analyses:

1. Changes in services due to price or volume change.

2. Changes in fixed costs due to the level of investment.

3. Changes in variable costs due to price or usage changes.

For example, these relationships should be recognized:

Net income = Revenue − Variable expenses − Fixed expenses
    and
Revenue = Variable expenses + Fixed Expenses + Net income

Using the data in the problem, what revenues are required to make a profit of $100,000?

Revenue to make = ($720,000/$1,200,000)(S) + $400,000 + $100,000
$100,000 profit

$$= \$1,250,000$$

Break-even analysis is used by banks to determine a pricing strategy when introducing a new product. Management can estimate volume levels and, considering costs, determine if the new product will at least recover these costs. Break-even analysis has also been used to estimate a lending rate based on loan characteristics and to establish the minimum balance requirements for interest-bearing demand deposit accounts. In these cases the variable and fixed costs of the service can usually be estimated, thereby providing basis for break-even analysis.

A specific application of break-even analysis to banking would be a situation where a bank needed to assess the checking or savings account balance level at which the actual annual handling costs of an account equals the income derived from using the balance on deposit. The Federal Reserve's Functional Cost Analysis defines four categories for transaction (regular checking and interest-bearing) accounts:

■ Checks written (on-us debits)

■ Deposits made

■ Transit checks deposited

■ Account maintenance

For savings accounts the cost categories are the following:

■ Deposits made

■ Withdrawals made

■ Interest postings

Figure 13-3
Break-Even Analysis

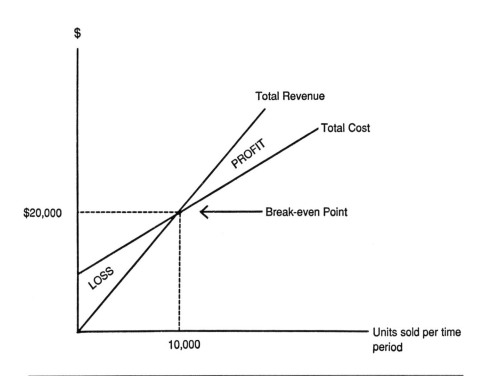

- Account openings
- Account closings
- Account maintenance

For each set there are variable and fixed costs. The fixed costs in each group are represented by account maintenance. The variable costs are based on the volume of items generated. The Federal Reserve's Functional Cost Analysis (average for all banks) provides an average volume of items generated for each category.

The break-even point is calculated as follows:

$$\left(\frac{\text{Annual variable cost per account*} + \text{Annual account maintenance cost}}{\text{Bank earning rate}} \right) \text{ divided by } 1 - \text{Reserve requirement}$$

*Checks written cost + deposit cost + transit check cost.

Break-even analysis is based on the following assumptions:

1. The cost-volume-profit relationships are linear over a wide range of production/services and revenues.

2. Expenses can be classified as either variable or fixed.

3. Prices, unit variable costs, and total fixed expenses will be unchanged during the period under consideration.

4. Volume is the sole cost driver. The influences of other possible cost drivers are held constant or regarded as insignificant. A cost driver is any factor whose change makes a difference in a related total cost.

5. The relevant range of volume is specified.

6. The sales mix of products will be unchanged during the period under examination. Sales mix is the combination of products and services that make up total revenue.

Margin of Safety

The margin of safety is the difference between current revenue and revenue at the break-even point. The margin of safety (M/S) represents the possible decrease in revenue that may occur before a loss is incurred; it can be expressed as follows:

$$\text{M/S in Dollars} = \text{Revenue} - \text{Revenue at Break-even point}$$

$$\text{M/S as Percent of Current Revenue} = \frac{\text{M/S}}{\text{Current Revenue}}$$

If the M/S is low, management knows that a small decline in revenue or volume or an increase in variable cost per unit or fixed costs can result in an operating loss and a loss of financial and operating flexibility. Operating risks are high if the M/S is low.

Multiproduct Enterprises

For a multiproduct enterprise, the horizontal axis of a break-even chart would be stated in dollars instead of physical units of output. Multiproduct analysis assumes that constant proportions of several products are sold and changes in the mixture as well as in costs or selling prices would generally make such a chart irrelevant.

CONTRIBUTION MARGIN ANALYSIS

Contribution margin analysis is a major decision-making tool. Contribution margin is defined as revenue less variable expenses and can be illustrated as

Revenue from services (50,000 units)	$100,000
Less: Variable expense	60,000
Contribution margin	40,000
Less: Fixed expenses	10,000
Net income	$ 30,000
Contribution margin per unit (50,000 units)	$0.80
Contribution margin rate (on revenue)	40%

The contribution margin receives its name because the excess of revenues over available expenses "contributes" to the payment of fixed expenses. Management's goal is to make the contribution margin as large as possible, other things being equal.

The contribution margin can be used in a variety of ways:

1. To help a bank decide on which products or services to push, de-emphasize, or discontinue

2. To appraise alternatives associated with price reductions, special discounts, special advertising campaigns, and the use of premiums (Compare added costs with the prospective additions in revenue.)

3. To estimate number of units required to be sold to obtain desired profits (Divide fixed costs plus desired profits by the contribution margin per unit.)

4. To utilize resources most profitably by determining the product or service that makes the largest total contribution to profit

5. To estimate the amount of variable costs allowed for a product or service and how much volume can be obtained

6. To help management understand the relationships among costs, volume, prices, and profits

7. To compute the break-even point in units or in dollars

The break-even point in units can be computed using the following contribution margin formula:

$$\text{Sales at break--even point} = \frac{\text{Fixed expense}}{\text{Contribution margin per unit}}$$

$$= \frac{\$10,000}{\$0.80(= \$40,000/50,000 \text{ units})}$$

$$= 12,500 \text{ units}$$

The contribution margin rate is computed as follows: contribution margin divided by sales. Sales at the break-even point in dollars can be computed using the contribution-margin rate as follows:

$$\text{Sales at break--even point in dollars} = \frac{\text{Fixed expense}}{\text{Contribution rate}}$$

$$= \frac{\$10,000}{40(= \$40,000/\$100,000)}$$

$$= \$25,000$$

Using data on contribution margin per unit, management can make quick estimates of the impact on net income resulting from changes in sales:

Change in net income = Change in volume × Contribution margin per unit

Change in net income = Change in sales revenue × Contribution margin rate

$$\begin{array}{l} \text{Change in selling price or unit cost} \\ \text{required to achieve a desired} \\ \text{contribution margin} \end{array} = \frac{\begin{array}{c}\text{Desired change in total}\\\text{contribution margin}\end{array}}{\text{Number of units to be sold}}$$

$$\begin{array}{l} \text{Sales required for desired} \\ \text{net income} \end{array} = \frac{\text{Fixed expenses + Desired net income}}{\text{Contribution margin rate}}$$

A cost-volume-profit chart (Figure 13-4) shows the profit or loss potential for an extensive range of volume. At any level of output, the profit or loss is the vertical difference between the sales line and the total cost line. The break-even point is the intersection of sales and total costs. The contribution margin at any level of output is the vertical difference between the sales line and the variable expenses line. The total expenses and variable expenses lines are parallel; the difference between them equals fixed expense.

Contribution margin analysis facilitates other decisions such as the utilization of scarce resources, make-or-buy equipment, and plant acquisition decisions. To illustrate several applications, assume the following data about a bank that can produce and sell three products or any combination thereof. However, the bank's production capacity is limited by the number of labor hours available to produce the products.

	Product A	Product B	Product C
Sales price per unit	$12	$15	$18
Variable expense per unit	7	9	10
Contribution margin per unit	5	6	8
Labor hours to produce one unit	5	3	16
Contribution margin per machine hour	$ 1	$ 2	0.80

Although Product C has the largest contribution margin per unit, Product B should be produced since it has the largest contribution per the constraining factor (labor hours).

The following illustration shows the income statement for a branch bank that has revenue but is operating at a $20,000 loss. This is considered a temporary situation. Should the branch continue operations or shut down? If the branch closes down, the fixed expenses will continue.

	Continue operations	Shut down
Revenue	$1,000,000	—
Less: Variable expense	900,000	—
Contribution margin	100,000	—
Less: Fixed expense	120,000	$120,000
Net loss	$ 20,000	$120,000

The bank should continue to operate the branch because the contribution margin is larger than zero. The contribution margin from continued operations helps pay some of the fixed expenses.

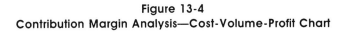

Figure 13-4
Contribution Margin Analysis—Cost-Volume-Profit Chart

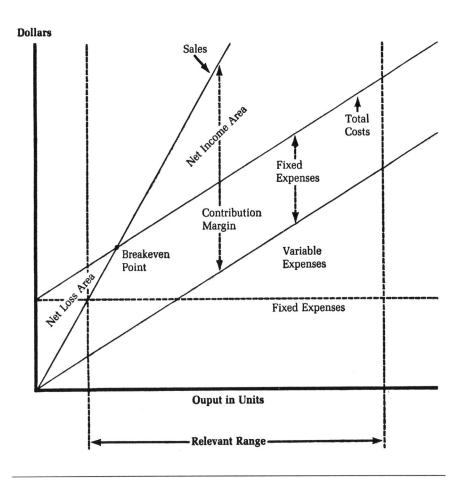

For banks, the net interest margin (the difference between interest income and interest expense) is an extremely important number in each bank. There is usually a greater opportunity for gain or loss in that number than in most if not all of the other opportunities. High margins are related to superior earnings. Contribution margin analysis can be applied to the interest margin of a bank with promising results. The analysis can be applied to loans, branches, departments, and other categories.

COST OF CAPITAL

The cost of capital usually refers to the cost of funds invested in a bank. In this sense the cost of capital is the weighted average of the cost of each type of debt and equity capital. The weight for each type of capital is the ratio of the market value of the securities representing that particular source of capital to the market value of all securities issued by the company. To illustrate and conceptualize the cost of capital, assume that the market value of a bank's common stock is $600,000 and the dividend yield is 10 percent. The market value of the company's interest-bearing debt is $400,000 with an average after-tax yield of 8 percent. The average cost of capital for the company can be estimated as follows:

Source	Proportion of Total Capital	Cost	
Common stock	0.60	0.10	0.06
Debt	0.40	0.08	0.032
Average cost of capital			0.092

Cost of capital also refers to the discount rate that equates the expected present value of future cash flows to common shareholders with the market value of the common stock at a specific time.

LEARNING CURVE

A learning curve describes the relationship between direct labor hours per unit and cumulative units produced. When accumulated volume doubles, the labor hours per unit decrease by a constant percentage. An 80 percent learning curve indicates that when cumulative volume doubles, labor hours per unit are reduced by 20 percent to 80 percent of the previous level. As workers become familiar with a specific task, their productivity increases. This learning process is particularly noticeable in new products or processes. The learning curve was first used in World War II in the aircraft industry. The learning curve can be described algebraically as follows:

$$y(x) = ax - b$$

where $y(x)$ =   direct labor hours required to produce x units
           x =   cumulative number of units produced
           a =   number of hours required to produce first unit
           b =   function the rate at which $y(x)$ decreases as cumulative production increases

Activities most subject to learning curve analysis include the following:

1.   Activities which have not been performed or not performed in their present operational form

2. Activities being performed by new employees and others not familiar with the operations

3. Activities which involve the use of a stated raw material for the first time or which involve a change in the way the material is used

4. Production runs of short duration, especially if these runs are repeated

To illustrate an application of the learning curve, assume that a bank estimates that it takes 4,000 labor hours to produce a product. The bank expects to build eight products for its customers. The company estimates that its learning curve is 80 percent after the first product is built. The effect of the learning curve on labor hours is computed as follows:

Cumulative Quantity	Cumulative Average Hours Per Product	Cumulative Hours
A	B	C
1	4,000	4,000
2	3,200 (4,000 × .80)	6,400
4	2,560 (3,200 × .80)	10,240
8	2,048 (2,560 × .80)	16,384

Column A = Double the cumulative quantity.
Column B = Multiply the cumulative averages by the learning curve percentage.
Column C = Multiply the cumulative average by the cumulative quantity.

A learning curve chart is illustrated in Figure 13-5.

A bank that accumulates experience the most quickly can benefit competitively over the long run. A knowledge of how the experience curve operates can help banks develop strategies for new products and processes, pricing, expansion, and other plans.

LEVERAGE

Leverage is used to explain a firm's ability to use fixed-cost assets or funds to magnify the returns to its owners. Leverage exists whenever a company has fixed costs. There are three types of leverage in financial management: operating, financial, and total leverage.

Financial leverage is a financing technique that uses borrowed funds or preferred stock (items involving fixed financial costs) to improve the return on an equity investment. As long as a higher rate of return can be earned on assets than is paid for the capital used to acquire the assets, the rate of return to owners can be increased. This is referred to as positive financial leverage. Financial leverage is used in many business transactions, especially where real estate and financing by bonds or preferred stock instead of common stock are involved. Financial leverage is concerned with the relationship between the firm's earnings before interest and taxes (EBIT) and the earnings available to common stockholders or other owners. Financial leverage is often referred to as "trading on the equity."

Figure 13-5
Learning Chart

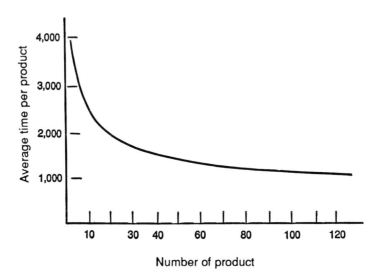

Number of product

Operating leverage is based on the relationship between a firm's sales revenue and its earnings before interest and taxes. Operating leverage arises when an enterprise has a relatively large amount of fixed costs in its total costs.

Total leverage reflects the impact of operating and financial leverage on the total risk of the firm (the degree of uncertainty associated with the firm's ability to cover its fixed-payment obligations).

Financial leverage arises as a result of fixed financial charges related to the presence of bonds or preferred stock. Such charges do not vary with the bank's earnings before interest and taxes. The effect of financial leverage is that an increase in the bank's earnings before interest and taxes results in a greater than proportional increase in the bank's earnings per share. A decrease in the firm's earnings has the opposite effect. The degree of financial leverage (DFL) is measured by the following formula:

$$DFL = \frac{\text{Percentage change in earnings per share}}{\substack{\text{Percentage change in earnings before} \\ \text{interest and taxes}}}$$

The degree of financial leverage indicates how large a change in earnings per share will result from a given percentage change in earnings before interest and taxes. Whenever the degree of financial leverage is greater than one, financial leverage exists. The higher this quotient, the larger the degree of financial leverage. Since debt financing incurs fixed interest charges, the ratio of debt to equity is considered a measure of financial leverage.

Operating leverage refers to the extent that fixed costs are utilized in the production process during an operating cycle. Operating leverage can also be used to measure the impact on earnings per share of having different levels of fixed to variable costs in manufacturing products. Earnings before interest taxes are related to changes in the variable cost to fixed cost relationship. As fixed operating costs are added by the firm, the potential operating profits and losses are magnified, and are ultimately reflected in the variation in earnings per share of stock. An enterprise with a large percentage increase in income relative to its increase in unit sales can expect to have large operating leverage. The degree of operating leverage (DOP) can be measured by the following formula:

$$DOP = \frac{\text{Percentage change in earnings before interest and taxes}}{\text{Percentage change in sales}}$$

The degree of operating leverage indicates how large a change in operating profit will result from a given percentage change in sales. As long as the degree of operating leverage is greater than one, there is positive operating leverage.

Figure 13-6 illustrates the application of leverage to a firm's income statement. Note that fixed expenses and interest expense remain unchanged. Note the sections of the statement associated with the computation of operating, financial, and total leverage. Note that what provides the leverage is fixed expenses and interest expenses. Note that the total leverage of 2.0 is the result of multiplying 1.2 (DOL) by 1.67 (DFL). If sales increase by 1 percent, earnings before interest and taxes will increase by 1.2 percent. EBIT increases by 10 percent, net income will increase by 16.7 percent. With total leverage of 2.0, to increase net income by 10 percent, sales must increase by 5 percent.

FINANCIAL FORECAST

A financial forecast for an enterprise is an estimate of the most probable financial position, results of operations and changes in financial position for one or more future periods. Most probable means that the forecast is based on management's judgment of the most likely set of conditions and its most likely course of action. A financial projection is an estimate of financial results based on assumptions which are not necessarily the most likely (SOP 75-4). A financial projection is sometimes used to present hypothetical courses of action for evaluation. A feasibility study is an analysis of a proposed investment or course of action (SOP 75-4).

A financial forecast presents a prediction of an entity's expected financial position, results of operations, and changes in financial position. A forecast is based on assumptions about expected conditions and expected courses of action, prepared to the best of the preparer's knowledge and belief. A financial projection differs from a financial forecast in that a projection depends upon one or more hypothetical assumptions. A projection responds to the question: "What might happen if . . . ?" Multiple projections consist of two or more projections based on a range of hypothetical assumptions.

Public accountants are primarily associated with forecasts and projects to lend their credibility to them. A client typically initiates the request that the accountant compile or review prospective financial information. In a review engagement by external accountants, the ac-

Figure 13-6
Financial, Operating, and Total Leverage

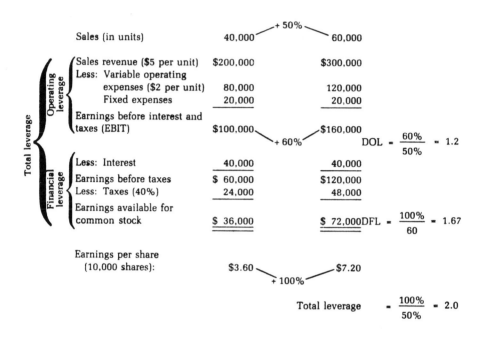

countant performs some procedures to achieve a level of assurance on which he or she bases an opinion. The accountant must perform inquiry and analytical procedures to achieve a reasonable basis for expressing limited assurance that there are no material modifications that should be made to the statements in order for them to be in conformity with generally accepted accounting principles or, if applicable, with another comprehensive basis of accounting. In a compilation service, the accountant performs few, if any, procedures; the accountant merely assists the client to "write-up" the financial information. Accountants are expected to render a report on compiled or reviewed prospective financial statements. The compilation report contains a disclaimer and offers no conclusions or any form of assurance. The review report gives the accountant's conclusions about proper presentation and about the reasonableness of the assumptions. The reports are either unqualified, adverse, or disclaimers resulting from scope limitations.

AICPA Rule of Conduct 201(e) prohibits an accountant from being associated with a forecast or projection which may lead readers to believe that the accountant vouches for the authenticity of the forecast or projection.

KEY DEFINITIONS

Activity accounting Responsibility accounting.

Accountability centers Responsibility centers.

Allocation Assigning items of cost or revenue to one or more segments of an organization according to a common cause, benefits received, or other rational measure of use.

ALM Asset/Liability management. A method of managing the net earnings impact of interest rate risk, liquidity risk, and capital adequacy risk (balance sheet risk). Managing both assets and liabilities simultaneously for the purpose of mitigating interest rate risk, providing liquidity, and to enhance the value of a bank.

Break-even point That point of activity where total revenues and total expenses are equal.

Budget A financial plan to estimate the results of future operations or capital project(s).

Budgeted statements Pro forma statements prepared prior to the accounting period.

Budget variance The difference between an actual amount and a budget amount.

Cap An interest rate cap is a financial arrangement that limits the exposure of a floating rate borrower to upward movements in interest rates.

Capital budgeting Long-term planning for capital expenditures and for the financing of such expenditures.

Contribution margin Revenue minus variable costs.

Control The action that a manager takes to ensure that actual results correspond to planned results.

Controllable item A cost, revenue, or investment item over which a manager has significant influence.

Cost-benefit A criterion for choosing among alternative systems. The basic rule: Additional benefits should exceed its expected additional costs.

Cost center A responsibility center where the manager can influence only costs and is held accountable for a specified output at a given cost level.

Cost of capital The required rate of return; average cost rate per year a company must pay for its equities.

Direct costing Variable costing.

Discounted cash flow A method of valuing expected future cash receipts and disbursements as of a common date.

Duration A technique used in ALM to analyze the cash flows of a balance sheet event. The weighted average term to maturity of all cash flows received from an investment(s) such as a bond, assets, or liabilities. Duration depends in part on maturity.

Duration drift The drift which occurs with the passage of time; the duration gets shorter as the bond approaches maturity.

Effective interest rate The actual rate of interest earned taking into consideration premiums or discounts on the debt.

Efficiency Optimal relationship between inputs and outputs.

Fixed cost Costs that are not affected by changes in volume of output.

Gap The difference between rate sensitive assets and rate sensitive liabilities expressed in dollars. Gap can also be measured in terms of duration.

Gross margin Excess of sales over the cost of goods sold.

Flexible budget A budget that recognizes varying levels of production and the costs that change with these levels. A series of static budgets for various production levels.

Internal rate of return The discount rate that equates the net present value of cash inflows and outflows to zero.

Investment center A responsibility center where the manager can influence revenues, expenses, and capital invested in the center to attain the desired performance.

Learning curve A cost function that describes the average cost per unit of output decline systematically as cumulative production increases.

Leverage An activity that borrows funds at a specified interest rate with the expectation of using these funds to earn a higher rate of return for the benefit of the enterprise.

Management accounting A form of accounting concerned primarily with how accounting can serve internal decision makers.

Margin of safety Excess of actual or budgeted sales over break-even sales.

Master budget A budget that summarizes the subunit budgets of an organization.

Net present value A method of calculating the expected utility of a project by discounting expected future cash flows to the present, using a predetermined minimum desired rate of return.

Operating budget A budget of the income statement along with supporting schedules.

Payback method A technique used to consider alternative capital expenditures that does not measure profitability but merely calculates the amount of time required to recover the initial net investment in an asset.

Performance reports Reports which measure actual results with budgeted amounts.

Planning The process of establishing goals, predictions, and results under various alternatives along with a decision of how to attain the desired results.

Profit center A responsibility center where the manager can influence both revenues and expenses for the center.

Profit planning A process in which a company's profit and growth objectives are established along with the means of attaining these objectives.

Responsibility accounting An accounting system in which the accountability for costs is assigned to a segment of the firm based on the amount of control possessed over costs. (Organizational centers are established for controlling revenues, costs, and profit.)

Sensitive analysis Attempts to assess the possible effects of risk or uncertainty on predicted cash flows.

Standard costs Costs which are assigned to the factors of production based on physical standards under efficient and effective operations to produce a product or service.

Static budget A budget prepared for a single volume of sales and production.

Transfer pricing The value placed upon goods or services transferred between profit centers of a decentralized company.

Variable costing Direct costing. A form of product costing that charges fixed factory overhead as incurred against the revenue of the period.

Yield Interest rate of return on a stream of cash flows.

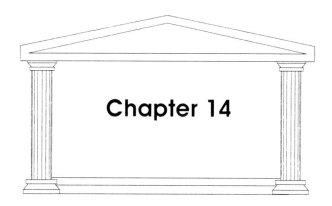

Chapter 14

Costs and Pricing

B anks are required to make numerous decisions relating to product costing and pricing. An understanding of concepts underlying these decisions is essential to making correct choices. The thrust of an efficient and effective cost management and pricing system is improved profitability and the attainment of the bank's mission, goals, and objectives. This chapter deals primarily with costing and pricing procedures.

COST

A cost is an expenditure (a decrease in assets or an increase in liabilities) made to obtain an economic benefit, usually resources that can produce revenue. A cost can also be defined as the sacrifice to acquire a good or service. Used in this sense, a cost represents an asset. An expense is a cost that has been utilized by the company in the process of obtaining revenues. (The benefits associated with the good or service have expired.)

Classification of Costs

Before costs can be controlled, they must be identified and classified. Costs can be classified in many ways and for different purposes including the following:

    1.   Direct, indirect, and full costs:

(a) Direct (traceable) costs are outlays that can be traced to a particular product, service, department, or activity. For example, the costs of material and labor that are identifiable with a particular physical product are direct costs for the product.

(b) Indirect costs are those outlays that cannot be identified with a specified product, department, or activity. Taxes, insurance, and telephone expense are common examples of indirect costs.

(c) Full cost of a good or service is the sum of its fixed and variable costs. Over the long run, a bank must recover its full costs.

2. Product and period costs:

(a) Product costs are outlays that can be associated with production. For example, the direct costs of materials and labor used in the production of an item are product costs.

(b) Period costs are expenditures that are not directly associated with production, but are associated with the passage of a time period. The president's salary, advertising expense, interest and rent expenses are examples of period costs.

3. Fixed, variable, and mixed (semivariable) costs:

(a) Fixed costs remain constant in total (not per unit) regardless of the volume of production or sales, over a relevant range of production or sales. Rent and depreciation are typically fixed costs. Total depreciation remains constant; depreciation per unit of output changes with changes in volume or activity. A bank's fixed costs include costs related to occupancy, dues, memberships, insurance, rent, etc. Fixed costs that arise from having property, plant, equipment and a basic organization are referred to as committed costs.

(b) Variable costs fluctuate in total (not per unit) as the volume of production or sales fluctuates. Direct labor and direct material costs used in production and sales commissions are examples of variable costs. Total commission expense varies with changes in sales volume; commission expense per unit of sales remains constant as sales volume changes.

(c) Mixed costs fluctuate with production or sales, but not in direct proportion to production or sales. Mixed costs contain elements of fixed and variable costs. Costs of supervision and inspections are often mixed costs.

4. Controllable and uncontrollable costs:

(a) Controllable costs are identified as a responsibility of an individual or department, and can be regulated within a given period of time. Office supplies would ordinarily be considered a controllable cost for an office manager. Over the long run, all costs are controllable.

(b) Uncontrollable cost are those that cannot be regulated by an individual or department within a given period of time. For example, rent expense is uncontrollable by the factory foreman.

5. Out-of-pocket costs and sunk costs:

   (a) Out-of-pocket costs require the use of current economic resources. Taxes and insurance are generally out-of-pocket costs.

   (b) Sunk costs are outlays or commitments that have already been incurred. The cost of equipment already purchased is a sunk cost.

6. Incremental and opportunity:

   (a) Incremental (or differential) cost is the difference in total costs between alternatives. Incremental costs can also be considered as the total cost added or subtracted by switching from one level or plan of activity to another. If a bank hires another teller for $25,000, the incremental cost is $25,000.

   (b) Opportunity cost is the maximum alternative benefit that could be obtained if economic resources were applied to an alternative use. If a bank funds a commercial loan, it gives up the opportunity of investing in a consumer loan. The opportunity cost of making the commercial loan is the going rate of the consumer loan.

7. Imputed and implicit costs:

   (a) Imputed costs are those costs that can be associated with an economic event when no exchange transaction has occurred. For example, if a company "rents to itself" a building that it might otherwise have rented to an outside party, the rent for the building is an imputed cost.

   (b) Implicit interest (versus imputed interest) is interest implied in a contract. It is neither paid nor received. The implicit interest rate is the rate that equates the present value of payments on a note with the face of the note. The implicit rate is determined by factors directly related to the note transaction. For example, assume that a dealer offers to sell a machine for $100,000 cash or $16,275 per year for ten years. By dividing the cash price by the annual payments (an annuity), a factor of 6.144 is computed ($100,000/$16,275). By referring to a Present Value of an Annuity of 1 in Arrears table, 6.144 appears in the 10 percent interest column when ten payments are involved. Therefore, the implicit interest rate in this offer is 10 percent.

8. Relevant cost:
   A relevant cost is an expected future cost and a cost that represents difference in costs among alternatives. Assume you purchased an airline ticket from New York to London at a cost of $300 and that you have made an unrefundable $75 downpayment on the ticket. The remaining $225 will be paid when you pick up the ticket. The ticket is nontransferable. You later discover that you can purchase a ticket to London on another airline for $200. Everything related to the two tickets is equal. The $75 downpayment is not relevant to this decision since it is not a future cost that differs among alternatives. You should buy the new ticket for $200.

9. Actual and standard costs:

(a)   Actual costs are the cost required to deliver a product or service to customers; the amounts determined on the basis of costs incurred (historical cost).

(b)   Standard costs are carefully predetermined costs that should be attained, usually expressed per unit. Banks often use the Fed's Functional Cost Analysis data as a proxy for the bank's standard costs. This data is usually six months or more old when available.

10.   Avoidable and nonavoidable costs:

(a)   Avoidable costs are costs that will not continue if an ongoing operation is changed or deleted.

(b)   Nonavoidable costs are the opposite of avoidable costs.

11.   Common and joint costs:

(a)   Common costs are cost of facilities and services shared by user departments.

(b)   Joint costs are cost of manufactured goods or services of relatively significant sales values that are simultaneously provided by a process or series of processes.

12.   Expired costs and unexpired cost:
Expired costs are expenses; unexpired costs are assets.

13.   Short-run costs and long-run costs:
Short-run cost vary as output varies for a given plant or operational capacity; long-run costs change costs associated with a given plant or operational capacity.

14.   Average cost and marginal cost:
Average cost is total cost divided by the number of units. Marginal cost is the cost to produce the next unit or the last unit.

Costs can also be categorized in a variety of ways, such as the following:

1.   By function, e.g., selling expenses, general and administrative expenses, and direct operating expenses

2.   By organizational unit, e.g., shipping department, loan department

3.   By product or service

Functional cost categories are a natural way to gather costs and can serve as a basis for controlling costs. Management uses cost classification by organization unit for control purposes and for developing product and service costs. When classified by organizational units, costs are assigned to areas of responsibility that are subject to control. Product costs are usually required for pricing decisions and profitability evaluations. The product or service cost classification is useful to establish a value on inventories or cost of goods sold or services provided.

Cost can also be classified as follows:

1.   On a basis of time:

(a)   Historical costs, i.e., when incurred.

(b)   Current costs, i.e., fair market value at current date

(c)   Budgeted cost, i.e., predetermined costs

2. As behavior in relation to activity (variable, fixed, and mixed costs)

3. By traceability (direct and indirect costs)

4. As charges against revenue (product and period costs)

5. As decision-making costs (not usually used for recording purposes):

    (a) Out-of-pocket vs. sunk costs

    (b) Avoidable vs. unavoidable costs

    (c) Relevant vs. irrelevant costs

    (d) Controllable vs. noncontrollable costs

    (e) Marginal and incremental (or differential) costs

    (f) Variable, fixed, and mixed costs

    (g) Imputed and implicit costs

    (h) Relevant costs

The Fed's Functional Cost Analysis System

The Fed's makes available on a no-cost basis a service available to all depository institutions from their regional Federal Reserve Bank. This service provided data about the costs of each banking function and compares those costs to average costs of peer banks. The cost analysis includes such items as check cashing, deposit taking, accounts maintenance, loan origination, deposit boxes and trust services, and transit checks collecting.

The Fed's service is especially useful for small or medium-sized banks as a measure of noninterest expenses. In essence, the service serves as a modified uniform cost accounting system.

COST BEHAVIOR

Various techniques are available for estimating the fixed and variable components of total costs. The least-squares regression analysis can usually be used to provide statistical estimates of fixed and variable costs based on data from previous periods. The equation for the determination of a straight line is given below:

$$Y = a + bX$$

The equation states that the value of Y is equal to a point (a) plus a percentage of variability applied to X. For example, if $30 is fixed cost for supplies expense, the percentage (b) is the change in Y in relation to the change in X. If Y increases $20 for each increase of 10 hours of activity, the percent of change is 200 percent (20/10). The equation now reads:

$$Y = \$30 + 200\%(X)$$

If X is given a value of 10, Y is equal to $50:

$$Y = \$30 + 2(10)$$
$$Y = \$50$$

The regression analysis can provide estimates of the standard deviation of the coefficient estimates. These estimated standard deviations can be used to test whether the coefficients (fixed or variable) are significant. For example, if the fixed-cost coefficient is not statistically significant, the cost account can be considered completely variable. The estimated standard deviation of the coefficients can also be used to establish a confidence interval on how large or small the variable-cost coefficient could be. The confidence interval could then be used in sensitivity analysis for cost and profit planning and forecasting. Some cost analysts use the estimated standard deviations to forecast the range of costs that would be expected for a given activity level.

COST ACCOUNTING

Cost accounting is a subset of accounting that develops detailed information about costs as they relate to units of output and to departments, primarily for purposes of providing inventory valuations (product costing) for financial statements, control, and decision making.

Standard cost systems are widely used by banks for pricing, budgeting, and performance evaluation purposes. For example, a cost system might be established for clerical and other employees where operational control is required. In a standard cost system product costing is achieved by using predetermined standard costs for material, direct labor, and overhead. Standard costs are developed on the basis of historical cost data adjusted for expected changes in the product, production technology, engineering estimates, and other procedures. Standards may be established at any one of the following levels:

1.   Ideal standards are set for the level of maximum efficiency.

2.   Normal standards are set to reflect the conditions that are expected to exist over a period of time sufficient to take into consideration seasonal cyclical fluctuations.

3.   Currently attainable standards are set at a level which represents anticipated conditions assuming efficient operations.

Because predetermined standards usually differ from actual costs incurred, a variance typically exists. An unfavorable variance results when actual cost exceeds standard cost; a favorable variance results when standard cost exceeds actual cost. The usual approach followed in standard cost analysis is to separate price factors from efficiency factors. When the actual amount paid differs from the standard amount, the variance is referred to as a price, rate, or spending variance.

The formulas for typical direct material, direct labor, and overhead variances are as follows:

1.   Direct material price variance = Actual quantities purchased × (Actual price − Standard price)

2.   Material quantity (or usage, efficiency) variance = (Actual quantity used − Standard quantity allowed) × Standard price

3.   Direct labor rate variance = Actual hours used × (Actual labor rate − Standard labor rate)

4. Direct labor efficiency variance = (Actual hours used − Standard hours allowed) × Standard labor rate

5. Volume variance = Standard fixed overhead rate × (Normal activity − Standard inputs allowed for output attained)

6. Budget variance = Actual overhead [Budgeted fixed overhead + (Standard variable overhead rate) × (Standard inputs allowed for output attained)]

A bank's revenues and costs are typically recorded and traced to individual units at the lowest level of the bank with primary day-to-day decision responsibility for a cost, revenue, profit or investment center, e.g., a check-processing department. Such a person or unit is usually in the best position to make decisions and influence actions. Unit costs are typically computed where control or pricing are the objective. Unit costs are calculated as follows:

$$\frac{\text{Estimated total costs for a budget period}}{\text{Average volume}} = \text{Unit costs}$$

Variances can be computed to identify any difference between planned and actual results. Because of the pyramid organization of banks, several levels of reports would ordinarily be necessary to summarize all activities.

For banks, fixed costs represent a sizeable percentage of all costs. Hence the total level of costs may not change as much for a bank as volumes of activities are changed (when excluding interest costs). Labor and interest costs are major expense items for a bank. For many banks a significant percentage of revenue is relatively fixed over a short period of time as a result of loan agreements and governmental regulations.

Costs and Productivity

Major factors related to efforts to improve productivity and performance include the following elements:

- Goals and objectives
- Standards
- Implementation
- Monitoring
- Feedback
- Evaluation
- Intervention
- Employee participation

Management reports are usually informational or performance reports. Informational reports often relate something about the organization in dollars, volume, costs, and so forth. Performance reports draws relationships, comparisons, and associations between data and how effectively or efficiently the task is accomplished. In banking reporting is often reflected in documents such as

- Financial statements and reports
- Budget summaries and variance analyses
- Volume and system related reports

Performance indicators are usually percentages that provide management with information that explains what occurs at various organizational levels. The indicators typically deal with productivity in the form of percentages. Examples of indicators include:

Percentage	Calculation
• Completion percent	Volume completed/Volume received × 100
• Efficiency percent	Standard hours required for work completed/Actual hours spent × 100
• Capacity percent	Standard hours required/Available hours × 100
• Utilization percent	Actual hours used/Available hours × 100

Aside from cost of funds to a bank which are subject to cost controls, overhead and administrative functions can have a direct impact on the cost and profitability of a bank. Significant cost savings in these two areas exist in banking because of (1) the extensive use of paper forms and records; (2) the requirements for extensive record keeping; (3) security and control; (4) sensitivity of the information handled; and (5) the fact that the principle activities are labor-intensive. Examples of where cost reduction potentials exist include a reduction in the number of records produced; a reduction in the number of copies prepared; and a reduction in the cost of preparation, storage, and retrieval. Costs reductions opportunities might also be found by establishing equipment inventory and control system to reduce loss and maintenance costs. A bank should also consider establishing written policies and procedures to standardize the work performed; establish accountability and controls; reduce costs associated with training new employees; establish controls to minimize loss from employee error or misconduct, and many others opportunities too numerous to list.

Many opportunities are available for cost improvement though an analysis of methods or systems employed by a bank. There are four basic elements to methods improvements: information, time, technique, and opportunity. Method improvement opportunities exist within every function of a bank. The opportunities for cost control standards as related to methods improvements for a bank can be summarized:

I.   Personnel

    A.   Employment and placement

    B.   Job classifications

    C.   Employee responsibilities

    D.   Training

    E.   Supervision

    F.   Procedures manual

II. General Standards

    A. Procedures (description of process, control features, action steps, and responsibility)

        1. Documentation

        2. Signatures

        3. Transfers

        4. Separation of duties

        5. Balancing procedures

    B. Other Standards

        1. Work and storage areas

            a. Access

            b. Vault regulations

            c. Extraneous items

            d. Wastepaper

            e. Storage containers/file cabinets

        2. Identification and control devices

            a. Identification devices

            b. Control devices

            c. Seals

        3. Watchers/observers

III. Functional Standards (Cash, securities, check stock, registered mail, etc.)

    A. Initial receipt

    B. Verification

    C. Storage, vault, or restricted access

    D. Internal transfers

    E. Processing

    F. Paying, shipping, and/or delivery

    G. Destruction/spoilage

    H. Records, audit trail

Source: *Bank Productivity*, Kent S. Belasco.

Needless to say, cost control, reduction, or elimination cannot take place unless there exists an environment and commitment at the highest level for such efforts. Properly used, costs are a useful tool for performance measurement and employee incentives. However, controlling costs is not an end in itself. Controlling costs has the danger of encouraging short-term management while losing sight of long-term mission, goals, and objectives. Controlling costs is a philosophy. Everything in banking is related.

PRICING POLICY

Pricing is a profit-planning opportunity in which management searches for alternative pricing policies and evaluates the profit consequences of the various alternatives before reaching a decision. Pricing policy refers to the principles and practices that determine pricing decisions. Theory and practice vary widely where pricing policies are determined, even within the same industry. Pricing should be viewed as a vehicle for profit improvement through fee revenue optimization.

Banks have found it expedient to have a pricing committee whose responsibilities are primarily limited to reviews of fee-based products of a noncredit nature. Credit-related products, such as loans, are usually reviewed by another committee, such as an asset/liability management committee. In reviewing a product for pricing, a pricing committee would take the following into consideration: profitability, product marketplace strategy, competition, perceived quality to the customer, regulatory considerations, community relations, customer base, impact on other bank products, and opportunities for cost reductions.

Bank pricing practices range from rule-of-thumb judgments (e.g., follow the competition), to conventional practices including cost-oriented and value- or demand-oriented models, to regulator-set versions, to the application of microeconomic principles. Many of these practices have some application to bank pricing practices and policies. Some of these practices are obviously more satisfactory than others as they relate to banking. However, an understanding of how prices have been set in various situations is valuable background information.

Establishing a Pricing Policy

The establishment of a pricing policy is the product of organizational goals, objectives, strategy, and tactics. Pricing objectives, or targets, as related to overall organizational objectives typically refer to

1. A rate-of-return objective
2. A profit maximization objective
3. Nonfinancial objective(s), e.g., growth, market share, high quality service
4. A combination of the above

Pricing theorists maintain that the primary purpose of using costs in pricing is to forecast the impact on profit of alternative prices. Costs usually set a minimum limit, or floor, to price. Costs can play a major role in special situations: product tailoring where the seller cannot affect the market price and so must adjust costs to make a profit; refusal pricing, where a product is designed for a single buyer; where a producer has a single buyer and the seller must price the product to prevent the buyer from making the product; and public utility pricing.

Costs for pricing purposes should have the following characteristics:

1. Costs should be expressed in terms of product or service units.
2. Product and nonproduct costs are relevant in pricing decisions.
3. Current or future costs are required for pricing; historical or standard costs are useful as guidelines.

Consumer demand is of major significance in establishing prices. Consumer demand is influenced by product differentiation and price elasticity.

The market situation plays a prominent role in pricing decisions. Prices are affected in different ways by competition, monopoly, monopolistic competition, and oligopoly.

Legal requirements imposed by laws, regulations, and commissions can have an impact on the pricing decision and must be complied with according to the law.

Social and ethical standards should be considered when pricing decisions are made. Banking does interface with society and the common good and this should be acknowledged by the professional banker.

Marketing theorists generally agree that the pricing process involves

1. Identifying markets to be targeted

2. Constructing the marketing mix

3. Selecting a pricing policy or objective

4. Determining price strategy and tactics

5. Establishing the specific price

Basic pricing strategies include the following:

1. Pricing low to limit competition and protect market share

2. Letting competition or market leader establish the price

3. Pricing below the market to provide a competitive edge

4. Pricing what the market will bear

When setting the final price for a service, management typically uses demand-based methods or cost-based methods. Demand-based methods include skimming, penetration; prestige, price lining (for a line of products), odd-even pricing, and demand-backward pricing (estimate the price that consumers will pay, work backward through margins and costs to establish the price).

Cost-based methods include markup pricing, cost plus percentage of cost, cost plus fixed-fee pricing, experience curve.

Profit-based methods include target profit pricing, target return-on-sales pricing, and target return-on-investment pricing. Competition based methods of pricing include (1) pricing at, above, or below the market, (2) loss leader pricing, (3) sealed bid pricing, and other forms.

A Formal Pricing Policy

Banks should develop a formal, written pricing policy for its products and services to obtain uniform pricing standards and procedures and to control and evaluate the pricing policy. Most banks assign the responsibility for establishing a pricing policy to a special pricing committee. This committee is composed of various high-level banking officials including the chief executive officer, the chair of the board of directors, controller, treasurer, marketing directors, and other persons who would be useful to the process. For example, the committee would be responsible for pricing new and established products and services. It would develop the bank's position on product and service profitability and how it is to be measured, monitored, and evaluated.

The committee would also be expected to develop policies for handling disputes related to pricing and for the discontinuance of products or services. The committee would be especially interested in evaluating customer profitability reports and documented exceptions made to the bank's pricing policy. The committee should meet at least monthly.

The bank's loan committee can provide valuable information to the pricing committee because it is in a position to evaluate and monitor the effect of pricing on loan making and loan risks. Other bank committees also interface directly or indirectly with the pricing committee, and their insights and inputs should be considered.

PRICING PRACTICES

Pricing goods and services is one of the most important strategic planning tools available to bank management. Without question, it has a major impact on the bank's bottom line. The controller should have a clear understanding of how prices are set in a market economy. A variety of pricing methods are presented here to give an overview of pricing as it applies to goods and services. Many of these pricing methods have an application to banking.

Economic Theory of Pricing

Demand for goods and services refer to the quantity that will be purchased at various prices at a given time. Demand is a function of price, income available for spending, prices of other commodities, and personal tastes. Generally, the higher the price of a good or service, the less the quantity of the item will be purchased. As prices rise, demand tends to fall off because (1) users of the product or service switch to substitutes and (2) present consumers reduce the consumption of most products. The lower the price, the more units of the product or service that will be demanded. When graphically presented, a demand curve appears with a downward slope. An increase in demand occurs when additional quantities of a product can be sold at the same price. A change in price alone can also change the quantity of a product demanded.

The impact of price changes on demand depends upon the price elasticity of a product or service. Price elasticity describes whether a given change in price will have a large, small, or no effect on demand.

The cost of production side of a bank can be combined with the demand side to determine the price and output of a commodity or service in the market place. However, a firm behaves differently under conditions of perfect competition, monopoly, monopolistic competition, and oligopoly. Before pricing under various market situations is discussed, it is necessary to define economic cost and revenue concepts:

1. *Total cost* (TC) is the sum of total fixed and total variable costs at a particular level of production.

2. *Average total cost* (ATC) is computed by dividing total costs by the number of units produced or by adding average fixed costs (AFC) and average variable costs (AVC).

3. *Marginal cost* (MC) is the increase in the total cost resulting from the production of one more unit of output.

4.   *Total Revenue* (TR) is the amount of revenue or income received from the sale of a given quantity of goods or services. It is computed by multiplying average revenue, or price, by the number of units sold.

5.   *Average revenue* (AR) is the revenue per unit sold, or price. It is computed by dividing the total revenue by the number of units sold.

6.   *Marginal revenue* (MR) is the increase in total revenue resulting from the sale of one more unit of output. It is computed by dividing the increase in total revenue resulting from the use of an additional unit of input by the increase in total product.

7.   *Total profit* is the difference between total revenue and total cost.

Pricing Under Perfect Competition

In perfect competition the price of a good or service is determined by the intersection of the market demand curve and the market supply curve for the commodity or product. Sellers have no pricing problems since their actions alone cannot change price. The firm should produce at a level that maximizes profit, i.e., at the point where total revenue exceeds total costs, which is also the point where marginal revenue is positive. Under perfect competition, the price a firm receives is identical with average revenue and marginal revenue.

Pricing Under Monopoly

In a monopoly the firm has one distinctly downward sloping demand curve. By varying its output, the monopolist can affect the price for its product. A monopoly has a marginal revenue curve that differs from its average revenue curve because each time a monopolist sells more output, it must reduce its price. The monopolist increases output as long as marginal revenue from the increased output exceeds the marginal cost of such output. On a graph this point is at the intersection of the marginal revenue and marginal cost curves. This point determines both output and price. Profit is the difference between average cost per unit and average revenue per unit.

Pricing Under Monopolistic Competition

Under conditions of monopolistic competition, a bank is able to differentiate its product or services from similar products or services. The bank has a downward-sloping demand curve (average revenue curve), which indicates that as prices decline, demand increases. In the short run firms operating under conditions of monopolistic competition have an equilibrium position similar to the monopolistic firm, i.e., at the point where MR = MC from below and where price is equal to or larger than average variable cost. Firms operating under monopolistic competition usually have excess capacity because they are not operating at a level of output where average cost is lowest. In the long run new firms enter the market because of the presence of economic profit. Firms do not operate at the optimum of their cost curves and so have not attained their greatest efficiency.

Pricing Under Oligopoly

Under oligopolistic market conditions, firms in the arrangement are interdependent and recognize this fact. Any action taken by one member will usually result in a reaction by the other member(s), which are rivals. The maximization of profit is usually achieved when

1. The firms recognize their interdependencies
2. Firms can easily agree
3. Other firms can easily enter.

There are no standard pricing models to illustrate oligopolies. Generally, output under oligopoly would be somewhat lower than under pure competition and more than under monopoly. Idle plant or productivity capacity exists and prices to the consumer will be higher than under competition.

Oligopolists often resort to nonprice competition to attract a larger share of a market so as not to alter established price structures or invite price wars. They attempt to do this through advertising, product differentiation, product innovation, and other means. Oligopolists often form cartels to establish price and output among the members. Policies are sometimes determined by a price or production leader.

Some economists argue that prices are inherently rigid under an oligopoly because if any one firm raises its price, no other firm would follow; hence the initial firm's revenues would fall. If any one firm lowered its price, all firms would follow thereby eliminating the anticipated revenue increase. Owing to this type of interdependence among oligopolistic firms, prices are inherently rigid. There is little empirical support for this theoretical notion, frequently call the kinked demand curve of oligopoly.

Administered Pricing

Administered pricing is a policy in which a provider of a service can exert an influence on the price charged for a service because of the absence of competition. Large and powerful providers are occasionally in a position to adopt administered pricing.

Conversion Cost Pricing

Conversion costs include direct labor and overhead costs. Costs of materials used in the product are not considered. Conversion costing is occasionally used when a customer provides the material. Conversion cost pricing requires that capacity is limited in terms of labor and overhead cost constrains. When conversion cost pricing is followed, companies direct their efforts to services requiring less labor and overhead (scarce resources) because more units can be produced and sold.

Cost-Plus Pricing

Cost-plus pricing requires a bank to add a predetermined markup to an established or known average cost. The size of the markup depends upon what the firm calculates it can obtain. This form of pricing usually establishes a target rate of return on its investment and uses this rate to establish prices. Cost-plus pricing generally does not take into consideration the elasticity of demand or the relationship of marginal cost to marginal revenue. As a result, the price established may not be the most profitable price attainable. Costs should be used in pricing primarily to forecast the impact on profits of alternative pricing policies. Cost usually refers to full costs. Cost-plus pricing is in essence a backward-cost pricing method. A desired percentage for profit is added to the full cost of the product or service to establish the price. Cost-plus pricing usually involves the difficult task of allocating fixed costs that cannot be traced directly to a project product or service.

A problem with full-cost pricing occurs when two or more products or services are produced or worked on. How should common costs be allocated to the products or projects and how large should the markup be? In spite of these and other problems, full-cost pricing is widely used because the economic model of pricing is difficult to apply, managers consider full-cost pricing to be safe, and intuitively managers believe that in the long run all costs, fixed and variable, must be recovered if the firm is to survive. However, full-cost pricing cannot guarantee any of these assumptions.

Differential Cost Pricing

A differential cost is the increase in total costs resulting from the production of additional unit(s). A desired markup based as a percentage of differential cost is added to full cost. Differential cost pricing focuses on the contribution to fixed costs and profit that an additional order will produce.

Direct Cost Pricing

Direct costs include the direct cost of material and labor along with variable overhead costs. When direct cost pricing is used, selling prices are set at a percentage above these direct costs incurred in producing the good or service. Direct cost pricing is valid if the cost characteristics of a bank's product lines are similar. If the indirect costs that should be allocated to each product line are not essentially the same percentage of direct costs, and if the assets employed by product lines are not similar, direct cost pricing can produce inequities in the pricing process. This method does not base pricing on indirect costs, which are often arbitrarily allocated to products.

Discounts

Discounts can be used as a pricing tool. Discounts, such as those for volume or bulk business and off-hours processing should be given close scrutiny in terms of profit contribution.

Fair Pricing

Fair pricing is an ethical concept of pricing goods and services. Under fair pricing an organization prices its goods and services at a price that allows the full recovery of all costs plus an equitable profit. Costs incurred for factors of production (land, labor, and capital) are supposed to be in amounts that provide for a fair standard of living for the parties involved. The concept of fair pricing is difficult to apply because what is fair or equitable is difficult to define.

Penetration Pricing

Companies have occasionally used penetration pricing in order to gain entrance into a market. In penetration pricing the company introduces a product or service at a low price and then hopefully moves up to a higher price. Penetration pricing is sometimes used when the competition dictates a price ceiling. Where a high volume of sales is required to make a product or service profitable, penetration pricing with its low prices might produce the necessary volume.

Price Leadership

Price leadership connotes a behavior where the dominant (leader) firm increases price as a signal for the other firms to follow. Such action, by itself, is not illegal. However, if it comes about as the result of collusion, it is illegal, just as price fixing is illegal.

Return on Assets

Some firms establish a price for their product or service based on a desired rate of return on assets employed in the company. The desired markup on cost can be determined according to the following formula and illustration: the company desires a 10 percent return on $60,000,000 assets employed in the business and annual costs total $45,000,000:

$$\text{Percent markup on cost} = \frac{\text{Assets employed}}{\text{Total annual cost}} \times \begin{array}{c}\text{Desired rate of}\\ \text{return on}\\ \text{Capital employed}\end{array}$$

$$\text{Percent markup on cost} = \frac{\$60,000,000}{\$45,000,000} \times 10\%$$

$$\text{Percent markup} = 13.3\%$$

The sales volume would then be computed using this formula:

$$\text{Sales volume} = \begin{array}{c}\text{Total annual}\\ \text{costs}\end{array} + \left(\begin{array}{c}\text{Total annual}\\ \text{costs}\end{array} \times \begin{array}{c}\text{Percentage}\\ \text{markup on cost}\end{array}\right)$$

Sales volume = $45,000,000 + ($45,000,000 × 13.3%)
Sales volume = $50,985,000 (rounded to $51,000,000)

If one million units are expected to be sold, the sales price should be $51.00 ($51,000,000/1,000,000 units).

Skim-Off-The-Top Pricing

If a bank's product or service is unique or novel, the bank may be able to take advantage of this situation until the market demand declines or competitors enter the field. Pricing under such conditions is referred to as skim-off-the-top pricing, or price skimming. As long as the bank maintains an exclusive market for this product, the company could charge a higher than normal price for the product in the early marketing stages. Generally, a higher price will produce a larger dollar volume of sales initially than would a low initial price.

Standard Costs

Standard costs are those that could be attained with efficient production methods at a normal capacity. In standard cost systems, a standard cost for material, labor, and factory overhead is developed. When a standard costs pricing policy is adopted, the company adds a desired markup to standard costs to establish a price.

Stay-Out, Floor, and Going-Rate Pricing

Stay-out pricing refers to low initial pricing, which is directed at discouraging potential competitors from entering the market. When stay-out pricing is used, profit margins are low, and competitors may find it difficult to compete under such circumstances.

Floor pricing involves lowering prices to meet competitors' prices. A floor-pricing policy frequently results in little or no profit but is justified on the basis that such pricing is required for the firm to keep its product(s) in the market.

Many firms simply adopt a manufacturer's or wholesaler's suggested retail price as a convenience or because contracts require it. Going-rate pricing requires a seller to base prices on prices established by competitors in the market.

Variable Cost Pricing

Variable costing is a form of product costing that charges fixed overhead immediately as incurred against the revenue of the period, without assigning it to specific units produced. Also called direct costing or marginal costing.

Variable cost pricing requires that a bank identify its variable and fixed costs. When this distinction can be made, a bank's contribution margin (sales minus variable costs) can be computed. The effect on contribution margins of different prices can be related to fixed costs. To illustrate a form of variable cost pricing, assume that a company produces two products and the variable cost of material, labor, and overhead for Product X is $20 and for Product Y is $30. If a 25 percent markup on variable cost is used, the sales price is

	Product X	Product Y
Full cost (assumed)	$50	$40
Markup on variable cost:		
10% x $20	2	
10% x $30		3
Sales price	$52	$43

A major advantage of variable cost pricing is that the difficult problem of allocating indirect, fixed costs can be avoided. Variable pricing is often useful in pricing a special order at a special price, in a dumping situation, or in a distress case. In difficult times a company may need to make some revenue above variable cost as an alternative to no revenue. Special-order pricing may involve discriminatory prices, which may have to be justified in order not to violate the Robinson-Patman Act.

BANK SPECIFIC PRICING PRACTICES FOR LOANS

Banks have used various loan-pricing models for evaluating pricing of loans. Three common procedures have been used:

1. *Pricing default risk* According to this concept, a profitable loan rate must compensate the lender for the time value of money, resource costs (loan processing, overhead, etc.), and the risk of default. A formula used to compute the contract rate (CR) follows where i = the nominal rate of interest and d = risk of default:

$$CR = (1 + i)/(1-d) - 1$$

   For example, a bank is considering a one-year loan. The T-bill rate is .10 percent and the expected probability of default is .01. The loan contract rate would be 11.1 percent (=1.1/.99)−1).

2. *Credit rationing* According to the credit rationing model, banks use flexible lending constraints or credit ceilings for borrowers and do not lend at any rate beyond those limits. The ceiling reflects a point where banks would not lend because in their judgment such rates would result in adverse loan selection and defaults which could reduce the expected return on the loan.

3. *Expected bank equity return under market conditions* Banks have used a capital-asset pricing model to determine loan prices based on the asset's contribution to portfolio risk. The same effect can sometimes be attained by bank credit analysis techniques.

TRANSFER PRICING

Divisions of an enterprise frequently buy and sell to one another. A transfer price is the price charged by one segment of an organization for a product or service that it supplies to another segment of the same organization. Various alternatives to establishing a transfer price include the following:

1. The transfer price should be set equal to the producing cost of the selling division.

2. The transfer price should be the amount the selling division could sell the product to an outside firm.

3. The transfer price should be the amount the buying division could purchase the product from an outside firm.

4. The transfer price should be a negotiated amount agreed upon by the buying and selling divisions.

5. The transfer price should be the costs incurred to the point of transfer plus the opportunity costs for the firm as a whole. The opportunity cost would be the next best alternative for the firm. For example, if the selling division was operating at less than full capacity, the opportunity cost would be zero. If the selling division was operating at full capacity, the opportunity cost would be the lost contribution margin

(selling price minus variable costs) resulting from forgoing outside sales to sell to the buying division.

The choice of method depends upon a number of factors, such as the autonomy allowed to divisions, the degree of market competition, the extent to which the goals of the division are expected to correspond to the goals of the firm, short-run supply and demand relationships, and how divisions are evaluated by the firm.

Internal Funds Transfer Pricing by Banks

Internal funds transfer pricing (FTP) is common among banks. FTP is an internal pricing mechanism that charges fund users interest and gives interest revenue credit to fund providers. FTP is often used in determining profitability, motivating staff, and facilitating the decision-making process. FTP also serves as a basis for assigning internal values and costs and for measuring earnings contributions of a bank's profit centers.

Major FTP methods used by banking include: single-pool method, multiple-pool method, matched funding, and contract spreads. Variations of these methods are also available.

Single-Pool Method

The single-pool method assumes a common pool of funds, into which all funds flow and from which all funds are provided. When the single-pool method is used, one rate is used for charging and crediting funds. This rate can represent the bank's effective cost of funds rate or an outside market rate. Many banks used a moving average of the rate on a short-term certificate of deposit to represent the marginal cost of funds spread over a reasonable period. The single-pool method is simple, easy to understand and administer. However, users of funds may be subjected to interest-rate risk due to fluctuations in the interest rate.

For example, assume that a bank uses a single-pool method in which the providers and users receive the same 10 percent rate. A bank branch provides $50,000 to the head office lending group. The lending group would pay 10 percent for use of funds. If the branch's average cost of funds is 8 percent, this would give the branch a 2 percent point profit spread. If the lending group is pricing its loans at 12 percent, it also has a 2 percentage point spread. If the FTP rate floats with the market, the lending group assumes an interest-rate risk.

Multiple-Pool Method

The multiple-pool method uses two or more rates in the transfer pricing process, i.e., a different rate for providers and users. Furthermore, rates could be stratified by a general maturity pool. The multiple-pool method provides a closer recognition of market reality by having two rates and provides more rate flexibility than the single-pool method.

Matched-Funding Method

Under matched funding, the bank's money desk goes to the money market and purchases funds for new loans. The funding and loans have the same maturity which locks in an interest rate on the funding so the spread or net interest margin should be stable through the life of the loan. The FTP pool administrator simulates a matched funding process.

The transfer-pricing mechanism selected should reflect the bank's management's objectives. The method selected can influence managerial behavior. For further information on FTP, refer to *Banker's Treasury Management Handbook* (Warren, Gorham & Lamont), Chapter 7.

COST OF FUNDS

The largest cost a bank incurred is its cost of funds. Various methods are used throughout the banking community to compute the cost of funds. Several of these methods will be discussed here.

Average Cost of Funds

A bank considers its average cost of funds to be the cost for all of its investable funds. A weighted averaging mathematical procedure is used to combine all sources of funds providing a number called the average cost of funds. The method is similar to that shown in the preceding section on cost of capital.

Incremental Cost of Funds

Incremental cost is the cost to the bank for funds to deal with its next major obligation or opportunity. For example, a bank has $1 million in saving deposits at 5 percent. The banks estimates that an additional $1 million in deposits could be obtained if the bank increased its borrowing rate to 6 percent. The bank was paying $50,000 on its original deposits; it will pay $120,000 on $2 million. The additional funds would cost the bank $70,000, a 7 percent rate.

Marginal Cost of Funds

The marginal cost of funds is the bank's cost for the next dollar of investable funds. Most banks consider the Fed's funds rate to be an approximation of a bank's marginal cost of funds. The U.S. Treasury bill auction is also considered to be an approximation of a bank's marginal cost of funds.

Opportunity Cost of Funds

The bank's opportunity cost of fund is the cost of choosing one alternative source of funds over another. For example, assume that a bank has an opportunity to sell $1 million in Fed funds at 7 percent. However, another investing opportunity arose and only $500,000 of the funds available were invested in Fed funds. The opportunity to make the new investment comes at a 7 percent opportunity cost.

ASSET/LIABILITY MANAGEMENT

Asset/liability management (ALM) has been defined as "a planning procedure which accounts for all assets and liabilities of a financial institution by rate, amount, and maturity. Its intent is to quantify and control risk. The focus is on the risk management of the net interest margin for profit." ALM planning impacts directly on the volume, mix, maturity, rate sensitivity, quality, and liquidity of a bank's assets and liabilities. It involves an integrated financial management policy. Emphasis is placed on positioning a bank's portfolio of loans and investments to maximize flexibility and return. In theory this requires that a bank secure funds at a particular rate of interest and employ those funds at a yield in excess of the cost for a maturity identical with that of the source of funds. To increase earnings, management must maintain a larger spread between the cost and use of funds while maintaining similar maturities. Asset/liability management also utilizes a process involving the mismatching of maturities between rate-sensitive assets and liabilities. For example, if a bank obtains fixed-rate liabilities and uses them in floating rate assets during a period of rising interest rates, earnings increases on the floating rate assets can be obtained.

Typical risks which ALM considers include those related to capital adequacy, liquidity, interest sensitivity, credit risk, foreign exchange risk, capital expenditure (acquisitions, branching), and service production risk (discount brokerage, trust). ALM attempts to produce an acceptable risk/reward ratio for a bank. Increased competition, inflationary pressure on profits, the volatility in interest rates, and deregulation have resulted in a renewed interest in ALM. Bank managers can adopt aggressive, defensive, or a middle ground approach to risk management.

Procedures vary for positioning assets and liabilities in ALM programs. One recommended procedure requires that (1) assets and liabilities be classified as rate-sensitive or non-rate-sensitive according to maturity, (2) each asset's and liability's interest rate yields (costs) and dollar volume be determined, and (3) measurement tools be used for analyzing this data and a format for interpreting the results. This procedure enables management to interpret the impact of interest rate changes on the profitability of its ALM program.

Interest-rate sensitive assets include floating rate loans, loans maturing, investments maturing, and fixed-rate loan amortization/payoffs. Maturing investments include federal funds, money market assets, government securities, and municipal securities, which mature during a forecast period and can be reinvested at current market rates. Interest-sensitive liabilities include short-term borrowing, maturing certificates of deposit and money market certificates, and floating rate liabilities. Certain assets and liabilities become interest-rate sensitive as they approach maturity.

Some banks use the following format or matrix, or some variation thereof, for rate sensitive analysis:

	3 mo.	6 mo.	9 mo.	1 year
Rate sensitive assets (dollars)				
Rate sensitive liabilities (dollars)				
Difference (RSA − RSL)				
Ratios:		(Data omitted)		
RSA/RSL				
RSA/Total assets				
RSL/Total liabilities				

The maturity matching of assets and liabilities can be analyzed using a format similar to the following to analyze any maturity gap and yield spread for a given time period:

Assets (same format for Liabilities)

($000) Amount	% of Total	Maturity	Weighted Factor	Yield (cost) of Funds	Weighted Factor

(Data omitted)

A weighted average maturity factor is computed for the assets and the liabilities by taking the proportion of assets and liabilities maturing within each maturity interval, and multiplying that percentage by the number of days to maturity. A weighted factor yield (cost of funds) factor can also be computed using the same procedure.

The difference between the weighted average asset maturity and the weighted asset liability maturity indicates a "GAP/ maturity mismatch." The difference between the weighted average yield and the weighted average cost of funds indicates any "net interest margin/spread." These ALM procedures can be used by management to develop rate tolerance policies to assist in evaluating and dealing with interest rate risks. A bank can influence its rate risk by modifying the maturity of its assets or liabilities, the volume of its rate sensitive assets or liabilities, the volume of its rate-sensitive assets or profits, the volatility in interest rates. Bank managers can adopt aggressive, defensive, or a middle group approach to risk management.

It is generally recognized that cash flows, profits, rates, balances, and time constitute the basic elements of any acceptable ALM program. Fund management and liquidity management are essential to sound ALM. Fund management established a close coordination of all aspects of funds acquisition and disposition. The consolidation of funds management operations facilitates efforts to centralize the management of interest rate risk. ALM also enables a bank to cultivate and develop direct sources of funds. Liquidity management relates primarily to the ability of a bank to meet maturing liabilities (GAP analysis), and customer demands for cash. A liquidity ratio is sometimes defined as

Assets maturing within 90 days + Readily salable assets
+ Deposit inflows expected in the next 90 days
+ Unused capacity to borrow – Net loan growth expected
in the next 90 days/Earning assets

Management would usually develop a liquidity ratio tolerance range. The liquidity ratio then would be managed, e.g., by adjusting the maturity of assets and liabilities or diversifying and broadening sources of funds.

Bank credit risk involves evaluating and managing the growth and diversification of loans and investments and establishing tolerance ranges for credit and investment ratios, such as the ratio of loan-loss allowance to total loans.

Many banks centralize the management of rate, credit, and liquidity risks through the use of profit centers in which departments, functions, or operating units "buy" and "sell" funds through a Treasury function. In the final analysis ALM is more an art than a science at its current developmental stage.

Bankers have developed a variety of analytical tools that are useful in ALM. The major objective of ALM is to optimize net interest income while minimizing liquidity risk, capital-adequacy risk, and interest-rate risk. These tools include the following:

1. *Asset allocation.* A method that matches liabilities and capital with assets according to interest rates, volatility, and maturities. Assets and liabilities are assigned to "maturity buckets" and variances are interpreted and dealt with. A funding source is allocated to assets and judgments made concerning its adequacy. The primary focus of ALM is liquidity. This method would typically allocate funds as follows:

Asset Allocation

	Amount	Fixed Assets	Other Nonearning	Cash and Due from	Mortgage Loans	Short-term Investments
Demand deposits						
Time deposits			(Data not provided)			
Purchased funds						
Equity						
Total						

2. *Gap management.* A method that assesses interest rate sensitivity according to maturities. Rate sensitive assets are associated with rate sensitive liabilities and any resulting gaps are identified. Funding surpluses and deficits are examined in "time buckets." The basic formula is: rate sensitive assets minus rate sensitive liabilities equals the interest rate sensitivity gap. The gap can represent either a surplus or a deficit. GAP refers to a specific time interval, such as a 30-day gap, which is the extent or degree to which assets maturing within 30 days exceed or fall short of liabilities maturing in 30 days. Its objective is to effectively position an institution's portfolio to maximize flexibility and profitability by identifying assets and liabilities that are interest sensitive. CAP analysis is typically short-term oriented and generally does not consider the reinvestment risk of the intermediate cash flows and long-term profitability. A simplified GAP report would appear as follows:

Maturity and Rate Sensitivity Analysis

	Rate	Balance	0-30	31-60	91-180	Other
Interest-Earning Assets:						
Real estate loans						
Commercial			(Data omitted)			

Rate	Balance	0-30	31-60	91-180	Other

Total (a)

Interest-Bearing
  Liabilities:

  Money market

  Time deposits

  Savings deposits

  Purchased funds

  Total (b)

Spread

Maturity Gap (a-b)

Cumulative Gap

3. *Duration Analysis.* A method that examines market price (value) changes resulting from interest rate shifts. When interest rates increase, the value of assets goes down. Duration analysis can provide an estimate of the weighted average maturity of an instrument or total portfolio. By matching durations, a bank can protect assets from the market value risk and the reinvestment risk. Duration analysis is discussed more fully in a following section of this chapter.

4. *Simulation.* A method of applying "what if" observations and previewing the impact of an operation or functions, enabling the impact of alternatives to be considered before implementation. Simulation is useful in making forecasts or projections.

5. *Optimization.* A powerful method for making economic decisions, which emphasizes the efficient allocation of resources to maximize or minimize an objective, such as maximizing profits or minimizing costs. The mathematical solution to such problems is optimization. Linear programming is one mathematical tool that is particularly effective in optimizing. Artificial intelligence is also a promising method.

DURATION ANALYSIS

Duration analysis is a technique of asset/liability management that involves measuring changes in capital values that follow from given changes in interest rates. The term "duration" was coined by Frederick Macauley in 1938. He questioned why changes in interest rates cause price changes in bonds that are not strictly proportional to the bonds' maturities. He determined that a bond's term to maturity is only a partial measure of the length of a debt instrument because maturity does not take into account the size or timing of intermediate cash flows. Macauley developed a set of formulas to explain, in a purely linear fashion, the relationship between bond prices and changes in interest rates. A key measure was a bond's duration, the weighted average maturity based on the present value of the cash flows rather than on the actual flows, as in the usual average maturity calculation. This set of concepts is the basis for duration analysis.

Measuring Duration

Every asset is exposed to several types of risk, including credit risk, liquidity risk, foreign exchange risk, and price risk. Cash flows from each asset are also subject to reinvestment risk. A bank's overall portfolio is also subject to interest rate risk.

Duration is a measurement of *interest risk* exposure based on *price risk* and *reinvestment risk.* Price risk is the chance that interest rates will rise, reducing the market value of an investment. Reinvestment risk is the chance that interest rates will fall, so that cash flows from the original instrument can only be reinvested at a lower rate than they had been earning. Price risk and reinvestment risk move in opposite directions. The decline in the price of a bond in relation to a change in interest rates can be tied directly to the duration of the bond.

The duration of the bond can be expressed mathematically as:

$$D = \frac{E(t \times PV(i))}{EPV(i)}$$

where t = time period (as distinguished from maturity), and PV(i) = present value of cash flow in period t.

To illustrate, consider the following example:

Principle value of instrument = $1,000

Market value = $1,000

Coupon rate = 10%

Yield to maturity = 10%

Maturity = 5 years

Interest paid annually = $100

Calculating the equation requires four steps:

1. Schedule the periodic cash flows.
2. Calculate the present value of each cash flow.
3. Multiply the present value of each cash flow by its period number.
4. Divide the sum of the results in step 3 by the market value of the instrument.

For the straightforward example given, the calculation would proceed as follows:

Period						Total
	1	2	3	4	5	Total
Interest	100	100	100	100	100	500
Principal	0	0	0	0	1,000	1,000
Present value	91	83	75	68	683	1,000

Period	Total					
Period × NPV	91	166	225	272	3,415	4,169

Thus,

$$\text{Duration} = \frac{4,169}{1,000} = 4.169$$

In this example the five-year bond can be thought of as comprising five annual cash flows plus a balloon payment. The first cash flow can be conceived as a one-year zero-coupon instrument, while the last cash flow can be considered a five-year zero-coupon instrument. Duration is a summary of all five cash flows into a single zero-coupon instrument.

Conceptually, by extension to a portfolio, a duration of 4.169 means that as of 4.169 years, regardless of fluctuations in interest rates, the asset portfolio will have yielded a return of 10 percent, because any change in reinvestment income during the first 4.169 years will be offset by the opposite change in market value at the 4.169th year, assuming that movements in and out of the portfolio are possible and practical. The ability to restructure the portfolio is necessary to maintain a portfolio duration of 4.169 and to correct for duration drift (the tendency of durations to change over time due to changes in cash flow patterns) and interest rate changes (for instance, a change in rates from 10 to 11 percent changes the duration of the example above to 4.0).

Given a concrete value for duration, what would be the change in market value of the asset portfolio if interest rates were to rise, say, 100 basis points? The equation for calculating the approximate change is:

$$\text{Change in market value} = \frac{-D(r) \times \text{current market value}}{(1 + r)}$$

where D = duration of the instrument, r = current interest rate, and r = change in interest rate. Applied to the present example:

$$\text{Change in market value} = \frac{-4.169\,(.01) \times 1,000}{(1 + .10)} = -37.90$$

In other words if rates increase 1 percent, the asset portfolio value decreases by about $37.90. The accuracy of this estimate declines as the duration becomes longer and the change in rates becomes larger (the precise figure for the decline in market value is $36.96 in the case above).

Viewed from a different perspective, the duration is the maturity date of a zero-coupon bond having the same yield to maturity as the coupon bond alternative and having the future value at duration of the compounded and discounted cash flows of the coupon bond to the duration date. The following table illustrates the calculation of the zero-coupon bond equivalent:

Year	Coupon Bond Cash Flow	Future Value at 4.169th Year
1	$ 100	$ 135.27
2	100	122.98
3	100	111.80
4	100	101.63
5	1,100	1,016.32
		$1,488.00

A change in interest rates will affect the present value of these two securities in an identical manner as long as the duration remains the same:

Interest Rate	Present Value of Coupon Bond Flows ($1,488 at 4.169th year)
9%	$1,039
10	1,000
11	963

Regardless of changes in the interest rate, however, a zero-coupon bond delivers the yield to maturity as of date of purchase not only on the initial investment but also on the reinvested interest. It is not subject to price or reinvestment risk if held to maturity.

An equivalent coupon bond will have the same characteristics, with the price risk at sale (4.169 years, in this example) offsetting whatever reinvestment risk exposure exists before then (assuming the interest rates move in parallel as they change). As cash payments are received from the coupon bond, however, its duration may change from that of the original zero-coupon equivalent, which will require a portfolio adjustment in order to maintain the zero-coupon.

Matching Assets and Liabilities

A simplistic approach to asset/liability management is to match-fund and asset with a liability of equal maturity at a positive spread, neglecting the periodic cash flows the asset throws off (and its duration). The higher the cash yield on an instrument, the higher its periodic cash flow and the shorter its duration, or period of cost recovery. More importantly, these cash flows will affect income as they are reinvested at rates above or below that on the original instrument and thus affect the actual yield to maturity on the initial investment.

In duration analysis the durations of asset/liability portfolios are matched rather than the maturities for assets and liabilities. For example, given a portfolio in which the market value of assets is 100, the market value of liabilities is 95, and that of equity (the residual figure) is 5, the durations of the assets and liabilities are calculated to be five years and four years, respectively. Suppose that interest rates increase 200 basis points. Using the equation for change in market value, the new value can be derived as:

	Change in market value	+	Original value		=	New value
For assets:	$\dfrac{-5(2.0) \times 100}{(1+.10)}$	=	-$9.09	$100		$91
For liabilities:	$\dfrac{-4(2.0) \times 95}{(1+.10)}$	=	-$6.90	95		$88
			Equity value			$ 3

In this scenario, because the asset value fell by a greater amount than the liability ratio, equity value declined from 5 to 3. The capital ratio, which had been 5 percent, dropped to 3.3 percent.

Equity value (in dollars) could have been protected from this loss in value if asset and liability durations had been set so that the duration of the equity would be zero—that is, so that equity is immunized from any change in interest rates. The equation to solve in order to accomplish this is

$$(^D\!A \times VA) = (^D\!L \times VL)$$

where the D terms represent durations, and the V terms represent market value. The term representing equity drops out because the duration of equity has been set at zero.

In a healthy bank the value of assets (VA) should exceed the value of liabilities (VL). Thus, to balance, the duration of assets (DA) must be less than the duration of liabilities (DL). Assuming the duration and value of the asset portfolio are 5 and 100, respectively, and the value of the liabilities portfolio is 95, as in the example above, the desired value for the duration of liabilities is

$$5 \times 100 = {}^D\!L \times 95$$
$$5.26 = {}^D\!L$$

Again, suppose interest rates rise by 200 basis points. The new values are:

	Change in market value	+	Original value		=	New value
	$\dfrac{-5(2.0) \times 100}{(1+.10)}$	=	-$9.10	$100		$91
	$\dfrac{-5.26(2.0) \times 95}{(1+.10)}$	=	$9.08	$ 95		$86
			Equity value			$ 5

The nominal equity has been protected from rate changes, and the capital ratio has now increased to 5.49 percent. (If the duration of the assets and liabilities had been matched, the value of the equity would have fallen but the equity-capital ratio would have remained 5 percent.) The durations of asset/liability portfolios will change in response to any change in interest rates, however, so a bank must restructure its portfolios accordingly to offset the changes in durations.

Duration Drift

Even if interest rates did not change, and the asset and liability portfolio durations were equal to begin with, the asset and liability durations would change over time because differences in intermediate cash flows (timing and amounts) of assets and liabilities will cause the portfolio durations to change over time. This change is called duration drift.

Duration drift is also caused by the difference in the rate of recovery of assets with intermediate cash flows and the single cash flow of zero-coupon bonds. The duration of an asset with intermediate cash flows will decline in a nonlinear fashion because the present value of the income received in the early years is greater than the present value of income received in later years. The duration of the zero-coupon bond declines in a linear fashion because of its single-payment feature. Although an asset portfolio might contain only zero-coupon bonds, the liability portfolio would not; therefore, the duration responses of the two to an interest rate change will differ and will tend to drift apart.

To keep the durations of its portfolios in balance so that equity duration is zero, a bank must constantly monitor the composition of its assets and liabilities, making appropriate changes in the maturities or coupon rates of assets, liabilities, or both (in opposite directions).

Evolution of Duration Analysis

The model described above is the first generation of duration models, usually known as Macaulay's duration. Underlying this model is the assumption that flat interest rate yield curves respond to random events with parallel shifts in the yield curves. This unrealistic assumption could lead to unrealistic results, however. A portfolio of very short-term and very long-term investments can be designed to have the same duration as a portfolio of medium-term investments. If changes at the ends of the yield curve are not the same as changes in the middle, the performance of the two portfolios can be quite different, as some investment officers have learned at great expense.

Second-generation duration analysis incorporates discounting the yield curve for relevant spot rates of zero-coupon bonds in each year until maturity. Each cash flow is then discounted by the relevant rate for the year in which the cash flow occurs. Third-generation duration analysis entails adjusting the relevant spot yield curve for zero-coupon bonds for historical average volatilities of rates and projecting these into the future. Fourth-generation duration analysis requires the empirical study of random events that influence the determination of short- and long-term rates and building a forecast of rate volatilities based on this study.

A common limitation of all these models is that, although the basic duration calculation is simple, deriving the proper values to use in the calculation is very complex. A bank must first have adequate portfolio data and use them to schedule cash flows over the term of the investments. Actual cash flows may differ from contractual cash flows, however, because of prepayments and defaults. The bank, therefore, must assess the probabilities of prepayments and defaults in order to estimate cash flows more accurately.

The next step is to discount this expected cash flow, which requires some assumptions about the behavior of yield curves. Several models are available of yield curves that are more complex than the simple flat curve, but no one of them can provide error-free duration calculations.

An additional complication is choosing appropriate rates by which to discount cash flows. Events affecting interest rates will have differing repercussions on long- and short-term rates.

This difference must be taken into account when calculating the effect of rate changes on the duration of any given portfolio.

Thus, duration analysis can not produce hard numbers, only estimates based on certain assumptions. It is not a panacea, but it can be a very useful tool of asset/liability management (Adapted from Leonard E. Wyderko, Jr., *A Duration Analysis Primer.* Chicago: Bank Administration Institute, 1985).

KEY DEFINITIONS

Asset/liability management A planning process that accounts for all assets and liabilities of a financial institution by rate, amount, and maturity. Its intent is to quantify and control risk.

Average fixed costs The total fixed cost divided by the number of units produced.

Average total cost Total cost divided by the number of units produced.

Average variable cost Unit variable cost; the total variable cost divided by the number of units produced.

Competition Rivalry among individuals and firms operating in a free enterprise system.

Cost An expenditure measured by the price paid or required to be paid to acquire goods or services. Numerous classifications and categories of costs are described in this chapter.

Cost accounting The process of classifying, summarizing, recording, reporting, and allocating current costs.

Cost behavior The functional relationship between changes in activity and changes in cost.

Demand curve A schedule of the quantities of goods that purchasers will purchase at different prices at a given time.

Duration analysis A technique of asset/liability management that involves measuring changes in capital values that follow from given changes in interest rates.

Elastic demand When prices change, the quantity changes by a greater percentage than the price changed so that the elasticity is numerically greater than one.

Equilibrium A stable flow of economic activity.

Equilibrium price The price at which quantity demanded equals the quantity supplied.

Increasing returns to scale A production situation in which output changes more than proportionately to a change in the scale of inputs.

Inelastic demand A relative change in price results in a smaller relative change in quantity.

Macroeconomics A discipline that deals with the aggregates of economics, such as total employment, the general price level, and total production.

Marginal cost The increase (decrease) in the total cost resulting from the production of one more (less) units of output.

Marginal efficiency of capital The expected rate of return on investments, or the expected profit from a given investment.

Marginal revenue The increase (decrease) in total revenue that results from the sale of one more (less) unit of output.

Macroeconomics A discipline that deals with the economic problems of the individual, the firm, and the industry.

Monopolistic competition An economic situation in which there are many purchasers who offer differentiated conditions to sellers.

Oligopoly A market condition in which relatively few firms produce identical or similar products.

Price The quantity of one good or service asked in return for a unit of another good or service.

Profit The incentive for using capital goods to produce goods and services.

Supply curve A line or curve showing the number of units of a good or service that will be offered for sale at different prices.

Transfer price A substitute for a market price used in profit accounting when one segment of a business sells to another segment. The transfer pricing problem requires setting prices so that both buyer and seller have goal congruence with respect to the parent organization's goals.

Utility The ability of a good or service to satisfy a want.

Variance The difference between actual costs incurred and the costs budgeted for the actual output attained.

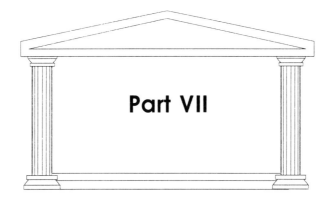

Part VII

Bank Accountability

Chapter 15

Bank Examinations and Audits

A   n audit is a systematic process of objectively obtaining and evaluating evidence about a specific entity for purposes of determining and reporting on the correspondence between assertions about economic events, actions, and other information and established criteria for reporting these assertions. A financial statement audit focus on the financial statements and management's communication with its publics. A statutory audit is an audit performed to comply with requirements of a governing body, such as a federal, state, or city government. Regulatory audits or examinations are performed by regulatory auditors.

An operational audit is a systematic review of an organization's activities for the purposes of assessing performance, identifying opportunities for improvement, and developing recommendations for improvement or further action. A compliance audit has as its objective the determination of whether the entity being audited is following procedures or rules established by a higher authority.

A social audit is an examination of an accounting entity in areas of social and environmental concerns, such as minority relations, waste managements, and so on. Internal auditing seeks to ensure that the company safeguards its assets, produces reliable accounting information, operates efficiently, and complies with company policies.

A bank's management is responsible for the contents of financial statements. Financial statements include the representations of management concerning economic transactions and events affecting the organization.

PART 1 EXAMINATIONS BY REGULATORY AUTHORITIES

Federal regulatory agency examination procedures can be found in the following major sources:

1. "Review of Regulatory Reports" Section 408 Comptroller's Handbook for National Bank Examiners.

2. "Applications" Section Q, Federal Deposit Insurance Corporation's DBS Manual of Examination Policies.

3. "Review of Regulatory Reports" Section 408 Federal Reserve System's Commercial Bank Examination Manual.

4. "Domestic and Other Reports to the Federal Reserve" Section 2250 Federal Reserve System's Bank Holding Company Supervision Manual.

THE BANK EXAMINATION

According to the Comptroller of the Currency, the essence of a bank examination is appraisal of the bank's assets and management, verification of its liabilities and determination of its adherence to law and sound banking principles. Examinations evaluate a bank's internal operations, internal audit programs, and investment and loan portfolios. At the end of every examination, examiners consult with bank management to point out weak practices of those not in conformity with sound banking. The object of examination is an appraisal of the soundness of management and of the bank's solvency and liquidity positions.

To reduce the risk of bank failure, commercial banks are subject to unannounced examinations by officials or various regulatory agencies at least once a year. The Office of the Comptroller of the Currency (OCC) is responsible for the examination of nationally chartered banks. The Federal Reserve (Fed) examines state-chartered banks that are members of the Federal Reserve System. The Federal Deposit Insurance Corporation (FDIC) examines FDIC-insured, state-chartered banks that are not members of the Fed. The Fed and the FDIC share the responsibility of examining state banks with the various state banking agencies.

Focus of Bank Examinations

Bank examinations focus on the identification and correction of possible problem areas within the operating procedures of a bank. They attempt to ensure that operating problems do not become a threat to the viability of the bank. Examiners evaluate the adequacy of internal controls against theft and fraud, look at how the bank conforms to banking regulations, and evaluate the quality of the bank's assets—especially its loans.

Rating Bank Performance

Since 1978 federal examiners have followed a uniform system of rating bank performance that looks at five major areas: capital adequacy, asset quality, management ability, earning quality, and liquidity level. This system is referred to by the acronym CAMEL.

Capital adequacy is measured by the level and trend in the bank's equity-to-debt ratio compared to similar financial institutions. Because bank capital serves as a cushion against loss, examiners normally will allow banks with better management and safer asset portfolios to offset these factors against a lower level of capital.

Asset quality focuses on the risk of the bank's asset portfolio. Examiners look closely at the loan portfolio of a bank in terms of its diversification and performance.

Management quality is examined in terms of competence of organization and internal controls, training, ability, willingness to comply with laws and regulations, and plans for management succession.

Earnings quality is measured by the level and trend in performance measures (such as return on assets and return on equity) relative to other similar financial institutions.

Bank liquidity is assessed by measuring likely future liquidity needs and the ability of the bank to meet those needs. The ability of a bank to meet its liquidity needs is measured by the level of cash and liquid securities in its portfolio plus the potential to raise funds quickly through short-term borrowings.

The Examination Process

Regulators review regulatory reports filed as part of their examination. The bank should be prepared to deal with requests made by regulators related to the reports. Efforts should be made to assist the examiners with the assistance possible to ensure the examiners understand the work papers, filed documents, and other data.

The examiner will verify the accuracy of reports submitted and insist on their being amended if material errors are found. A bank's consolidated reports of condition and income contain data required by the computer-based analysis system to properly detect changing patterns of behavior. The examiner will seek to determine that all reports submitted by the bank meet statutory and regulatory requirements. The examination will want to ascertain that the report was filed on a timely basis, was accurate, and agreed with the bank's general books. Banks should maintain an adequate internal control system and working paper documentation so that the examination can proceed without any unnecessary delays.

At the conclusion of the examination, regulators will prepare a report indicating the scope of the examination and conclusions drawn from the examination. Deficiencies are currently divided among safety, soundness, and compliance issues. Compliance issues can generally be taken care of by making the necessary changes in procedures. Safety and soundness issues typically require policy changes. Corrective actions generally fall into categories including changes in procedures and forms, changes in policy, charge-offs or loss of assets, and amending regulatory reports.

The bank's board should review the regulator's report and apprise management of their positions relating to the issues presented in the report. Regulators frequently give guidelines regarding changes and actions to undertake. The guidelines should be given the most serious consideration.

The External Auditor and Regulatory Engagements

Audit firms have policies and administrative procedures relating to SEC and other regulatory engagements. Audits of financial statements to be included in prospectuses, offering circulars, proxy, or information statements, and reports filed with various regulatory authorities require compliance with specific complex regulations and instructions. Prior to filing or release, certain financial statements and reports used for securities offering purposes with which the firm is to be associated should be reviewed by a designated technical reviewer. National CPA firms have a national director who is responsible for coordinating the firm's SEC and other regulatory agencies' practice.

The audit partner typically has the primary responsibility for the conduct and administration of each SEC and other regulatory engagements. This includes gaining an appropriate understanding of the circumstances peculiar to the client, determining the filing requirements and the firm's ability to meet them, and overseeing the engagement.

The SEC Practices Section (SECPS) of the AICPA has the authority to establish membership requirements for member firms with clients whose securities are registered with the Securities and Exchange Commission. For purposes of the SEC Practice Section requirements, SEC Clients are defined as

- Entities making initial filings under the Securities Act of 1933 or filing periodic reports with the SEC (except a broker dealer registered only because of Section 15(a) of the Securities Exchange Act of 1934)

- Banks or other lending institutions that file periodic reports with the Comptroller of the Currency, the Federal Reserve System, the Federal Deposit Insurance Corporation or the Federal Home Loan Bank Board, excluding entities (a) with less than $5 million in total assets on the last day of the issuer's three most recent fiscal years and less than 500 shareholders or (b) with less than 300 shareholders

- Companies whose financial statements appear in the annual report or proxy statement of an investment fund because it is a sponsor or manager of such fund, but which is not itself a registrant required to file periodic reports with the SEC

Auditors should be familiar with the numerous SEC publications including *Regulations S-X*, which is the principal accounting regulation of the SEC and governs the form and content of, and requirements for, financial statements in most filings with the SEC. *Regulation C* under the 1933 Act and *Regulation 12B* under the 1934 Act contain procedures that are used in preparing and filing registration and reporting forms. Other SEC publications include *Financial Reporting Releases, Accounting and Auditing Enforcement Releases, Staff Accounting Bulletins*, and the *SEC Docket*. There is also a series of special instructions relating generally to disclosures to be included in registration and reporting forms by registrants in specific industries, such as bank holding companies.

Part II THE EXTERNAL AUDIT

The basic function of a certified public accountant is auditing (also referred to as the attest function), which consists of examining and testing financial statements. The purpose of an external audit is to give the auditor's professional opinion as to whether the company's financial report fairly presents its financial position and results of operations. The audit report lends credibility to management's financial statements.

AN OVERVIEW OF THE EXTERNAL AUDIT

An external audit (attest or financial statement audit) is a systematic examination of financial statements, records, and related operations to ascertain adherence to generally accepted accounting principles, management policies, and other considerations.

An external or financial statement audit and the auditor's report provide additional assurance to users of financial statements concerning the information presented in them. Major national accounting firms that perform external audits are currently referred to as the Big Six:

Arthur Andersen

Coopers & Lybrand

Deloitte & Touche

Ernst & Young

Peat, Marwick, Main

Price Waterhouse

Other national, regional, and local accounting firms also provide quality external auditing services to banks and other business entities.

The Audit Committee

The audit committee is a significant part of a bank's organizational structure. The audit committee is formed by the bank's board of directors. It should ideally be composed of outside directors who have no active day-to-day operations function or role. The committee also serves as a liaison between the independent auditor and the board of directors. The committee advises the board in fulfilling its responsibility for public financial reporting and management oversight. The duties of an audit committee include the following:

- Approve the appointment and retention of the independent auditor
- Review the proposed scope of the audit
- Receive and review the findings of the audit (internal and external audits)
- Exercise oversight of the financial reporting process

The Audit Process

An independent auditor performs an examination of a client with the objective of issuing a report containing an opinion on the client's financial statements. The attest function of external auditing refers to the auditor's expressing an opinion on a company's financial statements. The criteria for judging an auditee's financial statement are generally accepted accounting principles. The typical audit leads to an attestation regarding the fairness and dependability of the financial statements, which is communicated to the officials of the audited entity in the form of a written report that accompanies the financial statements.

The auditing process is based on standards, concepts, procedures, and reporting practices. The auditing process relies on evidence, analysis, convention, and informed professional judgment. Auditing standards imposed by the American Institute of Certified Public Accountants are presented in Figure 15-1. The standards for internal auditors are established by the Institute of Internal Auditors. The General Accounting Office establishes audit standards for U.S. government auditors.

An auditor is expected to become familiar with the industry in which the client operates and with the client's organization and accounting system. The auditor generally proceeds with an audit according to the following process:

1. Plans the audit

2. Gathers evidence:

   (a) Studies, tests, and evaluates the firm's internal accounting control system

   (b) Performs and evaluates substantive tests including

   (i) Independent tests of account balances and transactions. Such tests include compliance tests that answer the question Were the accounting controls adequate and was the system operating as designed? Substantive testing answers the question Were the dollar amounts of the transactions correctly recorded?

   (ii) Other general procedures, including analytical tests (ratios and trends) and background information (to understand the client's business, operations, personnel)

3. Issues a report

Figure 15-2 shows a diagram of an audit.

In planning the audit, the auditor develops programs that identify and schedule audit procedures that are to be performed to obtain the evidence supporting the auditor's report. Audit evidence is proof obtained to support the audit's conclusion. Audit procedures include those activities undertaken by the auditor to obtain the evidence. Evidence-gathering procedures include observation, confirmation, calculation, analysis, inquiry, inspection, and comparison:

Observation	Evidence of existence of assets
Confirmation	Evidence of ownership
Calculation	Evidence of existence and valuation
Analysis	Evidence of reasonableness and relationships
Inquiry	Evidence of collaboration, support, investigation, and questioning
Inspection	Evidence of existence of assets, documentation, record keeping, etc.
Comparison	Evidence of similarity or difference

An audit trail is a chronological record of economic events or transactions that have been experienced by an organization. The audit trail enables an auditor to evaluate the strengths and weaknesses of internal control, system designs, company policies and procedures.

Figure 15-1
AICPA Auditing Standards

General Standards

1. The examination is to be performed by a person or persons having adequate technical training and proficiency as an auditor.

2. In all matters relating to the assignment, an independence in mental attitude is to be maintained by the auditor or auditors.

3. Due professional care is to be exercised in the performance of the examination and the preparation of the report.

Standards of Field Work

1. The work is to be adequately planned and assistants, if any, are to be properly supervised.

2. There is to be a proper study and evaluation of the existing internal control as a basis for reliance thereon and for the determination of the resultant extent of tests to which auditing procedures are to be restricted.

3. Sufficient competent evidential matter is to be obtained through inspection, observation, inquiries, and confirmations to afford a reasonable basis for an opinion regarding the financial statements under examination.

Standards of Reporting

1. The report shall state whether the financial statements are presented in accordance with generally accepted accounting principles.

2. The report shall state whether such principles have been consistently observed in the current period in relation to the preceding period.

3. Informative disclosures in the financial statements are to be regarded as reasonably adequate unless otherwise stated in the report.

4. The report shall contain either an expression of opinion regarding the financial statements, taken as a whole or an assertion to the effect that an opinion cannot be expressed. When an over-all opinion cannot be expressed, the reasons therefor should be stated. In all cases where an auditor's name is associated with financial statements the report should contain a clear-cut indication of the character of the auditor's examination, if any, and the degree of responsibility he is taking.

Figure 15-2
Diagram of an Audit

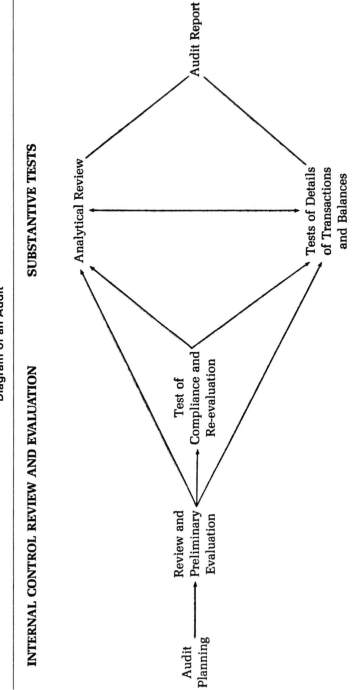

INTERNAL CONTROL REVIEW AND EVALUATION   SUBSTANTIVE TESTS

Audit
Planning

Review and
Preliminary
Evaluation

Test of
Compliance and
Re-evaluation

Analytical Review

Tests of Details
of Transactions
and Balances

Audit Report

Source: Kinney, William R., Jr., "Decision Theory Aspects of Internal Control System Design/Compliance, and Substantive Tests,"
          Journal of Accounting Research (Supplement, 1975), p. 16 (adapted).

The Audit Report

The independent audit report sets forth the independent auditor's opinion regarding the financial statements, that is, that they are fairly presented in conformity with generally accepted accounting principles applied on a basis consistent with that of the preceding year (or in conformity with some other comprehensive basis of accounting that is appropriate for the entity). A fair presentation of financial statements is generally understood by accountants to refer to whether

1. The accounting principles used in the statements have general acceptability

2. The accounting principles are appropriate in the circumstances

3. The financial statements are prepared so as to favorably affect their use, understanding, and interpretation

4. The information presented in the financial statements is classified and summarized in a reasonable manner

5. The financial statements reflect the underlying events and transactions in a way that presents the financial position, results of operations, and changes in financial position with reasonable and practical limits

The auditor's standard report identifies the financial statements audited in an introductory paragraph, describes the nature of an audit in a scope paragraph, and expresses the auditor's opinion in a separate opinion paragraph. A typical short-form audit report on financial statements covering a single year is illustrated in Figure 15-3.

Rule 2-02 of Regulation S-X sets forth the following requirements relating to audit reports:

- *Technical requirements* The accountant's report (1) shall be dated, (2) shall be signed manually, (3) shall indicate the city and state where issued, and (4) shall identify the financial statements covered by the report.

- *Representations as to the audit* The accountant's report (1) shall state whether the audit was made in accordance with generally accepted auditing standards and (2) shall designate any auditing procedures deemed necessary by the accountant under the circumstances of the particular case, which have been omitted, and the reasons for their omission. Nothing in this rule shall be construed to imply authority for the omission of any procedure which independent accountants would ordinarily employ in the course of an audit made for the purpose of expressing the opinions required by the following paragraph of this rule.

- *Opinion to be expressed* The accountant's report shall state clearly (1) the opinion of the accountant in respect of the financial statements covered by the report and the accounting principles and practices reflected therein and (2) the opinion of the accountant as to the consistency of the application of the accounting principles, or as to any changes in such principles which have a material effect on the financial statements.

Figure 15-3
Independent Auditor's Report

We have audited the accompanying balance sheet of X Company as of December 31, 19XX, and the related statements of income, retained earnings, and cash flows for the year then ended. These financial statements are the responsibility of the Company's management. Our responsibility is to express an opinion on these financial statements based on our audit.

We conducted our audit in accordance with generally accepted auditing standards. Those standards require that we plan and perform the audit to obtain reasonable assurance about whether the financial statements are free of material misstatement. An audit includes examining, on a test basis, evidence supporting the amounts and disclosures in the financial statements. An audit also includes assessing the accounting principles used and significant estimates made by management, as well as evaluating the overall financial statement presentation. We believe that our audit provides a reasonable basis for our opinion.

In our opinion, the financial statements referred to above present fairly, in all material respects, the financial position of X Company as of (at) December 31, 19XX, and the results of its operations and its cash flows for the year then ended in conformity with generally accepted accounting principles.

Signature

Date

■ *Exceptions* Any matters to which the accountant takes exception shall be clearly identified, the exception thereto specifically and clearly stated and, to the extent practicable, the effect of each exception on the related financial statements given.

The Audit Opinion

Various audit opinions are defined by the American Institute of Certified Public Accountants' Auditing Standards Board:

1. *Unqualified opinion* An unqualified opinion states that the financial statements present fairly, in all material respects, the financial position, results of operations, and cash flows of the entity in conformity with generally accepted accounting principles.

2. *Explanatory language added to the auditor's standard report* Circumstances may require that the auditor add an explanatory paragraph (or other explanatory language) to the report.

3. *Qualified opinion* A qualified opinion states that, except for the effects of the matter(s) to which the qualification relates, the financial statements present fairly, in all material respects, the financial position, results of operations, and cash flows of the entity in conformity with generally accepted accounting principles.

4. *Adverse opinion* An adverse opinion states that the financial statements do not present fairly the financial position, results of operations, or cash flows of the entity in conformity with generally accepted accounting principles.

5. *Disclaimer of opinion* A disclaimer of opinion states that the auditor does not express an opinion on the financial statements.

Internal Control

Internal control refers to the systems, procedures, and policies employed by an enterprise to help assure that transactions are properly authorized and are appropriately executed and recorded. Internal control applies to both administrative controls and accounting controls. Administrative (operating) controls include a plan of organization, procedures, and records that lead up to management's authorization of transactions. Accounting (financial) controls deal with the plans, procedures, and records required for safeguarding assets and producing reliable financial records. To evaluate internal controls, an auditor should have an understanding of the control environment, the accounting system, and control procedures. (Chapter 4, "The Accounting Model for Banks," contains additional relevant background material for internal controls.)

Auditing standards require that accounting controls be designed to provide reasonable assurance that

1. Transactions are executed in accordance with management's general or specific authorization

2. Transactions are recorded as necessary to permit preparation of financial statements in conformity with generally accepted accounting principles or any other criteria applicable to such statements and to maintain accountability for assets

3. Access to assets is permitted only in accordance with management's authorization

4. The recorded accountability for assets is compared with the existing assets at reasonable intervals, and appropriate action is taken with respect to any difference

Broad categories of control procedures that apply to both financial and administrative controls include the following:

1. Organizational structure:

    (a) Separation of duties

    (b) Clear lines of authority and responsibility

    (c) Formal policies

2. Adequate procedures:

    (a) Accounting checks

    (b) Proper documents and records

    (c) Error detection and correction procedures

    (d) Physical control over assets and records

3. Competent, trustworthy personnel (bonded where appropriate)

4. Performance goals and objectives:

    (a) Periodic reviews of performance

    (b) Comparisons of recorded accountability with assets

5. Independent review of the system

The Foreign Corrupt Practices Act passed in 1977 had a major impact on internal control applications in that it requires public companies to maintain reasonably complete and accurate financial records and a sufficient system of internal accounting controls. A major reason for this legislation was that Congress believed that public companies had inadequate controls to detect bribes and improper payments. See Chapter 2 for additional detail about this legislation.

A review of internal accounting controls is essential to an audit of financial statements. It enables the auditor to make a judgment concerning the reliance that can be placed on the records and for determining the nature, extent, and timing of various tests of the accounting data the system has produced.

Internal and external auditors should have an understanding of the internal control structure of the bank, including knowledge about the design and application of policies, procedures, and records.

The following Statements on Auditing Standards provide authoritative interpretations of internal control structures:

SAS No. 55, *Consideration of the Internal Control Structure in a Financial statement Audit (AU section 319)*

SAS No. 60. *Communication of Internal Control Structure Related Matters Noted in an Audit* (AU section 325).

Access to Reports of Regulatory Agencies

Accountants and attorneys hired by a bank and acting in their capacity as bank employees or agents are permitted to view an FDIC report without prior FDIC approval. Agents include accountants or accounting firms engaged by a bank's board of directors to perform an audit of the bank. Any contact by an auditor with the FDIC should be through the Chief Review Examiner in the FDIC region in which the bank is located. The OCC allows national bank examination reports to be made available to independent auditors.

Auditing EDP

Computers are widely used by banks to process financial information. The auditor should be able to evaluate and test a bank's electronic data processing system. The auditor must have knowledge of EDP terminology, systems, and audit procedures. Typically EDP auditing requires (1) the planning audit, (2) obtaining understanding of internal control and assessing control risks, (3) performing tests of controls and reassessing control risk, (4) performing substantive tests, (5) completing the audit, and (6) preparing and communicating the audit report. Chapter 4 has additional consideration related to auditing in a mini-computer environment.

INTERNAL AUDITING

Internal auditing is an independent appraisal function established by an organization to examine and evaluate its activities as a service to the organization. The internal auditing department of a bank provides the bank's internal auditing function. Internal auditors are employees of the organizations whose activities they evaluate. The internal audit department should not participate in bank operations. Auditors should be provided the independence they require to carry out their function effectively.

The *Statement of Principle and Standards for Internal Auditing in the Banking Industry* is the primary reference for evaluating the professional performance of internal auditors in the banking industry. The statement was prepared by the Audit Commission of the Bank Administration Institute. The statement and standards prescribe broad principles regarding the responsibilities and objectives of internal auditors and provide detailed organizational, personnel, performance, and communication standards and guidelines to direct the activities of internal auditors in the banking industry.

The primary focus of internal auditing is (1) the determination of the extent to which the organization adheres to managerial policies, procedures, or requirements and (2) safeguarding assets and ensuring that transactions are recorded correctly. Internal bank auditing should determine that controls and operating procedures are functioning to protect the bank from losses due to inefficiencies, inaccuracies, errors, irregularities, fraud, and manipulation. Internal auditors are frequently called upon to conduct special investigations and interrogations. The internal auditing department of a bank is expected to work within an EDP environment.

An internal audit department under the authority of the controller is normally used to perform the internal auditing function. The manager of the audit department often reports directly to the audit committee of the board of directors of the bank to protect the independent oversight function. Where a separate organizational structure is not provided, the board of directors receives a copy of each internal audit report and review's management's feedback to the audit report.

The designing of an effective internal auditing function by banks is especially important because banks have custody of large volumes of money and monetary items. Bank transactions are not only large in number and value but also varied in nature and complexity. The organizational structure of a bank with branches and departments increases the importance of strong internal auditing procedures. Needless to say, the fact that banks are regulated by government bodies enhances the significance of internal auditing.

A bank's internal auditing department should be knowledgeable enough about banking and banking related industries and practices to adequately assess the risks associated with banking. The auditor should be familiar with major banking risks: control risk, audit risk, credit risk, interest rate risk, liquidity risk, currency risk, country risk, compliance risk, and settlement risk.

The internal auditor uses many of the planning, control, and process procedures used by external auditors: observation, confirmation, calculation, analysis and so on. The auditor must give special attention to developing and monitoring effective internal control procedures, including documentation and recordkeeping. The internal auditing departments, of banks universally use checklists, internal control questionnaires, statistical samplings analyses, grading summaries, and other audit aids to assist in the performance of the auditing function. Banks prepare an internal auditing manual to provide the structure for a comprehensive audit program that enables the auditor to perform effective and efficient audits.

The internal audit report typically discloses the area, function, or subject audited, the objectives and scope of the audit, findings, grading summary, recommendations, and comments deemed applicable to the situation. Managers should respond to the audit report by taking whatever remedial action is appropriate and by reporting this action, providing an explanation of why the action is not possible or required or if audit finding are erroneous, if such is the case.

OPERATIONAL AUDIT

An operational audit focuses on the effectiveness and efficiency of bank management's operating procedures, not on recorded dollar amounts or reported financial information or the individuals conducting operating procedures. An operational audit is typically performed by internal auditors who are not governed by auditing standards. Audit procedures used in operational audits are similar to those used in external and internal auditing.

Operational audits focus on such matters as goals, objectives, policies, organizational structure, functions, products or services, regulatory compliance, cost and pricing decisions, and related matters. The audit report identifies the unit, function, or area audited; the purpose of the audit; audit objective(s), the scope of the audit; procedures used in conducting the audit; analysis procedures; findings, and recommendations, including comments.

COMPILATION

A compilation is presented by the auditor in the form of financial statements information that is the representation of management (owners) without the auditor expressing any assurance on the statements. A compilation requires that the auditor understand the industry and nature of the business in which the client is engaged, including the accounting records, qualifications of personnel, and the accounting basis on which the financial statements are presented. The accountant is not required to make inquiries or perform other procedures to verify, corroborate, or review information supplied by the client. A compilation report states that a compilation has been performed, describes a compilation, and states that no opinion or other form of assurance is expressed on the statements.

REVIEW

According to the AICPA, a review is the process of "performing inquiry and analytical procedures that provide the accountant with a reasonable basis for expressing limited assurance that there are no material modifications that should be made to the statements in order for them to be in conformity with generally accepted accounting principles or, if applicable, with another comprehensive basis of accounting." The objective of a review is to provide the accountant with a basis for expressing limited assurance that there are no material modifications that should be made to the financial statements.

THE AUDIT AND FRAUD

The fair presentation of financial statements does not mean that the statements are fraud proof. The independent auditor has the responsibility to search for errors or irregularities within the recognized limitations of the auditing process. An auditor understands that his or her examination based on selective testing is subject to risks that material errors or irregularities, if they exist, will not be detected.

The Commission on Auditors' Responsibilities addressed the question of an auditor's responsibility to a client for fraud of client personnel as follows:

> Under generally accepted auditing standards the independent auditor has the responsibility, within the inherent limitations of the auditing process . . . to plan his examination . . . to search for errors or irregularities that would have a material effect on the financial statements, and to exercise due skill and care in the conduct of the examination. The auditor's search for material errors or irregularities ordinarily is accomplished by the performance of those auditing procedures that in his judgment are appropriate in the circumstances to form an opinion on the financial statements; extended auditing procedures are required if the auditor's examination indicates that material errors or irregularities may exist . . . An independent auditor's standard report implicitly indicates his belief that the financial statements taken as a whole are not materially misstated as a result of errors or irregularities.

The Institute of Internal Auditors (IIA) in its *Standards for the Professional Practice of Internal Auditing* states:

> In exercising due professional care, internal auditors should be alert to the possibility of intentional wrong-doing, errors and omissions, inefficiency, waste, and conflicts of interest. They should also be alert to those conditions and activities where irregularities are most likely to occur ... Accordingly, the internal auditor cannot give absolute assurance that noncompliance or irregularities do not exist. Auditors sometimes perform social audits and statutory audits.

Congress enacted the Foreign Corrupt Practices Act of 1977 to deter various illegal activities including illegal foreign political contributions, bribes, kickbacks, and other violations. Specifically, it is a criminal offense to offer a bribe to a foreign official, foreign political party, party official, or candidate for foreign political office for the purpose of obtaining, retaining, or directing business to any person.

Bank frauds have also been tried under the Racketeer Influenced Corrupt Organization Act of 1970 (RICO). This act includes most patterns of racketeering (criminal) activities. The main features of this law are that the fraud must involve an organization (two or more criminals) and a pattern of criminal activities (two or more crimes). U.S. Attorneys must obtain permission from the Department of Justice before prosecuting a case under RICO. The maximum sentence that can be given under RICO is 20 years and a $250,000 fine on each count.

According to a report prepared by the U.S. House of Representatives, *Combatting Fraud, Abuse, and Misconduct in the Nation's Financial Institutions: Current Federal Efforts are Inadequate*, and other reports, the principal federal criminal statutes involving banks are

18 U.S.C. Section 215: kickbacks and bribes; unlawful for any officer, director, employee, agent, et al. (insiders) of a financial institution to solicit, accept, or give anything of value in connection with a transaction or the business of the institution.

18 U.S.C. 656; 961(c): theft, embezzlement or misapplication of bank funds willfully by an insider with the intent to injure or defraud the bank.

18 U.S.C. 1344: financial institution fraud; scheme or artifice to defraud a federally insured institution to take money, funds, credits, assets, securities, or other property by misrepresentation.

18 U.S.C. 1001: general false statements statute; knowingly and willfully falsifying or concealing a material fact or making a false statement, etc.

18 U.S.C. 1005: false entries in bank documents including material omission, with the intent to injure or defraud the commercial bank regulatory agencies' examiners or other individuals or companies.

18 U.S.C. 1014: false oral or written statements, such as a loan application, an agreement with the financial institution or another document, made knowingly for the purpose of influencing federally insured institutions.

18 U.S.C. 1341 and 1343: mail and wire fraud; a scheme or artifice to defraud that makes use of either the U.S. mail or electrical transmission.

18 U.S.C. 2, 3711: the general Federal aiding and abetting statute and general Federal conspiracy statute, often applicable when two or more persons are involved in the commission of an offense.

Major bank frauds are often related to large commercial and real estate transactions. They can involve insider participation. The Federal Bureau of Investigation identified five common types of schemes that can result in major bank frauds when connected with willful misapplication of funds, making false statements, willfully overvaluing property, and other illegal activities:

- *Nominee loans.* Loans obtained by one person on behalf of another, undisclosed, person. The nominee may have no involvement in the loan transaction other than to obtain the funds and pass them on to another party who does not want his or her identity known.

- *Double pledging of collateral* The same collateral is used at two or more financial institutions to obtain loans. The lenders are unaware of the double pledging of the collateral. The combined amount of the loans exceeds the value of the collateral.

- *Reciprocal loan arrangements* Loans made between insiders in different financial institutions that lend funds to each other or sell loans to other institutions with the agreement to buy loans from that institution. The purpose of such agreements is to conceal the loans or sales from bank examiners.

- *Land flips* The transfer of land between related parties to inflate the value of the underlying property fraudulently. The inflated land value is used as collateral for a loan. The amount of the loan frequently exceeds the actual value of the underlying property.

- *Linked financing* Large amounts of funds deposited in a financial institution, using brokered deposits or other means, with the understanding that the institution will make a loan conditioned on the deposit.

CIVIL AND CRIMINAL LIABILITY OF AUDITORS

In a litigious age external auditors are frequently involved in civil liability lawsuits for damages to clients and third parties. Lawsuits arise under common law, under the securities acts, and in connection with the responsibility for detection of fraud. The auditor's liability is often related to a breach of contract or tort liability (failure to carry out a duty).

An auditor's contractual responsibilities to the client may be expressed or implied. Implied responsibilities frequently are based on negligence. The legal test for negligence involves establishing whether the auditor has exercised reasonable care under the circumstances. Actual fraud requires the act or omission must have the intent to deceive. Constructive fraud involves acts or omissions resulting from gross negligence.

The legal responsibilities of the auditor are determined primarily by the following:

1. Specific contractual obligations undertaken

2. Statutes and the common law governing the conduct and responsibilities of public accountants

3. Rules and regulations of voluntary professional organizations

The auditor's civil liabilities can be outlined in terms of common law and statutory law liabilities:

Common Law

Client and third party beneficiaries	Third parties
Misleading financial statements	Misleading financial statements
Client's reliance	Client's reliance
Damages (loss) occurred	Damages (loss) occurred
Proximate cause linkage	Proximate cause linkage
Auditor's negligence	Auditor's gross negligence
Breach of contract	or actual fraud

Statutory Law

Securities Act of 1933	Sec. Exchange Act of 1934
Misleading financial statements	Misleading financial statements
Damages (loss)	Reliance
	Damages (loss)
	Proximate cause

Clients may usually recover damages if they can allege and prove the basis for the suit. Auditors' defenses under common law include due diligence, contributory negligence, and lack of causation. Under common law the burden of proof for negligence is on the plaintiff.

Certain defenses under statutory law include due diligence, lack of causation, lack of knowledge of misleading statements, and others. Under statutory law the burden of proof is on the defendant.

A crime involves both an act and criminal intent. Failure to exercise due diligence in the performance of tasks could be construed as a criminally fraudulent act, such as false and misleading statements and tax returns.

KEY DEFINITIONS

Attest A written statement that indicates a conclusion about an assertion of another party.

Audit A systematic process of objectively obtaining and evaluating evidence by a competent independent person about a specific entity for determining and reporting on the correspondence between assertions about economic events, actions, and other information and established criteria for reporting these assertions.

Audit committee A major committee of the board of directors of a corporation composed of outside directors who are assigned responsibilities to the audit and auditors.

Auditor One who conducts an audit to check the accuracy, fairness, and acceptability of accounting records and statements and attests to them.

Audit procedures Acts performed by an auditor to assure that objectives of the audit will be achieved.

Audit program Procedures followed in the conduct of an audit.

Audit risk The risk that the auditor may fail to appropriately modify his or her opinion on financial statements that are materially misstated.

Auditing around the computer Performing auditing procedures on the input and output data.

Auditing through the computer Performing tests of the controls built into the computer software to ascertain whether those controls are working properly.

Auditing with the computer Using the computer to perform certain audit procedures.

Auditing Standards Advisory Council An AICPA council that advises the AICPA on auditing matters.

Auditing Standards Board A committee of the AICPA that develops and promulgates auditing rules and procedures.

Audit trail A reference or guide to an underlying source record or document.

Bank confirmation A request signed by a representative of the client indicating the bank's record of amounts on deposit as well as amounts borrowed and other pertinent business transactions between the company and the bank, mailed to the bank for completion.

Bank cutoff statement A report for the period immediately after the balance sheet date. This statement could include deposit slips and canceled checks clearing the bank between the end of the fiscal period and the cutoff date.

Bank reconciliation A schedule showing the reconciliation of the difference between cash per bank and cash per books.

Confirmation A letter to a third party that verifies the existence of recorded amounts in the financial statements.

Continuing auditor An auditor who continues to be associated with a client over a period of years.

Errors Unintentional misstatements or omissions in financial statements, such as oversights, misinterpretation of facts, and mistakes in the application of accounting principles.

Evidence Anything that can influence the auditor's judgment regarding the conformity of a client's financial statements to GAAP.

Ethics A discipline dealing with moral duty, right, and wrong.

Generally accepted auditing standards Ten standards developed and approved by the AICPA: training, independence, professional care, planning, internal control, evidence, GAAP, opinion, disclosure, and consistency. These standards are classified as general standards, standards of field work, and standards of reporting.

Illegal acts Acts other than irregularities that are contrary to laws or governmental regulations.

Internal auditor An auditor who works within the client's organization to perform certain monitoring services for management.

Irregularities Intentional misstatements or omissions in financial statements, such as fraudulent financial reporting and defalcations.

Kiting A defalcation involving an amount withdrawn from one bank account and deposited in another without the withdrawal being reported in the book record for the first bank.

Lapping An irregularity arising when a person receiving cash temporarily misappropriates the cash and covers that act by delaying the credit to the customer's account in the accounts receivable subsidiary ledger.

MAS Management advisory services.

Negative accounts receivable confirmation A confirmation requested to be returned from a customer only if the customer disagrees with the balance being confirmed.

Operational audit A comprehensive examination and appraisal of an entitiy's operations to assure management that operations are performed in a manner that complies with established policies and objectives.

Opinion shopping Searching out an auditor if the management disagrees with the present audit regarding a financial reporting issue.

Performance audit An audit providing an independent view as to whether management and other personnel are efficient and effective in carrying out their responsibilities.

Principal auditor An auditor who audits the main components of an entity while other accountants audit some or all of the components.

Profession An association of people uniting a group with common goals and objectives relating to the public interest.

Pro forma statement Statements that reflect contemplated transactions or events.

Program audit A performance audit relating to a proposed or ongoing program.

Related party transactions Transactions between a reporting entity and persons who have the ability to materially influence that entity or who can be influenced by that entity.

Responsible party Management or others who are responsible for making assertions in prospective financial statements.

Special report A report requiring specific reporting procedures such as the following: (1) audits of financial statements prepared in accordance with a basis of accounting other than GAAP, (2) audits of specific accounts or items on financial statements, (3) reports on compliance with respect to contractual regulatory requirements, and (4) financial information presented in prescribed forms or schedules.

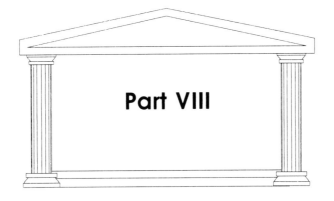

Part VIII

Compound Interest Concept

Chapter 16

The Time Value of Money

oney has time value. This is one of the most misunderstood phenomenon of finance today. Stated in the most elementary way, a dollar in your pocket that can be invested today is worth more than a dollar available one year in the future. This is so because the dollar received today can be invested to earn a return.

An historical reference illustrates the power of time and compounding interest on money. In 1626 Peter Minuit bought Manhattan Island from the Manhattan Indians for $24 worth of trinkets and beads. If the Indians had been able to invest that principal at 8 percent interest compounded annually, the principal would have grown to over $18 trillion in the early 1980s. This would have been enough money to buy back all of the property on the island of Manhattan today. Imagine the impact of compound interest on an IRA invested over 30 years. The principle is the same.

The concept of time value of money is the basis for

■ Interest income and expense calculations used in the day-to-day operations of a commercial bank

■ Models used for market valuation of bank assets and liabilities

Interest is a major costs to a debtor bank and an important source of revenue to a creditor bank. From a lender's viewpoint, interest is the excess money received over the amount loaned. From the borrower's viewpoint, interest is the excess money paid over the amount borrowed.

The increasing reliance of banking on mathematical models has made it necessary for bankers to have an understanding of major financial concepts related to compound interest and annuities. Money is a scarce resource and cannot be used free of charge. Interest is the cost of using money over time.

BANKING SPECIFICS

Compound interest and annuities have many business, banking, and personal applications. Examples include

1. Bonds: Issuance of and investing in
   (a) Prices of bonds issued at par, discount, or premium
   (b) Book value of a bond
   (c) Bond yield
   (d) Serial bonds
2. Sinking funds
3. Mortgage amortization
4. Implicit interest rates
5. Price of common and preferred stock
6. Life insurance settlement options
7. Capital budgeting decisions:
   (a) Discounted-cash-flow approach
   (b) Yield-on-investment approach
   (c) Net present value approach
8. Real estate transactions:
   (a) Debt service
   (b) Operating, capital, and leveraged leases
9. Internal rate of return
10. Imputing interest on noninterest-bearing notes
11. Valuing an asset or a business
12. Determining pension and post-retirement employee benefit obligations

INTEREST

Interest is a function of three variables:

1. The amount borrowed or invested (principal)

2.   The rate of interest, a percent of the principal

3.   The time period covered by the loan or investment (day, month, quarter, year, or period of years)

Simple interest is interest on the original principal (funds originally received or paid). Simple interest is computed according to the following formula:

$$\text{Interest} = \text{Principal} \times \text{Rate} \times \text{Time}$$

where time is either a year, a fraction of a year, or a multiple of years. For example, if you borrow $100 for one year at 10 percent, the interest for the year is $10 ($100 × .10% × 1).

Compound interest is the interest accrued on both the principal and the past unpaid accrued interest. When interest is compounded, it is earned each period on the original principal and on the interest accumulated for the preceding periods. The difference between simple interest and compound interest is illustrated in Figure 16-1.

PRESENT VALUE

Present value is the net amount of discounted expected cash flows relating to an asset or liability. Stated another way, present value is the principal that must be invested at time period zero to produce the known future value. The process of converting the future value to the present value is referred to as discounting. Present value problems can assume this form: If $1,688.96 is to be received four years in the future, what is its present value if the discount rate is 14 percent? Using a formula approach, the present value in this illustration can be computed by using the following formula:

$$pv = f \frac{1}{(1+i)^n}$$

where   pv = present value of any given future amount due in the future
         f = a future amount
         i = interest rate
         n = number of periods

The present value of $1,688.96 received at the end of four years discounted at 14 percent is $1,000 calculated as follows:

$$pv = (\$1,688.96) \frac{1}{(1+.14)^4} = \$1,000$$

or using the table in Figure 16-2:

$$pv = \$1,688.96 \times 0.592080 = \$1,000$$

An *annuity* is a series of equal cash flows (payments or receipts) occurring at equal intervals over a period of time, with compound interest on these payments. The equal cash flows are called rents. (The term *rents* refers to a series of equal receipts or payments; the term is not limited to payments on leased property.)

Figure 16-1
Simple Interest and Compound Interest Compared

End of Year	Interest Earned		Cumulative Interest	Balance
		SIMPLE INTEREST		
1	$1,000(.10) = $100		$100	$1,100
2	$1,000(.10) = 100		200	1,200
3	$1,000(.10) = 100		300	1,300
4	$1,000(.10) = 100		400	1,400
		COMPOUND INTEREST		
1	$1,000(.10) = $100.00		$100.00	$1,100.00
2	$1,100(.10) = 110.00		210.00	1,210.00
3	$1,210(.10) = 121.00		331.00	1,331.00
4	$1,331(.10) = 133.10		464.10	1,464.10

The present value of an annuity is the amount that must be invested now and, if left to earn compound interest, will provide for the receipt or payment of a series of equal rents at regular intervals. Over a period of time, the present value balance increases periodically for interest and decreases periodically for each rent paid or received.

If the present value of the series of cash flows or rents is determined one period before the receipt of the first rent, the series of rents is known as the present value of an ordinary annuity. The present value of an annuity due is determined on the date of payment of the first rent.

Tables are available that make present value computations relatively easy. Present value of $1 and present value of an annuity of $1 tables are presented in Figure 16-2 and 16-3, respectively. To illustrate, compute the present value of four rents of $1,000 with interest compounded annually at 14 percent. The first rent occurs on December 31, 1996, and the last rent occurs on December 31, 1999. This is an ordinary annuity (see Figure 16-3)

$$PV = \$1,000 \times 2.191371$$
$$= \$2,913.71$$

FUTURE VALUE

The future value (amount) of a single sum at compound interest is the original amount plus the compound interest thereon, stated as of a specific future date. For example, what will be the amount in a savings account on December 31, 1990, if $10,000 is invested at 14 percent interest on December 31, 1986? Using a Future Value of 1 table (see Figure 16-4) for $i = 14\%$ and $n = 4$, the future amount can be computed as follows:

$$\$10,000 \times 1.68896 = \$16,889.60.$$

Figure 16-2
Present Value of 1

PRESENT VALUE OF 1: $p = \dfrac{1}{(1+i)^n}$

n	1.5%	4.0%	4.5%	5.0%	5.5%	6.0%	7.0%
1	0.985222	0.961538	0.956938	0.952381	0.947867	0.943396	0.934579
2	0.970662	0.924556	0.915730	0.907029	0.898452	0.889996	0.873439
3	0.956317	0.888996	0.876297	0.863838	0.851614	0.839619	0.816298
4	0.942184	0.854804	0.838561	0.822702	0.807217	0.792094	0.762895
5	0.928260	0.821927	0.802451	0.783526	0.765134	0.747258	0.712986
6	0.914542	0.790315	0.767896	0.746215	0.725246	0.704961	0.666342
7	0.901027	0.759918	0.734828	0.710681	0.687437	0.665057	0.622750
8	0.887711	0.730690	0.703185	0.676839	0.651599	0.627412	0.582009
9	0.874592	0.702587	0.672904	0.644609	0.617629	0.591898	0.543934
10	0.861667	0.675564	0.643928	0.613913	0.585431	0.558395	0.508349
11	0.848933	0.649581	0.616199	0.584679	0.554911	0.526788	0.475093
12	0.836387	0.624597	0.589664	0.556837	0.525982	0.496969	0.444012
13	0.824027	0.600574	0.564272	0.530321	0.498561	0.468839	0.414964
14	0.811849	0.577475	0.539973	0.505068	0.472569	0.442301	0.387817
15	0.799852	0.555265	0.516720	0.481017	0.447933	0.417265	0.362446
16	0.788031	0.533908	0.494469	0.458112	0.424581	0.393646	0.338735
17	0.776385	0.513373	0.473176	0.436297	0.402447	0.371364	0.316574
18	0.764912	0.493628	0.452800	0.415521	0.381466	0.350344	0.295864
19	0.753607	0.474642	0.433302	0.395734	0.361579	0.330513	0.276508
20	0.742470	0.456387	0.414643	0.376889	0.342729	0.311805	0.258419
21	0.731498	0.438834	0.396787	0.358942	0.324862	0.294155	0.241513
22	0.720688	0.421955	0.379701	0.341850	0.307926	0.277505	0.225713
23	0.710037	0.405726	0.363350	0.325571	0.291873	0.261797	0.210947
24	0.699544	0.390121	0.347703	0.310068	0.276657	0.246979	0.197147
25	0.689206	0.375117	0.332731	0.295303	0.262234	0.232999	0.184249
26	0.679021	0.360689	0.318402	0.281241	0.248563	0.219810	0.172195
27	0.668986	0.346817	0.304691	0.267848	0.235605	0.207368	0.160930
28	0.659099	0.333477	0.291571	0.255094	0.223322	0.195630	0.150402
29	0.649359	0.320651	0.279015	0.242946	0.211679	0.184557	0.140563
30	0.639762	0.308319	0.267000	0.231377	0.200644	0.174110	0.131367

n	8.0%	9.0%	10.0%	12.0%	14.0%	16.0%	18.0%
1	0.925926	0.917431	0.909091	0.892857	0.877193	0.862069	0.847458
2	0.857339	0.841680	0.826446	0.797194	0.769468	0.743163	0.718184
3	0.793832	0.772183	0.751315	0.711780	0.674972	0.640658	0.608631
4	0.735030	0.708425	0.683013	0.635518	0.592080	0.552291	0.515789
5	0.680583	0.649931	0.620921	0.567427	0.519369	0.476113	0.437109
6	0.630170	0.596267	0.564474	0.506631	0.455587	0.410442	0.370432
7	0.583490	0.547034	0.513158	0.452349	0.399637	0.353830	0.313925
8	0.540269	0.501866	0.466507	0.403883	0.350559	0.305025	0.266038
9	0.500249	0.460428	0.424098	0.360610	0.307508	0.262953	0.225456
10	0.463193	0.422411	0.385543	0.321973	0.269744	0.226684	0.191064
11	0.428883	0.387533	0.350494	0.287476	0.236617	0.195417	0.161919
12	0.397114	0.355535	0.318631	0.256675	0.207559	0.168463	0.137220
13	0.367698	0.326179	0.289664	0.229174	0.182069	0.145227	0.116288
14	0.340461	0.299246	0.263331	0.204620	0.159710	0.125195	0.098549
15	0.315242	0.274538	0.239392	0.182696	0.140096	0.107927	0.083516
16	0.291890	0.251870	0.217629	0.163122	0.122892	0.093041	0.070776
17	0.270269	0.231073	0.197845	0.145644	0.107800	0.080207	0.059980
18	0.250249	0.211994	0.179859	0.130040	0.094561	0.069144	0.050830
19	0.231712	0.194490	0.163508	0.116107	0.082948	0.059607	0.043077
20	0.214548	0.178431	0.148644	0.103667	0.072762	0.051385	0.036506
21	0.198656	0.163698	0.135131	0.092560	0.063826	0.044298	0.030937
22	0.183941	0.150182	0.122846	0.082643	0.055988	0.038188	0.026218
23	0.170315	0.137781	0.111678	0.073788	0.049112	0.032920	0.022218
24	0.157699	0.126405	0.101526	0.065882	0.043081	0.028380	0.018829
25	0.146018	0.115968	0.092296	0.058823	0.037790	0.024465	0.015957
26	0.135202	0.106393	0.083905	0.052521	0.033149	0.021091	0.013523
27	0.125187	0.097608	0.076278	0.046894	0.029078	0.018182	0.011460
28	0.115914	0.089548	0.069343	0.041869	0.025507	0.015674	0.009712
29	0.107328	0.082155	0.063039	0.037383	0.022375	0.013512	0.008230
30	0.099377	0.075371	0.057309	0.033378	0.019627	0.011648	0.006975

Figure 16-3
Present Value of an Ordinary Annuity

PRESENT VALUE OF AN ORDINARY ANNUITY OF 1: $P_n = \dfrac{1 - \dfrac{1}{(1+i)^n}}{i}$

n	1.5%	4.0%	4.5%	5.0%	5.5%	6.0%	7.0%
1	0.985222	0.961538	0.956938	0.952381	0.947867	0.943396	0.934579
2	1.955883	1.886095	1.872668	1.859410	1.846320	1.833393	1.808018
3	2.912200	2.775091	2.748964	2.723248	2.697933	2.673012	2.624316
4	3.854385	3.629895	3.587526	3.545951	3.505150	3.465106	3.387211
5	4.782645	4.451822	4.389977	4.329477	4.270284	4.212364	4.100197
6	5.697187	5.242137	5.157872	5.075692	4.995530	4.917324	4.766540
7	6.598214	6.002055	5.892701	5.786373	5.682967	5.582381	5.389289
8	7.485925	6.732745	6.595886	6.463213	6.334566	6.209794	5.971299
9	8.360517	7.435332	7.268790	7.107822	6.952195	6.801692	6.515232
10	9.222185	8.110896	7.912718	7.721735	7.537626	7.360087	7.023582
11	10.071118	8.760477	8.528917	8.306414	8.092536	7.886875	7.498674
12	10.907505	9.385074	9.118581	8.863252	8.618518	8.383844	7.942686
13	11.731532	9.985648	9.682852	9.393573	9.117079	8.852683	8.357651
14	12.543382	10.563123	10.222825	9.898641	9.589648	9.294984	8.745468
15	13.343233	11.118387	10.739546	10.379658	10.037581	9.712249	9.107914
16	14.131264	11.652296	11.234015	10.837770	10.462162	10.105895	9.446649
17	14.907649	12.165669	11.707191	11.274066	10.864609	10.477260	9.763223
18	15.672561	12.659297	12.159992	11.689587	11.246074	10.827603	10.059087
19	16.426168	13.133939	12.593294	12.085321	11.607654	11.158116	10.335595
20	17.168639	13.590326	13.007936	12.462210	11.950382	11.469921	10.594014
21	17.900137	14.029160	13.404724	12.821153	12.275244	11.764077	10.835527
22	18.620824	14.451115	13.784425	13.163003	12.583170	12.041582	11.061240
23	19.330861	14.856842	14.147775	13.488574	12.875042	12.303379	11.272187
24	20.030405	15.246963	14.495478	13.798642	13.151699	12.550358	11.469334
25	20.719611	15.622080	14.828209	14.093945	13.413933	12.783356	11.653583
26	21.398632	15.982769	15.146611	14.375185	13.662495	13.003166	11.825779
27	22.067617	16.329586	15.451303	14.643034	13.898100	13.210534	11.936709
28	22.726717	16.663063	15.742874	14.898127	14.121422	13.406164	12.137111
29	23.376076	16.983715	16.021889	15.141074	14.333101	13.590721	12.277674
30	24.015838	17.292033	16.288389	15.372451	14.533745	13.764831	12.409041

n	8.0%	9.0%	10.0%	12.0%	14.0%	16.0%	18.0%
1	0.925926	0.917431	0.909091	0.892857	0.877193	0.862069	0.847458
2	1.783265	1.759111	1.735537	1.690051	1.646661	1.605232	1.565642
3	2.577097	2.531295	2.486852	2.401831	2.321632	2.245890	2.174273
4	3.312127	3.239720	3.169865	3.037349	2.913712	2.798181	2.690062
5	3.992710	3.889651	3.790787	3.604776	3.433081	3.274294	3.127171
6	4.622880	4.485919	4.355261	4.111407	3.888668	3.684736	3.497603
7	5.206370	5.032953	4.868419	4.563757	4.288305	4.038565	3.811528
8	5.746639	5.534819	5.334926	4.967640	4.638864	4.343591	4.077566
9	6.246888	5.995247	5.759024	5.328250	4.946372	4.606544	4.303022
10	6.710081	6.417653	6.144567	5.650223	5.216116	4.833227	4.494086
11	7.138964	6.805171	6.495061	5.937699	5.452733	5.028644	4.656005
12	7.536078	7.160725	6.813692	6.194374	5.660292	5.197107	4.793225
13	7.903776	7.486904	7.103356	6.423548	5.842362	5.342334	4.909513
14	8.244237	7.786150	7.366687	6.628168	6.002072	5.467529	5.008062
15	8.559479	8.060688	7.606080	6.810864	6.142168	5.575456	5.091578
16	8.851369	8.312559	7.823709	6.973986	6.265060	5.668497	5.162354
17	9.121638	8.543631	8.021553	7.119630	6.372859	5.748704	5.222334
18	9.371887	8.755625	8.201412	7.249670	6.467420	5.817848	5.273164
19	9.603599	8.950115	8.364920	7.365777	6.550369	5.877455	5.316241
20	9.818147	9.128546	8.513564	7.469444	6.623131	5.928841	5.352766
21	10.016803	9.292244	8.648694	7.562003	6.686957	5.973139	5.383683
22	10.200744	9.442425	8.771540	7.644646	6.742944	6.011326	5.409901
23	10.371059	9.580207	8.883218	7.718434	6.792056	6.044247	5.432120
24	10.528758	9.706612	8.984744	7.784316	6.835137	6.072627	5.450949
25	10.674776	9.822580	9.077040	7.843139	6.872927	6.097092	5.466906
26	10.809978	9.928972	9.160945	7.895660	6.906420	6.118183	5.480429
27	10.935165	10.026580	9.237223	7.942554	6.935155	6.136364	5.491889
28	11.051078	10.116128	9.306567	7.984423	6.960662	6.152038	5.501601
29	11.158406	10.198283	9.369606	8.021806	6.983037	6.165550	5.509831
30	11.257783	10.273654	9.426914	8.055184	7.002664	6.177198	5.516806

The future value (amount) of an annuity is based on equal periodic payments or receipts over equal intervals of time at compound interest. The computation involves adding the amounts to which each of the individual receipts or payments will accumulate at the end of a specified time period, assuming a specific compound interest.

The future value of an ordinary annuity is the total amount on deposit immediately after the last rent in the series is made. The future value of an annuity due is determined one period after the last rent in the series. To illustrate the computation of the future value of an ordinary annuity, assume four rents of $1,000 with interest compounded annually at 14 percent. The first rent occurs on December 31, 1996, and the last rent occurs on December 31, 1999 (see Figure 16-5).

$$FV = \$1,000 \times 4.92114$$
$$= \$4,921.14$$
$$FV = \$1,000(4.92114)$$
$$= \$4,921.14$$

PRESENT AND FUTURE VALUES OF ANNUITIES DUE

Tables are available for computing annuities due problems. However, the present value of an annuity due can be computed from a table of the present value of an ordinary annuity by adjusting the table.

To calculate the present value of an annuity due of n rents of $1, select the amount shown for n minus one period from the table of the present value of an ordinary annuity. To this amount, an additional rent of $1 would be added. For example, what is the present value of an annuity due of $1 at 5 percent for four periods?

First rent due immediately	1.0000
Add PV of 4 minus 1 (i.e., 3 rents) at 5%	+2.7232
PV of an annuity due of 4 rents of $1 at 5%	3.7232

The future value of annuity due can be computed using a table of the future value of an ordinary annuity after making certain adjustments:

1. Select from the table the future value of an ordinary annuity of n + 1 rents (where n equals the number of rents).

2. Subtract 1.0000.

Compute the future value of an annuity due of $1,000 at 5 percent compounded annually for two periods:

Future value of an ordinary annuity of 3 rents (2 + 1) at 5%	3.1525
Deduct one rent	−1.0000
Future value of an annuity due of 2 rents, at 5%	2.1525
Multiplied by the annual rent	× $1,000.00
Equals the future value of the annuity due	$2.152.50

Figure 16-4
Future Value (Amount) of 1 Table

FUTURE AMOUNT OF 1: $f = (1 + i)^n$

n	1.5%	4.0%	4.5%	5.0%	5.5%	6.0%	7.0%
1	1.015000	1.040000	1.045000	1.050000	1.055000	1.060000	1.070000
2	1.030225	1.081600	1.092025	1.102500	1.113025	1.123600	1.144900
3	1.045678	1.124864	1.141166	1.157625	1.174241	1.191016	1.225043
4	1.061364	1.169859	1.192519	1.215506	1.238825	1.262477	1.310796
5	1.077284	1.216653	1.246182	1.276282	1.306960	1.338226	1.402552
6	1.093443	1.265319	1.302260	1.340096	1.378843	1.418519	1.500730
7	1.109845	1.315932	1.360862	1.407100	1.454679	1.503630	1.605781
8	1.126493	1.368569	1.422101	1.477455	1.534687	1.593848	1.718186
9	1.143390	1.423312	1.486095	1.551328	1.619094	1.689479	1.838459
10	1.160541	1.480244	1.552969	1.628895	1.708144	1.790848	1.967151
11	1.177949	1.539454	1.622853	1.710339	1.802092	1.898299	2.104852
12	1.195618	1.601032	1.695881	1.795856	1.901207	2.012196	2.252192
13	1.213552	1.665074	1.772196	1.835649	2.005774	2.132928	2.409845
14	1.231756	1.731676	1.851945	1.979932	2.116091	2.260904	2.578534
15	1.250232	1.800944	1.935282	2.078928	2.232476	2.396558	2.759032
16	1.268986	1.872981	2.022370	2.182875	2.355263	2.540352	2.952164
17	1.288020	1.947900	2.113377	2.292018	2.484802	2.692773	3.1586.5
18	1.307341	2.025817	2.208479	2.406619	2.621466	2.854339	3.379932
19	1.326951	2.106849	2.307860	2.526950	2.765647	3.025600	3.616528
20	1.346855	2.191123	2.411714	2.653298	2.917757	3.207135	3.869684
21	1.367053	2.278768	2.520241	2.785963	3.078234	3.399564	4.140562
22	1.387564	2.369919	2.633652	2.925261	3.247537	3.603537	4.430402
23	1.408377	2.464716	2.752166	3.071524	3.426152	3.819750	4.740530
24	1.429503	2.563304	2.876014	3.225100	3.614590	4.048935	5.072367
25	1.450945	2.665836	3.005434	3.386355	3.813392	4.291871	5.427433
26	1.472710	2.772470	3.140679	3.555673	4.023129	4.549383	5.807353
27	1.494800	2.883369	3.282010	3.733456	4.244401	4.822346	6.213868
28	1.517222	2.998703	3.429700	3.920129	4.477843	5.111687	6.648838
29	1.539981	3.118651	3.584036	4.116136	4.724124	5.413388	7.114257
30	1.563080	3.243398	3.745318	4.321942	4.983951	5.743491	7.612255

Figure continues next page

FRACTION OF A YEAR

When the term of a debt is stated in months, the due date is the same date of the month as the initial date of the debt or the last day of the month. For example, a promissory note dated December 31 and having a term of two months comes due on the last day of February. When computing the term of a debt as a fraction of a year, several options are available including

1. Exact interest   Exact number of days/365
2. Bankers' rule interest   Exact number of days/360
3. Third option   Count each full month of the term as 30 days, adding any remaining days/360

Different financial institutions and financial instruments use different methods of determining fractions of a year in lending/investing situations. Some of these situations are identified here (exceptions are common):

Figure 16-4 (Continued)
Future Value (Amount) of 1 Table

n	8.0%	9.0%	10.0%	12.0%	14.0%	16.0%	18.0%
1	1.080000	1.090000	1.100000	1.120000	1.140000	1.160000	1.180000
2	1.166400	1.188100	1.210000	1.254400	1.299600	1.345600	1.392400
3	1.259712	1.295029	1.331000	1.404928	1.481544	1.560896	1.643032
4	1.360489	1.411582	1.464100	1.573519	1.688960	1.810639	1.938778
5	1.469328	1.538624	1.610510	1.762342	1.925415	2.100342	2.287758
6	1.586874	1.677100	1.771561	1.973823	2.194973	2.436396	2.699554
7	1.713824	1.828039	1.948717	2.210681	2.502269	2.826220	3.185474
8	1.850930	1.992563	2.143589	2.475963	2.852586	3.278415	3.758859
9	1.999005	2.171893	2.357948	2.773079	3.251949	3.802961	4.435454
10	2.158925	2.367364	2.593742	3.105848	3.707221	4.411435	5.233836
11	2.331639	2.580426	2.853117	3.478550	4.226232	5.117265	6.175926
12	2.518170	2.812665	3.138428	3.895976	4.817905	5.936027	7.287593
13	2.719624	3.065805	3.452271	4.363493	5.492411	6.885791	8.599359
14	2.937194	3.341727	3.797498	4.887112	6.261349	7.987518	10.147244
15	3.172169	3.642482	4.177248	5.473566	7.137938	9.265521	11.973748
16	3.425943	3.970306	4.594973	6.130394	8.137249	10.748004	14.129023
17	3.700018	4.327633	5.054470	6.866041	9.276464	12.467685	16.672247
18	3.996019	4.717120	5.559917	7.689966	10.575169	14.462514	19.673251
19	4.315701	5.141661	6.115909	8.612762	12.055693	16.776517	23.214436
20	4.660957	5.604411	6.727500	9.646293	13.743490	19.460759	27.393035
21	5.033834	6.108808	7.400250	10.803648	15.667578	22.574481	32.323781
22	5.436540	6.658600	8.140275	12.100310	17.861039	26.186398	38.142061
23	5.871464	7.257874	8.954302	13.552347	20.361585	30.376222	45.007632
24	6.341181	7.911083	9.849733	15.178629	23.212207	35.236417	53.109006
25	6.848475	8.623081	10.834706	17.000064	26.461916	40.874244	62.668627
26	7.396353	9.399158	11.918177	19.040072	30.166584	47.414123	73.948980
27	7.988061	10.245082	13.109994	21.324881	34.389906	55.000382	87.259797
28	8.627106	11.167140	14.420994	23.883866	39.204493	63.800444	102.966560
29	9.317275	12.172182	15.863093	26.749930	44.693122	74.008515	121.500541
30	10.062657	13.267678	17.449402	29.959922	50.950159	85.849877	143.370638

1. Ordinary interest (simple interest, 360 days):
   Banks
   Mortgages
   Certain installment loans
   U.S. agency bonds and notes

2. Exact interest:
   U.S. bonds and notes
   Municipalities

3. Bankers' rule interest
   Commercial paper
   Certificates of deposit
   Corporate loans
   Personal loans

4. Discount:
   U.S. Treasury bills

Figure 16-5

Future Amount of an Ordinary Annuity of 1: $F_O = \dfrac{(1+i)^n - 1}{i}$

n	8.0%	9.0%	10.0%	12.0%	14.0%	16.0%	18.0%
1	1.000000	1.000000	1.000000	1.000000	1.000000	1.000000	1.000000
2	2.080000	2.090000	2.100000	2.120000	2.140000	2.160000	2.180000
3	3.246400	3.278100	3.310000	3.374400	3.439600	3.505600	3.572400
4	4.506112	4.573129	4.641000	4.779328	4.921144	5.066496	5.215432
5	5.866601	5.984711	6.105100	6.352847	6.610104	6.877135	7.154210
6	7.335929	7.523335	7.715610	8.115189	8.535519	8.977477	9.441968
7	8.922803	9.200435	9.487171	10.089012	10.730491	11.413873	12.141522
8	10.636628	11.028474	11.435888	12.299693	13.232760	14.240093	15.326996
9	12.487558	13.021036	13.579477	14.775656	16.085347	17.518508	19.085855
10	14.486562	15.192930	15.937425	17.548735	19.337295	21.321469	23.521309
11	16.645487	17.560293	18.531167	20.654583	23.044516	25.732904	28.755144
12	18.977126	20.140720	21.384264	24.133133	27.270749	30.850169	34.931070
13	21.495297	22.953385	24.522712	28.029109	32.088654	36.786196	42.218663
14	24.214920	26.019189	27.974983	32.392602	37.581065	43.671987	50.818022
15	27.152114	29.360916	31.772482	37.279715	43.842414	51.659505	60.965266
16	30.324283	33.003399	35.949730	42.753280	50.980352	60.925026	72.939014
17	33.750226	36.973705	40.544703	48.883674	59.117601	71.673030	87.068036
18	37.450244	41.301338	45.599173	55.749715	68.394066	84.140715	103.740283
19	41.446263	46.018458	51.159090	63.439681	78.969235	98.603230	123.413534
20	45.761964	51.160120	57.274999	72.052442	91.024928	115.379747	146.627970
21	50.422921	56.764530	64.002499	81.698736	104.768418	134.840506	174.021005
22	55.456755	62.873338	71.402749	92.502504	120.435996	157.414987	206.344785
23	60.893296	69.531939	79.543024	104.602894	138.297035	183.601305	244.486847
24	66.764759	76.789813	88.497327	118.155241	158.658620	213.977607	289.494479
25	73.105940	84.700896	98.347059	133.333870	181.870827	249.214024	342.603486
26	79.954415	93.323977	109.181765	150.333934	208.332743	290.088267	405.272113
27	87.350768	102.723135	121.099942	169.374007	238.499327	337.502390	479.221093
28	95.338830	112.968217	134.209936	190.698687	272.889233	392.502773	566.480890
29	103.965936	124.135356	148.630930	214.582754	312.093725	456.303216	669.447450
30	113.283211	136.307539	164.494023	241.332684	356.786847	530.311731	790.947991

Banker's acceptances
Commercial paper
Certain municipal bonds and revenue bonds
Tax anticipation notes

TIME PERIODS

In the various tables presented the left-hand column refers to periods, not years. There can be compounding periods of less than one year, e.g., interest on savings accounts quarterly and on bonds semiannually. To use the tables in such cases, (1) divide the annual interest rate by the number of periods in the year and (2) multiply the number of periods in one year by the number of years. See Figure 16-6 for an illustration.

DEFERRED ANNUITY

A deferred annuity is an annuity that does not start to produce rents until two or more periods have passed. For example, an annuity of four annual rents deferred three years means that no rents will be paid (or received) during the first three years. The first of the four rents will be payable (or received) at the end of the fourth year.

The future value of a deferred annuity is the same as the future value of an annuity not deferred, since there is no accumulation or investment on which interest may accrue until the first rent. The deferred period is not used in computing the future value of a deferred annuity. The present value of a deferred annuity can be computed as follows:

1. Compute the present value of an ordinary annuity of one for the total periods involved.

2. Compute the present value of an ordinary annuity of one for the number of deferred periods.

3. Compute the difference between the amounts computed in steps 1 and 2 (the subtraction eliminates rents not received or paid during the deferral period).

4. Multiply the difference computed in step 3 by the amount of rent per period.

FINDING THE RENTS, NUMBER OF PERIODS, OR INTEREST RATE

In present value and future value of an annuity cases, if three of the following four factors are known, the fourth factor can be computed mathematically using the relationship of these factors to each other (for present value of an ordinary annuity):

1. The present or future value of an ordinary annuity.

2. The rents

3. The numbers of periods

4. The interest rate.

$$PV = \text{Periodic rent} \times \text{Present value factor}$$

Figure 16-6
Compounding Periods Less than One Year

Annual interest rate	Compounded (for 4 years)	Interest rate per compounding period	Number of periods			
12%	annually	$\dfrac{.12}{1} = .12$	4 yrs ×	1 period	=	4 periods
6%	semiannually	$\dfrac{.06}{2} = .03$	4 yrs ×	2 periods	=	8 periods
6%	quarterly	$\dfrac{.06}{4} = .015$	4 yrs ×	4 periods	=	16 periods
18%	monthly	$\dfrac{.18}{12} = .015$	4 yrs ×	12 periods	=	48 periods

The present value factor is found in the body of present value of an ordinary annuity table and is the juncture of an *n* column (number of periods) and the *i* row (interest rate).

RULE of 72, RULE of 69, and RULE of 78

The rule of 72 refers to the computation of the time it takes for money at interest to double. It is computed as (72/interest rate). For example, principal invested at 6 percent will double in approximately 12 years (72/6).

The rule of 69 states that an amount of money invested at *i* percent per period will double in $69/i + 0.35$ periods. For example, at 10 percent per period, a sum will double in $69/10 + 0.35 = 7.25$ periods.

The rule of 78 is a procedure followed by some finance companies for allocating interest on loans among the months of a year using the sum-of-the months' digits basis when equal monthly payments from the borrower are to be received. For example, the sum of digits from 1 through 12 is 78. Therefore, 12/78 of the year's earnings are allocated for the first month of the contract, 11/78 to the second month, and so on.

MERCHANTS' RULE AND UNITED STATES RULE

Two methods are frequently used for allowing interest credit on partial payments made on an installment debt (and variations of these methods are common):

1. *Merchants's rule* Both debt and all partial payments are considered to earn interest up to the final date. The final amount due is their difference.

2. *United States Rule* At the time of each payment, the accrued interest on the outstanding debt since the last payment is computed:

   (a) If the payment exceeds this accrued interest, the interest is paid and the difference is applied to reduce the outstanding debt, otherwise

   (b) The payment is held without interest and added to the next payment and the rule is applied to this total payment.

PERPETUITIES

A perpetuity is an annuity that continues indefinitely. Bonds that promise payment forever are called *consols*. The British and Canadian governments have issued perpetuties. A perpetuity can be in arrears or in advance. The only difference between the two is the timing of the first payment. If $1 is to be received at the end of every period and the discount is i percent, then the present value of the perpetuity is $1/i$. Future values of perpetuities are undefined.

KEY DEFINITIONS

Annuity A stream of level payments; cash flows that are equal in each year. Types of annuities include ordinary annuities and annuities due.

Annuity certain An annuity payable for a specified number of periods.

Annuity due An annuity whose first payment is made at the beginning of period 1.

Annuity in advance An annuity due.

Annuity in arrears An ordinary annuity whose first payment occurs at the end of the first period.

Compound interest Interest earned on principal and on accumulated interest of prior periods.

Compounding The process of computing the future value of a payment or a series of payments using compound interest procedures; the process of growth through reinvestment of earnings.

Deferred annuity A deferred annuity results when in a series of rents the first rent of an annuity is due after the expiration of two or more periods from the present.

Discount To find a present value; the difference between a principal sum and a future value.

Discounting The converting of future value(s) to the present value.

Discount rate The interest rate used in calculating the present value of a single amount or a series of payments.

Effective rate The true rate of interest, expressed as a percentage applicable for the life of the instrument.

Future value The present value compounded to a future time as a specified interest rate.

Future value of a single sum The original sum plus the compound interest thereon, stated at a specific future date.

Future value of an annuity A future amount accumulated at a certain time, assuming an equal periodic deposit and a specified interest rate.

Implicit interest rate The rate that equates the present value of the payments with the face of the note determined by factors directly associated with the note transaction; the internal rate of return.

Imputed interest rate The rate that equates the present value of the payments with the face of the note determined by factors not associated with the note transaction.

Interest Payments made on money borrowed or received on money loaned or invested; a fee for the use of money over time; the price of money.

Interest rate A percentage of the outstanding principal. Interest is usually expressed as an annual rate. When interest is shorter than one year, the interest rate for the shorter period must be determined.

Interpolate To derive a particular unknown value that lies between two given table values.

Net present value The present value of future sum(s) discounted at a specified rate of return minus the present value of the cost of the investment.

Nominal interest rate The contractual rate of interest.

Ordinary annuity An annuity whose first payment occurs one year in advance; an annuity in arrears.

Ordinary interest Interest computed on the basis of a 350-day year.

Perpetuity An annuity that continues indefinitely.

Present value The discounted value at the present time of a future sum of a stream of payments, using compound interest assumptions.

Present value of a single sum The principal that must be invested at time period zero to produce a known future value.

Present value of an annuity The present value of a series of equal rents made in the future.

Principal The amount borrowed or invested.

Rents A series of equal receipts or payments that occur at equal intervals of time.

Simple interest Interest computed only on the initial principal.

$$\text{Interest} = \text{Principal} \times \text{Rate} \times \text{Time}$$

Time The number of years or fractional portion of a year that the principal is outstanding.

Time value of money Money at the present time is more valuable than money at some point in the future.

Yield The internal rate of return on an investment; the compound return on investment.

Yield to maturity The internal rate of return on a long-term bond or investment.

Appendix A
Acronym Glossary

AAA American Accounting Association. A professional association of accountants who are primarily academics.

AAERs Accounting and Auditing Enforcement Releases (SEC).

ABA American Bankers Association. A major banking trade association located in Washington, D.C.

ABA Number American Bankers Association four-digit number (assigned to all financial institutions, administered by Rand McNally Corporation under contract with the American Bankers Association and the Federal Reserve System.

ABC Activity based costing. A method of assigning indirect costs to products and services. The method assumes that most overhead costs relate to activities within the firm and vary with *drivers* of those activities. The system assumes that all indirect costs are variable.

ABO Accumulated benefit obligation.

ABS Asset-backed securities.

ACH Automated clearing house. An automated system used for check clearing.

ACRS An accelerated depreciation method developed by Congress in 1981 and amended in 1986. The system provides percentages of the asset's cost to be depreciated each year for tax purposes. Salvage value is ignored.

AcSEC Accounting Standards Executive Committee. The senior technical committee of the AICPA authorized to speak in the area.

AFT Automated fund transfer of financial accounting and reporting including cost accounting.

AICPA American Institute of Certified Public Accountants. A major trade association for professional accountants.

AID Agency for International Development.

ALLL Allowance for loan and lease losses.

ALM Asset/liability management. A coordinated management system associated with a bank's assets and liabilities. Focus is on gap or duration position as related to changes in interest rates.

AMT Altercate minimum tax. A tax which applies to individuals, corporations, estates and trusts if it exceeds the taxpayer's regular tax liability. The AMT is the taxpayer's taxable income (1) increased by tax preference items and (2) adjusted for income, gain, deduction, and loss items that have to be recomputed under the alternative minimum tax system.

APB Accounting Principles Board. A generally accepted accounting principles standard setter replaced by the Financial Accounting Standards Board (FASB).

APR Annual percentage rate.

ARM Adjustable rate mortgage. Mortgage interest rate adjusts with market rate.

ARS Accounting Research Study. An AICPA study designed to provide professional accountants and others with a discussion of accounting problems.

ASB Auditing Standards Board (AICPA)

ASRs Accounting Series Releases. Pronouncements on accounting principles and practices put out by the SEC.

ATM Automated teller machine.

ATS Automated transfer service.

BA Bankers Acceptance.

BAI Bank Administration Institute. A major banking trade association.

BD Buydown.

BE Bond equivalent.

BEA Bureau of Economic Analysis.

BEY Bond equivalent yield.

BHC Bank holding company. An organization that owns and controls two or more banks.

BHCA Bank Holding Company Act of 1956.

BIF Bank Insurance Fund.

BIS Bank for International Settlements.

Bk Bank.

BKg Banking.

BLS Bureau of Labor Statistics.

BO Branch office.

BOP Balance of payments.

BOPEC The Fed's BHC rating system. B = bank subsidiaries; O = other or nonbank subsidiaries; P = parent company; E = consolidated earnings; C = consolidated capital.

BSA Bank Secrecy Act.

CA Chartered accountant. A title used in Australia, Canada, and the United Kingdom for an accountant who has satisfied various requirements to qualify to serve as a public accountant. Current assets.

CAMEL A bank regulatory rating system. C = capital; A = asset quality; M = management; E = earnings; L = liquidity.

CAP Committee on Accounting Procedure. A predecessor of the APB which established GAAP from 1939 through 1959.

CAPM Capital asset pricing model. A statistical model for pricing systematic risk.

CapMAC Capital Markets Assurance Corporation.

CAR Capital appropriation request.

CARDs Certificates of amortizing revolving debts.

CARs Certificates of automobile receivables.

CASB Cost Accounting Standard Board. A board of five members authorized by Congress to promulgate cost-accounting standards designed to achieve uniformity and consistency in the cost-accounting principles followed by defense contractors under federal contract.

CATs Certificates of accrual on Treasury certificates.

CBCT Customer-Bank Communications Terminal.

CBO Congressional Budget Office. Collateralized bond obligation.

CCO Commodity Credit Corporation.

CD Certificate of deposit.

CEA Council of Economic Advisers.

CEBA Competititve Equality Banking Act of 1987.

CEO Chief executive officer.

CETA Comprehensive Employment and Training Act.

CF Cash flow.

CFA Chartered financial analysts.

CFO Chief financial officer.

CFTC Commodity Futures Trading Commission.

CHIPS Clearing House Interbank Payments System. A clearing system for wire transfers.

CIA Certificate of Internal Auditing.

CIF Customer information file. A file on customer relationships, settlements, and demographics.

CLEOs Collateralized lease equipment.

CLO Collateralized loan obligation.

CMA Certificate in Management Accounting.

CMO Collateralized mortgage obligation.

CMT Constant maturity treasury.

COF Cost of funds.

COLA Cost-of-living adjustment. A form of indexation measuring changes in the cost-of-living.

COPS Covered option securities.

Corp. Corporate; corporation.

COUGRs Certificates of government receipts.

CPA Certified Public Accountant; customer profitability analysis.

CPI Consumer price index.

CPR Constant repayment rate; conditional prepayment rate.

CPU Central processing unit that performs the basic functions of a computer.

CR Credit.

CRA Community Reinvestment Act. An act to encourage banks to help meet the credit needs of their communities.

CSBS Conference of State Bank Supervisors.

D&B Dun & Bradstreet.

DCF Discounted cash flow. A measure of the value of future expected cash expenditures and receipts at a common date.

DDA Demand deposit account.

DIDMCA Deposit Insurance Deregulation and Monetary Control Act (1980).

DIF Deposit insurance fund.

DIP Debtor-in-possession.

DISC Domestic International Sales Corporation. A domestic corporation that earns most of its income from exports.

DR Debit.

E&O Erros & Omissions.

EBIT Earnings before interest and taxes.

ECC European Economic Community.

ECOA Equal Employment Opportunity Act.

ECP Eurocommercial paper.

EDGAR Electronic Data Gathering, Analysis, and Retrieval system. A Fed system used to automate the receipt, processing, and public dissemination of reports filed with the SEC.

EDP Electronic data processing.

ECOA Equal Credit Opportunity Act.

EEOC Equal Employment Opportunity Commission.

EFT Electronic funds transfer.

EFTS Electronic funds transfer system.

EITF Emerging Issues Task Force. A task group of the FASB which issues pronouncements associated with emerging accounting EOP.

EOQ Economic order quantity.

EPA Environmental Protection Agency.

EPS Earnings per share.

ERISA Employee Retirement Income Security Act.

ESOP Employee Stock Ownership Plan. A stock bonus plan 9 (or combination of stock-bonus and money purchase plans) which is qualified under Section 401 (a) and is designed to invest primarily in employer securities.

ESOT Employee Stock Ownership Trust. A trust fund created by a corporate employer that can provide various tax benefits to the corporation while providing for employee stock ownership.

EXIMBANK Export-Import Bank of the United States.

FAC Federal Advisory Concil.

FAF Financial Accounting Foundation (oversees GASB and FASB).

FASB Financial Accounting Standards Board.

FASB Statement A FASB Statement of Financial Accounting Standards. Also referred to as SFAS.

FCA Farm Credit Administration.

FCPA Foreign Corrupt Practices Act.

FCRA Fair Credit Reporting Act.

FDEPS Fully diluted earnings per share.

FDIC Federal Deposit Insurance Corporation.

Fed Federal Reserve System. The central bank in the United States and a major regulator of banks.

FedWire A Fed system designed to handle domestic wire transfers.

FEI Financial Executives Institute. An organization of financial executives.

FFCB Federal Farm Credit Bank.

FFIEC Federal Financial Institutions Examination Council.

FGIC Financial Guaranty Insurance Corporation.

FHA Federal Housing Authority.

FHLBB Federal Home Loan Bank Board. Federal regulator of savings and loan associations that oversees the FSLIC.

FHLMC Federal Home Loan Mortgage Corporation. Freddie Mac.

FICA   Federal Insurance Contribution Act.   Source of social security taxes and benefits.

FIRREA   Financial Institutions Reform, Recovery, and Enforcement Act.

Five Cs   Character, capacity, collateral, capital, and conditions. A basis for analyzing the credit ability of a borrower.

FLB   Federal land banks.

FMV   Fair market value. The amount that would be realized from the sale of property at a price that is agreeable to both buyer and seller in an arm's length transaction.

FNMA   Federal National Mortgage Association. Fannie Mae.

FOB   Free on board.

FOIO   Freedom of Information Act.

FOMC   Federal Open Market Committee.

FRB   Federal reserve bank.

FRENDS   Floating rate enhanced debt securities.

FRNs   Floating rate notes.

FRR   Financial Reporting Releases (SEC).

FSC   Foreign Sales Corporation. A corporation that provides significant tax incentives to encourage the export of U.S. goods and services.

FSF   Financial services industry.

FSI   Financial-services industry.

FSLIC   Federal Savings and Loan Insurance Corporation. It is currently bankrupt and may be merged with the FDIC.

FTC   Federal Trade Commission.

FTE   Full-time equivalent staff. Staff equivalency expressed in decimal fractions based on hours.

FUTA   Federal Unemployment Tax Act. An act which provides for taxes to be collected at the federal level to subsidize states for their unemployment compensation programs.

FX   Foreign exchange.

FY   Fiscal year.

GAAP   Generally accepted accounting principles. Rules and guidelines accepted as authoritative by the accounting profession.

GAAS   Generally accepted auditing standards.

GAGAS   Generally accepted government auditing standards.

GAO   General Accounting Office (U.S.).

GAP   Ratio measure of the relationship between rate-sensitive assets and rate-sensitive liabilities computed over a specific maturity or duration period. It measures the interest-rate sensitivity for deposit institutions. Dollar GAP = RSA − RSL; gap ratio − RSA/RSL.

GASB Governmental Accounting Standards Board. The major developer of generally accepted accounting principles for state and local governments.

GATT General Agreement on Tariffs and Trade.

GEM Growing equity mortgage.

GNMA Government National Mortgage Association. Ginnie Mae.

GNP Gross national product.

GO General obligation.

GUNs Guaranteed underwriting facilities. An entity that assures that notes will be paid at maturity.

HELOC Home equity line of credit.

HDGS High dollar group sort. A procedure set up by the Fed to accelerate the collection of items drawn on major banks located outside major cities.

HLT Highly leveraged transaction.

HMDA Home Mortgage Disclosure Act.

HUD Department of Housing and Urban Development.

IASC International Accounting Standards Committee. An organization that establishes international accounting standards.

IBAA Independent Bankers Association of America.

IBF International banking facility.

IC Internal control.

ICC Interstate Commerce Commission.

ICONs Indexed currency option notes.

IFC International Finance Corporation.

IIA Institute of Internal Auditors.

IMA Institute of Management Accountants.

IMF International Monetary Fund.

I/O Input/output.

IRA Individual retirement act.

IRC Internal revenue code.

IRR Internal rate of return.

IRS Internal Revenue Service.

ITC Investment Tax Credit.

JIT Just-in-time inventory. A system of managing inventory where each component is purchased or manufactured just before it is used.

KPI Key performance indicator.

LBO Leveraged buyout. A transaction in which investors use debt (leverage) to buy out existing owners of a company.

LC Letter of credit.

LCL Lower of cost or market.

LCM Lower of cost of market. An inventory method that values inventory at the lower of cost or market.

LDC Less developed country.

LIBOR London Interbank Offered Rate; a rate at which Eurocurrency banks lend to each other.

LM Liability management. A technique used by banks to develop borrowing arranged profitably.

LP Linear programming.

LPO Loan production office.

MACRS Modified Accelerated Cost Recovery Systems. A computer based retrieval system containing the complete text of most public corporate annual reports and Forms 10-K. The system is available through the AICPA.

M&A Mergers and acquisitions.

MAS Management Advisory Services. Services provided by public accounting firms and others to assist management in a variety of areas.

MIS Management information system.

MMDA Money market deposit account.

MMP Money market preferred stock or dutch auction preferred stock.

M1 A definition of money that includes the means of payment.

M2 A definition of money that includes both means of payment and time deposits.

M3 M2 money plus large-denomination time deposits and specialized money market mutual funds for institutional investors.

MO Money order.

MTG Mortgage.

NAARS National Automated Accounting Research System.

NABCA National Association for Bank Cost Analysis.

NASDAQ National Association of Securities Dealers Automated Quotation.

NBS National Bureau of Standards.

NBSS National bank surveillance system. A system used by the Office of the Comptroller of the Currency to monitor national banks.

NC No charge.

NCCB National Consumer Cooperative Bank.

NCD   Negotiable certificate of deposit.

NCUA   National Credit Union Administration.

NIF   Note issuance facility.

NII   Net interest income. The spread between interest income and interest expense available for covering a bank's loan losses, overhead, securities losses, taxes, dividends, capital source, and other requirements.

NIM   Net interest margin. Net interest income/earning assets.

NOL   Net operating loss. A loss that occurs when business expenses exceed business income for a taxable year.

NOW Account   Negotiable Order of Withdrawal. A savings account on which orders to pay can be drawn.

NPV   Net present value. A summary measure of the effect of an individual investment of capital on the present worth of an investment.

NSF   Not sufficient funds.

NYSE   New York Stock Exchange

O/H   Overhead.

OAPEC   Organization of Arab Petroleum Exporting Countries.

OASD(H)   Old Age, Survivors, Disability and (Hospital) Insurance.

OCC   Office of the Comptroller of the Currency. A federal regulator of national banks.

OD   Overdraft.

OID   Original issue discount obligations. A security issued at a discount to face value at the time the instrument is originally issued.

OLEM   Other loans especially mentioned.

OMB   Office of Management and Budget (U.S.)

OREO   Other real estate owned.

OSHA   Occupational Safety and Health Act. The act that governs working conditions in industry and commerce.

OTC   Over the counter stock.

OTS   Office of Thrift Supervision.

P/E   Price-earnings ratio. Ratio of market price to earnings per share (EPS). A major measure of the market's evaluation of a company.

P&L   Profit and loss statement. An income statement.

PBB   Program plan budgeting.

PBGC   Pension Benefit Guarantee Corporation. A federal corporation that guarantees basic pension benefits in covered pension plays.

PBO   Projected benefit obligation.

PCPS   Private Companies Practice Section (AICPA).

PEPS   Primary earnings per share.

PERLS   Principal exchange-rate-linked securities.

PERT   Program evaluation review technique. A form of network analysis which include the optimistic time, the most likely time, and the pessimistic time used to estimate an expected completion date for a project within a probability range.

PHC   Personal holding company. A tax designation for a corporation that (1) has 5 or fewer shareholders who own more than 50 percent of the outstanding stock at any time during the last half of its tax year; and (2) has personal holding company income that is at least 60 percent of its adjusted ordinary gross income for the tax year. The tax on a PHC is equal to 28 percent of the undistributed personal holding company income. The purpose of the tax is to prevent a closely held corporation from converting an operating company into a nonoperating company.

PIK   Pay in kind preferred stock.

PIN   Personal identification number.

PM   Profit margin. Ratio of net income to total income.

PO   Principal only.

POS   Point of sale. A device to automatically transfer funds between a customer's account and a merchant's account. Used with a debit card.

PSC   Personal service corporation. A corporation whose principal activity is the performance of personal services.

PV   Present value of 1.

PVI   Present value index. A profitability index. Present value of cash inflows/present value of capital invested.

R&D   Research and development. Costs related to research and development activities.

RAN   Revenue anticipation note.

RAP   Regulatory Accounting Practices (or Principles). Accounting principles established by regulatory authorities.

RE   Retained earnings.

REIT   Real estate investment trust.

REMIC   Real estate mortgage investment conduit. A form of collateralized mortgage obligation that splits up the cash flow on a mortgage in various ways.

REO   Real estate owned.

REPOS   Dealers repurchase agreement.

RESPA   Real Estate Settlement Procedures Act.

ROA   Return on assets. Net income/total assets. Measures profitability in relation to assets employed.

ROE   Return on equity.

ROI Return on investment. A ratio of expected return on an investment or project: income divided by average cost of assets devoted to a project.

RP Repo/Repurchase agreement. An agreement involving the sale of a security sold under an agreement to repurchase, often used in short-term debt management.

RSA Rate-sensitive assets. Assets subject to interest rate changes and repricing.

RSL Rate-sensitive liabilities. Liabilities subject to interest rate changes and repricing.

RTC Resolution Trust Corporation.

S corporation A tax designation for corporations that elect to be taxed like a partnership for federal income tax purposes.

S-X The SEC's regulation setting forth the form and content of financial reports to the SEC.

SABs Staff Accounting Bulletins (SEC).

SAIF Savings Association Insurance Fund.

S&L Savings banks and savings and loans. Financial institutions originally organized to accept savings deposits and to make loans mainly to households.

SAR Summary annual report.

SARs Stock appreciation rights.

SAS Statement of Auditing Standards. Auditing standards promulgated by the AICPA.

SBA Small Business Administration.

SDRs Special drawing rights. Liabilities of the International Monetary Fund that serve as international fiat money.

SEC Securities and Exchange Commission. A federal agency established to protect shareholders. The SEC's accounting requirements are provided in its *Accounting Series releases (ASR)*, *Financial Reporting Releases* (FRR), Accounting and Auditing Enforcement Releases, *Staff Accounting Bulletins*, Regulation S-X, and Form 10-K.

SECPS SEC Practice Section.

SEP Simplified employee pension plan.

SFAC Statement of Financial Accounting Concepts. An FASB document which describes underlying accounting concepts.

SFAS Statement of Financial Accounting Standards. An FASB document that describes major generally accepted accounting principles associated with various topics.

SIC Standard industrial classification.

SIPC Securities Investor Protection Corporation.

SNAFU Situation normal, all fouled up.

SPINs Standard and Poor's indexed notes.

SOP Statement of Position (AICPA).

SQCS Statements on Quality Control Standards (AICPA).

SRPT   Statements on Responsibilities in Tax Practice. Ethical standards of practice and compliance established by the Tax Division of the AICPA. The statements do not bind legally.

SSARS   Statement on Standards for Accounting and Review Services. Pronouncements of the AICPA on unaudited financial statements and unaudited financial information of nonpublic entities.

SSMAS   Standards for Management Advisory Services.

STAGS   Sterling transferable accruing government securities.

STRIPS   Separate trading of registered interest and principal of securities.

SWOT   Strengths, weaknesses, opportunities, threats. Self-analysis criteria used in strategic planning.

SYD   Sum-of-the-years'-digits. A depreciation method.

TA   Trade acceptance.

T-account   A general ledger account form shaped like the letter T. Debits are shown to the left of the vertical line, credits to the right.

TAN   Tax anticipation note.

T-bill   Treasury bill.

TCMP   A stratified random sample used to select tax returns for audit.

TE   Tax-equivalent. A technique for converting tax-free rates to compare with taxable rates. Tax free rate/(1 − marginal tax rate).

TEFRA   Tax Equity and Fiscal Responsibility Act of 1982.

10-k   The annual report required by the SEC of most publicly held corporations.

TIGRs   Treasury investment growth certificates.

TILA   Truth in Lending Act.

TIN   Taxpayer identification number.

TRA   Tax Reformat Act of 1986.

TT&Ls   Treasury tax and loan accounts. U.S. government accounts at local banks.

TVA   Tennessee Valley Authority.

UBPR   Uniform Bank Performance Report. A report referencing unusual or significant changes in a bank's financial condition.

UCC   Uniform Commercial Code.

UCCC   Uniform Consumer Credit Code.

ULPA   Uniform Limited Partnership Act.

UPA   Uniform Partnership Act.

U.S.C.   United States Code.

VA   Veterans Administration.

VAT   Value added tax.

X-C Ex coupon.

X-D Ex dividend.

X-I Ex interest.

X-Rts. Ex rights.

YLD Yield.

YTC Yield to call.

YTM Yield to maturity.

ZBA Zero balance accounts. A cash management technique in which a bank automatically transfers funds from a designated master account as checks are presented against the parable and payroll accounts.

ZBB Zero-based budgeting. Also, zero bracket account (tax).

ZCRO Zero cost ratio option.

ZEBRAs Zero coupon eurosterling bearer or registered accruing certificates.

Appendix B
Index of References to APB and FASB Pronouncements

Accounting Principles Board Opinions

Date Issued	Opinion Number	Title
Nov. 1962	1	New Depreciation Guidelines and Rules
Dec. 1962	2	Accounting for the "Investment Credit"; Accounting Principles for Regulated Industries
Oct. 1963	3	The Statement of Source and Application of Funds
Mar. 1964	4	Accounting for the "Investment Credit"
Sep. 1964	5	Reporting of Leases in Financial Statements of Lessor
Oct. 1965	6	Status of Accounting Research Bulletins
May 1966	7	Accounting for Leases in Financial Statements of Lessor
Nov. 1966	8	Accounting for the Cost of Pension Plans
Dec. 1966	9	Reporting the Results of Operations
Dec. 1966	10	Omnibus Opinion—1966
Dec. 1967	11	Accounting for Income Taxes
Dec. 1967	12	Omnibus Opinion—1967
Mar. 1969	13	Amending Paragraph 6 of APB Opinion No. 9, Application to Commercial Banks
Mar. 1969	14	Accounting for Convertible Debt and Debt Issued with Stock Purchase Warrants
May 1969	15	Earnings per Share
Aug. 1970	16	Business Combinations
Aug. 1970	17	Intangible Assets
Mar. 1971	18	The Equity Method of Investments in Common Stock
Mar. 1971	19	Reporting Changes in Financial Position

Date Issued	Opinion Number	Title
July 1971	20	Accounting Changes
Aug. 1971	21	Interest on Receivables and Payables
Apr. 1972	22	Disclosures of Accounting Policies
Apr. 1972	23	Accounting for Income Taxes—Special Areas
Apr. 1972	24	Accounting for Income Taxes—Investments in Common Stock Accounted for by the Equity Method (Other than Subsidiaries and Corporate Joint Ventures)
Oct. 1972	25	Accounting for Stock Issued to Employees
Oct. 1972	26	Early Extinguishment of Debt
Nov. 1972	27	Accounting for Lease Transactions by Manufacturer or Dealer Lessors
May 1973	28	Interim Financial Reporting
May 1973	29	Accounting for Nonmonetary Transactions
June 1973	30	Reporting the Results of Operations
June 1973	31	Disclosures of Lease Commitments by Lessees

Accounting Principles Board Statements

Date Issued	Statement Number	Title
Apr. 1962	1	Statement by the Accounting Principles Board (on Accounting Research Studies Nos. 1 and 3)
Sep. 1967	2	Disclosure of Supplemental Financial Information by Diversified Companies
June 1969	3	Financial statements Restated for General Price-Level Change
Oct. 1970	4	Basic Concepts and Accounting Principles Underlying Financial Statements of Business Enterprises

Financial Accounting Standards Board
Statements of Financial Accounting Standards

Date Issued	Statement Number	Title
Dec. 1973	1	Disclosure of Foreign Currency Translation Information
Oct. 1974	2	Accounting for Research and Development Costs
Dec. 1974	3	Reporting Accounting Changes in Interim Financial Statements
Mar. 1975	4	Reporting Gains and Losses from Extinguishment of Debt
Mar. 1975	5	Accounting for Contingencies

Date Issued	Statement Number	Title
May 1975	6	Classification of Short-Term Obligations Expected to be Refinanced
June 1975	7	Accounting and Reporting by Development Stage Enterprises
Oct. 1975	8	Accounting for the Translation of Foreign Currency Transactions and Foreign Currency Financial Statements
Oct. 1975	9	Accounting for Income Taxes-Oil and Gas Producing Companies
Oct. 1975	10	Extension of "Grandfather" Provisions for Business Combinations
Dec. 1975	11	Accounting for Contingencies-Transition Method
Dec. 1975	12	Accounting for Certain Marketable Securities
Nov. 1976	13	Accounting for Leases
Dec. 1976	14	Financial Reporting for Segments of a Business Enterprise
June 1977	15	Accounting by Debtors and Creditors for Troubled Debt Restructuring
June 1977	16	Prior Period Adjustments
Nov. 1977	17	Accounting for Leases-Initial Direct Costs
Nov. 1977	18	Financial Reporting for Segments of a Business Enterprise-Interim Financial Statements
Dec. 1977	19	Financial Accounting and Reporting by Oil and Gas Producing Companies
Dec. 1977	20	Accounting for Forward Exchange Contracts
Apr. 1978	21	Suspension of the Reporting of Earnings Per Share and Segment Information by Nonpublic Enterprises
June 1978	22	Changes in the Provisions of Lease Agreements Resulting from Refunding of Tax-Exempt Debt
Aug. 1978	23	Inception of the Lease
Dec. 1978	24	Reporting Segment Information in Financial Statements That Are Presented in Another Enterprise's Financial Report
Feb. 1979	25	Suspension of Certain Accounting Requirements for Oil and Gas Producing Companies
Apr. 1979	26	Profit Recognition on Sales-Type Leases of Real Estate
May 1979	27	Classification of Renewals or Extensions of Existing Sales-Type or Direct Financing Leases
May 1979	28	Accounting for Sales with Leasebacks
June 1979	29	Determining Contingent Rentals
Aug. 1979	30	Disclosures of Information About Major Corporations
Sep. 1979	31	Accounting for Tax Benefits Related to U.K. Tax Legislation Concerning Stock Relief

Date Issued	Statement Number	Title
Sep. 1979	32	Specialized Accounting and Reporting Principles and Practices in AICPA Statements of Position and Guides on Accounting and Auditing Matters
Sep. 1979	33	Financial Reporting and Changing Prices
Oct. 1979	34	Capitalization of Interest Cost
Mar. 1980	35	Accounting and Reporting by Defined Benefit Pension Plans
May 1980	36	Disclosure of Pension Information
July 1980	37	Balance Sheet Classification of Deferred Income Taxes
Sep. 1980	38	Accounting for Preacquisition Contingencies of Purchased Enterprises
Oct. 1980	39	Financial Reporting and Changing Prices: Specialized Assets-Mining and Oil and Gas
Nov. 1980	40	Financial Reporting and Changing Prices: Specialized Assets-Timberlands and Growing Timber
Nov. 1980	41	Financial Reporting and Changing Prices: Specialized Assets-Income-Producing Real Estate
Nov. 1980	42	Determining Materiality for Capitalization of Interest Costs
Nov. 1980	43	Accounting for Compensated Absences
Dec. 1980	44	Accounting for Intangible Assets of Motor Carriers
Mar. 1981	45	Accounting for Franchise Fee Revenue
Mar. 1981	46	Financial Reporting and Changing Prices: Motion Picture Films
Mar. 1981	47	Disclosure of Long-Term Obligations
June 1981	48	Revenue Recognition When Fight of Return Exists
June 1981	49	Accounting for Product Financing Arrangements
Nov. 1981	50	Financial Reporting in the Record and Music Industry
Nov. 1981	51	Financial Reporting by Cable Television Companies
Dec. 1981	52	Foreign Currency Translation
Dec. 1981	53	Financial Reporting by Producers and Distributors of Motion Picture Films
Jan. 1982	54	Financial Reporting and Changing Prices: Investment Companies
Feb. 1982	55	Determining Whether a Convertible Security Is a Common Stock Equivalent
Feb. 1982	56	Designation of AICPA Guide and Statement of Position (SOP) 81-1 on Contractor Accounting and SOP 81-2 Concerning Hospital-Related Organizations as Preferable for Purposes of Applying APB Opinion 20
Mar. 1982	57	Related Party Disclosures

Date Issued	Statement Number	Title
Apr. 1982	58	Capitalization of Interest Cost in Financial Statements That Include Investments Accounted for by the Equity Method
Apr. 1982	59	Deferral of the Effective Date of Certain Accounting Requirements for Pension Plans of State and Local Governmental Units
June 1982	60	Accounting and Reporting by Insurance Enterprises
June 1982	61	Accounting for Title Plant
June 1982	62	Capitalization of Interest Cost in Situations Involving Certain Tax-Exempt Borrowings and Certain Gifts and Grants
June 1982	63	Financial Reporting by Broadcasters
Sep. 1982	64	Extinguishments of Debt Made to Satisfy Sinking-Fund Requirements
Sep. 1982	65	Accounting for Certain Mortgage Banking Activities
Oct. 1982	66	Accounting for Sales of Real Estate
Oct. 1982	67	Accounting for Costs and Initial Rental Operations of Real Estate Projects
Oct. 1982	68	Research and Development Arrangements
Nov. 1982	69	Disclosures About Oil and Gas Producing Activities
Dec. 1982	70	Financial Reporting and Changing Prices: Foreign Currency Translation
Dec. 1982	71	Accounting for the Effects of Certain Types of Regulation
Feb. 1983	72	Accounting for Certain Acquisitions of Banking or Thrift Institutions
Aug. 1983	73	Reporting a Change in Accounting for Railroad Track Structures
Aug. 1983	74	Accounting for Special Termination Benefits Paid to Employees
Nov. 1983	75	Deferral of the Effective Date of Certain Accounting Requirements for Pension Plans of State and Local Governmental Units
Nov. 1983	76	Extinguishment of Debt
Dec. 1983	77	Reporting by Transferors for Transfers of Receivables with Recourse
Dec. 1983	78	Classification of Obligations That Are Callable by the Creditor
Feb. 1984	79	Elimination of Certain Disclosures for Business Combinations by Nonpublic Enterprises
Aug. 1984	80	Accounting for Future Contracts

Date Issued	Statement Number	Title
Nov. 1984	81	Disclosure of Postretirement Health Care and Life Insurance Benefits
Nov. 1984	82	Financial Reporting and Changing Prices: Elimination of Certain Disclosures
Mar. 1985	83	Designation of AICPA Guides and Statement of Position on Accounting by Brokers and Dealers in Securities, by Employee Benefit Plans, and by Banks as Preferable for Purposes of Applying APB Opinion 20
Mar. 1985	84	Induced Conversion of Convertible Debt
Mar. 1985	85	Yield Test for Determining Whether a Convertible Security is a Common Stock Equivalent
Aug. 1985	86	Accounting for the Costs of Computer Software to Be Sold, Leased, or Otherwise Marketed
Dec. 1985	87	Employers' Accounting for Pensions
Dec. 1985	88	Employers' Accounting for Settlements and Curtailments of Defined Benefit Pension Plans and for Termination Benefits
Dec. 1986	89	Financial Reporting and Changing Prices
Dec. 1986	90	Regulated Enterprises-Accounting for Abandonments and Disallowances of Plant Costs
Dec. 1986	91	Accounting for Nonrefundable Fees and Costs Associated with Originating or Acquiring Loans and Initial Direct Costs of Leases
Aug. 1987	92	Regulated Enterprises-Accounting for Phase-In Plans
Aug. 1987	93	Recognition of Depreciation by Not-for-Profit Organizations
Oct. 1987	94	Consolidation of all Majority Owned Subsidiaries
Nov. 1987	95	Statement of Cash Flows
Dec. 1987	96	Accounting for Income Taxes
Dec. 1987	97	Accounting and Reporting by Insurance Enterprises for Certain Insurance Enterprises for Certain Long-Duration Contracts and for Realized Gains and Losses from the Sale of Investments

May 1988	98	Accounting for Leases:
		    Sale-Leaseback Transactions Involving Real Estate
		    Sales-Type Leases of Real Estate
		    Definition of the Lease Term
		    Initial Direct Costs of Direct Financial Leases

Sep. 1988	99	Deferral of the Effective Date of Recognition of Depreciation by Not-for-Profit Organizations

Date Issued	Statement Number	Title
Dec. 1988	100	Accounting for Income Taxes-Deferral of the Effective Date FASB Statement No. 96
Dec. 1988	101	Regulated Enterprises-Accounting for the Discontinuation of Application of FASB Statement No. 71
Feb. 1989	102	Statement of Cash Flows-Exemption of Certain Enterprises and Classification of Cash Flows from Certain Securities Acquired for Resale
Dec. 1989	103	Accounting for Income Taxes-Deferral of Effective Date of FASB Statement No. 96
Dec. 1989	104	Statement of Cash Flows-Net Reporting of Certain Cash Receipts and Cash Payments and Classification of Cash Flows from Hedging Transactions
Mar. 1990	105	Disclosure of Information About Financial Instruments with Off-Balance-Sheet Risk and Financial Instruments with Concentrations of Credit Risk
Dec. 1990	106	Employers' Accounting for Postretirement, Benefits Other Than Pensions
Dec. 1991	107	Disclosures About Fair Value of Financial Institutions
Dec. 1992	109	Accounting for Income Taxes
Dec. 1992	110	Reporting by Defined Benefit Pension Plans of Investment Contracts

Financial Accounting Standards Board
Statements of Financial Accounting Concepts

Date Issued	Statement Number	Title
Nov. 1978	1	Objectives of Financial Reporting by Business Enterprises
May 1980	2	Qualitative Characteristics of Accounting Information
Dec. 1980	3	Elements of Financial Statements of Business Enterprises
Dec. 1980	4	Objectives of Financial Reporting by Nonbusiness Organizations
Dec. 1984	5	Recognition and Measurement in Financial Statements of Business Enterprises
Dec. 1985	6	Elements of Financial Statements

Appendix C
References

American Institute of Certified Public Accountants, New York:

Accounting for Options.
Accounting Principles Board Opinions.
Accounting Principles Board Statements.
Accounting Interpretations.
Accounting Research Bulletins.
Accounting Trends & Techniques
Accounting Terminology Bulletins.
AICPA Audit and Accounting Manual.
Audits of Banks. Industry Audit Guide.
Audits of Investment Companies. Industry Audit Guide.
Journal of Accountancy.
Savings and Loan Associations. Audit and Accounting Guide.
Technical Practice Aids.

Antrim, P. S., and Johannes, M. *A Banker's Guide to Meeting Capital Requirements.* Rolling Meadows, IL: Bank Administration Institute, 1989.

Austin, D. V., and Simoff, P. L. *Strategic Planning for Banks.* Rolling Meadows, IL: Bankers Publishing Co., 1990.

Bankers Publishing Company/Probus Publishing Company:

A Banker's Guide to Meeting Capital Requirements.
Accounting, Budgeting, and Finance.
Accounting Policies for Non-Performing Loans.
A Desktop Reference Manual of Compliance Terms.
A Duration Analysis Primer.
A Guide to TIN Compliance.
Anticipatory Auditing Using Key Indicators.
A Practical Guide to Duration Analysis.

Asset/Liability Management.
Asset/Liability Management Techniques.
Bank Productivity.
Bank Regulatory Management Deskbook.
Bank Secrecy Act Compliance.
Bank Soundness.
Cost analysis and Control in Banks.
EDP Auditing Guide.
Effective Asset/Liability Management for the Community Bank.
Effective Teller Management.
Evaluating Commercial Bank Performance.
Handbook of Earnings Enhancement for Financial Institutions.
How to Analyze a Bank Statement.
How to Interpret Financial Statements for Better Decisions.
Information Reporting and Compliance.
Internal Auditing for the Community Bank.
Internal Auditing in the Banking Industry (3 volumes).
Management Accounting in Banks.
Modern Banking.
Option Pricing and Investment Strategies.
Overview of Risk-Based Capital Requirements.
Profitability Measurement for Financial Instruments.
Regulatory Management Compliance Audit Deskbook.
Report Writing for Internal Auditors.
Risk-Based Internal Auditing for Depository Institutions.
Statement of Principle and Standards for Internal Auditing in the Banking Industry.
Strategic Planning for Banks.
Teller Management.
Teller Operations Manual.
Teller Performance.
Teller World.
The Banker's Complete Credit and Loan Administration.
The Complete Encyclopedia of Accounting, Finance, Investing, Banking and Economics.
The Electronic Future of Banking.
Trust Audit Manual.

Banker. R. E., and others. *Advanced Financial Accounting.* New York: McGraw-Hill, 1993.

Bank Performance Annual. Boston, MA: Warren, Gorham & Lamont, Annual.

Bavishi, V.B. *International Accounting and Auditing Trends.* Princeton, NJ: Center for International Financial Analysis & Research, Inc., 1989. Two volumes.

_____. *Who Audits the World.* Latest edition.

Beams, F. A. *Advanced Accounting.* Englewood Cliffs, NJ: Prentice Hall, 1992.

Belasco, K. S. *Improving Performance by Managing Non-Interest Expense.* Rolling Meadows, IL: Bankers Publishing Co., 1990.

_____. *Earnings Enhancement Handbook.* Chicago, IL: Bankers Publishing Company, 1991.

Bernstein, L.A. *Financial Statement Analysis.* Englewood Cliffs, NJ: Prentice Hall. Latest edition.

Bierman, H., and Smidt, S. *The Capital Budgeting Decision.* New York, NY: Macmillan Publishing Co., 1988.

Binder, B.F. *Banker's Treasury Management Handbook.* Boston, MA: Warren, Gorham & Lamont, 1988.

Bisk, N.M. *Auditing.* Tampa, FL: National Institute of Accountants. Latest edition.

Blanding, S. L. *Acquisitions.* Chicago, IL: Probus, 1991.

Board of Governors of the Federal Reserve System. *Annual Report.*

_____. *Commercial Bank Examination Manual.*

_____. *The Federal Reserve System in Brief.* Federal Reserve Bank of San Francisco.

_____. *Welcome to the Federal Reserve.*

Bollenbacher, G. M. *The New Business of Banking.* Chicago, IL: Bankers Publishing Company, 1992.

Brown, A. J. *High Performance Banking: How to Improve Earnings in Any Bank.* Rolling Meadows, IL: Bankers Publishing Company, 1990.

Burton, J.C., and others. *Handbook of Accounting and Auditing.* Boston, MA: Warren, Gorham & Lamont, Inc., 1988.

Carlson, John H., and Fabozzi, Frank J., eds. *The Trading and Securitization of Senior Bank Loans.* Chicago, IL: Probus, 1992.

Center for Banking Issues and Strategies. *Analyzing Success and Failure in Banking Consolidation.* Rolling Meadows, IL: Bank Administration Institute, 1990.

Chew, Donald, ed. *New Developments in Commercial Banking.* Cambridge, MA: Blackwell, 1991.

Ciliberti, A.N. *Bank Internal Auditing Manual.* Boston, MA: Warren, Gorham & Lamont. Latest edition.

Comptroller of the Currency. *Annual Report.*

_____. *Comptroller's Handbook for Compliance.*

_____. *Comptroller's Handbook for National Bank Examiners.*

_____. *Comptroller's Manual for Corporate Activities.*

_____. *The Director's Book—The Role of a National Bank Director.*

_____. *A Director's Guide to Board Reports: Red Flags and Other Points of Interest.*

_____. *FFIEC EDP Handbook.*

_____. *Handbook for National Bank Examiners.*

_____. *Weekly Bulletin* (annual subscription)

Call report illustration booklets (FFIEC):
Commercial Banks with Domestic/Foreign Offices
Domestic Offices only/total assets 300 Million or More
Domestic Only/Assets 100, but Less Than 300 Million
Domestic Only/Assets Less Than 100 Million
Other:
Quarterly Journal. Four issues of the quarterly Journal make up of the OCC's annual
report. The March issue contains the report of operations for the previous year.
Supervisory references:
Comptroller's Handbook for Consumer Examinations
Comptroller's Handbook for Fiduciary Activities
FFIEC EDP Handbook
Regulatory subscriptions:
Banking Circulars
Banking Bulletins & Circulars (Annual subscription)
Examining Bulletins
Examining Circulars
Interpretations and Actions (Annual subscription)
Banking references:
Commercial Bank Entry into Revenue Bond Underwriting
Complimentary publications
A Director's Guide to Board Reports: Red Flags & Other Points of Interest
A Partnership Approach to Neighborhood Commercial Reinvestment
Basic Banking Services and Government Check Cashing
Money Laundering: A Banker's Guide to Avoiding Problems
OCC Organizational Directory
Opportunities and Issues Banks in Affordable Housing

Coopers & Lybrank. *Guide to Financial Instruments.* New York, NY: Cooper & Lybrand, 1988.

DeRosa, D. *Managing Foreign Exchange Risk.* Chicago, IL: Probus, 1991.

Deutsch, G. M., and Mecimore, C. D. *Bank Controller's Manual.* Austin, TX: Sheshunoff
Information Services, 1990.

Dyckman, T. R., and others. *Intermediate Accounting.* Chicago, IL: Irwin, 1992.

Ernst & Whinney. *International Accounting Standards.* Cleveland, OH: Ernst & Whinney,
1986.

Fabozzi, Frank J. *Fixed Income Mathematics.* Chicago: Probus, 1993.

_____, ed. *Investing: The Collected Works of Martin L. Leibowitz.* Chicago, IL: Probus,
1992.

Federal Deposit Insurance Corporation. *Annual Report.*

_____. *Manual of Examination Policies.*

Federal Financial Institutions Examination Council. *Annual Report.*

Federal Reserve System. *Annual Report.*

_____. *Bank Holding Company Supervision Manual.*

_____. *Commercial Bank Examination Manual.*

_____. *The Federal Reserve System: Purposes & Functions.* Latest edition.

Financial Accounting Standards Board. *Accounting Standards: Original Pronouncements.* Norwalk, CONN: Financial Accounting Standards Board, latest edition.

_____. *Statements of Financial Accounting Concepts 1-6.*

The First Boston Corporation. *Handbook of U.S. Government and Federal Agency Securities.* Chicago, IL: Probus, 1990.

Fitch, Thomas. *Dictionary of Banking Terms.* Hauppauge, NY: Barron's Educational Series, 1990.

FMCG Capital Strategies. *Analyzing Success and Failure in Banking Consolidation.* Rolling Meadows, IL: Bank Administration Institute, 1990.

Foster, G. *Financial Statement Analysis.* Homewood, IL: *Advanced Accounting.* Latest edition.

Gitman, L. J., and Joehnk, M. D. *Fundamentals of Investing.* New York: Harper & Row, 1990.

Gup, B. E. *Bank Fraud.* Rolling Meadows, IL: Bankers Publishing Co., 1990.

Horngren, C.T., and Harrison, W.T. *Cost Accounting.* Englewood Cliffs, NJ: Prentice Hall. Latest edition.

Howcroft, B., and Storey, C. *Management and Control of Currency and Interest Rate Risk.* Chicago, IL: Probus, 1990.

Howe, Donna M. *A Guide to Managing Interest-Rate Risk.* New York: New York Institute of Finance, 1992.

Huber, S. K. *Bank Officer's Handbook of Government Regulation.* Boston, MA: Warren, Gorham & Lamont, 1992.

Hull, John. *Options, Futures, and Other Derivative Securities.* Englewood Cliffs, NJ: Prentice Hall, 1989.

Institute for Strategy Development. *A Banker's Guide to Meeting Capital Requirement.* Washington, DC: Institute for Strategy Development, 1989.

Jarnagin, B. D. *Financial Accounting Standards.* Chicago, IL: Commerce Clearing House, latest edition.

Johnson, Hazel J. *The Bank Valuation Handbook.* Chicago, IL: Bankers Publishing Company, 1993.

Johnson, H.T., and Kaplan, R.S. *Relevance Lost: The Rise and Fall of Management Accounting.* Cambridge, MA: Harvard Business School, 1987.

Kieso, D. E., and Weygandt, J. J. *Intermediate Accounting.* New York: John Wiley & Sons, 1992.

Konishi, A., and Dattatreya, R. E., eds. *Handbook of Derivative Instruments.* Chicago, IL: Probus, 1991.

Konishi, A., and Fabozzi, R. J., eds. *Asset/Liability Management.* Chicago, IL: Probus, 1991.

Kramer, J. L., and Phillips, L. C. *Federal Taxation.* Englewood Cliffs, NJ: Prentice Hall, 1992.

Management Accounting.

Martin, John D., and others. *Basic Financial Management.* Englewood Cliffs, NJ: Prentice Hall, 1991.

McCafferty, T. A., and Wasendorf, R. R. *All About Futures.* Chicago, IL: Probus, 1992.

Miller, M. A. *Comprehensive GAAP Guide.* San Diego, CA: Harcourt Brace Jovanovich, latest edition.

Miller, P. B., and Redding, R. J. *The FASB: The People, the Process, and the Politics.* Homewood, IL: Irwin, 1988.

Moore, C.L., and others. *Managerial Accounting.* Cincinnati, OH: South-Western Publishing Co. Latest edition.

National Credit Union Administration. *Annual Report.*

Newell, J., and others. *Encyclopedia of Mortgage and Real Estate Finance.* Chicago, IL: Probus, 1991.

Nikolai, L. A., and Bazley, J. D. *Intermediate Accounting.* Cincinnati, OH: South-Western, 1992.

Office of Thrift Supervision. *Annual Report.*

_____. *Thrift Activities Regulatory Handbook.*

Perry, L.G., and Hajrnek, R.F. *SEC Accounting and Reporting Manual.* Boston, MA: Warren, Gorham & Lamont, Inc., 1988.

Pointer, L.G., and Schroeder, R.G. *The FASB: The People, the Process, and the Politics.* Homewood, IL: Irwin, 1987.

Practical Accountant.

Regulatory Compliance Associates, Inc. *A Desktop Reference Manual of Compliance Terms* Rolling Meadows, IL: Bankers Publishing Company, 1990.

_____. *Overview of Risk-Based Capital Requirements.* Rolling Meadows, IL: Bank Administration Institute, 1989.

Ricketts, Don, and Gray, Jack. *Managerial Accounting.* Boston, MA: Houghton Mifflin, 1991.

Santoro, N. J. *Finding and Exploiting Profit Opportunities Inside Your Bank.* Chicago, IL: Probus, 1992.

Securities and Exchange Commission. *Annual Report.*

_____. *SEC Accounting Rules.*

_____. *SEC Docket.*

_____. *Statistical Bulletin.*

Securities Regulation and Law Report. Washington, DC: Bureau of National Affairs. Weekly.

Sinkey, J.F. *Commerical Bank Financial Management.* New York, NY: Macmillan, 1988.

Schroeder, M. R. *Bank Officer's Handbook of Commercial Banking Law.* Boston, MA: Warren, Gorham & Lamont, 1992.

Simons, W. K., and Nadolmy, N. Z. *Regulatory Management Compliance Audit Deskbook.* Chicago, IL: Bankers Publishing Company,

Stevenson, T. H. *The Board of Directors.* Rolling Meadows, IL: Bankers Publishing Company, 1990.

_____. *The Bank Regulatory Management Deskbook.* Chicago, IL: Bank Publishing Company, latest update.

_____. *The Deposit Compliance Deskbook.* Chicago, IL: Bankers Publishing Company, 1992.

Thau, A. *The Bond Book.* Chicago, IL: Probus, 1992.

United States Government Manual. Washington, DC: U.S. Government Printing Office. Annual.

Vickman, T.W. *Handbook of Model Accounting Reports and Formats.* Englewood Cliffs, NJ: Prentice Hall, 1987.

Wendell, P.J. *Corporate Controller's Manual.* Boston, MA: Warren, Gorham and Lamont, 1989.

_____. *SEC Accounting Report.* Boston, MA: Warren, Gorham & Lamont. Monthly.

Williams, J.R., and others. *Intermediate Accounting.* New York, NY: The Dryden Press. Latest edition.

Woelfel, C. J. *Financial Statement Analysis.* Chicago, IL: Probus, 1988.

_____. *Accounting, Budgeting, and Finance: A Reference for Managers.* New York, American Management Association, 1990.

_____. *The Desktop Guide to Money, Time, Interest and Yields.* Chicago, IL: Probus, 1988.

_____. *Encyclopedia of Banking and Finance.* Ninth Edition. Chicago, IL: Probus Publishing Company, 1991.

Wolk, H. I., and others. *Accounting Theory: A Conceptual and Institutional Approach.* Cincinnati, OH: South-Western, 1992.

Appendix D
Directory

African Development Bank
Abidjan, Ivory Coast

American Accounting Association
5717 Bessie Drive
Sarasota, FL 33583

American Bankers Association
1120 Connecticut Avenue, NW
Washington, DC 20036

American Institute of Certified Public
  Accountants
1211 Avenue of the Americas
New York, NY 10036

Asian Development Bank
6 ADB Avenue, 1501
Mandaluyong, Metro Manila, Philippines
632-711-3851

Association of Government Accountants
727 23rd Street
Arlington, VA 22202

Bank Administration Institute
One North Franklin
Chicago, IL 60606
312-553-4600

Congressional Budget Office
Second and D Streets S.W.
Washington, DC 20515
202-276-2621

Council of Economic Advisers
Old Executive Office Building
Washington, DC 20500
202-395-5084

Department of Commerce
Constitution Ave and Tenth St NW
Washingtion, DC 20530
202-514-2000

Department of Housing and Urban
  Development
451 Seventh Street SW
Washington, DC 20410
202-708-1422

Department of Justice
Constitution Avenue and Tenth Street NW
Washington, DC 20530
202-514-2000

Department of Labor
Bureau of Labor Statistics
Washington, DC 20212

Department of the Treasury
1500 Pennsylvania Avenue NW
Washington, DC 20220
202-566-2000

Farm Credit Administration
1501 Farm Credit Drive
McLean, VA 22012-5090
703-883-4000

Federal Deposit Insurance Corporation
550 Seventeenth Street NW
Washington, DC 20429
202-393-8400

Federal Financial Institutions Examination
 Council
Suite 850B
1776 G Street NW
Washington, DC 20006
202-357-0177

Federal Financing Bank
15th Street and Pennsylvania Avenue NW
Main Treasury Building
Washington, DC 20220
202-566-2468

Federal Reserve System
Twentieth Street and Constitution Avenue
 NW
Washington, DC 20551
202-452-3000

Federal Trade Commission
Pennsylvania Avenue at Sixth Street NW
Washington, DC 20580
202-326-2222

Financial Accounting Standards Board
High Ridge Park, P.O. Box 3821
Stamford, CT 06905

Financial Executives Institute
10 Madison Avenue, Box 1938
Morristown, NJ 07960

General Accounting Office
441 G Street NW
Washington, DC 20548
202-275-5067

Governmental Accounting Standards Board
Hidge Ridge Park
Stamford, CT 06905

Government Printing Office
North Capitol and H street NW
Washington, DC 20401
202-275-2051

The House of Representatives
The Capitol
Washington, DC 20515
202-224-3121

Institute of Internal Auditors
Altamonte Centre
249 Maitland Ave.
Altamonte Springs, FL 32701

Institute of Management Accountants
570 City Center Building
Ann Arbor, MI 48104

Inter-American Development Bank
1300 New York Avenue NW
Washington, DC 20577
202-623-1000

Internal Revenue Service
1111 Constitution Avenue NW
Washington, DC 20224
202-566-5000

International Accounting Standards
 Committee, American Institute
 of Certified Public Accountants
1211 Avenue of the Americas
New York, NY 10036

International Bank for Reconstruction
 and Development
1818 H Street NW
Washington, DC 20433
202-477-1234

International Finance Corporation
1818 H Street NW
Washington, DC 20433
202-477-1234

International Monetary Fund
700 Nineteenth Street NW
Washington, DC 20431
202-623-7000

National Credit Union Administration
1776 G Street NW
Washington, DC 20456
202-682-9600

Office Management and Budgets
Executive Office Building
Washington, DC 20503
202-395-3080

Office of the Comptroller of the Currency
250 E Street SW
Washington, DC 20219
202-874-5000

Office of Thrift Supervision
1700 G Street NW
Washington, DC 20552
202-906-6913

Pension Benefit Guaranty Corporation
2020 K Street NW
Washington, DC 20006
202-778-8800

Resolution Trust Corporation
801 Seventh Street NW
Washington, DC 20434
202-416-6900

Securities and Exchange Commission
450 Fifth Street NW
Washington, DC 20549
202-272-3100

The Senate
The Capitol
Washington, DC 20510
202-224-3121

Superintendent of Documents
Government Printing Office
Washington, DC 20402-9325
202-523-5230

Thrift Depositor Oversight Board
Suite 600
1777 F Street NW
Washington, DC 20232
202-786-9661

United Nations
New York, NY 10017
212-963-1234

Index